Sex
and
Love
in Intimate
Relationships

Sex and Love

in Intimate Relationships

Robert W. Firestone

Lisa A. Firestone

Joyce Catlett

American Psychological Association • Washington, DC

Published by
American Psychological Association
750 First Street, NE
Washington, DC 20002
www.apa.org

To order
APA Order Department
P.O. Box 92984
Washington, DC 20090-2984
Tel: (800) 374-2721
Direct: (202) 336-5510
Fax: (202) 336-5502
TDD/TTY: (202) 336-6123
Online: www.apa.org/books/
E-mail: order@apa.org

In the U.K., Europe, Africa, and the
Middle East, copies may be ordered from
American Psychological Association
3 Henrietta Street
Covent Garden, London
WC2E 8LU England

Typeset in Goudy by World Composition Services, Inc., Sterling, VA

Printer: United Book Press, Inc., Baltimore, MD
Cover Designer: Naylor Design, Washington, DC
Project Manager: Debbie Hardin, Carlsbad, CA

The opinions and statements published are the responsibility of the authors, and such opinions and statements do not necessarily represent the policies of the American Psychological Association.

Library of Congress Cataloging-in-Publication Data

Firestone, Robert.
    Sex and love in intimate relationships / Robert W. Firestone, Lisa A. Firestone, Joyce Catlett.
        p. cm.
    Includes bibliographical references and index.
    ISBN 1-59147-286-5
    1. Sex. 2. Love. 3. Intimacy (Psychology) I. Catlett, Joyce. II. Title.

HQ801.F553   2005
306.7—dc22   2005003228

British Library Cataloguing-in-Publication Data
A CIP record is available from the British Library.

Printed in the United States of America
First Edition

CONTENTS

ACKNOWLEDGMENTS

We wish to express our appreciation to Tamsen Firestone, Jo Barrington, Susan Short, and Jo Linder-Crow for their brilliant editing of the manuscript. We are grateful to Susana Buckett for her efforts in researching the vast literature on sexuality, intimate relationships, and gender issues and for her help in producing the final manuscript. We also wish to thank Anne Baker, who worked closely with us to complete the manuscript; Margaret McMurtrey, for her help in copy editing the final draft; and Jina Carvalho, who, assisted by Joni Kelly, is responsible for disseminating an expanding body of written and filmed works through the Glendon Association.

We want to thank Gary VandenBos and Jon Carlson for producing the American Psychological Association (APA) video on Sexual Health with coauthor Lisa A. Firestone, which provided the initial impetus for writing this book. We also wish to acknowledge our indebtedness to Susan Reynolds, acquisitions editor at APA Books, for her continued encouragement and support and to Judy Nemes, development editor, for her insightful suggestions regarding stylistic, organizational, and editorial changes.

We express our gratitude to the people whose stories are recounted throughout this book. We thank them for their openness and honesty in describing their feelings, thoughts, and opinions about their sexual lives and intimate relationships in interviews, psychotherapy sessions, and discussion groups. These individuals were strongly motivated to make the insights they gained available so that others might benefit from their experiences.

The names, places, and other identifying facts contained herein have been fictionalized, and no similarity to any persons, living or dead, is intended.

Sex
and
Love
in Intimate
Relationships

INTRODUCTION

Although sexuality can be one of the greatest pleasures in life, and a very special opportunity for gratification and fulfillment, it also represents an aspect of life that is complex and difficult and sometimes even traumatic. In this regard, the renowned psychiatrist Laing quipped in a number of his workshops that "the bedroom is the most dangerous place on earth." Both men and women are confused about themselves as sexual beings and are vulnerable to destructive internal "voices"[1] or self-attacks that have been incorporated during their developmental years. Furthermore, because of a generalized suppression of communication on the subject, people receive little feedback about the subject of their sexuality. Cultural influences reinforce negative attitudes toward the body, nudity, and sexuality, giving sex a "dirty" connotation. The unnecessary and unnatural suppression and distortion of sexuality in Western society lead to an exaggerated, prurient interest in sexuality, dirty jokes, perverse attitudes and actions, and a general increase in aggressive acting out behavior (Prescott, 1975).

The so-called sexual revolution of the 1960s was replaced with a conservative backlash that served to compound the problems in sexual relationships. Over the years, sex has been used in marketing commercial products, as well as other manipulations of public opinion. Sex on the Internet, allowing for arousal separate from human contact, has become a profitable commodity. In modern society, there is often more sex, but less feeling. Young people refer to "hooking up" (Brooks, 2003), a term that suggests the lack of feeling in sexual relating. Men and women today are suspicious and distrustful of one another, which negatively affects their sexual relationships and prohibits real intimacy. Most find it difficult to combine sex and love and sustain genuine closeness.

Human sexuality is a simple and pleasurable combination of attitudes and actions that involves giving and receiving for both parties. If not corrupted by ignorance, prejudice, childhood trauma, or outright sexual abuses, people can enjoy this natural function. The main thesis of this volume is that sexuality is often limited or damaged in an individual's upbringing, and the resultant unresolved emotional pain gives rise to long-standing psychological defenses. These defenses, both self-protective and self-nurturing, preclude personal vulnerability and interfere with full and uninhibited participation in sexual relating.

Most men and women profess that they desire a close, loving sexual relationship that is active and long-lasting. We have found that, in actuality, relatively few can tolerate loving or being loved. For those who have been damaged as children, living defensively, maintaining distance, and warding off closeness can become lifelong behavior patterns that seriously affect their relationships and sexual lives.

Our purpose in writing this book is to shed light on the often trouble-some subject of sexuality, sharing knowledge gained from more than 40 years of combined clinical experience and a unique longitudinal study of three generations of individuals, couples, and families.[2] Based on our work, we will describe the developmental issues that affect a child's sexual identity, point out the problems in establishing intimacy, define a healthy sexual relationship, enumerate the factors involved in developing oneself and in selecting a mate, and describe a treatment modality for sexual problems and conflicts that is effective in improving sexual relationships. In short, we wish to provide information that clinicians can use to help their clients become more fully loving and sexual.

Sex and Love in Intimate Relationships is different from the large majority of books on sex, which tend to focus on the technical aspects of sexual relationships. Currently there is a dearth of information regarding the important emotional or psychological dimensions of human sexuality. This book does not focus on evaluating or perfecting sexual performance. Instead, it deals with sex in a much broader sense by focusing on how people feel about themselves as men and women and how they interact in their close relationships.

We view sex as a physical and emotional exchange and describe sexuality as a form of intimate communication. This book delineates both the psychological factors that contribute to satisfying sexual experiences and those that interfere with the ability to achieve sexual and emotional intimacy. It provides an in-depth understanding of why the unique combination of love and sex, although challenging, offers the most fulfillment. This work is based on a theoretical model that integrates psychodynamic and existential systems of thought, that points out the relationship between psychological defenses and sexual difficulties. We provide numerous case studies and personal accounts to illustrate this perspective.

This book offers information gathered from a large number of individuals, both in and out of couple relationships, in both clinical and nonclinical settings. The diverse population represents a broad mental health spectrum, ranging from healthy individuals and those with minor emotional problems, to people with more serious disturbances. They recounted their experiences in a variety of situations, including psychotherapy sessions, individual and couple interviews, formal and informal discussions, and specialized seminars organized for the purpose of gathering data on such issues as subjects' feelings, opinions, attitudes toward sex, and sexual practices.

ORGANIZATION OF THE BOOK

Sex and Love in Intimate Relationships is divided into four sections. Part I, "Exploring Sexuality and Love," addresses fundamental questions such as what is healthy sexuality and what is the meaning of the word "love." The chapters also deal with components of a "healthy" sexual relationship, qualities to further develop in oneself and to look for in an "ideal" partner, and characteristics of an "ideal" sexual experience. We offer our conceptualization of love and its manifestations in a close, personal relationship.

Part II, "Factors Influencing Sexual Development and Adult Sexual Functioning," delineates crucial interpersonal factors that affect children's sexual development. The topics under discussion include parents' emotional hunger and its effect on the child's emerging sexuality and other parental attitudes and behaviors that can generate a sense of shame in children. Many of the case studies in this section recount painful experiences people endured in their early lives. In some cases, these incidents may appear to be relatively mild; nevertheless, they had a serious impact on the sexual development and adult sexual functioning of the individuals involved. Other cases describe experiences that were, in fact, traumatic and that had severe and long-lasting effects on the sexual lives of the people involved.

We argue that the hurt and fear resulting from such experiences may lead to a defensive posture and a tendency to depersonalize that often have a profound adverse effect on the willingness to remain vulnerable and close during intimate moments. We propose that problems in sexuality are closely related to overall defenses; for example, children who have been emotionally deprived or rejected early in life tend to experience problems forming attachments and difficulties in combining love and sex as adults.

This section also addresses issues of sexual stereotyping and its effect on couple relationships and describes differences as well as similarities between men and women. We offer our views regarding the psychodynamics involved in the development of sexual dysfunctions and review a number of other theoretical approaches to the etiology of these dysfunctions and problems in sexual relating.

Part III, "The Defensive Process and Sexuality," describes the key element of our theoretical approach—the fantasy bond—an illusion of connection to the mother or primary caregiver. This primary defense or illusion of fusion leads to a pseudoindependent posture that later interferes with closeness with others. We show how an awareness of the existential issues of aloneness and death reinforce the primary defense or fantasy bond. This section also introduces the concept of the voice—a secondary defense—that supports the fantasy bond and self-parenting process. We describe how debilitating critical voices are introjected during early family interactions and discuss the role that these negative views of self and others play in a variety of sexual problems.

Another chapter discusses the relationship between psychological defenses, sexual withholding, and symptoms of low sexual desire, a disorder that is prevalent in Western society. Also we explore the ways that men and women experience painful feelings of sexual jealousy. Lastly, we provide an in-depth discussion of our views regarding the advantages and disadvantages of exclusive versus nonexclusive sexual relationships.

Part IV, "Therapeutic Approaches to Problems in Sexual Relating," describes the therapeutic methodology called voice therapy. We delineate the five steps in voice therapy as they have been applied in the context of couples therapy and provide case studies to illustrate assessment, treatment strategy, and outcome. We describe corrective suggestions, journaling exercises, and other homework assignments that can help partners learn to tolerate more intimacy in their relationship. The epilogue summarizes our approach and briefly reviews the major concepts and methods elucidated throughout this work.

To conclude, in both the clinical and nonclinical populations we studied, many people reported being confused and insecure about their sexuality. Often they believed they were the only ones struggling with this issue. In this book, we explore in depth the experiences that damage individuals in their sexuality and provide methods for understanding and coping with the problems that result from these early experiences. We have found that by identifying and challenging destructive thought processes or "voices" that interfere with closeness and optimal sexual functioning, people can learn to combine love and sexuality and achieve that special combination that is so desirable in their intimate relationships.

NOTES

1. The concept of the "voice" (Firestone, 1988) refers to a system of thoughts, beliefs, and attitudes, antithetical to self and hostile toward others, that is at the core of all forms of maladaptive behavior. When verbalized in the second person format, the contents of this destructive thought process are generally accompanied by varying degrees of anger and sadness.

2. For a description of participants in the longitudinal study, see Firestone, Firestone, and Catlett (2003) and Firestone and Catlett (1999).

I

EXPLORING SEXUALITY
AND LOVE

1

WHAT IS HEALTHY SEXUALITY?

Sexual health is the integration of the somatic, emotional, intellectual, and social aspects of sexual well-being, in ways that are positively enriching and that enhance personality, communication, and love.

—World Health Organization
(1975; cited in Slowinski, 2001, p. 273)

A healthy sex life is central to one's sense of well-being and a potential source of pleasure, happiness, and fulfillment. The enjoyment of passion, eroticism, and sexual intimacy and the giving and receiving of affection are fundamental aspects of being human. The special combination of loving sexual contact and genuine friendship that can be achieved in an intimate relationship is conducive to good mental and physical health and is a highly regarded goal for most people.

On the other hand, sexual relationships can be risky emotional investments because they also have the potential for causing distress and grief. Indeed, a good deal of human misery centers around sexuality and the difficulties that most people encounter in attempting to achieve and sustain satisfying sexual relationships. Disturbances in sexual relating have serious consequences, affecting every aspect of a person's life, including activities and pursuits far removed from the sexual domain.

DEFINING "NORMAL" SEXUALITY

In contemporary discourse about sex, the terms "normal," "natural," and "healthy" have all been used to describe sexual behavior in human beings. It is important to draw some distinctions between these terms. "Normal" is a word generally used to indicate the statistical norm, that is, what most people do, whereas the terms "natural" and "healthy" are more likely to be used as value judgments regarding the moral dimensions of a given sexual behavior or practice (Strong, DeVault, & Sayad, 1999).

Sex researchers have stressed the enormous diversity of sexual behaviors and practices across different cultures (Suggs & Miracle, 1993). Obviously, what is considered "normal," "natural," or "moral" in one society may well be considered "abnormal," "unnatural," or "deviant" in another. Furthermore, what was considered abnormal in the past may be considered normal and acceptable today. Indeed, during the past several decades, the frequency with which people engage in certain sexual activities has changed substantially. For example, Laumann, Gagnon, Michael, and Michaels (1994) reported that

> The emergence of oral sex as a widespread technique practiced by opposite-gender sex partners probably began in the 1920s and over the past seventy years it has become more common in various social contexts and among most social groups. (p. 102)

Similarly, people's evaluations of the "morality" of these sexual practices have significantly changed (Stone, 1985).[1] According to Marty Klein (1992), "What was considered abnormal only forty years ago: vibrators; touching oneself during intercourse; couples masturbating together; women enjoying oral sex . . . are now considered fairly routine in many parts of the country" (p. 163).

In discussing how to evaluate the morality of a specific sexual practice, Klein (1992) cited three criteria as a basis for making a responsible choice: "Is it consenting (and is the other person really in a position to give consent)? Is it exploitative? Is it self-destructive?" (p. 5). In *Sex: A Philosophical Primer*, Singer (2001) also addressed the subject of morality and sexual ethics, asserting that

> All means of satisfying one's sexual urges should be considered equally moral, equally permissible, provided that they entail no harm to any one else. . . . Nevertheless, society has an undeniable obligation to protect minors against sexual molestation, and the same applies as well to adults who have or would have withheld their free consent in relation to activities abhorrent to them. (p. 119)

Our views regarding "moral" and "natural" sexuality are congenial in many respects to the sentiments expressed by Klein and Singer. In the following pages, we expand on Klein and Singer's definitions and describe our views regarding healthy sexuality.

OUR PERSPECTIVE ON HEALTHY SEXUALITY

We define healthy sexuality as a mode of sexual relating that represents a natural extension of affection, tenderness, and companionship between two people (Firestone, 1990c; Firestone & Catlett, 1999). When both partners are fully present, in close emotional contact with each other, and enjoying the spontaneous giving and receiving of affection and sexual pleasure, their lovemaking contributes significantly to their emotional well-being and overall satisfaction in life.

In our work, we focus on the psychological factors that tend to give sexuality its depth and meaning. From this perspective, healthy sexual relating involves two individuals who have mature attitudes toward sex and do not view it as an activity isolated from other aspects of their relationship. They see sex as a fulfilling part of life and lovemaking as an opportunity to offer pleasure to each other and to experience pleasure themselves. They are sexually aware and informed, relatively uninhibited, and largely unself-conscious in their emotional and sexual responses, and they are therefore free to enjoy the physical contact, excitement, and passion of the sexual encounter. Both partners have an active desire for sex, a positive body image, and congenial attitudes about themselves and their partner that are relatively free of distortion or bias.

Healthy sexuality also implies incorporating sexuality into one's daily life, rather than consigning it solely to the sex act itself. In an ongoing sexual relationship, both partners would be aware of the important role that sex plays in their lives, not as an exaggerated area of focus but as a simple human experience.

In our work with individuals and couples, we observed that an individual's attitude toward sex is usually reflected in his or her level of vitality, overall appearance, and expressions of tenderness and affection. Sexual desire adds zest to people's lives, whereas diminished or inhibited sexual desire can detract from their enthusiasm for living and make life seem flat and uninteresting. Indications of sexual desire and a lively interest in sex can be observed in a person's facial expression, smile, friendly manner, sense of humor, playfulness, spontaneity, and enthusiasm. People who enjoy an active sex life seem more energetic and vivacious and are generally more appealing than those who are inhibited sexually or have little interest in sex.

We believe that "natural" or "healthy" sexuality includes an acceptance of our animal nature and a positive attitude toward our bodies, our nudity, and our sexual urges. It implies seeing sex as a simple and pleasurable act and giving it a high priority in our lives. In a culture or society that viewed sex as a natural, pleasurable activity, the subject would be openly talked about and personal feelings and preferences would be discussed in an adult fashion.

OTHER DESCRIPTIONS OF THE SEXUALLY
HEALTHY INDIVIDUAL

Mental health professionals, sex therapists, and sex educators have attempted to conceptualize the sexually healthy individual in terms that encompass many personal qualities, attitudes, behaviors, and lifestyles (LoPiccolo, 1994; Zilbergeld, 1999). Schnarch (1991) has described healthy sexual functioning as being closely related to an individual's "capacity for intimacy" and his or her ability to attach "profound emotional meaning to sexual experience" (p. 19). The Sexuality Information and Education Council of the United States (2002) recently published a broad definition of healthy sexuality. The council delineated a wide range of characteristics of the sexually healthy adult individual, who would

> Appreciate one's own body. Seek further information about reproduction as needed. Affirm that human development includes sexual development that may or may not include reproduction or genital sexual experience. Interact with both genders in respectful and appropriate ways. Affirm one's own sexual orientation and respect the sexual orientation of others. Express love and intimacy in appropriate ways. Develop and maintain meaningful relationships. Avoid exploitative or manipulative relationships. (p. 7)[2]

Another definition of healthy sexuality can be found on the University of Illinois Web site (University of Illinois Board of Trustees, 2004) that cited sex therapist Maltz's definition of healthy sexuality as

> Positive, enriching, and about how we communicate and accept and give love. It means having the ability to enjoy and control our sexual and reproductive behavior without guilt, fear or shame. Sexual expression is a form of communication through which we give and receive pleasure and emotion. . . . Healthy sex requires that these conditions be met: Consent, Equality, Respect, Trust, and Safety. (p. 1)

CRITERIA COMMONLY USED TO EVALUATE SEXUALITY

The frequency of sexual relations is often considered to be a criterion for healthy sexuality or an indicator of "normality." Indeed, many men and women are curious about how often the average person makes love. There are a multitude of sex surveys that report the frequency of sexual relations for single, cohabiting, and married people.

Stritof and Stritof (2004) reported highlights of one recent survey (the 2003 Durex Survey), which found that the average American couple has sex about once a week. The survey also showed that unmarried couples living together have sex 146 times a year, while married couples make love 98 times a year on average. Results from another survey (Laumann et al., 1994) showed 13% of married couples having sex a few times per year, 45% reported making love a few times per month, 34%, 2 to 3 times per week, and 7%, 4 or more times per week.[3]

The types of sexual activities that couples engage in are often used as criteria for normality. The survey conducted by Laumann et al. (1994) found that the large majority of men and women (95% and 97% respectively) engaged in vaginal intercourse; approximately three quarters of both men and women practiced oral sex; and one quarter of men and one fifth of women reported engaging in anal sex. Among men and women who reported having sex with a same-gendered partner in the past 5 years, active and receptive oral sex were practiced by between 72% and 82% of respondents. Active and receptive anal sex were practiced by between 62% and 64% of the male respondents. For women in same-gendered partnerships, "the rates and pattern of oral sex are quite similar" (p. 319) to those reported by male respondents in same-gendered partnerships.

Many individuals evaluate the "success" of their sexual performance in terms of whether or not their lovemaking culminates in orgasm for both partners. In the study cited above, Laumann et al. (1994) found that "Three-quarters of the men report that they always have orgasm during sex" (p. 114). The survey also uncovered an interesting discrepancy: 29% of women said they always have an orgasm with this specific partner. This rate was "46 percentage points lower than that of men" (p. 114). In commenting on this discrepancy, Laumann et al., stated, "To the extent that female orgasm is now considered both a right (for women) and a responsibility (for men), this discrepancy undoubtedly constitutes a source of considerable intergender/ interpersonal tension" (p. 114). These findings raise another important question: do most men and women consider orgasm to be the ultimate goal or criteria for a "healthy" or an ideal sexual experience?

DIMENSIONS OF AN IDEAL SEXUAL EXPERIENCE

In describing the dimensions of healthy sexuality, researchers have recently turned their focus to evaluating emotional satisfaction or dissatisfaction attained by adult individuals during a sexual experience rather than focusing solely on physical satisfaction as in previous surveys. One extensive survey (Laumann et al., 1994), for example, assessed the degree of physical and emotional satisfaction. Results from interviews with 3,432 men and women showed that 47% of men and 41% of women reported that their "specific partnerships could be accurately characterized as 'extremely' physically pleasurable" (p. 118), while only 41% of the men and 37% of women reported the partnership as emotionally satisfying. What dimensions of a sexual experience or relationship contribute to its being satisfying both physically and emotionally?

In the following pages, we offer material from ongoing specialized seminars about sexuality and from interviews in which people discussed their opinions, feelings, and experiences. During these interviews and seminars, men and women were asked, "How would you describe the ideal sexual relationship or experience?"

Elliott: I think a sexual experience is ideal when it's part of sharing the day and then being affectionate, then there's more affection, and then you're sexual. Afterwards, you're affectionate, and you're friends; it's a smooth continuum like that.

Diana: I think that an ideal sexual experience would be one where both partners would feel appreciative to one another for being given something that made them happy and made them feel good.

Brad: For me, the ideal sex experience would include feelings of friendliness and closeness, combined with passionate lovemaking, and talking freely and directly to your sexual partner about your personal feelings, both positive and negative, as they arise.

Andy: I think that for me the thing that makes sex an ideal experience is if my girlfriend is really interested and really lets me make her feel good.

Renee: An ideal sexual experience has an even deeper meaning, because to be fully sexual makes you feel so alive. You feel it everywhere in your life. When I'm sexual, I really feel my body. I love that feeling, I love feeling the other person. I love feeling my own body, just physically, my skin against his skin and the physical sensations. But also it makes me feel alive and very sensitive to everything around me, to my life. If I'm not motivated to be sexual, I become dull, my senses become dulled.

Vivian: I feel like the most important thing is just being there and not being inside my head, being with my husband and feeling really close. Those times feel really special.

Christopher: [to his girlfriend] When it's nice between us, it is so wonderful for me and I feel both excited and close, and I also feel very free. It's interesting that what comes with the really gratifying sexual experience is a sense of feeling really free afterwards too. I feel happy to see you throughout the day and my feelings of affection and closeness continue for quite a while.

Maria: Sex would be a simple part of life. It's not separate, it's not serious, it's not in a dark room, it's a fun, easy, close experience.

Jason: For me to have a really, really satisfying sexual experience, I need intimacy, whether it's physical or verbal, outside of the bedroom first. I think sex is better when there's a connection there. It might be more aggressive and physical, or more calm and tender, depending on the situation. Also I feel satisfied when I get some acknowledgment that my boyfriend was pleased.

Kevin: I feel that the ideal sexual relationship is made up of friendship, continuity, and affection. And spontaneity is a key part of it. Anything that routinizes the relationship, I feel, kills the sexuality.

The general consensus obtained from these interviews and discussions seemed to indicate that to be a fully satisfying experience, the sexual relating had to include emotional closeness. Healthy sexual experiences appear to be characterized by an uninterrupted flow of pleasurable sensations and feelings throughout the act. There is a notable absence of inhibition at any time during the process, beginning with the initial expressions of physical affection, and continuing through foreplay, intercourse, and the time immediately following the experience. Partners feel free in undressing, being looked at, and being touched. They are not worried about making sounds indicating their pleasure, nor are they fastidious about smells or focused exclusively on having an orgasm.

In an "ideal" sexual encounter, partners would proceed naturally from one plateau of arousal to the next undisturbed by negative thoughts about their bodies, their sexuality, their performance, or their partner. Both partners would tend to be spontaneous in their sexual responses, and neither person would try to inhibit or control any aspect of the sex act. Because both individuals would take responsibility for their own sexual desires and needs and indicate their wants, there would be a feeling of equality inherent in their interaction that would contribute to their overall sense of well-being and individuality. Ideally, there would be an absence of guilt, self-critical ruminations, or hostile attacks on one's partner about the experience. Following a gratifying sexual encounter, partners would tend to experience a mixture of happiness, sadness, relaxation, and fulfillment, and they would probably express their mutual appreciation, verbally and nonverbally, for the pleasure they received.

A satisfying sexual encounter can be playful, carefree, sensuous, affectionate, serious, sad, or a combination of these qualities and emotions.

Although there is a wide range of sexual experience that men and women enjoy, many have described their ideal experience as one that combines tenderness, warmth, friendship, and sexual satisfaction. For example, in one group discussion, Maria talked about aspects of her sexual relationship with her husband that she found especially gratifying and meaningful.

> In our lovemaking, there is such an absolute lack of control. It's almost a magical experience, because going into it, I never know what's going to happen. There's no timing, there's no order of anything; we're simply two people together, and I never know ahead of time exactly how it's going to work. But if we're both close, really there in the situation, it really does feel to me like something magical happens.

Satisfying, mature sexual relations are not necessarily limited to long-term relationships. For example, a sexual encounter between two people who have just met can be satisfying on both an emotional and physical level. In general, a positive or healthy sexual experience, whether casual or not, includes close emotional contact with one's partner, a sense of mutual give and take, and feelings of fulfillment and well-being following the experience. In the same discussion, Jeremy expressed his ideas about what he considered to be the "ideal" sexual experience.

> The "ideal" sexual experience can go from being fun and playful to being a very deep emotional experience. I've had a few "ideal" sexual experiences with a woman who I didn't develop a long-term relationship with. But in that moment there was an intimacy, there was a togetherness, and you lose a self-consciousness in that intimate moment with someone like that. You're two people equally sharing that experience. But, at the same time, you have a tremendous awareness of the other person's vulnerability, and their being so open and receptive to you. There is something so touching about that awareness and that experience—that's what makes it ideal.

Another participant, Cliff, described the contrast between what he considers an "ideal" and a less-than-ideal sexual experience:

> When sex is simple and easy, I feel very happy with my girlfriend, and I don't have a lot of thoughts in my head about being able to satisfy her. But then there are times when it's not like that, and it feels like there are six of us in the bedroom, like in that movie, *The Story of Us*, when Bruce Willis and Michelle Pfeiffer's "parents" suddenly appear and interrupt an intimate moment with their hostile messages. When that happens to me, there's so much going on in my head, it's confusing and I get muddled.

As is obvious from Cliff's description, obstacles can arise during sex that interfere with sexual fulfillment. For example, at those times when people get into their heads (thinking negative thoughts or just worrying), lovemaking can come to a complete standstill, leaving partners frustrated and confused.

In listening to individuals talk about their sexual experiences, we learned a great deal about what interrupts the smooth flow of feelings and sensations during lovemaking. For example, people described the kinds of negative thoughts that often intruded into their thinking at various points, distracting them from the full enjoyment of the experience. In many cases, these critical thoughts were directed toward their sexual performance and increased any anxieties they might have had regarding having an orgasm and/or satisfying their partner.

Satisfying sex and emotional intimacy may elicit a myriad of emotions—feelings of tenderness, excitement, pleasure in satisfying the wants and needs of the other, and joy in sharing a meaningful experience. An especially close sexual interaction, one that combines "eyes-open" emotional intimacy with passionate sex, may approach a spiritual level (Chessick, 1992; Schnarch, 1991). We believe that during those moments when ecstasy and exhilaration combine with poignant feelings of sorrow and existential pain, lovers never feel more together and more alone. Indeed, this unique blending of eroticism and love represents a powerful antidote to the existential despair inherent in the human condition.

ESSENTIAL PERSONAL QUALITIES FOR HEALTHY SEXUAL RELATING

Any attempt to synthesize the information gathered through years of discussions and interviews with couples can sound prescriptive and simplistic, an attitude that is personally offensive to us and incongruent with our perspective and purpose. Nevertheless, it is valuable to delineate the factors that we have found to be the most significant in contributing to positive or healthy sexual relating. It is obvious that the success or failure of an intimate relationship is strongly influenced by the personal qualities one brings to the relationship as well as by one's choice of a partner. Taking both of these perspectives into account, there are a number of personality characteristics that each partner might strive to further develop within him- or herself.

Nondefensiveness and Openness

In our work with couples, we have found that two qualities essential in achieving a satisfying and fulfilling relationship are openness and a lack of defensiveness. Nondefensiveness may be defined as a receptivity to feedback without being guarded or hypersensitive about any topic. The negative impact of making certain subjects taboo and excluding them from one's communications in a close sexual relationship cannot be overstated. Because most people are self-critical in the area of their sexuality, they often overreact to any negative feedback, mild or harsh, from an intimate partner, whether it is related to their appearance, body, sexual practices, or performance. Therefore, they tend to exclude these subjects from their communications. The resulting censorship in the partners' dialogue leads to increased tension and tends to reverberate through other areas of the relationship.

Studies by Gottman and Krokoff (1989) have shown that many couples find it uncomfortable to communicate about sex. In some cases, one partner's defensiveness about sex predisposes the withdrawal of the other person, while in other instances defensiveness leads to an escalation of conflict between partners. Defensiveness may be expressed through refusal to talk about the subject, anger, tears, "falling apart," and victimized pleas for more understanding. There may be expressions of defeat and hopelessness through statements such as, "Well, if that's how you really feel about me," "Why do you have to be so picky? You're always finding fault with me," or other statements that make a partner regret ever having broached the subject.

Openness includes the ability to be forthright in expressing feelings, thoughts, dreams, and desires. Individuals who are direct in stating their sexual wants and needs have a good effect on their partner and the relationship. Men and women who are motivated to develop beyond their defenses against intimacy, especially in their communications, are generally not secretive or self-protective, nor are they embarrassed or ashamed to disclose their fears or doubts about sexual matters to their partner. However, people who are resistant to change may be more secretive and less open to feedback when communicating with their partner. In terms of their sexuality, these men and women may develop habitual or routinized modes of interacting sexually because they are afraid of being vulnerable and emotionally close to their partner.

Honesty and Integrity

Dishonesty and deception are perhaps the most hurtful qualities manifested by sexual partners. Because deception fractures another person's sense of reality—the belief in the veracity of his or her perceptions—the personal qualities of honesty and integrity are fundamental to the emotional well-being and mental health of both partners and vital to the quality of their relationship. For example, deception about the other's sexual alliances can destroy the betrayed partner's basic sense of trust in him- or herself and other people.

Real honesty requires considerable self-knowledge and an intolerance of any falseness or insincerity in oneself. It is manifested in a nonduplicitous style of communication. People who have achieved a high level of integrity in their lives also have a realistic evaluation regarding the extent to which they are capable of accepting loving sexuality in their relationships. They represent themselves accurately and do not condone discrepancies between their words and actions.

Double messages such as proclamations of love that are not congruent with loving behaviors are confusing and ultimately destructive to the trust between sexual partners. Studies of communication within couples (Canary, Cupach, & Messman, 1995; Gottman, 1979; Gottman & Krokoff, 1989; Keeley & Hart, 1994) have found that the greater the discrepancy between the manifest content (seemingly positive verbal messages) and their underlying or latent meaning (in particular, body language indicating negativity), the greater the potential for disturbance. In the area of sexuality, as in other areas of the relationship, partners may have implicitly agreed not to notice the discrepancy between statements of love and behaviors that express underlying hostility. This further confuses the issue and creates additional problems in the sexual interaction. As Bach and Deutsch (1979) said, "There is a tendency of both parties to disavow the crazymaking experience, to deny it and smooth over its ill effects" (p. 23).

Respect for One's Partner as a Separate Individual

In an ideal relationship, each partner values the other person, separate from his or her own interest, and places the other's wants, desires, and satisfaction on an equal basis with his or her own. Furthermore, each partner feels congenial toward the other's overall goals in life. In relating sexually, neither attempts to manipulate or control the other's responses. In seeking a potential partner, one would be well advised to seek out someone who is independent and self-reliant, because these qualities are needed to develop this type of mature perspective on relationships. The ideal partner would be aware that feeling his or her separateness is an integral part of having a sensitive, tender feeling toward his or her partner.

Individuals who have developed a high level of self-differentiation show, through words and actions, a genuine respect for the boundaries, wants, and priorities of their mate. They take pleasure in seeing their partner flourish in areas of his or her life that are separate from them. There is an awareness that to be close to another person, one must have a sense of one's separateness and autonomy.

To develop the ability to maintain independence and autonomy while relating closely with another, a person would first need to achieve insight regarding important events in his or her childhood, for example, in relation to any losses, separations, or trauma experiences that may have occurred. The resolution of past trauma entails gradually developing a coherent narrative about experiences with significant attachment figures and making sense of aversive childhood events. Findings from recent research (Karr-Morse & Wiley, 1997; Main & Goldwyn, 1984; Main & Solomon, 1986; Siegel, 1999) have shown the necessity for retrieving painful childhood memories as well as the emotions associated with these memories to achieve maturity in one's attitudes and behaviors in an adult relationship.[4] In addition, individuals need to challenge defensive attitudes and sexual biases formed early in life that may still influence their ways of relating to their partner.

In discussing problems encountered by many individuals who are struggling to preserve their autonomy and sense of themselves in their relationships or marriages, Wallerstein and Blakeslee (1995) proposed that the first task of intimate partners is separating emotionally from the family of origin. In explaining what this entails, they wrote: "Psychological separation means gradually detaching from your family's emotional ties. . . . This emotional shift from being a son or daughter to being a wife or husband is accomplished by *internally* reworking your attachments to and conflicts with your parents" (p. 53) [italics added]. In other words, even though a person is physically distant from parents and other family members, unless he or she has achieved a certain degree of emotional emancipation from the family, there will inevitably be limitations on his or her sexual life. Bowen (1978) and Kerr and Bowen (1988) have also called attention to this important factor in personal development, emphasizing that emotional emancipation from the parental family is an important step toward becoming a more differentiated self or autonomous human being.

Empathy, Compassion, and Understanding

Empathy, compassion, and understanding are related concepts; however, some authors have discriminated between these terms. Empathy is defined by Siegel and Hartzell (2003) as

> Understanding the internal experience of another person; the imaginative projection of one's consciousness into the feelings of another person or object; sympathetic understanding. This is a cognitively complex process that involves mental capacities to imagine the mind of another. Empathy may depend on the capacity for mindsight, mediated by the integrative right hemisphere and prefrontal regions of the brain. (p. 224)

Siegel and Hartzell define compassion as

> The ability to feel with another. . . . Compassion is a caring stance toward the distressful emotional experience of another person. Compassion may depend on mirror neuron systems, which evoke an emotional

state in us that mirrors that of another person, enabling us to feel another person's pain. (p. 224)

Understanding involves an awareness and appreciation of the commonalities and differences that exist between two people. According to Duck (1994),

The more one comprehends another person, the more one learns not only about the person's mind but also about the range of social actions that the person finds acceptable. In turn one can modify one's style of behavior in order to respond more appropriately to the person in the extended interactions of a relationship. (p. 131)

Duck's description of the elements that make up understanding is similar in many respects to Siegel and Hartzell's (2003) concept of "Mindsight—the capacity to 'see' or image, the mind of oneself or another, enabling an understanding of behavior in terms of mental processes" (p. 224). In expanding the concept of empathy, Eagle and Wolitzky (1997) contended that "there are different components and aspects of empathy, including the empathic experience of the listener, received empathy, empathic communication, and so on" (pp. 241–242).

When both partners are empathic and capable of communicating with compassion and respect for the other person's wants, attitudes, and values, each partner feels understood and validated. In an ongoing sexual relationship, they are able to candidly discuss their differences as well as their commonalities. As a result, their communications, both during sex and in other parts of their life together, have the positive effect of making each person feel acknowledged and unique.

The Capacity to Give and Receive Love, Affection, and Sex

Ideally, personal growth and increased self-differentiation would facilitate an increase in a tolerance for closeness and an enhanced potential for enjoying sexual intimacy in one's relationship. The act of making love involves a particularly close physical and emotional exchange between two people. To be fully engaged in this powerful transaction, an individual needs to develop his or her capacity to both give and receive physical affection and to enjoy the emotional exchange that occurs during a sexual experience.

The ability to love—to feel empathy and to express kindness, generosity, and tenderness toward another person—requires first learning to value oneself and one's experiences. This can be a difficult task because the ability to see oneself as having worth and one's life as having value is often damaged early in life. Thus, the process of learning to love is an ongoing endeavor directed toward transforming negative attitudes toward oneself and one's sexuality into a more compassionate, less restrictive view.

In our opinion, this process of expanding one's capacity to love another is a skill that must be developed, just as one develops any other skill. However, learning to love can be difficult and complicated for men and women who, as children, may have been damaged in their feelings about themselves. For example, it may be difficult to accept tenderness and sexual responses from another person because such affection causes a resurgence of painful feelings from the past. We believe that to preserve a loving, sexual relationship, both partners must be willing to face the threat to their defense system that being loved and appreciated poses. Both must be willing to change negative images of themselves formed in the family and to give up defenses they once may have felt were necessary for their psychological survival.

The Capacity for Being Vulnerable

It is important to develop the capacity to be vulnerable in close sexual experiences rather than trying to protect oneself against the possibility of being hurt or rejected. Individuals who have been damaged early in life and who lack trust in others are often afraid to take a chance on being close emotionally and sexually in a relationship. They may be especially intolerant of combining love, affection, and satisfying sex in an intimate relationship.

The ability to maintain emotional contact with one's partner while making love presupposes a willingness to experience poignant feelings that invariably arise during a meaningful sexual encounter. We have found that the special combination of sexuality, affection, and emotional closeness can serve to remind people that they are truly alive, that they really do exist. Giving value to their existence tends to make them acutely aware of the fragility of life and the ultimate separation, through death, from loved ones and from the self. Frightened by these issues of death and dying, people often turn their backs on their sexuality and retreat emotionally, rather than embrace life to its fullest.

CONCLUSION

In answering the question, what is "normal" or "natural" sexuality, it is well to remember that these definitions have changed during the past century, as they have in every period of history. As historian Stone (1985) rightly observed: "What is absolutely certain . . . is that over the long history of Western civilization, there has been no such thing as 'normal sexuality.' Sexuality is a cultural artifact that has undergone constant and sometimes dramatic changes over time" (p. 42). Normality or abnormality in relation to sexuality is embedded in people's beliefs about the morality or immorality of certain sexual practices, and these beliefs can vary tremendously across cultures, social classes, ethnic groups, and historical eras.

In describing our conceptualization of "healthy sexuality," we expanded on definitions of healthy sexuality previously adopted by several organizations and public health officials and included other important psychological and relational dimensions. An understanding of healthy sexuality enables one to visualize personal qualities and behaviors in each partner that would contribute to a loving and sexually fulfilling relationship. In an ongoing intimate relationship, healthy sexual experiences based on love, affection, and friendship have an overall positive effect on both partners. In addition, mature loving sexuality is manifested in an appreciation and respect for the true nature of the other person and support for his or her personal freedom pursuant to his or her personal goals in life. Individuals who strive to develop themselves and their full potential and who seek partners with strength and independence are more likely to succeed in their quest for love and sexual intimacy.

A combination of sexuality, close emotional contact, and personal communication is an ideal in couple relationships. However, relationships that combine genuine love and sexuality are difficult to find and even more difficult to tolerate or accept. Although people feel especially gratified when a sexual experience has also been emotionally satisfying, they have a good deal of resistance to that combination. This resistance arises in part because genuinely loving sexuality represents a significant intrusion into people's psychological defenses. Lovers frequently feel uniquely vulnerable to the possibility of future loss or rejection when they remain close to each other during sex. They are deeply touched to be gratified by another, yet are painfully aware of how much they stand to lose.

As men and women become more aware of these seemingly paradoxical reactions to love and sex, they expand their boundaries and experience more satisfaction in life. For example, during the course of our clinical study, we observed that many clients altered their attitudes toward sex in a positive direction. In challenging their defenses against closeness and intimacy, they gradually changed many ways they had limited or controlled expressions of love and sexuality in their intimate relationships. They increasingly came to value love and sexual intimacy and viewed these aspects of their relationship as a fundamental part of life. In essence, they came to perceive sexual love as "a way of *being* together" as Keen (1997) described it, that is, "not *having* (mutual possession) or *doing* (exercising skills), but being present and vulnerable in the fullness of [one's] being" (p. 207) [italics added].

Moreover, we found that, in general, as individuals develop and work through childhood conflicts and trauma, they become less fearful of physical and emotional closeness. As they mature emotionally and modify defensive behaviors, they tend to make better choices and progressively develop more fulfilling sexual relationships. As their potential for eroticism and emotional closeness increases, they are likely to seek partners who manifest strength and independence and who can also tolerate relatively high levels of intimacy.

It has been our experience that people can learn to tolerate the anxiety evoked by passionate, loving sexual experiences and maintain a real closeness with their partner and a natural, healthy desire for sex. In differentiating themselves from their families-of-origin and strengthening their point of view in relation to their sexuality, they can develop and sustain more deeply fulfilling sexual relationships than they previously thought possible.

NOTES

1. According to historian Stone (1985),

   To a young male citizen of Athens in the fifth and fourth centuries B.C., it was perfectly proper and moral to use the body of a male or female slave for any sexual pleasure that took his fancy—whether it be sodomy, fellatio, or whatever. . . . [From the 4th to the 18th century] it was generally held that passionate sexual love between spouses within marriage was not only indecent but positively sinful. (p. 35)

2. The other characteristics listed by the Sexuality Information and Education Council of the United States (2002) are

   Make informed choices about family options and lifestyles. Exhibit skills that enhance personal relationships. Identify and live according to one's values. Take responsibility for one's own behavior. Practice effective decision-making. Communicate effectively with family, peers, and partners. Enjoy and express one's sexuality throughout life. Express one's sexuality in ways congruent with one's values. Discriminate between life-enhancing sexual behaviors and those that are harmful to self and/or others. Express one's sexuality while respecting the rights of others. Seek new information to enhance one's sexuality. Use contraception effectively to avoid unintended pregnancy. Prevent sexual abuse. Seek early prenatal care. Avoid contracting or transmitting a sexually transmitted disease, including HIV. Practice health-promoting behaviors, such as regular check-ups, breast and testicular self-exam, and early identification of potential problems. Demonstrate tolerance for people with different sexual values and lifestyles. Exercise democratic responsibility to influence legislation dealing with sexual issues. Assess the impact of family, cultural, religious, media, and societal messages on one's thoughts, feelings, values, and behaviors related to sexuality. Promote the rights of all people to accurate sexuality information. Avoid behaviors that exhibit prejudice and bigotry. Reject stereotypes about the sexuality of diverse populations. (p. 7)

Also see "Defining Sexual Health: A Descriptive Overview" (Edwards & Coleman, 2004).

3. Laumann et al. (1994) reported results from a comprehensive survey of the sexual habits of people in the United States. They conducted 90-minute, face-to-face interviews with 3,432 Americans between the ages of 17 and 59, asking them about their sexual practices and beliefs. The University of Chicago Harris School (1994), in a summary of Laumann's results, reported that "Approximately one third have sex a few times a year or not at all, a third have sex once or several times a month, and another third have sex at least two or more times a week" (p. 2).

4. See Main and Solomon (1986) and Siegel (1999) regarding the relationship between the ability to construct a coherent narrative of one's attachment history, the elicitation of deep feeling, and the resolution of early trauma and loss. In discussing ongoing attachment research conducted with the Adult Attachment Interview, Siegel (2001) stated,

> The finding that the coherence of the adult's autobiographical narrative is the most robust predictor of the child's attachment with the parent can help us shed light on the importance of neural integration for both mental health and nurturing interpersonal relationships. Coherent narratives can be seen to reflect the ability of the "interpreting" left hemisphere to utilize the autobiographical, mentalizing, and primary emotional processes of the right hemisphere in the production of "coherent" autonoesis, or self-knowledge. (p. 89)

2

WHAT IS LOVE?

The great aim of every human being is to understand the meaning of total love. Love is not to be found in someone else, but in ourselves; we simply awaken it. But in order to do that, we need the other person. The universe only makes sense when we have someone to share our feelings with.

—Coelho (2004, p. 116)

For centuries, philosophers, poets, novelists, and social scientists have attempted to define the meaning of the word "love," describe the emotions accompanying the subjective experience of falling in love, and elucidate how love is manifested in human relationships of every kind. Reik (1941) called attention to the problem of defining love in his book *Of Love and Lust*:

Love is one of the most overworked words in our vocabulary. There is hardly a field of human activity in which the word is not worked to death. . . . There is no doubt as to which science is qualified to give us the desired information and insight, but psychology seems to be extremely reticent on the subject. (pp. 9–10)

Writing about love in his personal journal, Laing (personal communication, July 1989) expressed sentiments similar to those of Reik:

Psychology. . . . No where within the network of its assumptions and terminology is there any possibility of even conceptualising mutual love. . . . Freud stated his position perfectly clearly: "Simple human love is impossible" (Future of an Illusion). Most of his followers are too cowardly, dull, and dishonest to be so candid.

Let us move on. Let's take a few breaths of fresher air. Let's start with the belief, hope, wish, that mutual love is possible.

PHENOMENOLOGICAL DESCRIPTIONS OF LOVE

Volumes have been written about the nature of love and how love is manifested in an intimate relationship. The philosopher Singer (2001), in *Sex: A Philosophical Primer*, asserted that

> There is no single entity, no discernible sensation or emotion, that is love. . . . There is no feeling, no unique and explicit datum, such that love exists if and only if it is present. Love is a form of life, though often short-lived, a disposition, a tendency to respond in a great variety of ways, many overlapping but none that is necessary and sufficient. It is a propensity to have affirmative and corroborative responses, thoughts, and inclinations to act without being limited to any one paradigmatically. (pp. 84–85)

In *The Four Loves*, Lewis (1960) wrote about Eros (or what many refer to as passion), describing it as "that state which we call 'being in love'" (p. 91). He observed that "the lover desires the Beloved herself, not the pleasure she can give" (p. 94).

> Without Eros sexual desire, like every other desire, is a fact about ourselves. Within Eros it is rather about the Beloved. . . . [It is] entirely a mode of expression. It . . . [is] something outside us, in the real world. . . . One of the first things Eros does is to obliterate the distinction between giving and receiving. (pp. 95–96)[1]

In *You Can't Go Home Again*, Wolfe (1934) gave "love" great significance when he eloquently described the basic nature of human beings:

> Man loves life, and loving life, hates death, and because of this he is great, he is glorious, he is beautiful, and his beauty is everlasting. He lives below the senseless stars and writes his meanings in them. . . . Thus it is impossible to scorn this creature. For out of his strong belief in life, this puny man made love. At his best, he *is* love. Without him there can be no love . . . no desire. (p. 411)[2]

In a conversation with Arnold Toynbee (Gage, 1976), Daisaku Ikeda, former president of Soka Gakkai International, a Buddhist organization, described a version of the Buddhist conception of love:

> The word *love* has been highly conceptualized and made very abstract. Just as charitable works without love can do harm, so abstracted love without practical application can be meaningless. I believe that the

Buddhist concept of compassion . . . defined as removing sorrow and bringing happiness to others . . . gives love substantial meaning. . . .

Yoraku—the second component of compassion in the Buddhist sense—means the giving of pleasure. . . . It is the joy of living . . . the ecstacy of life. It includes both material and spiritual pleasure. Without the deep feelings of fulfillment and the ecstacy generated by the emotions of life, pleasure in the truest sense is impossible. (pp. 357–358)

There are also many Judeo-Christian conceptualizations of love. Perhaps the most familiar are the statements attributed to the apostle Paul in I Corinthians 13 (World English Bible):

Love is patient and is kind; love doesn't envy. Love doesn't brag, is not proud, doesn't behave itself inappropriately, doesn't seek its own way, is not provoked, takes no account of evil; doesn't rejoice in unrighteousness, but rejoices with the truth; bears all things, believes all things, hopes all things, endures all things. Love never fails. . . . But now faith, hope, and love remain—these three. The greatest of these is love. (vv. 4–13)

OUR VIEW OF LOVE

But what is love, really? What does it mean to love someone? Defining love in operational or behavioral terms is a challenging undertaking. In *Altruism and Altruistic Love*, Post, Underwood, Schloss, and Hurlbut (2002) raised an important question: "What is at the very core of human altruistic love?" Their answer was that love might be conceptualized as "affirmative affection."

We all know what it feels like to be valued in this way, and we remember loving persons who conveyed this affective affirmation through tone of voice, facial expression, a hand on the shoulder in time of grief, and a desire to be with us. . . . Love implies benevolence, care, compassion, and *action*. (p. 4) [italics added]

In our view, actions that fit the description of a loving relationship are expressions of affection, both physical and emotional; a wish to offer pleasure and satisfaction to one's mate; tenderness, compassion, and sensitivity to the needs of the other; a desire for shared activities and pursuits; an appropriate level of sharing of one's possessions; an ongoing, honest exchange of personal feelings; and the process of offering concern, comfort, and outward assistance for the love object's aspirations.

Love includes feeling for the other that goes beyond a selfish or self-centered interest in the object. As such, love nurtures and has a positive effect on each person's self-esteem and sense of well-being. Love is truth and never involves deception, because misleading another person fractures his or her sense of reality and is therefore a serious human rights violation that adversely affects mental health.

Our thinking regarding the nature of love is congenial with the words written by Fromm (1956) in *The Art of Loving*. Fromm observed that "There is only one proof for the presence of love: the depth of the relationship, and the aliveness and strength in each person concerned; this is the fruit by which love is recognized" (p. 87). These manifestations of love can best be personified in the following description of one man's feelings for his wife after 25 years of marriage:

> When I first met Annette, I thought that she was attractive and she appeared to be a very nice person. At the time, however, I wasn't especially drawn to her; in fact, she seemed a little boring. Yet for some bizarre reason, a crazy thought came into my mind and it came up repeatedly: "You're going to marry this girl." It was so odd and out of character to the way I usually think that I told my friends about it and we all laughed. For one thing, my life was stable, I felt content, and I was already involved in a romantic relationship at the time. Besides, I considered the words that came to me to be rather corny.
>
> Nothing came of this incident, but later on, Annette became involved in my social circle and we actually became friends. One day, on our way to meet friends for a day sail, Annette and I found ourselves alone together, an unusual circumstance. While we were driving to the marina, I suggested that we stop for a moment to look at the ocean conditions. Parked by the breakwater, I leaned toward her and we kissed. From that moment on we were in love.
>
> In our love, a remarkable transformation took place in both of our lives. For one thing, her looks changed radically; indeed, in love, she developed into an exceptionally beautiful woman and I wasn't the only one who noticed the difference. All of our friends commented on it. Now it's close to thirty years later since we first met and she's still beautiful, but it's not just her physical beauty.
>
> For me, my life changed radically. We did get married, my friendships expanded, and I was inspired in my work. I had the courage to forge ahead in many new and creative endeavors.
>
> Annette is an incredibly sensitive, psychologically sophisticated and sweet person, very affectionate and naturally responsive sexually. She has an unusual capacity for pleasure in being touched and is easily orgasmic. I love her body and her responsiveness. I know that it's hard to believe, but after all of these years, I'm still as sexually attracted as I was originally.
>
> There are many other qualities in Annette that I discovered as our relationship unfolded. Annette is exceptionally intelligent, free-thinking, creative, and has an incredible sense of humor. She can turn

an unfortunate or embarrassing situation into something poignant and special. She has a unique feeling and respect for people's sexual nature and it has a powerful effect on both women and men. She has the knack of making women feel more feminine and men feel manly.

In our relationship there has always been a sense of equality and mutual respect. We fully believe in the personal freedom of each other and pose no limits on each other's development. This has been a guiding principle for us even when it caused us inconvenience or pain. I think that's why our relationship is still fresh and exciting. In that respect, we feel different from what we see in so many other couples. They appear to be so much more possessive and intrusive on each other and act different in each other's company than otherwise. I find the company of most couples to be boring. They seem to cancel out each other's sexuality and appear deadened in each other's presence.

From what I have said, you might think that life for us has always been happy. It has certainly been good overall, but we have had our bad times. When I first suggested that we have children together, Annette became emotionally distraught, even hostile. I had never seen her like that before and it shocked her as well. She had never been defensive and caught on that something was radically wrong with her response. But that didn't change things. We had trouble for months after that. Her feelings were all over the place and it practically ruined us. Luckily she got help and worked out her fears about having children. The result was that we now have four grown daughters who have turned out well.

And the trouble about having children wasn't our only problem. Whenever the issue of death came up—a movie, something on the news or information about the tragedy of someone we knew—she would become cold and unaffectionate. I would be hurt at those times and it was difficult for both of us.

Even at other times she would shy away from being romantic and back away from closeness, and this caused me a lot of pain. She was shy about showing our relationship in public, especially if her women friends were around. She didn't want to stand out exactly. She even said that she felt like she didn't want to be too important to anyone or too valued. At those times, she would pull inward to protect herself.

There were occasions when I was shaken up, too, because I had never been so vulnerable in a relationship. But eventually we sweated out these difficult times together because we really cared deeply for one another. To this day, we are lovers and the best of friends, rely on each other for support and companionship, and are a vital part of each other's lives. I know that she knows me and loves me and that I make her happy. She says that her life would be impossibly dull without me. I can barely imagine the horror of living life without her.

The relationship between this man and woman was inspirational to all of their friends and acquaintances and was illustrative of what we conceive to be the essence of a loving style of relating. Both parties were kind, generous with one another, independent, self-reliant, warm, respectful, sexually responsive, not restrictive or intrusive, and nondefensive. Although this example illustrates love between a couple, many of the same qualities apply to love between friends and family members and can be extended to a love for humanity.

WHAT GENUINE LOVE IS NOT

To better understand what genuine love is, perhaps we should also describe what it is not. Love is not what we mean when one is told by a family member that "mommy or daddy really loves you but he/she just doesn't know how to show it." Love is not selfish, possessive, or demanding, or a proprietary right over the other. Love is never submission or dominance, emotional coercion, or manipulation. Love is not the desperate attempt to deny aloneness or the search for security that many couples manifest in their desire for a fused identity.

Lawrence (1920) stressed this theme in his work:

> Why should we consider ourselves, men and women, as broken fragments of one whole? It is not true. We are not broken fragments of one whole. (p. 271)

> Fusion, fusion, this horrible fusion of two beings, which every woman and most men insisted on, was it not nauseous and horrible anyhow, whether it was a fusion of the spirit or of the emotional body? Why could they not remain individuals, limited by their own limits? Why this dreadful all-comprehensiveness, this hateful tyranny? Why not leave the other being free, why try to absorb, or melt, or merge? One might abandon oneself utterly to the *moments*, but not to any other being. (p. 391)

Love is not to be confused with emotional hunger, that is, a desperate, immature need for dependence on another that drains the other person's vitality. Nor is it to be confused with a deep longing to find total confirmation of oneself in the other. In *The Denial of Death*, Becker (1973/1997) described the results of finding such an "ideal" love:

> If you find the ideal love and try to make it the sole judge of good and bad in yourself, the measure of your strivings, you become simply the reflex of another person. You lose yourself in the other, just as obedient children lose themselves in the family. . . . When you confuse personal love and cosmic heroism you are bound to fail in both spheres. . . . How can a human being be a god-like "everything" to another? (p. 166)

In "Projecting Our Other Half," Sanford (1980/1985) discussed the other side of the coin of "ideal love." He argued that

> To the extent that a relationship is founded on projection, the element of human love is lacking. To be in love with someone we do not know as a person, but are attracted to because they reflect back to us the image of the god or goddess in our souls, is, in a sense, to be in love with oneself, not with the other person. Real love begins only when one person comes to know another for who he or she really is as a human being, and begins to like and care for that human being. (p. 88)

Love is not a word to be bandied about as in a couple's collusive attempt to maintain control of one another. It does not relate to an inner state of mind that has no recognizable outward manifestations.

In our experience, we have found that many people fail to reach a level of emotional maturity that would allow them to be capable of offering love, and they are also afraid of accepting or receiving love. In working with couples in initial intake sessions, we have observed that one or the other will outline a number of objections that amount to a fairly extensive annihilation of the other's character, only to be followed by an equally denigrating attack by the other partner. As the session progresses, we often notice their mistreatment of one another firsthand and tend to agree with both parties' assessment of each other, as these negative behaviors become more obvious. In other words, they have described each other fairly accurately, as it turns out, and manifest considerable hostility. Yet when we ask these warring couples why they stay together when they find each other so objectionable, they typically respond by saying, "Because we love each other." However, the destructive behaviors these people manifest toward one another do not fit any acceptable definition of the word love. Why call it "love" when the behavior toward the love object is neither affectionate nor respectful, lacks communication and companionship, violates the personal boundaries of the other, and is often insensitive or outright hostile or abusive?

However, our views also resonate with those of Laing (1967), who expressed cautious optimism when describing couples who lived their lives based primarily on illusions of love. In *The Politics of Experience*, he wrote, "Perhaps men and women were born to love one another, simply and genuinely, rather than to this travesty that we call love" (p. 76).

OTHER CONTEMPORARY VIEWS ON PSYCHOLOGICAL AND BIOLOGICAL COMPONENTS OF LOVE

The subjective experience of being in love involves a multitude of biological, environmental, and social factors. Love encompasses both an emotional experience and behavioral responses. Feelings of love, as with other feelings, arise involuntarily and are experienced as sensations in the body (Firestone, Firestone, & Catlett, 2003). As Greenberg (2002) succinctly put it: "Emotions go coursing through people's bodies whether they like it or not" (p. 14). The various components that impact the experience of emotions, including love, have been studied by researchers, including bodily (physical) components (Fosha, 2000; Valliant, 1997) and components involving evaluation, perception, sensation, and feeling (Greenberg & Safran, 1987).

In their work, Hatfield and Rapson (1993) make a distinction between two basic types of love. They defined passionate love as a "hot," intense emotion: "A state of intense longing for union with another. Passionate love is a complex functional whole including appraisals or appreciations, subjective feelings, expressions, patterned physiological processes, action tendencies, and instrumental behaviors" (p. 5). In contrast, these researchers defined companionate love as a "warm" emotion, "the affection and tenderness we feel for those with whom our lives are deeply entwined" (p. 9).

Attachment researchers who focus on the role of love in caregiving and attachment behavioral systems have proposed several hypotheses about the behavioral responses associated with love. For example, Kirkpatrick (1998) observed that "Many behaviors exhibited by adult lovers resemble behaviors of infants interacting with their primary caregivers. Adult lovers engage in kissing, cuddling, nuzzling, 'baby talk,' holding hands, and a variety of other behavior patterns commonly observed in mother-infant dyads" (pp. 362–363). However, Kirkpatrick also noted that adult romantic attachments may be qualitatively different from infant–parent attachments. "Romantic relationships might involve neither the caregiving system nor the attachment system per se, but rather are organized around a single component shared by those systems: the emotional bond of love" (p. 361).

Research into specific physiological and neurological underpinnings of love has only recently been undertaken by the scientific world.[3] According to Insel (2002) despite "nearly 50 years of research on the neuroendocrinology of sex," there is a dearth of studies regarding "where or how the brain mediates love" (p. 254). Insel also noted that

> Love, whether considered as attachment, such as a pair bond, or viewed as a form of self-sacrificing altruism, is difficult to define operationally. . . . Although most of us may recognize love as the most powerful psychological and biological experience of our lives, how do we quantify this experience? (pp. 254–255)

In spite of these obvious difficulties, several researchers have attempted to identify the physical or neurological correlates of love as manifested both in attachment behaviors between parent and child and in adult romantic attachments (Fisher, 1992, 2000, 2004; Fisher, Aron, Mashek, Li, & Brown, 2002; Lewis, Amini, & Lannon, 2000; Love, 2001; Pines, 1999). In a review of these studies, Lewis and colleagues (2000) offered a thoughtful account of how physiological and psychological factors may interact to create not only the experience of love, but also an individual's core sexual identity:

> From birth to death, love is not just the focus of human experience but also the life force of the mind, determining our moods, stabilizing our bodily rhythms, and changing the structure of our brains. The body's physiology ensures that relationships determine and fix our identities. Love makes us who we are, and who we can become. (p. viii)

Being in love and falling in love may involve different biochemical processes. Research studies have focused on determining biological components underlying emotions that people experience during the "falling in love" phase. For example, Pines (1999) noted that the process of "falling in love" involves two basic components, arousal and labeling.

> All strong emotions [including love] have two components, one is physiological and has to do with the body, the other is cognitive and has to do with the mind. The physiological component is a state of arousal. The cognitive component is a label that explains the arousal. (p. 14)

Pines cited a series of studies conducted by Aron (role-play experiments in a natural setting and in the laboratory) that investigated the cognitive components of arousal and the important role played by labeling in partner selection, attraction, and the subjective experience of falling in love. In one such experiment, called the "creaky bridge" experiment, Dutton and Aron (1974) asked one group of men to cross either a "flimsy suspension bridge" five feet wide and some 250 feet above jagged boulders and river rapids of the Capilano Canyon in Vancouver, British Columbia, or a broad, low bridge farther upstream. Fisher (2004) described the experiment as follows:

> In the middle of each bridge stood a beautiful young woman (part of their research team) who asked each passing man to fill out a questionnaire. After each man completed the survey queries, she casually told him that if he had any further questions about the study, he should call her at her home. She gave each her telephone number. None knew the woman was part of the experiment. Nine out of thirty-two men who walked the narrow, wobbly high bridge were attracted enough to call the woman in her home. Only two of those who met her on the low, solid bridge contacted her. (p. 193)

Fisher conjectured that the attraction was linked to a physical change in the body that is associated with danger: "Danger stimulates the production of adrenaline, a bodily stimulant closely related to dopamine and norepinephrine" (p. 193).[4] As psychologist Hatfield (1988) stated, "Adrenaline makes the heart grow fonder" (p. 204). In other words, the sense of danger created a sense of excitement similar to the experience of "falling in love."

In discussing brain chemicals or neurotransmitters that may contribute to the rapid heartbeat associated with this type of arousal, Liebowitz (1983) hypothesized that the euphoric state of falling in love or infatuation may be induced by phenylethylamine (PEA). According to Liebowitz,

> Drugs that raise norepinephrine, dopamine, and PEA levels at times cause overstimulation, in which people need only a few hours' sleep, tend to feel very optimistic about the future. . . . Interestingly, this is similar to what happens to people when they get promoted, win a lottery, or fall in love. (pp. 37–38)

In her book, *Why We Love*, Fisher (2004) stressed the fact that

> We still know so little about this madness of the gods. . . . But of one thing I am convinced: no matter how well scientists map the brain and uncover the biology of romantic love, they will never destroy the mystery or ecstasy of this passion. I say this from my own experience. (p. 218–219)

CONCLUSION

Learning to love wholeheartedly is a most worthwhile endeavor but requires considerable devotion, time, and energy. As Rilke (1908/1984) observed,

> It is also good to love: because love is difficult. For one human being to love another human being: that is perhaps the most difficult task that has been entrusted to us, the ultimate task, the final test and proof, the work for which all other work is merely preparation. (p. 68)

Serious resistance will be encountered as clients strive to learn how to love and be loved more fully because when people have been hurt in the past, they are reluctant to trust and be open to being hurt again. They feel self-protective and fear being vulnerable and open to emotional pain. In describing this learning process, Coelho (2004) wrote

> Everyone knows how to love, because we are all born with that gift. Some people have a natural talent for it, but the majority of us have to re-learn, to remember how to love, and everyone, without exception, needs to burn on the bonfire of past emotions, to relive certain joys and griefs, certain ups and downs, until they can see the connecting thread that exists behind each new encounter; because there is a connecting thread. (p. 139)

A person who overcomes self-limiting defenses and learns to give and receive love experiences the most satisfaction in life. Indeed, as we noted in the previous chapter, love is the antidote to existential pain and aloneness. When love is sincere and real, it reaches spiritual proportions that give value and meaning to life.

NOTES

1. Excerpt from *The Four Loves*, Copyright © 1960 by C. S. Lewis, renewed 1988 by Arthur Owen Barfield, reprinted by permission of Harcourt, Inc.
2. Quotation from chapter 27, p. 411, from *You Can't Go Home Again*. Copyright 1934, 1937, 1938, 1939, 1940 by Maxwell Perkins as Executor of the Thomas Wolfe estate. Copyright renewed © 1968 by Paul Gitlin. Reprinted by permission of HarperCollins Publishers, Inc.
3. To some people, these investigations are unwelcome because they threaten to destroy the "mystery of love." In their book *Brain Sex*, Moir and Jessel (1989) called attention to the fact that

   Senator Proxmire . . . in opposing a grant request from the National Science Foundation into the nature of love . . . said: "200 million Americans want to leave some things a mystery, and right at the top of those things we don't want to know is why a man falls in love with a woman and vice versa." (p. 101)

4. Fisher (2000) found that these parallels suggest that "levels of CNS dopamine are rising in the infatuated individual as their beloved takes on special meaning" (p. 99). In a functional magnetic resonance imaging (fMRI) experiment, Fisher found that the caudate nucleus, which intensifies the experience of romance, "became active as our lovesick subjects gazed at the photos of their beloveds" (p. 149). Fisher (2000) also reported studies showing that "increased concentrations of dopamine in the central nervous system (CNS) are associated with exposure to a novel environment . . . as well as with heightened attention, motivation, and goal-directed behaviors" (p. 99). Two hormones, oxytocin and vasopressin, have also been shown to be activated during sexual intercourse and are also associated with feelings of attachment. According to Love (2001), "Oxytocin is largely responsible for why you feel closer to your partner and more 'in love' when you have regular sex" (p. 115).

II

FACTORS INFLUENCING SEXUAL DEVELOPMENT AND ADULT SEXUAL FUNCTIONING

3

FACTORS THAT AFFECT AN INDIVIDUAL'S SEXUALITY

Sexuality teaches us, more than any other human experience, about self—who am I and why do I exist?

—Harvey and Weber (2002, p. 55)

What is sexuality? What precisely does the word refer to? A certain ambiguity seems to be associated with its meaning and common usage. According to Zoldbrod (1998) "Sexuality means a dimension of personality instead of referring to a person's capacity for erotic response alone" (p. 2). Aanstoos (2001) defined sexuality as being "like an atmosphere, in the sense that it is an ever-present background—a horizon of existence. . . . Just as we *are*, we *are sexual*" (p. 78).

Human sexual development and sexuality are topics far broader in scope than the act of sexual intercourse per se. Sexuality encompasses an individual's basic identity as well as the dimensions of healthy sexuality delineated in chapter 1. Indeed, the ways that people express themselves sexually play a significant role in all relationships, including those between women and men, women and women, and men and men. As Harding (2001) cogently noted, "Whenever two people find themselves together they have to negotiate the hetero-erotic or the homo-erotic potential of their relationship in some way" (p. 1). In the discussions of sexual relating throughout this book, we refer to all interpersonal relationships and all types of sexual encounters between adults. Our goal is to examine psychological and social factors that influence the wide range of sexual experiences and intimate associations that human beings are involved in.

In our work, we have found that the fundamental issues in disturbed sexual relationships are closely related to an intolerance of intimacy based on each partner's psychological defenses and his or her negative attitudes toward self and others. Fears of aloneness, abandonment, rejection, and potential loss manifested by both partners are significant factors at the core of the problems they encounter in relating sexually. In particular, the combination of love and sex is a difficult goal for most people to achieve because it revives painful memories and feelings from childhood. It also arouses the dread of potential loss through rejection and ultimately, through death. In addition, an intimate sexual relationship, in which the lover sees the other in a realistic, positive light, threatens the defense system by interrupting negative fantasies about the self and disrupting psychological equilibrium (Firestone & Catlett, 1999).

When one constructs a powerful defense system, which often happens when there has been anxiety and emotional deprivation in one's early years, there is a compelling need to hold on to and protect that system of defenses. Fears, anxieties, and insecurities also drive individuals to reenact their parents' defensive style of interacting and destructive, stereotypical attitudes toward each other in their closest relationships. The tendency to emulate negative parental attitudes and behaviors, together with the process of retreating to a defensive, self-protective posture, interferes with the ability to develop and sustain fulfilling sexual relationships characterized by feelings of compassion and equality.

In this chapter, we explore the factors that contribute to the difficulties that many individuals encounter in developing and maintaining, or even tolerating, intimate, loving sexuality. The chapter begins with a brief description of some biological factors that may contribute to the development of gender identity and other aspects of adult sexual functioning. Next we describe how painful childhood experiences and interpersonal attitudes in the family impact the sexual development of children and predispose the formation of psychological defenses. From a developmental perspective, we describe how identification and imitation processes operating within the family can influence gender role expectations and boys' and girls' sexual identities and sexuality. We also explain how sexual abuse affects children's emerging sexuality. The chapter ends with a discussion of the diverse cultural and societal influences on people's sexuality and sexual lives, including the impact of the media and popular culture.

SOME BIOLOGICAL FACTORS THAT AFFECT
HUMAN SEXUALITY

Sexual behavior is based on an innate biologically determined drive. As with any other animal, human beings have a natural drive to be sexual and reproduce (Fisher, 1992, 2000, 2004; S. Freud, 1905/1953; Hazan & Shaver, 1987). In addition, a person's sexual behavior, sexual desires, and gender identity are psychosomatic, that is, they encompass aspects of the mind as well as the body (Fausto-Sterling, 2000).

In their attempts to explain the course of a child's sexual development and its culmination in an adult's sexual functioning, philosophers, psychologists, and others have focused on the mind or the body, or on an interaction between the two (Everaerd, Laan, & Spiering, 2000). For example, philosopher Giddens (1992) proposed that "The body, plainly enough, is in some sense—yet to be determined—the domain of sexuality" (p. 31), while psychologist Michael Bader (2002) argued that "Sex begins in the mind and then travels downward. . . . It is the imaginative power of the mind that transforms our biological imperatives into the actual experience of sexual pleasure" (p. 5).

Even though human beings have evolved beyond estrus (which drives sexual behavior in other species), "the biological imperative to *reproduce and to multiply* still gives shape to our sexual desires" (H. Kaplan, 1995, p. 24). For example, testosterone is recognized as the libidinal hormone for both men and women. According to Moir and Jessel (1989), "The more testosterone, the greater the sexual urges already present, be they homosexual or heterosexual, orthodox or deviant" (pp. 103–104). Neuroendocrinologist Olsen (1992) noted that "Hormones secreted by the testes during a critical developmental period have masculinizing and defeminizing effects on sexual behaviors" (p. 1).

According to Fisher (2004), dopamine and norepinephrine are brain chemicals that initiate sexual desire, probably through increasing testosterone levels. As noted in the previous chapter, oxytocin and vasopressin also appear to be involved in sexual responses as well as tendencies to form an intimate attachment. H. Kaplan (1995) asserted, for example, that oxytocin in particular is probably the "'glue' that attaches babies and mothers as well as lovers to each other" (p. 31).

As is true with other innate human capacities, the diverse manifestations of an individual's sexuality are multidetermined; they are powerfully influenced or controlled by a wide range of genetic, environmental, and social factors. These factors interact with each other to determine the ways in which each person expresses his or her sexuality. As sex researcher Bancroft (1999) correctly observed, "We cannot expect to understand human sexuality unless we consider both biology and culture (and it is important to stress culture, not just environment) and the interface between them as it affects the individual, the dyad, and the group" (p. 226).

INTERPERSONAL FACTORS THAT AFFECT CHILDREN'S EMERGING SEXUALITY

During their formative years, children are faced with pain and anxiety from two major sources: (a) negative experiences in the family and (b) fundamental human issues such as the evolving awareness of aloneness, aging, and death as inevitable processes in life (Firestone, 1997a). A major source of the problems that plague adult sexual relationships can be traced to adaptations that children necessarily make to early interpersonal pain, separation experiences, and other losses. Later in the developmental sequence, children learn about death, the ultimate separation. At this point, the defenses they formed originally in relation to interpersonal stress are powerfully reinforced. Thereafter, disturbances in emotional and sexual functioning, resulting from the process of defending oneself against interpersonal and existential pain, are retained throughout life, predisposing serious problems in one's intimate relationships.

The Effects of Parental Attitudes and Behaviors

Emotional damage to children is a complex phenomenon (Belsky, 1980) and no single pattern of parent–child interaction is fully explanatory in relation to adult sexual functioning. However, there are a number of interpersonal factors that cause children to form defenses that affect their body image, emerging sexuality, and future choice of partners.

It is important to recognize the fact that parents have a fundamental ambivalence in relation to their offspring. Parents' feelings and attitudes toward their children, like their feelings and attitudes toward themselves, are both positive and negative (Chen & Kaplan, 2001; Firestone, 1990b; R. Parker (1995); Rohner, 1986, 1991). On the basis of cross-cultural studies encompassing 35 cultures, Rohner (1991) found that parents' attitudes could be assessed along a continuum ranging from parental warmth and acceptance to indifference, rejection, and hostility. He concluded that parental rejection has a universal effect on children and that it can be measured intergenerationally.

The fact that parents have strong desires to nurture and care for their children does not negate the hostility or indifference they feel at times toward them (Firestone & Catlett, 1999). In the process of growing up, all children experience varying degrees of emotional pain in their early family relationships. Even in "ideal" families there is unavoidable frustration and pain, for example, in reaction to inevitable separation experiences and existential concerns, and most family constellations are less than ideal (Beavers & Hampson, 1990; Tedeschi & Felson, 1994).

Children's hurt or angry response to their parents becomes transformed into defensive behaviors that are later elaborated in many areas of their adult lives, including their sexuality. This defensive incorporation of parental characteristics and behaviors is heightened during times of unusual stress and emotional pain. The dynamics underlying the child's strong tendencies to imitate a parent's more negative traits and behaviors can be understood in terms of the defense of identifying with the aggressor (Ferenczi, 1933/1955; A. Freud, 1966). Under stressful or abusive conditions, the small child ceases identifying with him- or herself as the weak, vulnerable child and instead identifies with the powerful parent. In the process, the child incorporates the parent's aggression and hostility and takes on the parent's defenses, behaviors, and traits as his or her own.

Parental Rejection and Hostility

Obviously, parents vary widely in their responses to their infants and children. At times parents are warm and affectionate toward their child, while at other times they may be unresponsive or even cruel. When parents are consistently warm and accepting in their interactions with family members, children generally grow up with a sense of well-being and healthy self-esteem, and they are likely to feel accepting of their bodies and sexuality. However, when parents are inconsistent and erratic in their responses, children learn to expect rejection or punishment and tend to withdraw so they will not be hurt. This anticipation of being hurt or rejected persists into adulthood, influencing individuals' responses in close interpersonal relationships.

Parental attitudes of rejection, indifference, and/or hostility toward a child can result in feelings of being unlovable. These feelings are later often manifested in negative feelings toward various body parts that lead to critical thoughts about these specific areas. Subsequently, when these parts are touched or otherwise stimulated, a state of anxiety or tension, or even physical pain may be aroused rather than feelings of pleasure (Orbach, 2004).[1]

James: My girlfriend is a very affectionate person, but sometimes I can hardly stand her touch, especially when she touches my face. When I started exploring the reasons for this, I remembered that when I was a little kid, I really wanted to be close to my mother and wanted to show her affection. When she would be watching TV, I'd want to lay my head in her lap, but she was so tense that she couldn't just relax and sit there. She'd tell me to move over, to get away from her. When I thought about those times, I had more understanding about why I feel uncomfortable with my girlfriend's touch.

There are a number of reasons why many well-intentioned parents hold back affection from their children. Parents who were deprived of affection and love during their childhood often lack the emotional resources to provide affection, love, direction, and control for their children. In addition, the aliveness and spontaneity of infants and children threaten their parents' defenses by reawakening suppressed feelings from the past. In an attempt to avoid these painful emotions, many parents unintentionally maintain a certain distance from their children by being indifferent, rejecting, critical, or even hostile toward them. In fact, frequently parents find themselves treating their offspring with many of the same destructive behaviors they experienced during their formative years. There is also evidence that parents experience discomfort when their child passes through stages of development that were particularly painful or traumatic for the parents themselves. During this time period, they can become unusually insensitive or punishing to the child (Gerson, 1995).

In addition, many parents experience feelings of discomfort and pain when their children express physical affection toward them. To cope with these feelings, they may pull away or even become punitive in their responses. Children who experience this type of response gradually learn to inhibit the expression of their positive feelings. Many children come to believe that there is something wrong with their loving feelings or that their affection or their physical nature or bodies are somehow unacceptable.

Parents' discomfort and anxiety are transmitted to their infant through physical touch, facial expressions, and other behavioral cues. Observers have noted a form of withdrawal in mothers who appear to be unaffected or unmoved by the emotional experience of feeding or caring for a child, and who avoid eye contact with their infants (Bolton, 1983; Welldon, 1988). Other studies have investigated the ways that a mother's feeling state is transmitted to her infant (Beebe & Lachmann, 2002; LeDoux, 1996; D. Lott, 1998; Schore, 1994; Siegel, 1999; Siegel & Hartzell, 2003; Stern, 1985, 1995).[2]

A number of theorists and researchers (Fosha, 2000; Gewirtz & Hollenbeck, 1990; Harlow, 1958; Harlow, Harlow, & Suomi, 1971; Montagu, 1986; Orbach, 2004; Stern, 1985, 1994, 1995) have emphasized the importance of bodily touch as well as parental acceptance of the infant's body. According to Orbach (2004), "We therapists know how absolutely critical benign and loving touch is in both early development and in life in general"

(p. 37). She also emphasized that "The body that is not received, the body that has no body to meet in its development becomes a body that is as precarious, fractured, defended, and unstable as a precarious psyche" (p. 27). Inhibitions resulting from a "precarious" body image and a sense of being unlovable often cause people to hold back their love, affection, and sexual responses in their closest, most intimate associations.

Harsh Attitudes Toward a Child's Body and Developing Sexuality

Early experiences with diapering and toilet training play a significant role in an individual's image of his or her body. Negative attitudes or overt disgust expressed by parents contribute to a sense of shame that persists into adult life. The genital area becomes imbued with an anal connotation, confused with excretory functions, and is therefore considered dirty. Shameful feelings are extended to anything below the waist.

> Melissa: Recently, I found a photograph of myself as a baby, strapped to the toilet. I couldn't have been more than a few months old. My mother used to brag to her friends that I was toilet-trained before I was a year old. Later, when I was older, there was a bottle of some kind of liquid, it smelled like peroxide, on the back of the toilet. She told me I had to thoroughly cleanse myself with it every time I went to the bathroom. After I was married, I continued to worry about cleanliness. I used douches daily, or sometimes more often, because I had a basic feeling that I was dirty "down there."

We have found that excessive control or domination, as well as an overconcern with cleanliness and orderliness, can damage children's sense of autonomy and their feelings that their bodies belong to them (Firestone, 1990b). Other clinicians have described tendencies on the part of some parents to take over the child's body and bodily functions in this manner. For example, according to Fisher and Fisher (1986), "Such parents may express their anger and suspicion by imposing unreasonable body controls. What is terribly confusing to the child is that such controls are invariably disguised as something that is being done 'for your own good'" (p. 79). In his extensive studies of shame, M. Lewis (1992) called attention to the fact that parents often express disgust or contempt when socializing their children, especially during toilet training. He explained that if parents are unable to reason with their children or feel it is unacceptable to express anger, they may employ disgusted or contemptuous facial expressions, usually unconsciously, as a solution to disciplinary problems. The child incorporates these negative parental attitudes that often generalize to an overall feeling that he or she is basically bad, undesirable, and unlovable.

Imitation of Parents' Distorted Views
of Sexuality and the Human Body

Parental attitudes toward nudity, masturbation, and sex play have a powerful impact on children's ongoing sexual development. Developmental psychologists have stressed the fact that during early childhood, masturbation and sex play are normal and typically not problematic (Bonner, 2001; Martinson, 1994; Zoldbrod, 1998). However, on an emotional level, many parents still find it difficult to think of masturbation and sex play as normal, as not harmful to children, and they tend to respond accordingly. Other parents find nudity in young children to be problematic and by their attitudes, convey the message to their child that his or her body is shameful. When parents have repressive attitudes and rigid dogmatic religious beliefs, these attitudes, together with their sexual tensions, are covertly or overtly conveyed to the child, usually with negative consequences (Firestone, 1990b; Davidson & Darling, 1993; Gagnon, 1985; Kelsey & Kelsey, 1991; Zoldbrod, 1998).[3]

> *Carlos:* Once when I was about 12 years old, I walked into my parents' bedroom and my mother was taking a shower in the bathroom. I didn't know she was in there, and when she came out, she yelled at me for being in their bedroom and ran past me very quickly to get a robe to cover herself with. For the whole time I was growing up, there was always a big fuss being made about me getting dressed quick, to cover up my body. So even now to this day, if I'm in the locker room at the gym, or if it's the first time that I'm with a woman and we're getting undressed, my first thought is that they're going to see that there's something weird about me, and it leaves me feeling really awkward and shy, especially in a sexual situation.

Attitudes Toward Sex

Virtually every individual, to some degree, has developed a negative point of view about sexuality and the body, especially the sexual areas. Children witness their parents' distorted attitudes, which they assimilate. These attitudes take sex out of the realm of a natural human function and relegate it to a separate and distinct area of life. Within many families, there is little or no indication that the parents enjoy an affectionate, active sexual relationship. In the extreme, some parents are reluctant to express physical affection in front of their children. Many parents feel that children should learn healthy attitudes about sex, but few discuss sex openly and personally with their children (Firestone, 1990b; Friday, 1977; Galinsky, 1981; Schiffer, 2004).

We have noted that, in some families, parents go to the opposite extreme and overemphasize sex, which can be as damaging as the more repressive attitudes of more rigid families. Parents who have a distorted focus on sexuality and an overly sexualized style of relating extend those attitudes to their children. For example, an adolescent girl recalled that when she was five, her "open-minded" parents provided her with detailed information about sex that was inappropriate for her age. Although they subscribed to the view that sex is simply a natural function of the human body, their sexual attitudes and activities were promiscuous. Later, the young woman revealed that she had grown up thinking that all interactions between a man and a woman were sexual and had no idea that friendship or affection could exist without a sexual component being present.

Attitudes Toward One's Body

Negative views held by parents in relation to the human body and nudity predispose the development of a sense of shame and guilt in children. In turn, this formation of a negative body image significantly affects sexual attitudes and feelings in one's adult life. Theorists have emphasized that sexual identity and self-esteem have their foundations in one's image of one's body (Orbach, 2004; Storr, 1968; Whitaker & Malone, 1953). According to Storr (1968), an individual's self-esteem is chiefly rooted in sexuality. "We cannot escape our physical natures; and a proper pride in oneself as a human being is rooted in the body through which love is given and taken" (p. 69).

When observing infants and toddlers, one can see that they enjoy a sense of freedom and a lack of self-consciousness about being naked. Yet by the time they are five or six, many children are embarrassed to be seen without clothes. The effects of children imitating their parents' attitudes and internalizing shameful feelings about their own bodies can be observed in the negative thoughts and feelings many men and women have about themselves. We have found that most people have critical thoughts about various parts of their bodies. These internal attacks often impair their ability to feel sensations in certain areas of their body or complicate a potentially gratifying sexual experience.

When parents dislike themselves, have a negative view of their bodies, and are ashamed of their productions, they will inadvertently pass on the shame they feel about themselves and their physical nature to their children. It is natural for a person to extend his or her subjective views about him- or herself to his or her creations. In addition, many parents tend to disown negative attitudes toward their bodies and project them onto their offspring.

As a result of assimilating these distorted views early in life, many men and women still suffer from feelings of sexual inferiority and inadequacy.

Most have secret doubts about their sexuality and countless criticisms about their bodies.

> *Jonathan:* I have critical thoughts about myself, about practically everything about me, my shoulders, chest, legs, and especially my penis. The attacks [inner voices] are like, *You're so small, you're not like other men. Just look how small your penis is. It doesn't look like a man's penis, and everything else about you is wrong, everything else about you is like a little boy. How can you possibly expect to attract women if you look like this?* I'm constantly looking at other men and thinking to myself that every man looks more masculine than me or more attractive to women than me.
>
> I remember that my father had a low opinion of himself as a man. I think he extended the feelings he had about himself to me because he always seemed embarrassed by me, especially by the way I looked. Actually I was a really skinny kid. One summer when I was about 10 years old, we were at the beach, and my father humiliated me by ridiculing me in front of all my friends, pointing out how "skinny and scrawny" I was. So today many times I feel like hiding. I literally don't want to be recognized, because I'm afraid in that recognition and in any comparison with any other man, I have to lose.

Similarly, many women have serious doubts about their appearance, their ability to attract a sexual partner, and the size and shape of their body. For example, Rosa revealed negative thoughts she experiences during lovemaking:

> I start having picky, critical thoughts about my breasts, like *You're so strange-looking. You don't have breasts like normal women, there's really something wrong with your breasts, they're not big enough, they're so small and they're not the right shape.* I think this stuff a lot, but it feels hard to say. I feel ashamed to say it.
>
> Also I'm really critical of myself about being short. I think I use it to feel like I'm not like a real woman or that I don't really have a real woman's body. The thoughts go like this, *You're deformed in some way because you're small, and it makes you different. You don't look the same as other women.*

Men and women who have negative attitudes toward their bodies and sexuality feel confused and lack confidence. Any criticism of how men are sexually, any sign of sexual dissatisfaction on the part of their partner, or any hint of rejection reinforces men's inner doubts about their manhood. Men's concerns appear to center on the theme of sexual inadequacy, which in some cases may be related to their fathers' views of their own bodies and their attitudes toward sex. Many women have similar doubts about their femininity. Based on the strong identification with the mother, the female child internalizes her mother's critical attitudes toward her body and toward sexuality. As an adult, she often experiences these attitudes as derogatory thoughts about her weight, breast size and shape, genitals, and overall sexual performance (Fenchel, 1998; Friday, 1977; Rheingold, 1964).

To summarize, many men and women have grown up in families where they were taught distorted views about the human body and sex. In turn, they pass these views on to their offspring. Thus, for many men and women, the simple act of sex is often contaminated by a harmful socialization process that inhibits spontaneity and fosters feelings of self-consciousness and shame.

Identification With and Imitation of Same Sex Parent

Parents' importance as role models for their children has long been emphasized in the literature (Bandura, 1986; Maccoby & Jacklin, 1974). Both the strengths and weaknesses of mothers and fathers are transmitted through the generations within the family context, with parents serving as positive and negative role models for the sexual attitudes and behavior of their children. Parents' positive traits and behaviors are readily imitated by children and assimilated without conflict into their personalities and behavior repertoires. However, the most pervasive influences on the sexual functioning of both women and men may lie in their identification with, and imitation of, the negative characteristics and behaviors of the parent of the same sex (Bandura, Ross, & Ross, 1961).

Children closely observe and incorporate the ways in which their parent of the same sex relates to his or her mate. If interactions between the parents are generally hostile, sons tend to identify with and imitate their father's negative attitudes and behaviors in relation to the mother and other women, whereas daughters take on their mother's negative views and behaviors toward the father and men in general.

Mothers and Daughters

The relationship between mothers and daughters is based on an identification that is intense and powerful (Firestone, 1990b; Mendell, 1998). According to Mendell (1998), "The mother-daughter tie is the most archaic, difficult, and in some ways the most important and lasting relationship in a woman's psychic life" (p. 227). This strong identification can have positive as well as negative consequences in a woman's life, especially in her relationships with men (Fenchel, 1998; Welldon, 1988). Girls learn by observation and imitation to be like the mother and feel strange or uncomfortable when they are different from their role model.

In addition, girls who suffer maternal deprivation carry elements of exaggerated need into subsequent relationships with men. The anger, resentment, and search for nurturance continue to complicate friendships and relationships with women as well. Paradoxically, the more painful and frustrating the interactions with a rejecting or withholding mother, the more the daughter tends to incorporate her mother's toxic attitudes and behaviors. Left unchallenged over time, the distinction between the daughter's personality and the incorporated negative traits becomes less and less obvious until the defended posture of the mother becomes dominant and the pattern is repeated with her children.

The effects of this imitative process can be observed in couple and family relationships. For example, when a mother represents herself as an asexual woman and allows herself to deteriorate physically, it has a destructive effect on her daughter's sexuality. During a discussion group, several women reported that as they were growing up they were bothered by their mother's lack of attention to appearance and apparent disinterest in sex. An awareness of these negative attitudes, traits, and behaviors in their mothers caused these women considerable guilt and self-recriminations that often took the form of self-critical thoughts.

> Allison: I remember that my sister and I used to think of ways to try to get my mother to care more about herself. We used to actually talk about what we could do to try to get her to bathe more often because we were aware of her body odors. It was actually a topic of conversation between my sister and me, because we knew she never cared about herself and it made us feel terrible.

> Joan: I was angry that my mother didn't just lose weight, that she didn't take care of herself. I remember being repelled by the way she looked. But at the same time, it made me really critical of myself. I'm really critical of my body because I think I look like her a lot and I feel heavy like her, even though I'm not that overweight.

Repercussions of the destructive elements in the mother-daughter bond have a negative effect on a woman's relationship with men and later, with her children. However, it is more important to emphasize the powerful limitation this bond may impose on each woman's sense of self. Its stultifying impact on a daughter's sexuality and feelings of self-worth and competency is far greater than many people realize (Firestone, 1990b).

Fathers and Sons

Fathers play an influential role in their son's sexual development, just as mothers do with their daughters. Boys who experience their father as angry and abusive in relation to their mother are often fearful of becoming like him. As adults, they may inhibit their natural assertiveness and attempt to hold back their angry reactions to provocations from their partners on the one hand; on the other hand, they may find themselves acting out abusive behavior in relation to their partners, just as their fathers did.

A boy may observe his father's hostile, patronizing, and defensive attitudes toward women and may identify with him when he is in conflict with his wife. Some men have a paternalistic or judgmental style of relating to their wives, which their sons imitate and later reenact in their relationships with women. For example, David recalled that while he was growing up, his father was punitive and harsh toward him and his mother.

> David: I remember how my father related to my mother. He was condescending and super-critical of her. He yelled at her at lot, telling her she had no right as a woman to do thus and so, or implying that she had no right to speak her mind or have opinions. So it's been painful for me to recognize that that was the way I treated my wife when I was married. I always acted superior to her and ordered her around and directed her, telling her, in effect, what she could and could not do. Also I never listened to her or thought she had anything worthwhile to say.
>
> One day after she had been seeing a therapist for a while, she was telling me what she would like to do that evening, and I got very angry at her, I guess simply for having an opinion of her own. I yelled at her and insisted that she had no right to say what she was saying. In fact, I told her in no uncertain terms that I didn't want to hear another word out of her. Instead of cowering like she usually did, she just looked puzzled, and, actually slightly amused. She said, "David, you're talking to me like I'm a child." I realized then that my being a parent in relation to her being like a child was over.

If the father is passive or subordinate to the mother, boys closely observe and incorporate his style of relating to her; boys are acutely aware of the times when their father caters to their mother, is intimidated by her tears, or surrenders to her control. In families where this dynamic predominates, the son may imitate his father's subservient role.

Competition and Oedipal Issues

Parents' unresolved feelings about competition are often acted out in relation to their offspring. Intense covert feelings of rivalry, resentment, or hatred toward a child on the part of the parent of the same gender, the parents' overall retreat from competitiveness and sexuality, and their lack of sexual fulfillment, are debilitating forces affecting the child's attitude toward competing and his or her sexuality as an adult.

S. Freud (1909/1957) observed that children exhibit competitive and sexually rivalrous feelings toward parents of the same sex as they strive for the attention of the opposite sex parent and noted that these rivalrous feelings engender a fear of retaliation in children. However, parents' rivalrous, competitive feelings toward their children have been seen as less acceptable and are less documented in the literature. Clearly, there are some exceptions, including Bloch (1985), Firestone (1990b, 1997a), Kestenberg and Kestenberg (1987), A. Miller (1979/1981), Rheingold (1964, 1967), and Shengold (1989) among others.

Historically, the incest taboo came into existence as an attempt to suppress rivalry within the family system (DeMause, 1991; Fox, 1983/1993; Levi-Strauss, 1969/1993).[4] Yet these highly charged competitive feelings are not eliminated by restrictive codes and continue to exist within families. In couple relationships where the quality of the sexual relating has decreased or there is excessive dependency or possessiveness, the partners often experience considerable jealousy in relation to rivals or competitors (Bloch, 1978; Firestone, 1994a). The birth of a child brings a third party into the situation, which can disturb the sense of equilibrium and security of one or both parents. In addition, immature and narcissistic parents are threatened by the child's demands for attention from the other partner as well as the partner's response to such demands.

Most parents find it difficult to admit feelings of anger, jealousy, and rivalry in relation to their children. Therefore, parents generally attempt to suppress their negative wishes or urges to rid themselves of the unwanted rival. Nevertheless, children sense this covert aggression, and it has a detrimental effect (Bloch, 1978; A. Miller, 1979/1981, 1980/1984a; Rheingold, 1964, 1967; Welldon, 1988). Later, as adults, when they are involved in competitive situations, these individuals may experience irrational fears and self-attacks. Because of this, many people pull back from competing, especially in sexually rivalrous situations. For example, in a 12-year study involving more than 2,500 women, Rheingold (1964) found that many recalled childhood fears of parental aggression, especially fears of retaliation on the part of a jealous, vindictive mother. In explaining these fears and their consequences in the lives of adult women, Rheingold noted that "the child's greater dependency upon the mother causes her attitudes and acts bespeaking rejection to be the more threatening" (p. 19). "The threat of retaliation . . . forces her [the daughter] to abandon her aspirations and surrounds all woman-roles with danger" (p. 267).

A mother who is insecure may experience feelings of jealousy and envy in observing her husband's attentiveness to the daughter. In this situation, when she senses her mother's anger, the daughter becomes fearful of her mother's envy and her potential for acting out vindictive behaviors. Later, as an adult, she may fear retaliation from other women who represent symbolic substitutes for the mother.

> *Tina:* I can clearly recall the hatred that my mother directed toward me. She knew I was my father's favorite. She was always telling me that I was too old to sit on his lap or give him a hug. I also know how my father felt toward me, so I can imagine that she was even more resentful than I was aware of at the time. I know that I felt afraid of her a lot of the time. Now, whenever I walk into a room where there's that kind of competition going on, or if I sense another woman watching in the background, I feel the same fear and panic, and I feel like running.

We have found that many women take their cues from other women in the interpersonal environment in terms of their emotional state. Therefore, when women observe other women being self-denying, unattractive, or distant from the men in their lives, they are more likely to imitate those types of behaviors.

Similar dynamics may be operating in the male child who is regarded as a competitor by the father. As adults, these men often project the aggression that was originally directed toward them from their fathers onto other men in their present-day life. Therefore, they have an exaggerated fear of retribution and tend to retreat from competitive situations (Firestone, 1994a). For example, a father, who was insecure and jealous of the attention his wife paid to their son (Sam), constantly criticized his son and ridiculed any qualities that his wife responded to. At times, the father became explosively angry, threatened punishment, and on occasion was physically abusive toward Sam. Later, the son projected fears of his father's wrath onto other men.

> *Sam:* Recently I began to realize that there are reasons why I don't actively compete in my everyday life. My fear of my father has followed me ever since childhood and it still affects me now. I can see how I've transferred my fear onto every other man in my adult life and onto every situation, especially in relation to my girlfriend. I have a gut level feeling of not being able to successfully compete for her especially if there's another guy in the picture. I have an irrational fear that he's going to kill me, or at the very least, deeply humiliate me. But I'm beginning to realize that these fears have nothing to do with my real life now, they have to do with the past.

Parents' Exploitive Use of the Child to Fulfill Their Emotional and/or Sexual Needs

Parents' or other adults' exploitive use of children for emotional and/or sexual satisfaction can be particularly damaging to a child's sexual development. Even in the absence of actual sexual abuse, a parent's seductive behavior or exaggerated focus on a child also leads to feelings of inadequacy or fears of being depleted later in life. Numerous sexual dysfunctions and disorders of sexual desire have been correlated with childhood sexual abuse and emotional incest. This type of abuse is especially devastating when the parent, the person most responsible for the safety of the child, is the person who has betrayed the child's trust (Courtois, 1999; Dorais, 2002; Freyd, 1996; Herman, 1981, 1992; Sarwer & Durlak, 1996).

Emotional Hunger

Many children suffer from the debilitating effects of a parent's emotional hunger, desperation, and intrusiveness. Emotional hunger is a desperate longing, based on parents' unmet needs from the past, to demand love from their child rather than offer love and affection. Generally speaking, immature or emotionally hungry parents exert a strong pull on their offspring to try to meet their (the parents') dependency needs (Firestone, 1990b; G. Parker, 1983; Tronick, Cohn, & Shea, 1986; West & Keller, 1991). Psychoanalysts (Masterson, 1985; A. Miller, 1979/1981) have stressed the fact that children who are "used" or exploited in this manner feel compelled to gratify their parents' unconscious primal needs at their expense. In describing this important dynamic of family life, Fenchel (1998) contended that "Any infant is an enigma at birth, but the infant is a total object for the parents' needs. The narcissistic investment of the loving parent represents a demand on the child for support of the parents' self-esteem" (p. 152).

Emotional hunger may be manifested in a wide range of behaviors. Parents may try to live through their child, have a proprietary interest in the child, or exhibit anxious overconcern and overprotection, intrusiveness, and affectionateless control. A needy parent may also exclude the other parent from the mother–child or father–child dyad, as will be described in chapter 4. In some cases, as children develop, parents may portray a need for their child to actually take care of them—"parentification" (G. Parker, 1983).

The detrimental effects of parents' emotional hunger that have been observed in adolescents and adults can include feelings of insecurity and of being suffocated, drained, or depleted (Firestone, 1990b). Immature and emotionally hungry parenting can result in sexual problems for both men and women. One of the most significant outcomes in adulthood related to experiencing a parent's emotional hunger is an intolerance of physical and emotional closeness. Individuals with this intolerance will often unconsciously distance themselves by withholding or inhibiting their responses.

There is a difference between genuine affection and the kind of affection and physical touch that reflects a parent's underlying feelings of emotional hunger (Firestone, 1985, 1990b; Firestone & Catlett, 1999). The child being caressed by an emotionally hungry, needy parent who is sexually or emotionally immature does not feel loved, cared for, or secure. Such a child may become refractory to physical touch and may feel trapped by close relationships later in life. These feelings of claustrophobia in combination with guilt are also common in children who have been made to fill the role of confidante to a parent.

For example, Neil began experiencing problems in his relationship with Elizabeth as the couple became closer. Evidently, their sexual relationship had been exciting initially, but Neil reported feeling increasingly awkward and self-conscious as time went on. In a session, he revealed that it was becoming difficult for him to respond to Elizabeth as she became more demonstrative and wanting sexually.

> *Neil:* I've never felt uncomfortable in any sexual situation until the last few months as Elizabeth and I started getting closer. Even the specifics are embarrassing. Just everything, her touching me feels like it's wrong, and I feel shaken up by it.

As Neil explored the problem further, he experienced deep feelings of sadness and anger as he traced his feelings of self-consciousness to interactions with his mother.

> *Neil:* I think that I know where this comes from. I felt that kind of self-consciousness with my mother, even recently. It's a very uncomfortable kind of feeling. I can't have a normal conversation with her, and our hugs are always very intense. I'll kind of pull away and then she'll kind of pull me back and then I don't know what to do.

In recalling the ways in which his mother was emotionally hungry toward him, Neil began to achieve insight into some of the reasons why he was having problems in his sexual relationship with Elizabeth.

Emotional Incest

Covert incest or "emotional incest" (Love, 1990) is closely related to emotional hunger. An emotionally incestuous relationship is basically a sexualized relationship, "even when there is no clear-cut, explicit sexual activity between the individuals" (Gartner, 1999, p. 26). Manifestations of emotional incest in a parent or parents include flirtatiousness, sexualized affection, inappropriate touching and handling of the child's body and clothing, sexual innuendos, possessiveness, jealousy of other people in the child's life, a strong preference for and focus on the child, and sexualized excitement when close to the child. According to Love (1990), emotional incest has two defining features "The parent is using the child to satisfy needs that should be satisfied by other adults" (p. 9), and "The parent is ignoring many of the child's needs" (p. 10). In their writing, Bolton, Morris, and MacEahron (1989); A. Miller (1979/1981); Love (1990); and Shengold (1989) have shed considerable light on the subject of enmeshed families and emotionally incestuous relationships.

Hannah's parents divorced when she was 10, and she would visit her father on holidays. When she was 13, her father became blatantly inappropriate in relating to her.

> *Hannah:* When I was 13, I stayed at my father's apartment in London for two weeks during the summer. The first night I was there, he said that as a treat, he was taking me out to dinner at his favorite restaurant. He told me I could even wear make-up. The day before I arrived, he had bought me a really stylish black dress and beautiful earrings, which he insisted I wear. I remember being really excited. I felt like I was being treated as special by him. He even put up my hair himself.
>
> His favorite restaurant turned out to be the corner pub. That was the first disappointment. Then as soon as we sat down in a booth, some guys came over, friends of his, and he introduced me as his "new girlfriend." At first I thought he was just joking around, but then I saw that he wanted his friends to think I was his girlfriend. I was horrified! I felt so uncomfortable, but I could not say a word. I just smiled and kept quiet, afraid of making him mad and of losing his attention. At the time, I could see that he was using me in a way that seemed kind of weird. I felt so nervous and self-conscious I could barely eat. But we went out practically every night of those two weeks to the same pub and the same scene was repeated. I couldn't wait until the holiday was up and I could return to boarding school. I never told anybody about this, it was too embarrassing.
>
> Today I realize how those "dinners out" with my father must have affected me. It's clear to me now that he was totally insensitive to my feelings. It's obvious that there were sexual overtones to what he did. I really came to believe that my looks were the most valuable thing I had. I was a nobody, except for how I looked.
>
> Today I feel that I'm always focused on how I look and try to figure out new ways to dress to attract men. But whenever a

man seems to fall for me, for my looks, I soon became bored with him. I start to pick him apart. It's sad, because the man I broke up with recently wanted to get married and have a baby with me. He really liked me, for me. We enjoyed activities together, like skiing, taking walks. I became extremely critical of him. I became disgusted with him. I could not stand his looking at me, his touching me. Eventually the relationship ended and I lost a chance to have something valuable in my life because I can't accept real love from a man. My father's perverted use of me left me unable to accept real love and closeness. I protect myself by getting rid of any man who gets too close to me.

Emotionally incestuous parents injure the child's capacity for wanting and his or her desire to seek satisfaction in a mature sexual relationship. Individuals who were damaged in this way may unconsciously inhibit their sexual responses in their adult relationships. In particular, as a sexual relationship becomes emotionally closer and more meaningful to them, they may experience a diminution in sexual desire or an increasing aversion to making love. In discussing sexual problems that are common among victims of emotional incest, Love (1990) argued that in some cases, these children later become involved in "brief, clandestine affairs with relative strangers." Others tend to repress their sexuality. "The man may be impotent or disinterested in sex. The woman may be afraid of sex or have difficulty achieving an orgasm" (p. 54).

> *Gabrielle:* To me, my father's attentions seemed competitive, especially when I started to date. He always told me that my skirts were too short and would measure the distance from my knees to the hem of my skirts before I left on a date. Once when I was in my late teens, our family went on vacation together. An older family friend asked me to take a walk with him into town. This was in broad daylight and as we turned the corner some blocks from our hotel, I noticed my father walking half a block behind, stalking us. I tried to pretend nothing unusual was going on, but the friend I was with finally noticed. He was outraged at my father's behavior and his suspicious nature and actually confronted him when we got back to the hotel. Of course, that led to a completely humiliating scene.
>
> Even before I got married, I had a lot of sexual problems. It was difficult for me to feel very much sexually, especially after my boyfriend and I started living together. Then after we were married, it got even worse. On the rare occasions that I was sexually responsive, I would feel guilty, but I

didn't know why. Then the next time, I would be completely unresponsive. After that, I would feel guilty for pulling away from him. Much later, I realized that my sexual inhibitions were related to the way my father had felt about sex and especially the way he viewed my sexuality. It was like it somehow belonged to him.

Overreactions to Natural Feelings of Attraction That Occur Within the Family

There are feelings of attraction that naturally accompany the close contact that parents have with their children (Dix, 1985; Firestone, 1990b, Friday, 1977). The feelings of love and affection that we are describing here are different from sexual feelings. Obviously, behaviors based on sexual feelings, including inappropriate touching or handling of a child and overt sexual child abuse, are destructive to children.

Emotionally healthy parents who have satisfying adult sexual relationships are comfortable with these feelings and can express loving affection to their children. In spite of the fact that these feelings naturally occur, some parents may still feel discomfort when such feelings arise. For example, some mothers report feeling uncomfortable with physical sensations they experience when their baby is nursing (Dix, 1985). Other mothers and fathers avoid expressing physical affection to an older child because they are confused or alarmed at any indications of sexual attraction. We have observed some children who were punished as though they are to blame for arousing these "forbidden" emotions in parents. Parents need to become more aware that fears associated with taboos against physical closeness between family members can effectively limit them in their ability to accept the child's expressions of love and affection. As noted earlier, in such situations, the child internalizes a feeling that there is something unlovable or unacceptable about him or her and learns to hold back or inhibit love, affection, and other positive responses.

Physical affection and contact are vital and valuable for a child's development. There is, of course, an obvious distinction between warmth, affection, and tenderness and sexualized attention to a child. In this context, it is important to mention that the focus on incidents of sexual child abuse, while leading to necessary identification of cases, treatment, and prevention, has also had an inhibiting effect on people who work closely with children. Acting on this self-consciousness and fear may be detrimental to psychotherapy with children and can often pose a problem for child psychologists, teachers, day-care providers, and other professionals who have close contact with young children (Orbach, 2004). In many cases, children who grow up in conditions of neglect and abuse turn to a favorite teacher or mentor as their only source of affection and positive role-modeling. If these adults hold back their natural warmth and affection out of a fear of being misinterpreted, they inadvertently inflict further damage on those children most in need; indeed, they may well harm every child they would otherwise positively influence.

Child Sexual Abuse and Incest

Child sexual abuse is the sexual exploitation or victimization of a child by an adult, adolescent, or older child. The difference in age and sexual knowledge between a child and an older person makes informed consent to sexual activity impossible. Child sexual abuse was defined by Steele and Alexander (1981) as "the misuse of the immature child by the adult for the solving of problems and satisfying of adult needs, while disregarding the appropriate needs and developmental state of the child" (p. 233). Incest is child sexual abuse that takes place within the family context. Incidents of child sexual abuse and incest are far more prevalent than previously recognized. Faller (1999) reported, "Estimates are that one in three or four women is sexually abused during the course of her childhood and one in six to 10 men" (p. 4).

Child sexual abuse can involve both fathers and mothers as well as other adults and parental substitutes and includes abuses toward same-sex children. According to Whealin (2004),

> Men are found to be perpetrators in most cases, regardless of whether the victim is a boy or a girl. However, women are found to be perpetrators in about 14% of cases reported against boys and about 6% of cases reported against girls. (Who Are the Perpetrators of Child Sexual Abuse section, ¶ 5)

In some industrialized countries, people do not report child sexual abuse, and it is believed by many clinicians and researchers that sexual abuse is under-reported in the United States as well.

Sexual Abuse of Female Children

In her descriptions of incest involving female children, Freyd (1996) proposed that profound amnesia for sexual abuse and related events may occur when there has been a betrayal of trust in cases where the perpetrator is an attachment figure, such as a parent or caregiver: Zurbriggen and Freyd (2004) also noted, "According to betrayal trauma theory, survivors of childhood abuse by a caretaker have learned to cope with social conflicts they cannot escape by being disconnected internally" (p. 145). Wilsnack, Wonderlich, Kristjanson, Vogeltanz-Holm, and Wilsnack (2002) found that "Among women who report [child sexual abuse], forgetting and subsequently remembering abuse experiences is not uncommon" (p. 139). Similarly, Courtois (1999) called attention to the fact that sexually abused children often forget the incidents of maltreatment.[5]

Ogilvie (2004) reported that "Estimates of female-perpetrated child sexual abuse based on a variety of surveys of the general population . . . place the percentage of sexual contact by females at . . . approximately 5 percent . . . for female children" (pp. 3–4). With respect to female sexual abuse of girls, she also noted that "Recent research suggests that mother-daughter incest is not rare; it is underestimated and underreported because its occurrence involves the breaking of two taboos, incest and homosexuality" (p. 4).

Sexual Abuse of Male Children

The problem of estimating the prevalence of child sexual abuse among boys is compounded by the fact that these cases are likely to be under-reported (Purcell, Malow, Dolezal, & Carballo-Dieguez, 2004). In fact, according to Dorais (2002) "For a long time, it was thought that sexual abuse of boys was still a marginal phenomenon. This is not so. . . . [But] boys are more reluctant than girls to disclose the fact that they have been abused" (pp. 16–17). Gartner (1999) also observed that "the sexual victimization of boys . . . is even more universally minimized, underestimated, and ridiculed than the abuse of girls" (p. 3). Gartner further noted that "Boys are socialized to believe that men want sex whenever it is offered to them. The sexual behavior of adults with boys has often been misunderstood and underreported because it is not considered abusive or even unwelcome" (p. 42). Being abused by an adult male presents special problems for boys. According to Gartner, "Molestation by a man is likely to undermine a boy's sense of his gender identity and orientation, whether he is predominantly heterosexual or homosexual" (p. 96).

Sexual abuse by a woman may be even more problematic for young males. "The traumatic impact of abuse of boys by women is particularly minimized in our culture" (Gartner, 1999, p. 46). When the perpetrator is the boy's mother, the damage to the boy's psyche and sexuality is especially destructive (Miletski, 1995). According to Gartner (1999), "Maternal sexual betrayal of a son often occurs covertly, in the guise of some aspect of caretaking and nurturing, as when a mother gives her son unneeded enemas or spends too much time washing his genitals" (p. 52).

IMPLICATIONS OF CHILD SEXUAL ABUSE FOR ADULT FUNCTIONING AND SEXUAL RELATING

The implications and long-term effects of incest and child sexual abuse are pervasive, far-reaching, and extend beyond the sexual sphere. Significant correlations have been found between child sexual abuse and higher rates in adult life of depressive symptoms, anxiety symptoms, dissociation, substance abuse disorders, eating disorders, posttraumatic stress disorders, bipolar disorders, and suicide (Bergen, Martin, Richardson, Allison, & Roeger, 2003; Fergusson, Horwood, & Lynskey, 1996; Gold, Lucenko, Elhai, Swingle, & Sellers, 1999; Hyun, Friedman, & Dunner, 2000; Mullen & Fleming, 1998; Oates, 2004; Romans, Martin, Anderson, Herbison, & Mullen, 1995; Safran, Gershuny, Marzol, Otto, & Pollack, 2002; Spak, Spak, & Allebeck, 1998; Thakkar, Gutierrez, Kuczen, & McCanne, 2000; Twomey, Kaslow, & Croft, 2000).

Studies have shown that female adolescents who were sexually abused as children tend to develop secondary sexual characteristics (breasts and pubic hair) earlier and begin menstruating at an earlier age than their nonabused peers (van der Kolk, personal communication, April 2004). They experience themselves as different, in the negative sense, from other girls, and as a result have very few or no female friends. Instead they gravitate toward friendships with boys who they relate to in a sexualized way. Mullen and Fleming (1998) also reported evidence showing that in "those whose abuse has been particularly gross (in terms of physical intrusiveness, frequency, duration or closeness of relationship to abuser), there is an increased risk of precocious sexual activity with its attendant risks of teenage pregnancy and social ostracism" (p. 8).

Specific outcomes in terms of adult sexual functioning and problems in intimate relationships have been delineated by several clinicians and researchers (Doll, Koenig, & Purcell, 2004; Heiman & Heard-Davison, 2004; Kirschner & Kirschner, 1996; Meston, Heiman, & Trapnell, 1999; Purcell et al., 2004; Roberts, O'Connor, Dunn, & Golding, 2004).[6] These effects include "sexual aversion or avoidance, decreased sexual desire or sexual self-esteem, inhibited sexual arousal or orgasm, vaginismus, dyspareunia, and negative attitudes toward sexuality and intimate relationships in general" (Meston & Heiman, 2000, p. 399). Kirschner and Kirschner (1996) found that "86 percent [of child sexual abuse survivors] had difficulties dealing with close relationships" (p. 408).[7] Other studies cited by Kirschner and Kirschner found that "67 percent of female survivors experienced an aversion to sex. Briere (1992) reported that 42 percent of his sample experienced low sexual desire" (p. 409).

Herman (1981) has found that the ongoing effects in adolescent and adult women's lives from sexual abuse and incest range from feelings of being set apart from other people, isolation due to the incest secret, promiscuity, revictimization by other relatives and adults, rape, deep feelings of shame, depression, and suicide attempts. In Herman's sample, "Many oscillated between periods of compulsive sexual activity and periods of asceticism and abstinence" (p. 100). Incest, in particular, interferes with the child's ability to form a secure attachment either with the abusing parent and the "enabling" nonabusing parent, preventing the development of a basic trust in other people. Both limitations clearly have negative consequences in the exploited child's adult relationships. Mullen and Fleming (1998) asserted that "In those abused by someone with whom they had a close relationship, the impact is likely to be all the more profound" (p. 9). These researchers also noted that the consequences of this breach in basic trust can often be observed in the types of attachments people develop in their adult sexual relationships.

The long-term effects of childhood sexual abuse on the lives of boys and men have recently become the target of research. Purcell et al. (2004) reported that "The effects of CSA [child sexual abuse] on diverse emotional and social domains are pervasive and long-lasting" (p. 94). Cross-sectional studies of sexually abused men show elevated levels of hypersexuality and high-risk sexual behavior, including prostitution, unprotected sex, and having many sexual partners. According to Purcell et al., gay men and bisexual males are "more likely to have been abused than heterosexual men, and . . . are particularly likely to have been abused by men" (p. 97). In an in-depth study of 26 male survivors of childhood sexual abuse, Lisak (1994) found that the men expressed a "basic sense of badness in myriad forms: As a feeling of inferiority, of insignificance, of being unacceptable and unlovable. . . . For some men, sexual intimacy was frightening because it re-evoked feelings related to the abuse" (pp. 541–542).

Research studies have been conducted to explore the long-term cumulative effects of experiencing physical, emotional, and sexual abuse, as well as exposure to family and community violence (Briere, 1992; Briere & Elliott, 2003; Cole & Putman, 1992; Mullen & Fleming, 1998). These three forms of child maltreatment frequently occur together. For example, Felitti et al. (1998) found that the probabilities that children who were exposed to child sexual abuse were also exposed to psychological abuse and physical abuse were 24% and 22%, respectively.[8]

We believe that any kind of sexual abuse is clearly damaging psychologically to both boys and girls; however, the effects are compounded by the secrecy that surrounds incestuous relationships (Conte, 1988; Firestone, 1990b; A. Miller, 1981/1984b; Newberger & deVos, 1988). The consequences of these acts are exacerbated when denial and dishonesty within the family take precedence over concern for the child. In an interview, Melanie, 45, described the secrecy that surrounded the ongoing incestuous relationship she had with her father that began when she was 9 years old. When she entered therapy at 29, Melanie was suffering from feelings of emptiness, diminished sexual desire, and compartmentalized feelings about her sexuality and her body. Melanie explores the shame and guilt that had led to her secrecy.

I had been in therapy several months when I brought up the subject of my sexual relationship with my father. My therapist was the first person I had ever told since I left home. In all the years of silence, it was like I had been keeping my sexual life a secret even from myself.

My father would take me to his workshop behind the garage, and the whole thing was very secretive. We pretended to everyone and even to ourselves, I think, that we were engaged in practical work that had to be done and that I was his helper. I didn't tell my mother for years. Then when I finally told her, there was a big family upheaval: I could hear them yelling and talking about divorce and about him going to prison. I thought I had ruined the whole family. The next day, my mother took me aside and said "Just don't tell anybody. Don't tell anybody ever. Not even your best friend."

For about two weeks after that, my mother didn't let me out of her sight, so I wasn't exposed to my father. But then one night, we were in the kitchen doing dishes and she said that he wanted some help in the workshop, so I should go and see if I could help him. I was so confused, I couldn't believe she said that, but I went anyway. And the sexual thing started up all over again. When I was in therapy and looking back on that time, I had to face the fact that she essentially gave me over to him. So it made sense to me that I never brought up the subject again to her.

I tried to rationalize away my guilt by reminding myself that my father never had actual intercourse with me, and so I was able to preserve my "virgin" status. But I worried endlessly that the relationship had damaged me sexually and that I would never be sexually "all right."

After I left home, I was involved with lots of guys. Sex was very exciting for me. I felt really passionate and it seemed like everything was fine. But then I met a man I really was drawn to, and we fell in love. At first, things were okay, but as we got closer, I started having a lot of trouble feeling any sexual sensations. Then after we married, I started avoiding situations where we would ordinarily be sexual. When we did make love, I sometimes would feel like pushing him away, especially when he was saying loving, tender things to me. That's when I decided I had to go to therapy.

Distorted cultural and familial attitudes toward sex also contribute to and complicate the resultant psychological and sexual problems (Firestone, 1990b; Herman, 1992; Spiegel, 2003). As Miller (1980/1984) put it,

> It is not the trauma itself that is the source of illness but the unconscious, repressed, hopeless despair over not being allowed to give expression to what one has suffered and the fact that one is not allowed to show and is unable to experience feelings of rage, anger, humiliation, despair, helplessness, and sadness. (p. 259)

The optimal response in terms of ameliorating the impact of child sexual abuse would be for parents to show empathy and understanding toward the child rather than maintaining secrecy through denial or by invalidating the child's experience. Lieberman (2004), in describing her "relational diathesis model," emphasized that one condition necessary to achieve resolution of sexual abuse trauma and resume developmental momentum is "the caregiver's capacity to provide comfort and assuage fear" (p. 345).

CULTURAL AND SOCIETAL INFLUENCES ON SEXUALITY

In the process of evolving groups and societies, individual patterns of defense are pooled and combine to form specific world views, cultural attitudes, and social mores. Cultural prerogatives and social mores based on defense formation then reflect back on each member of society, further reinforcing people's defenses and depriving them of vital experiences necessary for achieving their true potential (Billig, 1987; Billig et al., 1988; Firestone, 1985, 1997a).

These types of institutionalized attitudes and conventions act on people in the form of negative social pressure and support their distorted views of sex and their defenses against being close sexually and emotionally in a personal relationship (Francoeur, 2001; Shea, 1992). Commenting on the impact of culture on sexuality, Bancroft (2002) stated, "Here we can assume that learning plays a crucial mediating role; the culture provides guidelines or scripts for appropriate sexual responses, and the individual learns them accordingly" (p. 19).[9]

It appears that societies in the Western world (with few exceptions) perceive sex in ways that sensationalize it and imbue it with a "dirty" connotation. At the same time, numerous social sanctions function to suppress honest, realistic discourse regarding sex, place serious prohibitions on sex education for young people and discourage an open discussion of sexual abuse and incest (Herman, 1981). We agree with Prescott (1975) and A. Miller (1980/1984a) who argued that a suppressive society leads to an increase rather than a decrease in the pervasiveness of problems in sexual relating, perversion, child abuse, and rape, the very effects it attempts to avoid.

On a societal level, there is still considerable support for the point of view that sex is inherently bad (Francoeur, 2001). This concept of sexuality continues to influence conventional secular thinking despite the sexual revolution and scientific, social, and medical advances regarding sexuality during the past 50 years (Tiefer, 2001). In some traditional religious belief systems, for example, sex is perceived as an expression of the baser or sinful nature of human beings. Regarding these negative views of sex, Shea (1992) called attention to the historical fact that, in contrast to ancient Babylonian, Egyptian, Greek, and Roman cultures, "The Christian era, influenced by pagan philosophies, brought the Western world a negativity to sex that is unique among the great cultures of history" (p. 72). For generations, this negativity, combined with inaccurate, distorted views of human sexuality, has functioned to alienate people from their bodily sensations and feelings (Pagels, 1988, 1995; Vergote, 1978/1988).

In our opinion, religious teachings originally meant to enhance spiritual and human qualities have been misinterpreted in a way that has contributed to people's tendencies to lead a self-denying, self-sacrificing life. Theologians have used St. Augustine's revision of the creation myth, in which he postulated that death was the punishment for Adam's act of disobedience, to hold out the promise that if one denies sexual desire and bodily pleasures, one's soul will triumph over the body and survive death (Pagels, 1988). Goldenberg, Cox, Pyszczynski, Greenberg, and Solomon's (2002) approach is congenial to our point of view stated above: "Although virtually all cultures restrict and disguise sexual behavior in some ways, some seem more restrictive than others. Similarly, some cultures seem to go to great lengths to distance humans from other animals, whereas others do not" (Cultural Variability section, ¶ 1). Goldenberg, Pyszczynski, Greenberg, and Solomon (2000) concluded,

> Thus we may be in a catch-22 in which we must control anxiety to be able to embrace the potential for pleasure that our bodies provide, but we must largely forsake our bodies and cling to the world of cultural symbols and standards [religious belief] to control that anxiety. (p. 215)

Anthropologist Manson (1994) observed that "With the exception of the moral conservatism of the Victorian era, Western culture has generally experienced a gradual relaxation of sexual mores since the Renaissance" (p. 86). However, in spite of this positive evolution, restrictive attitudes toward a wide range of sexual behaviors still exert considerable influence in contemporary society. These social mores obviously have destructive effects on an individual's sexual development. For example, negative views of sex often have the effect of suppressing natural curiosity and aliveness about sexuality and increasing guilt about sex (Calderone & Johnson, 1989; Gunderson & McCary, 1979). In general, repressive social mores in relation to nudity, the human body, and sexuality continue to play a crucial role in each child's sexual development in spite of an accumulated body of knowledge regarding biological aspects of sex. As a result, nearly every individual in our culture has learned to feel shame regarding his or her body, body parts, and sexuality, and these imposed views have generated a variety of sexual problems and fears related to sexual performance (Calderone & Johnson, 1989; Firestone, 1990b, 1990c).

PERCEPTIONS OF SEXUALITY REPRESENTED IN THE MEDIA AND OTHER FORMS OF POPULAR CULTURE

Each person growing up today is affected by repressive and exploitative attitudes toward sexuality. Distorted beliefs about sex and prejudicial, sexist views of men and women are widely disseminated through books, magazines, popular music, radio, television, the internet, and other areas of popular culture. For example, Kernberg (1995) has suggested that in the mass media, there was a substantial increase in "mutual distrust between male and female groups" (p. 187) during the 1990s.

Sex as presented in numerous film and television productions is all too often sensationalized and trivialized and is at times presented in conjunction with scenes of violence. This combination desensitizes viewers and blurs the distinction between appearance and reality. In a policy statement, the American Academy of Pediatrics (2001) announced that "In film, television, and music, sexual messages are becoming more explicit in dialogue, lyrics, and behavior. In addition, these messages contain unrealistic, inaccurate, and misleading information that young people accept as fact" (Abstract). "The average American adolescent will view nearly 14,000 sexual references per year, yet only 165 of these references deal with birth control, self-control, abstinence, or the risk of pregnancy or STDs" (American Academy of Pediatrics, 2001, Media and Sexual Learning section).

Pornography in the United States is now a $8 billion a year business. According to He (2001), in this country pornography is accepted as part of the adult culture and is legally and morally tolerated. "Pornographic material is legally available to anybody over eighteen in bookstores, newsstands, video stores, X-rated movie theaters, adult cable channels, pay TV and even international computer networks such as the Internet and World Wide Web" (p. 132).

There have been mixed reviews and opinions concerning the effects of pornography and other nonpornographic print media on adolescent and adult attitudes and sexual behavior. Historically, the sexual content in literary works has consistently elicited concern and censorship throughout the 20th century in the United States. For example, *Fanny Hill* was banned in the United States until 1966, and James Joyce's *Ulysses* was subject to censorship on national and local levels (Stern & Handel, 2001).

In recent years, the Internet has evoked similar concern, providing the impetus for studies to determine its positive and negative effects on Web surfers. For example, Stern and Handel (2001) reported that

> Researchers are divided on whether or not this [the interactive feature of the Internet] is a blessing or a problem. . . . Some researchers, however, warn that the combination of anonymity and rewarding intimacy can lead to deviant sexual misconduct (Durkin & Bryant, 1995) and disruptions in marital relations (Young, 1998). (p. 289)

The above analysis is not meant to convey the impression that most, if not all, electronic and print media contain negative or distorted messages about sex. To the contrary, many literary works, films, television programs, and Web sites convey accurate information and positive messages about sexuality to readers and media consumers. For example, Anderson-Fye (2003) reported a longitudinal study of adolescent girls in Belize that revealed how they were positively affected by viewing American television talk shows, especially *Oprah*. Several girls in the study, after viewing *Oprah*, were able for the first time to accurately identify some of their experiences with male relatives as sexual abuse. They were then able to work through the resulting symptoms of posttraumatic stress disorder that emerged and help change their families for the better. They also felt empowered to not accept abuse from men. In the print media, hundreds of poems, novels and essays depict the potential emotional richness and meaning of people's sexual lives. Unfortunately, because of their wide audience appeal, films and TV programs that distort or trivialize sex may have far more influence on individual members of society than do more realistic, positive views set forth in many literary works.

CONCLUSION

An individual's sexuality and his or her sexual development are determined through the complex interaction of many biological, psychological, and social factors. Sexual behavior is based on a biologically determined drive; similarly, sexual desire and sexual arousal contain physical and cognitive components and are experienced in the body as well as the mind. Sexual feelings, as with all feelings "arise involuntarily and are experienced as sensations in the body" (Firestone, Firestone, & Catlett, 2003, p. 107).

In this regard, we believe that people who are close to their feelings are better able to respond positively to loving and being loved in an intimate relationship than those who have less access to their feelings. Furthermore, research (Oatley, 1996; Parrott & Harre, 1996) has shown that feelings are closely related to people's motivations, that is, to their wants, needs, and desires. When children are hurt early in life, they develop defenses to protect themselves against painful emotions. However, the defenses that function to reduce painful emotions also cut people off from experiencing other feelings as well. In other words, one cannot selectively defend oneself against feelings of pain and frustration without diminishing one's capacity for experiencing the whole gamut of emotions. Thus, remaining connected to one's feelings is crucial to pursuing the satisfaction of one's wants and needs in a sexual relationship.

In working with patients and in observing individuals and families in their everyday lives, we have become increasingly impressed with the prevalence of sexually related disturbances in our culture. These disturbances are related to a variety of factors that influence children's development as sexual beings. For example, in socializing their children, parents may feel under pressure from society to teach restrictive, negative views of sexuality. On an intellectual level, most people recognize that negative attitudes toward the human body, nudity, masturbation, and sex play between children are the results of social learning. Yet these views continue to be transmitted to children and exert a powerful influence on their emerging sexuality.

Moreover, the majority of adults in Western society have grown up in families where they assimilated negative perceptions of sexuality and distorted views about sex. These attitudes persist, generally on the unconscious level, and interfere with the achievement and maintenance of sexually and emotionally fulfilling relationships.

In addition, many children endure sexual abuse at the hands of immature adults who themselves may have been victims of destructive sexual attitudes and sexual maltreatment. This form of abuse contributes to a wide range of sexual dysfunctions and emotional disturbances in adults. Sexual abuse also interferes with children developing a healthy, secure attachment to their caregivers. Their insecure attachment patterns are often manifested in their adult relationships and cause problems in their sexual relating.

Many problems in adult sexuality and in couple relationships are related to even more fundamental disturbances in parent-child relationships. These sexual problems and disturbances might never arise if parents, because of their limitations, did not need to defend themselves in their interactions with their children. For example, children whose parents love and accept them for who they are and allow them to freely express their love and affection toward them are unlikely to develop sexual problems as adults or feel confused about their sexuality. Children whose parents do not exploit or use them to fulfill their (the parents') emotional or sexual needs will be unlikely to grow up with persistent fears of love and sexual intimacy. Parental defenses, including emotional hunger and an intolerance of being loved, are perhaps the most powerful factors impacting their children's emerging sexuality. Children react to the resultant hurt and frustration by forming defenses, which in turn, predispose disturbances in their sexual functioning that can persist into adulthood.

NOTES

1. For example, Orbach (2004) has addressed this dynamic in reporting a case of vaginismus, or painful intercourse.

2. When examining and coding an infant's behavioral and feeling reactions during selected close interactions with its mother, Stern (1985) noted that the mother's internal emotional state had a powerful influence on her baby's state of arousal and emotional responses. Overstimulation from an intrusive mother, understimulation from a depressed mother, or chaotic, inconsistent stimulation from an anxious mother tended to disrupt the relaxed, alert state in the infant, referred to as a state of "going on being" by Winnicott (1958).

3. Regarding parents' views of sex, Zoldbrod (1998) described a continuum of family attitudes toward sex, ranging from an ideal environment through a predominantly nurturing environment, evasive environment, permissive environment, negative environment, seductive environment, to an overtly sexual environment and outlined several outcomes in terms of potential disturbances in adult sexual functioning.

4. See theories on the evolution of the incest taboo in Suggs and Miracle (1993), in particular the papers by Fox (1983/1993) and Levi-Strauss (1969/1993). According to Levi-Strauss (1969/1993), "The prohibition of incest is less a rule prohibiting marriage with the mother, sister or daughter, than a rule obliging the mother, sister or daughter to be given to others" (p. 229). The rule or taboo functioned as a kind of "alliance assurance" to cement cooperative ties with other members of the tribe and incidentally increased gene variability.

5. There is still considerable controversy regarding the veracity of recovered memories and the concept of "repression" as the defense mechanism responsible for periods of "forgetting" traumatic childhood events, including incidents of child sexual abuse. See Loftus and Ketcham (1994) and Pope and Brown (1996).

6. Spiegel (2003) found that more than 50% of outpatients and from 50% to 70% of inpatients have histories of child sexual abuse. A study conducted by Kinzl, Traweger, and Biebl (1995) with 202 female university students found that victims of multiple child sexual abuse reported sexual desire disorders and orgasmic disorders more frequently than did single-incident victims and nonvictims. In addition, Mullen and Fleming (1998) found that

> Significantly more child sexual abuse victims believed their attitudes and feelings about sex caused problems or disrupted their satisfaction

in sexual relationships. . . . There was also a significant increase in the frequency with which the victims complained of what they perceived as negative and disruptive attitudes in their partners that caused sexual difficulties. (pp. 7–8)

7. See Doll et al. (2004), who asserted that

An emerging body of literature suggests that children who are [sexually] abused also face increased risk of physical health problems in adulthood, including negative sexual and reproductive health consequences such as unwanted pregnancy, sexually transmitted diseases including HIV infection, and adult sexual violence. (p. 3)

Cobia, Sobansky, and Ingram (2004), in their study of female survivors of child sexual abuse, found that "Many women internalize the psychological coercion from the abuse, overgeneralizing the abusive experience to other potential sex partners and to a general aversion or avoidance of sexual activity" (p. 314). See also Reissing, Binik, Khalife, Cohen, and Amsel (2003), who cited a study involving three groups of women showing physical distress related to sexual functioning. "More women in the vaginismus group reported a history of childhood sexual interference and held less positive attitudes about their sexuality" (p. 55).

8. The Adverse Childhood Experiences (ACE) Study conducted by Felitti et al. (1998) found "a strong dose response relationship between the breadth of exposure to abuse or household dysfunction during childhood and multiple risk factors for several of the leading causes of death in adults" (p. 251). "The prevalence and risk [of] . . . ≥50 intercourse partners, and history of a sexually transmitted disease increased as the number of childhood exposures increased" (p. 250).

9. With respect to other societal influences on an individual's sexuality, Herdt (2004) noted that

Less obvious are the forces of poverty, racism, or heterosexism that disproportionately impact upon minorities or certain social classes or sexual cultures not in the majority, creating conflict, turmoil, uncertainty, and anxiety that inflect sexual development. Among the outcomes of such conditions in contemporary society are sexual abuse, sexual risk taking that introduces unintentional pregnancy early in development, and exposure to major STDs. (p. 53)

4

MEN, WOMEN, AND
SEXUAL STEREOTYPES

At this contentious moment in the history of male–female relationships, it is important for us to note that there is not one set of elements for men and another for women. Society has wounded and rewarded men and women differently. But when it comes to practicing the art and discipline of love, we are equally challenged.

—Keen (1997, p. 32)

During the past 50 years, a significant transformation has taken place in the way men and women relate sexually (Hyde & Oliver, 2000; Schoenewolf, 1989; Solomon & Levy, 1982; Walsh, 1997; Young, 1999). Numerous cultural developments have contributed to these changes, among them the feminist movement, the men's movement, and women's ongoing and increasing involvement in the workplace (Bly, 1990; Sheehy, 1998). Since the 1960s, surveys indicate that many men have become more sensitive and less detached while many women have become more self-assertive and less dependent than their predecessors (Rubin, 1990). Commenting on the many real gains for both men and women that may be attributed to the "sexual revolution" Rubin stated,

> For the first time in our history, women were not just permitted but exhorted to experience the full force of their sexuality, to take pleasure in its expression, to celebrate it publicly rather than to conceal it as some private shame. . . . [For men] there was the possibility for sex among equals, sex with a "good" woman who made a free choice, a woman who was neither guilt-ridden nor shamed by the expression of her sexuality, a sexual connection that was also a freely given emotional exchange. (p. 93)

However, as social critic Young (1999) observed, these gains are far from complete: "Too many countries around the world still deny women the basic rights of adult members of society (though it's worth remembering that men's lot in these countries usually is not too enviable either)" (pp. 265–266).

Despite the movement toward gender equality, many people still lack a fully developed sense of self and the autonomy necessary to sustain a loving and sexually fulfilling relationship. Men and women are currently living within a society that is in transition between a traditional patriarchal social structure and a system that reflects more equality between the sexes (Silverstein, Auerbach, & Levant, 2002). As a result, many are confused about their gender roles, relationships, and sexuality.

It is beyond the scope of this book to examine the multitude of recent societal changes with respect to gender roles and expectations or to comment on their implications for sexual relationships. However, in this chapter, we describe an overall view of sexual stereotyping in our society and show how these distorted views create animosity between men and women. We provide a brief review of findings from gender studies and a critique of gender studies that we believe may perpetuate stereotypic attitudes. We offer our views regarding similarities and differences between the sexes. Our focus is on exploring these similarities and differences in terms of men's and women's psychosexual development, adult sexual functioning, and ways of expressing their sexuality in relationships. In addition, we explore how boys and girls learn their parents' defensive styles of relating with each other through the process of imitation. Also we examine conflicting hypotheses about how children are socialized into their respective gender roles and the differential developmental tasks they encounter during their formative years. Lastly, we briefly review several conjectures proposed by evolutionary psychologists regarding differences in male and female sexual strategies and preferences in mate selection.

SEXUAL STEREOTYPES: AN OVERVIEW

As described in chapter 3, psychological defenses established early in life later combine with the defenses of other individuals to produce cultural attitudes and social mores that shape a society. Once established, cultural prerogatives and social institutions reflect back on each member of society (Billig, 1987; Billig et al., 1988; G. Mead, 1934/1967). Sexist attitudes and sexual stereotypes are a significant part of this defensive apparatus and are transmitted through succeeding generations within the family context. If parents have sexist attitudes, their children assimilate these views, both explicitly through verbal communications and implicitly through the processes of identification and imitation. These defensive views are then projected into the social mores and institutions of the larger society. Sexism

essentially represents the extension of each individual's biased, hostile attitudes toward the opposite sex into a social framework. Negative attitudes
toward lesbian, gay, bisexual, or transsexual orientations are also still commonplace in our culture (Friedman & Downey, 2002).

Although changes have occurred in the roles of men and women in
our society, there are still remnants of sexist views that portray men as
masterful and powerful yet paternalistic and uncommunicative, and women
as emotionally responsive and communicative yet childlike, helpless, and
incompetent (Aries, 1997; Beyer & Finnegan, 1997; Kupers, 1997).[1] Sexual
stereotypes are confusing because they assign men and women to artificial
categories. Clearly, some stereotypes do correspond to research findings
regarding specific differences between men and women. However, when
these findings are exaggerated or overgeneralized in the popular media
(Tiefer, 2000); and when perceptions of men and women take on a connotation of cynicism and denigration, they generate hostility between people
and undermine their relationships.

According to Lott (1997), some gender research has perpetuated biased
attitudes toward women and men. She commented that, in general "Cataloging sameness and differences does not serve the interests of a science of psychology, first, because we well know that behavior always occurs in a context
and that the situation or circumstance makes a significant difference" (p. 19).
Lott went on to note that societies that encourage beliefs "in gender-related
traits (regardless of whether they are said to be learned or innate)" tend to
justify the continuation of "separate spheres for women and men" (p. 22).

The majority of adults have been raised in families in which they
learned inaccurate information about themselves and about the opposite sex.
Social psychologist Geis (1993) noted that people hold numerous implicit
hypotheses and beliefs about men and women that they use to "interpret
perceptions of males and females from the time they are born" (p. 14).
Moreover, these beliefs about gender differences influence people's behavior
in ways that are limiting or restrictive (Deaux, 1999). For example, Fiske,
Bersoff, Borgida, Deaux, and Heilman (1997) have pointed out that "*prescriptive* or normative sex stereotypes (e.g., women should be nice and passive;
men should be strong and aggressive)" (p. 322) are harmful for both women
and men.

Despite changes in family life because of increased equality between
the sexes, the ways that many boys and girls are socialized into their respective
gender roles may still adversely affect the quality of their relating in adult
associations. For example, Ickes (1993) has reported "*a growing body of
research evidence indicating* that the relationships of men and women with
traditional gender roles are far from optimal" (p. 71).

In general, sexist attitudes tend to foster a "us/them" polarization and
reflect an underlying negativity and hostility that can be as damaging to

human relations as racial prejudice. In a recent interview (American Association of Marriage and Family Therapy Staff, 2002), Keen strongly criticized sexist attitudes and traditional gender role expectations of men and women that remain in popular thought today: "I would no longer use words like masculinity and femininity. They are very deceptive" (p. 33).

> People go into therapy asking the questions they've been taught to ask, so you get these simplistic things, like "men are from Mars and women are from Venus." Come on! I have 2 daughters and 2 ex-wives—don't tell me that women are always from Venus. In some of the groups I've worked with, I've met good, assertive women, making their place in the world and after a while they say, "I don't feel feminine." And there are the men who are very sensitive and tell me that they don't feel masculine. . . . They have all these stereotypes. I try to lead them to their own stories—to own their own autobiography, rather than think in terms of these archetypes. (p. 35)

DISTORTED VIEWS OF MEN AND WOMEN

In exploring the sources of stereotypic views of men and women, it is worthwhile to briefly summarize recent social and economic trends.

A Historical Perspective on Men

During the late 1960s, a number of social forces converged to set into motion a cultural movement that has come to be known as the "men's movement." The movement evolved in part as a response to the women's liberation movement and was also inspired by the youth movement's opposition to the status quo and the Vietnam War. Currently, the men's movement is divided among several major organizations that promote differing ideologies and have diverse psychological underpinnings and political agendas.

Distorted Views of Men

Despite the efforts of many factions in the men's movement to promote gender equality and challenge sexual stereotypes, there are still strong tendencies to malign and depreciate men in contemporary society. Glick and Fiske (2001) have cited findings showing that men and women alike have more positive views of women than of men. Some early proponents of the feminist movement also expressed hostile attitudes toward men. As feminist bell hooks [sic] (1984/2001) observed, many women liberationists originally insisted on a "'woman only' feminist movement and a virulent anti-male stance" (p. 527). "Men, they argued, were all-powerful, misogynist oppressors—the enemy. Women were the oppressed—the victims" (p. 527). According to Young (1999), "The new feminism [beginning in the 1980s] . . . focuses on the evil that men do to women" (p. 5).

Many people still view men as powerful, aggressive, insensitive, non-communicative, and misogynous and as being interested only in sex, not in intimacy or close relationships (Allen, 1997; Aries, 1997; Felson, 2002; Kupers, 1997; Rubin, 1983). It is not uncommon to see gender issues discussed, in both the professional and popular literature, from a biased point of view that perceives men as being less sensitive, feelingful, communicative, and empathic than women. For example, in attempting to make people more aware of the ways that commonly accepted stereotypes about men affect the raising of boys, Levant (1992) delineated the "seven traditional male role norms" (p. 380). Among the characteristics he described that fit these male role norms are "restrictive emotionality" and "nonrelational attitudes toward sexuality" (p. 380).

Linguist Tannen (1990), who bases her work on findings from selected gender studies, has argued that women feel that men do not communicate. Tannen (1997) attributes the problem to differences in conversational style. Her use of the terms "*report-talk* and *rapport-talk*" to depict these differences may have the effect of supporting stereotypic views. She contended that "For most men, talk is primarily a means to preserve independence and negotiate and maintain status in a hierarchical social order. . . . For most women . . . conversation is primarily a . . . way of establishing connections and negotiating relationships" (p. 88).

Such discussions also tend to portray men as generally being less willing than women to commit to a relationship. This same bias depicts men as being primarily interested in their careers, sporting activities, and practical matters and as being less interested than women in marriage and parenthood. We believe that these sexist attitudes prevent people from developing a genuine understanding or a realistic picture of men's personal qualities. Moreover, many men accept these generalizations as foregone conclusions and have internalized the associated negative emotional loading or bias. As a result, they subscribe to society's stereotypical and negative views of themselves, which causes them to turn against themselves and other men.

For example, in comparing men and women in terms of self-esteem, it is interesting to note that a study by Rudman and Goodwin (2004) showed that "women strongly implicitly prefer their own gender, whereas men do not" (p. 508). In an interview, Rudman further explained, "'A clear pattern shown in all four studies is that men do not like themselves automatically as much as women like themselves'. . . . 'This contradicts a lot of theoretical thinking . . . [and suggests] that negative male stereotypes can promote greater liking for women'" (quoted in Dittmann, 2004, p. 11).

During the developmental years and throughout their lives, boys and men attempt to adjust their behavior according to these negative stereotypes about men (Pleck, 1995).[2] For example, Silverstein et al. (2002) have emphasized that men develop gender role identity as a result of strong social pressure to conform to cultural norms and stereotypes.[3] According to Pollack (1998), the myth that boys are "toxic" includes a perception of men as "psychologically unaware, emotionally unsocialized creatures" (p. 62). In his work, Pollack stresses the fact that men and women alike are damaged by accepting these stereotypes as real representations of boys and men.

There are also numerous stereotypes about men pertaining to their sexuality. In our society, men are generally perceived as being more sexually oriented than women, having more sexual experiences and fantasies than women, being more sexually aggressive, more random, more impersonal in their sexual encounters than women, and relating to women as sex objects (Levant, 1992; Pleck, 1995). Although research does tend to support the premise that men indicate more interest in sex than women,[4] the information is often misinterpreted or exaggerated. The same is true when people over-generalize or exaggerate research findings suggesting that men have more sexual experience and more sexual fantasies than their female counterparts, are more random in selecting partners, and desire more variety (Buss & Schmitt, 1993).

In relation to child-rearing, many men who believe that they are less nurturing or loving toward children than women may retreat from the paternal role and leave most of child-rearing functions to women. Some women reinforce this stereotype by subtly conveying that women understand better than men how best to raise a child (Pollack, 1998).[5] In describing how traditional gender roles based on cultural stereotypes have been manifested in fathering, Silverstein et al. (2002) commented, "Because a 'real' man must avoid 'sissy stuff,' a traditional father limits his involvement in child care. He might 'baby-sit' if his wife has to be away, but he does not actively manage the children" (p. 362).

Although family life has changed in recent years, partly as a result of women's increasing involvement in the workplace, internalized stereotypes and behaviors based on these biased views are difficult to overcome because they are deeply entrenched in people's thinking. In a series of interviews and discussion groups, several men and women revealed the ways in which distorted views of men were transmitted to them in the context of early interactions within their family-of-origin.

> Colin: I've been thinking lately about how my mother's attitude toward men affected me while I was growing up and how I'm still struggling with that in my adult life. I had a view of my father through my mother's eyes, and it was not a very good view. She really saw him as a critical, angry man.

So I grew up seeing him, and almost all men, through her eyes. I didn't even know what a strong man was. To me, viewed through her eyes, strong men were mean. Strength was meanness.

Evan: I can identify totally with what Colin said. Anything that I do that feels male, I identify as being mean. I grew up in a household in which my father was at work all the time. When I was 8 years old, my father died and from then on I was surrounded by women who saw men as lechers. I picked up their point of view, and I've got that point of view toward other men. I've taken on that point of view toward myself, and it really restricts me. If I have a sexual urge that I feel like acting on, not even necessarily the physical act of sex per se, but just talking with a woman that I'm attracted to sexually, I feel totally constrained. I feel like if I make a move that I'm infringing on someone else's territory. I feel that it's wrong for me to do, it's mean for me to do and that I just don't belong there.

Kimberly: Whenever I feel interested in meeting a man or pursuing a relationship, I have a lot of cynicism about my prospects. I remember my mother lecturing me about men. I never thought much about her lectures at that point and I thought they had no effect on me whatsoever. But now I find myself thinking things like: "You're never going to find any man who is nice because there are no men who are like that. They're all horrible. They all want to make a fool out of you. They all do. They're all just going to drop you and toss you aside for somebody else. They all are."

Jennifer: My father didn't have any sexual experience before he married my mother when he was 23. He really believed the stereotype that men were out of control sexually. He was always telling me "You have to be really careful with men, because the least little thing you do to them is going to trigger them and they're going to be out of control and they won't be able to stop themselves."

Eric: Up until I was about six or seven, my sisters and I slept in the same room, and then we were separated. At that time, my younger sister was my best friend. I remember I could not understand what was going on. Also I remember I had a feeling I was being separated because I was changing into a person that could not control himself and I was going to do something bad. There was this unspoken feeling in my family that "Men get to a stage where once they become a sexual person it's something they can't control. They become like an animal, and you have to separate them from girls really early so that nothing happens in the family." And I know that as I grew older, I kept on waiting for this mysterious thing to happen to me that I was going to turn into an animal in terms of being sexual and not be able to hold myself back.

A Historical Perspective on Women

The feminist movement (a revival of the original 19th century women's movement) has lobbied for better child care, abortion rights, and ratification of the Equal Rights Amendment and has taken an aggressive stand against patriarchism (Yanak, 2004).[6] On the socioeconomic level, feminists have contributed significantly to women's goals of achieving personal freedom and equal status with men (Showalter, 2001).

Living within a patriarchal society has indeed had a significant impact on women's lives (Bigler, 1999; Gilligan, 1982, 1996). For many centuries, women were denied access to power and influence in many important spheres of life and therefore many adopted indirect or passive means in attempting to fulfill their human potentialities (Chesler, 2001). As Rubin (1983) noted more than twenty years ago, "Not only are women economically and socially disadvantaged when compared to men, but social definitions insist that passivity and dependency are the core of femininity while aggressiveness and independence are the central features of masculinity" (p. 141). Today, many women still find it difficult to break out of this stereotypic mold, often for reasons that are more psychological than social (Gilligan, 1991).[7]

Distorted Views of Women

Women are continually being shaped and directed by stereotypes in destructive ways that cause alienation between the sexes. For example, in Western society, attitudes that portray females as helpless and unstable are still commonplace and have both a direct and indirect influence on economic as well as sexual equality between the sexes. Many feminists predict that it will take considerably more time to alter basic attitudes about being a woman in a patriarchal society (Chodorow, 1978; J. Miller, 1976; Spence, 1999; Young, 1999).

Admittedly, it is difficult to alter, within one or two generations, deeply held sexist beliefs based on a centuries-old patriarchal social order. One reason for this difficulty lies in the fact that many sexist attitudes are implicit and exist on an unconscious level. As noted previously, unconscious, implicit beliefs held by parents are internalized by their children and, in turn, are reinforced by stereotypic views still prevalent in most modern societies. In fact, some theorists argue that sexist views against women based on patriarchism have changed little during the past 100 years. For example, according to Rosenberger (1998), "Freud's . . . [1905/1953] evaluation of women as possessing weaker superego development reflected the prevailing social context of womanhood. . . . This paradigm is little changed today and little varied across cultures" (p. 66).

In terms of physical strength and overall body size, women are clearly the weaker sex. Originally, these biological factors undoubtedly contributed to the formation of an unequal power structure based on the division of labor by sex difference. However, women who exhibit overly passive or compliant traits and behaviors have probably been influenced more by suppression, social prejudice, and stereotypic views than by these biological determinants. Fiske et al. (1997) described the effects on women of trying to follow "prescriptive" stereotypes or "female role norms": "[Women's] competence is undervalued if they behave in traditionally feminine ways, while their interpersonal skills are derogated and their mental health is questioned if they behave in traditionally masculine ways" (p. 322).

In the area of sexuality, women are invariably thought of as having less sexual desire and fewer sexual fantasies, and as being more passive sexually than men. They are viewed as having little interest in casual sexual encounters and as only wanting sex if they are in love or involved on a deep level (Buss & Schmitt, 1993; Daly & Wilson, 1983; Ridley, 1993). In their relationships, they are believed to be more loving and faithful than men. Society views with criticism and suspicion those women whose sexual preferences and behaviors fail to conform to these stereotypes. According to Reid and Bing (2000), most people still rely on these stereotypes when defining women's roles:

> Women have been represented on one polarity as asexual madonnas, and at the other end as highly sexual, alluring sirens. . . . They are either good or evil. The good woman will be represented biologically as virginal (i.e., pure, innocent, and naive) and psychologically as a self-effacing, self-denying earth mother. The evil woman is seen as a whore; she is a scheming, ambitious, and a clever seductress. (pp. 141–144)

Clearly, not all of the social prejudice that women face is hostile; some paternalistic attitudes toward women as the weaker sex are seemingly positive. For example, although women are typically perceived as more childish, melodramatic, scatterbrained, or irrational than men, on the positive side, they are seen as sensitive, empathic, and intuitive, as easily forming deep emotional attachments, and as primarily interested in a long-term relationship and parenthood. As Glick and Fiske (2001) pointed out, "Benevolent sexism (a subjectively favorable, chivalrous ideology that offers protection and affection to women who embrace conventional roles) coexists with hostile sexism (antipathy toward women who are viewed as usurping men's power)" (p. 109). (Views of men as strong, masterful, and rational are also "benevolent.")

According to Glick and Fiske, many women willingly accept this stereotypic view of themselves. "Benevolent sexism, after all, has its rewards; chivalrous men are willing to sacrifice their own well-being to provide for and to protect women" (p. 115). Indeed, both men and women tend to endorse "benevolent" sexist beliefs that perceive women as basically weaker than men in areas that go beyond size and strength and as needing special protection and care.[8]

We have found that although most women believe on a conscious level that they are as competent and as intelligent as their male counterparts, on an unconscious level, many still hold internalized stereotypic beliefs that are diametrically opposed to their conscious attitudes. Despite the fact that women are increasingly assuming leadership positions in the business and professional world, in their personal lives and in their intimate relationships, some women continue to relate to men as "ultimate rescuers" and feel they need to be taken care of on some level. In a meta-analysis that investigated gender differences in helping behaviors, Eagly and Crowley (1986) found indications of this tendency. "In general men helped more than women and women received more help than men" (p. 283).

In calling attention to traditional stereotypes and conventional views of gender roles that alienate men and women, Keen (1997) argued that "Women, we are told, want to talk about their feelings and problems, and men just want to solve them. Women want relationship, and men need to maintain autonomy. We suffer from different communication strategies, tongues, languages" (p. 12). Keen went on to say that

> There is widespread resentment about the ways we [are] wounded by the gender roles we inherited. Men were taught that they could earn love only by providing, taking charge, being in control, and protecting women and children. Women were taught that they could earn love only by being nurturing, sexy, submissive, and passive. (p. 26)

In a similar vein, Marmor (2004) has criticized the negative sexist views of women still promulgated in society, many of which were based on findings in previous research: "The degree of cultural and/or intellectual accomplishment on the part of women as compared to men is *not* dependent on any presumptive inherent biological or psychosexual inferiority, nor has it ever been" (p. 19).

A BRIEF CRITIQUE OF GENDER RESEARCH

In recent years, a number of researchers have critiqued many of the widely publicized findings obtained from gender studies. We suggest that the ways in which some studies were designed probably contributed to the contradictory and inaccurate findings previously reported in the literature. For example, Grossman and Wood (1993) manipulated instructions to subjects in two experiments. They discovered that any gender differences in emotional expressivity were largely related to subjects' endorsement of gender-role expectations. In other words, subjects in the two experiments responded as they believed they were "supposed" to respond, according to the popular gender stereotypes.

In addition, Burn (1996) reported that measures of empathy used in some studies found larger sex differences on self-report questionnaires than on physiological measures. Her finding suggested that males may "be unwilling to portray themselves as empathic on a self-report measure, because doing so is inconsistent with the male gender role" (p. 57). We contend that this finding could also be explained by the fact that men may be reluctant to reveal feelings of empathy or be emotionally expressive because they have come to accept without question the stereotypical view of themselves as being less empathic and emotionally expressive than women.

Other recent gender studies have shown that many stereotypes negatively comparing men with women in terms of their ability to express emotion are blatantly inaccurate, while others have interpreted inconclusive findings as being definitive (Barrett, Robin, Pietromonaco, & Eyssell, 1998; Carpenter & Addis, 2000; Conway, 2000).

In studies that examined men's and women's communication styles, Burleson, Kunkel, Samter, and Werking (1996) found few differences in key aspects of communication. In particular, Dindia and Allen (1992), in their meta-analysis of 205 studies involving 23,702 subjects, found that "sex differences in self-disclosure are small" (pp. 117–118). These findings contradicted Tannen's (1990) hypotheses regarding differences between men and women in their communications styles as described in the previous section. Hook, Gerstein, Detterich, and Gridley (2003) concluded that "Men and women were similar in their level of comfort with both giving and receiving emotional support in relationships" (p. 471). In relation to men's and women's views of love, Fehr and Broughton (2001) found that "Unexpectedly, both women and men embraced companionate kinds of love as representing their view of love" (p. 134).

In terms of sexuality, it does not appear that women are innately less interested in sex or more sexually inhibited than men. In fact, when men and women are surveyed, there is tremendous overlap in their sexual propensities and preferences. For example, contrary to the popular stereotype that men have far more sexual experiences than women, a recent survey (Smith, 1998) showed that since the early 1900s, women have gradually become more experienced sexually. In 1998, 51.5% of women between the ages of 15 and 19 had engaged in premarital sex, as compared with 60% of the men in the same age group.

In a meta-analysis of research in this area, Hyde and Oliver (2000) concluded that "The bottom line is that the theories reviewed . . . do not make strong differential predictions regarding patterns of gender differences in sexuality. Rather, they yield similar if not identical predictions" (p. 73).[9] In other words, there appear to be more similarities than differences between men and women in areas pertaining to sexual interest and sexual behavior.

Attachment research has provided conflicting findings regarding differences between men and women in their attachment patterns in adult romantic relationships. For example, Shaver, Papalia, et al. (1996) found some gender differences in attachment styles, particularly in individuals categorized as being insecurely attached, while others (Gentzler & Kerns, 2004; Schmitt, Alcalay, et al., 2003) found no gender differences in individuals categorized as avoidantly attached.

Lastly, in terms of child-rearing, Silverman (2003) reported findings from numerous studies, including research conducted by Lamb, showing no differences between fathers' and mothers' desire and ability to parent their children. For example, in summarizing their research, Lamb and Lewis (2004) reported, "Most men in a variety of cultural settings clearly adapt positively to parenting" (p. 278).

We believe that it is important to explore the differences that do exist between the genders, separate from the stereotypic biases, overgeneralizations, and frequently politicized interpretations of research findings regarding such differences.

OUR VIEWS

Our observations of men and women have led to the conclusion that many gender stereotypes are exaggerated and destructive. Our interviews and discussions with individuals, couples, and family members resulted in information that often contradicted widely accepted generalizations about how women and men view emotions, sex, relationships, and child-rearing, and how they relate in an intimate association. For example, we found that although most males traditionally have been taught to mask their emotions, including feelings of empathy, compassion, and sadness, they are as emotionally expressive as females in settings where such feelings are acceptable. In spite of this, some of the men we interviewed still tended to underestimate their sensitivity and their capacity for experiencing emotion and, to some extent, they idealized women with respect to these qualities.

In terms of committing to a relationship, the large majority of men reported that they desired a long-term association with another person, were as interested in marriage and raising children as their female counterparts, and wanted to share the responsibilities of child-rearing with their partner. We also found that, contrary to stereotypic thinking, men were not indifferent to women's feelings and moods. In fact, most of the men we interviewed showed a consistent concern for their partner's well-being and reported feeling the most happy and contented when their partners were feeling strong and self-confident.

In relation to child-rearing, both men and women indicated a strong interest in and feeling for children. Moreover, many women reported having the same anxieties about handling newborns as men did. They did not feel that they possessed an inherent maternal quality that made them more sensitive or attuned to their infants and children than their mates. In fact, there tended to be wide variation among mothers as well as fathers in their capability to care for their offspring. We also noted that many men gave child-rearing functions a high priority and tried to spend as much time as possible with their children. Our findings with respect to men's involvement in child-rearing functions are supported in part by Pleck's (1997) findings that there have been "Clear increases in paternal engagement and responsibility, especially over the past three decades" (p. 75).

We also found that in general, both men and women reported feeling guilty and were self-critical when they felt they were not living up to popular societal stereotypes. Moreover, many said that they felt resentful and angry when a partner failed to conform to certain gender role expectations.

We suggest that there may be differences between men and women with respect to the ways that they express themselves in a sexual situation. For example, a sexually healthy, emotionally mature man would be comfortably assertive and responsive during sex. This term refers to the capacity to respond spontaneously and sensitively to indications of the woman's increasing excitement and to an ability to remain emotionally close throughout the experience and afterward. This emotional contact can be preserved through verbal and/or nonverbal communication.

Being comfortably active indicates an absence of self-doubts, feelings of inadequacy, and anxieties related to feeling completely responsible for satisfying one's partner. It also implies a freedom from the fear that some men experience in the presence of a passionate, wanting woman.

In fact, many men report experiencing the highest levels of sexual arousal when their partner becomes excited or aroused. At the same time they enjoy receiving physical affection, touching, and sexual caressing from their partner.

A sexually healthy, emotionally mature woman would tend to be actively receptive during lovemaking. This implies a willingness to remain fully open to her partner during sex and the ability to stay in touch with one's bodily sensations and feelings rather than to retreat into one's mind. Women who are self-possessed and able to remain emotionally close to their partner during sex can be described as being actively receptive. During lovemaking, they are neither overly aggressive nor passive. Active receptivity as described here is representative of an internal state of wanting and the desire to enter into an equal physical and emotional transaction with another person. It is important to emphasize here that receptivity does not mean passivity. As Marmor (2004) noted, "Receptivity and passivity are not synonymous. It is a striking commentary on the power of a cultural prejudice that both male and female classical Freudians have always assumed that the vagina, as a hollow organ, *had* to be a passive receptacle" (p. 16).

If a woman is in this receptive state, that is, allowing herself to completely experience feelings of sexual desire, she tends to elicit a strong sexual response from her partner. Ideally, this receptivity and openness are part of her overall style of relating to her partner. In other words, these behaviors and traits of openness and vulnerability would extend beyond the bedroom into the couple's daily life and significantly contribute to harmony in their relationship. When making love, ideally both partners, if emotionally mature and sexually healthy, would be fully engaged in an equal transaction in terms of both giving and receiving affection and sexual pleasure, and each would be responsible for asking for what he or she wanted sexually.

In a discussion group, Ken talked about feeling that his girlfriend, Lauren, was not open to receiving pleasure from him.

> *Ken:* The one thing I've had a hard time saying is that I don't see our sex life as being as exciting as I would like it to be. I don't feel excited when I think about making love. I feel that some of the things you do make me not want to be with you. When I thought more about it, I realized that it seems difficult for you to receive pleasure from me during the sexual act. I haven't been able to explain it very well or talk about it with you until now.
>
> I don't feel critical of you, or critical about the reasons why I don't feel attracted to you. I have an idea of what it is. I think it's difficult for you to let me make you feel good, to have an orgasm. It's hard for me to feel like I can give you an orgasm. I feel like you take it from me [sad]. Then I feel gypped out of being able to make you feel good. I feel upset, different than how I like to feel with you. Instead, what I end up doing is avoiding being sexual with you.

We also learned that a man's emotional and sexual responses appeared to be strongly related to the woman's genuine sexual desire. A woman may act interested or aggressively pursue sex, but without feeling and genuine desire for the man, her partner will have difficulty responding sexually. Most men blame themselves for sexual failures and tend to deny their partner's influence, even when intellectually aware of her potential effect. We also found that the way women feel about themselves and their physical appearance has considerable impact on their partner's sexual desire. Women also revealed that they experienced less sexual desire and often found it difficult to feel excited or aroused when their partner was cold or withdrawn, became overly dependent, seemed to value work over personal and family life, or felt victimized.

Therefore, there are several definitive differences between men and women and these differential behaviors and propensities are influenced by a multitude of biological, environmental, and cultural factors. As Chiland (2004) argued,

> Mead [Mead, 1948] shows that every society has a concept of how males and females should feel and behave and how, through the educative and other child-rearing procedures it sets up, it shapes children in such a way that they become the men and women that society expects. (p. 86)

The socialization process within the family, differential developmental tasks, and social learning through identification with and imitation of parental role-models are all formative influences that interact to generate different sexual attitudes and behaviors in men and women.

PARENTAL IMPACT ON ADULT SEXUALITY

In this section, we focus on the dynamics operating in the earliest relationships of both male and female children that impact their later development as sexual beings. It is important to note that social learning in relation to sexuality and differential sexual behavior takes place in the context of role modeling and imitation, especially of the traits, attitudes, and behaviors manifested by the same-sex parent. Hogben and Byrne (1998) stressed the fact that "As children are more likely to be reinforced for same-sex imitation, they tend to pick up same-sex behaviors, which leads to the cognitive association of particular behaviors with male versus female sexuality" (Hogben & Byrne, 1998, Theoretical Models and Research Outcomes section, ¶ 9). According to learning theory, "children imitate same-gender adults more than other-gender adults, so that the gender-role behavior of the previous generation perpetuates itself in the next generation" (Hyde & Oliver, 2000, p. 61). Thus, an exploration of parent–child relations can facilitate a better understanding of same-sex identification and imitation processes that contribute to adult sexual functioning of individuals of both genders.

Fathers and Sons

In attempting to establish a relationship with their father, many boys experience serious inner conflicts: they long for tenderness, love, and nurturance from their fathers, yet in some families, there may be a taboo against fathers being physically affectionate to their sons. According to Pollack (1998), "Because of the way we as a society view boys and men . . . many fathers, especially in public settings, may feel inhibited about showing the empathy they *naturally* feel for their sons" (p. 116).[10]

Competitive feelings between family members can have a negative effect on boys' sexual development. Boys may experience envy, hostility, and feelings of rivalry directed toward them from their fathers and may have competitive feelings toward their fathers as well (Firestone, 1994a). We have found that both sets of feelings can contribute to the sense of alienation that many boys feel in relation to their fathers. As adults, their friendships and associations with other men are often influenced by emotional residuals of this conflict. For example, a son's awareness that as an adult he is now enjoying a more satisfying intimate relationship than his father had can lead to guilt and anxiety about surpassing his father. Men's achievements in their professional and personal lives and in their relationships can activate powerful feelings of fear and guilt, as well as a sense of loss.

In addition, fathers serve as role models for their sons in terms of both positive and negative behaviors they exhibit. For example, in a study of more than 80 adolescent boys, D'Angelo, Weinberger, and Feldman (1995) found that sons of fathers who were aggressive and who lacked self-control exhibited numerous problems as adolescents and adults. Included in these problematic behaviors were "poor peer relations . . . at-risk behaviors . . . multiple sexual partners . . . [and] poor conflict resolution skills" (p. 883).

Boys observe and identify with a father's hostile and defensive attitudes toward their mother and other women, as noted in chapter 3. A father's weakness as a role model poses a serious limitation on the son's ability to develop a strong sense of male identity. Moreover, many fathers unknowingly support the mother's stereotypic views of men as uncommunicative, harsh, and unfeeling. Many women reinforce this sexist attitude when they use their husbands as agents of punishment. As a result, many children, boys and girls alike, learn to view male strength in a negative light. With respect to these conflicting views of masculinity that boys are presented with, Park (1995) emphasized that

What the boy needs is a father's help in dealing with the emotional pressures that come from his mother. He needs to learn that there are other views of masculinity than those which she propounds, and that what she says to him has more to do with her own past experiences than with him. (p. 23)

Some fathers manifest intrusive child-rearing practices when relating to their sons. Barber and Harmon (2002) have described a form of "psychological control" that they observed in many family constellations. According to Barber and Harmon, psychological control includes such parental behaviors as possessiveness, protectiveness, love withdrawal, control of the child's personal life, and erratic emotional behavior. Barber and Harmon reported preliminary findings from a number of studies that investigated the negative effects of paternal psychological control on male adolescent behaviors, particularly tendencies to be aggressive in peer relationships. Although their results are still inconclusive because of the limited number of samples studied thus far, there are indications that this type of control on the part of fathers is detrimental to the psychosocial development of their male offspring.

Other fathers exert harsher forms of behavioral control in interactions with their sons. For example, in his work, G. Parker (1983) observed a number of fathers who exerted "affectionateless control" over their sons.[11] Parker defined affectionless control as a harsh parenting style that appears to represent a diminished caring on the part of fathers. For example, Jain, Belsky, and Crnic (1996) reported a group of fathers who they described as traditional in their child-rearing practices. "The traditional men were those classified as disciplinarians and as uninvolved. . . . [They were] over-reactive to typical toddler behavior, resulting in almost exclusively disciplinary interactions or avoidance of their sons altogether" (p. 440).

As a result of these influences, many men feel isolated and alone in their suffering and may try to mask their pain with a tough, defensive exterior (Jolliff & Horne, 1999; Pollack, 1998; Silverstein et al., 2002). They are convinced that other men do not experience the same feelings of inadequacy, desperation, and fear that torment them. Because they feel alienated, they often find it difficult to relate to other men on more than a superficial level.

Pollack (1998) delineated several negative consequences in male development stemming from absent or uninvolved fathers. He noted that "Father absence has been correctly linked to a host of ills for boys . . . [including] difficulties with emotional commitments" (pp. 124–125). As noted, interactions between parents can have both positive and negative effects on their male offspring. Alienation between parents, argumentative interactions, and marital distress in general can interfere significantly with a boy's relationship with his father. For example, one study reported by Cummings, Goeke-

Morey, and Raymond (2004) showed that "Marital conflict predicted more disruptions in father-son than in mother-son interactions" (p. 200).

In general, the anxiety and insecurity from these early childhood experiences with their fathers are perpetuated in men's adult relationships. The defenses that they formed to cope with this pain and hurt interfere with their achieving real intimacy and adult sexual relating.

Mothers and Daughters

In the traditional family constellation, the mother still has the role of primary caregiver and therefore exerts the greater influence on children (Mendell, 1998). Mothers' strengths as well as their weaknesses are transmitted intergenerationally to their daughters through the processes of identification and imitation. In general, girls tend to form a stronger identification with their mothers than do boys (Chodorow, 1978; Fenchel, 1998; Hudson & Jacot, 1995). According to Genevie and Margolies (1987), mothers "form this primary relationship more readily with their daughters whom they view as extensions of themselves" (p. 291). This phenomenon has the potential for perpetuating mature, positive personality characteristics through succeeding generations of women. However, the negative effects of this identification process often outweigh the positive (Fenchel, 1998; Firestone, 1990b; Welldon, 1988).

Mothers who are intrusive and violate the boundaries of their children damage their daughters' ability to develop independence and autonomy as adult women. For example, an emotionally immature mother may attempt to merge her identity with her daughter and overstep the boundaries between them (Fenchel, 1998; Rubin, 1983; Westkott, 1997).[12] If a mother seeks to fulfill herself through her children, her daughter often feels drained of her emotional resources and angry at the mother's intrusiveness and control. Many girls react to their mother's exaggerated focus by repressing their anger and becoming more passive and compliant. As adults, they tend to unconsciously hold back their affection and sexual responses in intimate relationships, with little or no understanding of the underlying reasons.

> Emily: Recently I started thinking about my relationship with my mother and how I was always her baby and I was her best friend and I was her everything. I remember going to the store in high school and crossing the street and her holding my hand and feeling totally humiliated and being so afraid my friends were going to see me holding my mother's hand crossing the street. And she'd always make a big deal about it. Anything I did, she was right there.
>
> One time my boyfriend and I—we were totally in love— we were at my Mom's house and we laid down on the floor to

watch TV, and my mother came and laid right between us. Then she laughed and said, "Oh silly me. What have I done?"

Today I feel still guilty about falling in love. Getting to know a man is okay, but once the relationship deepens, then I feel guilty and I want to step back. Each time this happens, it's hard for me to maintain the closeness. Something comes between us. It sounds strange, but it's almost like she gets in the way. It's like somehow she possesses me or something like that. I feel like she's still here, she's still getting in my way, and she still wants me. She doesn't want me to have anything, except for her.

Paradoxically, the more the daughter resents the mother and suffers in interactions with her, the more she tends to imitate her behavior. Her attempts to remain close to the mother lead to the formation of a fantasy bond or imagined connection with her (Firestone, 1990b). As a result of this negative identification, the daughter tends to incorporate and compulsively act out her mother's most negative characteristics, traits that were not necessarily representative of her mother's personality as a whole. This alliance or imagined fusion with the mother can play a significant part in limiting the daughter's ability to assume the role of an adult sexual woman. For example, some women experience profound separation anxiety when they symbolically or literally move away from the mother as they reach higher levels of self-differentiation and become more individuated.

In other cases, a daughter may fear her mother's feelings of hostility, jealousy, and envy as she moves toward sexual maturity. She may actually be afraid of retaliation from the mother for seeking adult sexual fulfillment. In our experience, we have found that both separation anxiety and fear of the mother's envy or vindictiveness are often experienced by women at crucial points in their sexual development. Caplan (1981) has described how a daughter may adjust to her mother's envy: "Often, she does one of two things (or tries both at different times): she reduces her efforts to achieve (or at least begins to conceal them from her mother), and she puts emotional or physical distance between herself and her mother" (p. 120).

Guilt reactions may also become more evident as young women take tentative steps toward independence or move away from emotional ties with the family. In the case of adolescent girls, the guilt involved in breaking away or "leaving her mother behind" is often intense and debilitating, especially when the mother is depressed, self-denying, self-destructive, or immature in her orientation (Richman, 1986).

Thus, each step in the daughter's movement toward self-differentiation and separation from the mother, entering into a sexual relationship with a man, getting married, starting a family of her own, can create varying degrees of guilt, fear, and separation anxiety. During such critical periods, these powerful emotions often cause women to retreat to a sameness with the mother. Similarly, each step that women take toward sexual maturity is filled with conflict. Most women are necessarily ambivalent; they are torn between expressing their love and sexual desire in relation to a man, which represents a symbolic separation from the mother, and holding back their loving responses, which affirms the imaginary connection with her (Firestone, 1990b; Rubin, 1983). In reporting data from interviews with pregnant women, Rheingold (1964) described the consequences of preserving the imagined connection with one's mother:

> A woman may bring any number of assets to marriage—compassion, wisdom, intelligence, skills, an imaginative spirit, delight-giving femininity, good humor, friendliness, pride in a job well done—but if she does not bring emancipation from her mother, the assets may wither or may be overbalanced by the liability of the fear of being a woman. (p. 451)

Over many generations, women have tended to internalize compliant, yet inwardly defiant, behavior patterns that have been as detrimental to their personal development as the social forces that made their use necessary. These passive–aggressive tendencies often give rise to withholding patterns that may only be partially conscious; yet these behaviors act as barriers to harmonious relations between men and women. Although many women still feel restricted or oppressed by the inequities that continue to exist within society, we believe that much of the damage to their initiative and sexuality can be traced to limitations imposed by identification with negative traits in the mother and fears of separating from the imagined connection or fantasy bond with her (Firestone, 1990b).

Mothers and Sons

A significant aspect of maternal influence on male offspring is the propensity of some mothers to be overprotective, overly involved, intrusive, or nervously focused on their children, and on their sons in particular. This overprotective stance may originate from benevolent maternal attitudes, however, it can also arise because of a mother's lack of involvement in other parts of her life. As French psychoanalyst and social critic Kristeva (Oliver, 2002) commented,

> Nobody knows what the good-enough mother is . . . but I would try to suggest that maybe the good-enough mother is the mother who has something else to love besides her child; it could be her work, her husband, her lovers, etc. If for a mother the child is the meaning of her life, it's too heavy. (p. 336)

Investigations into the long-term effects on boys of maternal overprotection and control have shown that "psychological control was positively related to both depression and antisocial behavior" in older boys (Barber & Harmon, 2002, p. 19). As adults, men who were affected by their mothers' anxious concern, intrusiveness, and exaggerated focus may exhibit a wide range of defensive reactions. To varying degrees, they may experience painful feelings of inadequacy or have a fear of being smothered or dominated by a woman. They may even become critical of sexually responsive women and unconsciously averse to forming relationships with them.

We have found that men tend to experience feelings of sexual inferiority when the mother has been inappropriate or seductive in her behavior during the formative years. It has been shown that a seductive relationship with the mother often stimulates intense oedipal rivalry and leads to increased fear of competing and powerful feelings of inadequacy in the growing boy (Love, 1990; A. Miller, 1979/1981; Park, 1995). This type of provocative relationship on the part of some mothers can predispose sexual problems in adult males, including either an avoidance of sex, or a tendency to be overly compliant or submissive in relationships with women. In general, these family dynamics lead to considerable hostility between men and women and can seriously undermine their sexual relationships. On the basis of 150 in-depth interviews with men during a period of two years, Park (1995) found that for many men, "The experience of being truly close to someone else, whether man or woman, puts him at risk of experiencing again the same bewildering emotions that he knew in infancy" (p. 3). Specifically, with respect to overly solicitous and emotionally seductive mothers, Park noted that

> Men [from these enmeshed families], who generally have so much of mother, tend to experience her presence as sometimes smothering, stifling and demanding. In their later relationships, the pull towards intimacy and sexual union is powerfully countered by the fear of being submerged or swallowed up. They cannot get close because they do not think they will survive the experience. (p. 125)

In some families where the mother tends to form an exclusive relationship with her son, the father is often pushed into the periphery of the boy's life. We have found that although the father may feel distressed and angry at the way his son is being overprotected or indulged, he also feels excluded from the relationship and finds it difficult to intervene, and he may develop resentment toward both his wife and son (Firestone, 1990b).

A mother who is intrusive in this way exerts a strong pull on the son that leaves him feeling empty. The same person that a son would naturally turn to for love and care is instead seeking nurturance, care, and love from him (Love, 1990). Therefore, as an adult, he may self-protectively pull back from women and turn away from potential sources of gratification in close relationships (Firestone & Catlett, 1999). Men who have been damaged in this way may develop habitual patterns of holding back their affection and sexual responses because they perceive their partner's sexual interest as a demand.

Emotional unavailability, rejection, or withholding on the part of mothers also have detrimental consequences for male children (Fenchel, 1986; Park, 1995; Pollack, 1998; Pollack & Levant, 1998). For example, if a mother withholds her affection and love from her son, his hurt and angry response may cause him to suppress his affectionate feelings for her. In other cases, he may become clingy, desperate, and overly dependent on her. Subsequently, as an adult, he may be uncomfortable with dependent feelings in himself.

Many men continue to search for gratification of their unfulfilled longings for affection, tenderness, and love. The desperation and dependency they felt toward their mother is now directed toward the primary woman in their lives. In their adult associations, these men seek symbolic safety and reassurance in an imagined connection or fantasy bond with women (maternal substitutes) to their own detriment and that of their sexual relationship (Firestone, 1985). According to Rubin (1983), the man's sexual involvement with a woman

> Calls up the memory of the infantile attachment to mother along with the old ambivalence about separation and unity, about emotional connection and separateness. It's likely therefore that it will elicit an intense emotional response—a response that's threatening even while it's gratifying. . . . It's also what they fear. For it threatens their defenses against the return of those long-repressed feelings for that other woman—the first connection in their lives. So they hold on to the separation between the sexual and emotional and thereby keep the repression safe. (pp. 105–106)

Fathers and Daughters

Fathers also play a significant role in their daughters' development. It has been found that paternal warmth and involvement in the family are important factors influencing the development of femininity in young girls (Cramer, 1997). In explaining the importance of fathers in the lives of their female offspring, Rubin (1983) stresses that fathers are crucial in helping their daughters successfully differentiate from the mother. She noted that

> In childhood, a girl handles the threat [of separation from the mother] by turning to father to help her make and maintain the necessary separation. . . . It's this difference, and the importance it holds in her

separation struggle, that helps to define a girl's sexual orientation. . . .
A father affirms the femaleness of his daughter. (pp. 147–148)

There is also some evidence showing that paternal neglect, emotional unavailability, or indifference are hurtful to female children. One study (Manlove & Vernon-Feagans, 2002) of fathers and infant sons and daughters found that fathers were available to their sons significantly more than to their daughters. The fathers in this sample were also much more involved in caregiving or child-rearing tasks in relation to their sons than their daughters.

In a seminal article, Ellis et al. (2003) posed the question: "Does father absence place daughters at special risk for early sexual activity and teenage pregnancy?" These researchers conducted longitudinal studies in the United States and New Zealand in which community samples of girls were followed prospectively from early in life (5 years) to approximately age 18. It was found that the answer to this question is yes. "First, in both the U.S. and New Zealand samples, there was a dose-response relationship between timing of onset of father absence and early sexual outcomes," (p. 815), including teenage pregnancy. Cramer (1997) also emphasized that "fathers contribute heavily to their daughter's representations of gender identity and of relations between the sexes," but she qualified her statement as follows: "The degree of cohesion [agreement] or of conflict between female images carried by mother and father will in great part determine the future woman's fate" (p. 388).

In many areas of female psychosexual development, it appears that on the one hand, fathers can provide confirmation of their daughter's feminine characteristics, while on the other, they can denigrate these same potentialities. For example, several women participants in our seminars reported feeling humiliated by fathers who depreciated or ridiculed them. Often these humiliating events occurred early in the girl's life:

Jacqueline: When I was about five years old, my sister and I were arguing in our bedroom while we were getting dressed and my father was yelling for me to come into the living room. I didn't have any clothes on yet, but I was so afraid to not respond right away when he called that I went out into the living room. I was naked when I walked in there, and when he saw me, he started laughing. I remember feeling humiliated and there was nothing I could do to cover myself up either.

Paula: My father teased me all the time about my body, especially when I got to be a teenager. If I got dressed up to go to a party and was wearing a padded bra, he would notice and invariably say "Hey, it looks like you're getting help today." I was always very embarrassed about my breasts being small anyway, so I would feel totally humiliated when he said that. His teasing made me feel terrible about myself and I thought I was so inadequate, that something was really wrong with me, that my body wasn't right somehow.

Obviously, in families where the father has an overly sexualized involvement or actually acts out incestuous feelings, he has a profoundly harmful effect on his daughter's developing sexuality. In relation to father–daughter incest, Herman (1981) suggested that: "The actual sexual encounter may be brutal or tender, painful or pleasurable; but it is always, inevitably, destructive to the child. The father, in effect, forces the daughter to pay with her body for affection and care which should be freely given" (p. 4).

In summarizing this section, we suggest that the psychodynamics operating in the father-daughter and father-son dyads described above are complicated and often difficult to untangle. As Lamb and Lewis (2004) commented, "Because the two parents' behaviors, attributions, and attitudes are complexly interrelated, it is hard to identify paternal effects" (p. 290). However, these researchers also stressed the fact that "The evidence to date suggests that . . . earlier paternal involvement predicts their adult children's feelings of satisfaction in spousal relationships" (p. 290).

GENDER-ROLE SOCIALIZATION AND DEVELOPMENTAL TASKS

The ways that children learn to conform to their gender roles are largely determined by familial and cultural influences; however, there is considerable controversy regarding how male and female children are socialized into their respective gender roles. Some theorists suggest that society's patriarchal influences still direct the socialization of boys and girls (Nealer, 2002; Pollack, 1998), whereas others claim there is little difference in how male and female offspring are being raised in today's families (Geary, 1998). In addition, social learning theorists have hypothesized that differences in mothers' and fathers' styles of relating to each other must "somehow help boys and girls acquire gender-appropriate behavioral repertoires" (Lamb & Lewis, 2004, p. 287).

A number of research studies have been conducted addressing the question of whether or not remnants of patriarchism have differential effects on boys and girls. In particular, many researchers have focused their attention on how society and families influence young children's development of emotional expressiveness and empathy. These personal qualities and/or behaviors are important because they affect one's ability to establish and maintain intimacy in an adult romantic relationship as well as influencing one's style of sexual relating.

Male Psychosexual Development and Gender-Role Socialization

Research findings related to the ways that boys are raised in our culture are contradictory. There are at least three competing theories that attempt to explicate the socialization of a male child into the masculine gender role. For example, in a review of research into child-rearing practices in the traditional family, Pollack (1998) asserted, "Studies show that boys at a very early age are pushed to suppress their vulnerable and sad feelings, they also demonstrate that boys are pressured to express the one strong feeling allowed them—*anger*" (p. 44). In other words, Pollack's findings showed that in more traditional families, boys are taught to act brave, strong, and tough and to not show weakness, and therefore to stay away from tender feelings. In Pollack's opinion, our patriarchal society also places a strong emphasis on male children separating emotionally from the mother at an early age. Other research (Levant, 1998) has indicated that male infants may be more emotionally expressive than female infants before this separation.[13] According to Levant, this research also showed that "Despite this initial advantage in emotional expressivity, males learn to tune out, suppress, and channel their emotions" (p. 39).

In contrast, Kiselica (2001) has criticized Pollack's and Levant's findings and their interpretations of such findings. According to Kiselica, boys and girls differ only in *how* they express feelings of empathy. In his work, Kiselica observed that "boys are just as likely as girls to help a crying peer" and concluded that male children and adolescents are "quite capable of responding prosocially when their fellow human beings are in some kind of trouble" (p. 15).

Geary's (1998) findings also contradict Pollack's and Levant's position. Geary discovered no differences between male and female infants and toddlers in their expressions of empathy in situations where they had caused the distress in another baby. In addition, he reported studies showing that the ways boys and girls are socialized to their gender roles are becoming increasingly similar, and that in general, parents "treat boys and girls in very similar ways" (p. 252).

Thus, it appears that many of the findings regarding socialization practices briefly reviewed here are ambiguous and largely inconclusive. We suggest that there is a need for further, carefully designed, observational studies of emotional expressiveness and empathy in adult males and their proposed antecedents in infants, toddlers, and young boys.

Psychoanalytic and object relations theorists have suggested that the different developmental pathways by which boys and girls attain sexual maturity may contribute to gender differences with respect to emotional responsiveness, attitudes toward sex, and sexual behavior (Benjamin, 1995;

Chodorow, 1978, 1989; Kernberg, 1995).[14] For example, Kernberg (1995) contended that the developmental tasks faced by boys (resolving the oedipal conflict) are substantially different from those that girls encounter. However, Kernberg also noted that all children, regardless of gender, face a similar developmental task—that of emancipating themselves from the effects of their parents' attitudes toward the opposite sex and their prohibitions regarding sexuality: "In short, overcoming fear and envy of the other gender represents, for both men and women, the exhilarating experience of overcoming the prohibitions against sexuality" (p. 54).

Mendell (1998) also stressed similarities between male and female development: "Both girls and boys must grapple with the issue of separating from the mother, first in order to attain object constancy and its associated autonomy and then in the service of becoming separate, differentiated, genital sexual beings" (pp. 231–232). The son, in differentiating himself from the mother, gradually shifts his identification to the father.

Female Psychosexual Development and Gender-Role Socialization

In contrast to theoretical approaches to male development, there is considerable agreement about the important social and cultural factors that continue to affect girls and women through the life span. Hyde and Oliver (2000) observed that "Central to the message conveyed to girls and women is that sex for them is legitimate only in the context of a committed relationship, whereas men are allowed more sexual freedom" (p. 71).

The results of this differential socialization would indicate that "women are punished for sexual activities such as having numerous partners or engaging in casual sex, whereas men are less likely to be punished, or perhaps are positively reinforced (through admiration or increased social status), for such behaviors" (p. 61). Hyde and Oliver (2000) noted, however, that this "double standard" has eased in recent years, being replaced by a more relaxed standard in which premarital or extramarital sex is tolerated for both men and women, yet these sexual involvements are acceptable for women only if they are in love or engaged.[15] Social role theory proposes that throughout childhood and beyond, girls learn implicitly and explicitly what will be expected of them as sexual women, including expectations based on the double standard described above (Bussey & Bandura, 1984; Fagot & Hagan, 1991). In addition, according to Reid and Bing (2000), girls are taught that they need to be cared for and protected because they are the "weaker" sex.

Attachment researchers have also explored gender differences in studies comparing the personality traits and behaviors in infants who are securely attached to their mothers with those of infants categorized as insecurely attached. One study found that at age 4, insecurely attached girls showed greater compliance and less assertive behavior than insecurely attached boys

(Turner, 1991). However, Gilligan (1982) found that compliant behavior is manifested at a later stage in girls' development than was suggested by Turner.[16]

Psychoanalytic and psychodynamic theorists have approached the issue of female psychosexual development from a number of different perspectives. Early psychoanalysts proposed that girls needed to maintain their original identification with the mother in order to attain a decisive female identity and appropriate feminine gender role. At the same time, they also needed to make "libidinal connections to the father and—unlike boys—[girls need] . . . to overcome the rivalry with the mother" (Fenchel, 1998, p. xvi).

In contrast to classical psychoanalytic perspectives, early revisionists and critics of Freud's male-oriented theories (Chodorow, 1978; Horney, 1967) asserted that the most significant factor is not how girls resolve the triangular situation of the oedipal complex but rather how they respond to events and experiences that occur much earlier, during the pre-oedipal phase. Recently, Benjamin (1999) who endorses Horney's revisionist views, argued that "The girl reaches the [oedipal] complex by way of her libidinal strivings toward the father rather than through the narcissistic injury of not having a penis" (p. 88). Benjamin also noted that the anxiety of separating from the mother is more important than castration anxiety as a formative influence in female sexual development.[17]

French psychoanalyst Chodorow (1978, 1989) concluded that boys and girls have different gender-related experiences because women care for children. She contended that,

> As a result of being parented by a woman, both sexes are looking for a return to this emotional and physical union. A man achieves this directly through the heterosexual bond which replicates for him emotionally the early mother-infant exclusivity which he seeks to recreate. . . . Women have different and a more complex set of relational needs, in which exclusive relationship to a man is not enough. This is because women experience themselves as part of a relational triangle in which their father and men are emotionally secondary, or at most equal, in importance to their mother and women. Women, therefore, need primary relationships to women as well as to men. (1989, p. 77)

Chodorow further asserted that, in contrast to boys, it is not necessary for girls to sever the attachment to the mother in order to develop a feminine identity; instead they need to preserve the attachment to the mother.[18]

We agree, albeit only in part, with Chodorow's analysis of the differential outcomes of early developmental tasks for boys and girls. We contend that because male and female children face differential developmental tasks during their formative years, as adults they tend to have a conflict of interest when they enter into a sexual relationship with one another. As Chodorow asserted, for a man, a close sexual relationship can symbolize the fulfillment of his desire for close, affectionate contact with the mother that he has longed for since early childhood. However, this illusion that he is achieving a reunion with the mother is often based more on a childlike fixation than on a healthy, adult desire for companionship. We emphasize that for a woman, a mature sexual relationship with a man can symbolize separation and a loss of fantasized connection with the mother, which arouses considerable fear, guilt, and anxiety. In such instances, men and women are at odds with each other in forming a committed sexual relationship, especially one that includes emotional closeness and satisfying sexuality. To avoid the blending of love and sexuality, one or both partners may withdraw either sexually or emotionally from the other person.

EVOLUTIONARY PSYCHOLOGISTS' CONJECTURES ABOUT DIFFERENTIAL MATING STRATEGIES

One difference between men and women suggested by evolutionary psychologists is that men and women employ different strategies in selecting mates (Buss & Barnes, 1996; Buss & Schmitt, 1993; Kriegman, 1999). These psychologists propose that prehistoric men and women needed to solve different types of adaptive problems (Buss, 1994; G. Miller, 2000). Describing the reasoning behind their conjectures, Buss and Schmitt (1993) explain that for more than two million years, our ancestors' choices evolved through a process of natural selection. During evolutionary history, both women and men have pursued short- and long-term mating strategies necessary for solving problems of adaptation. Their preferences for desirable qualities in a potential mate evolved from those strategies that best solved problems related to each gender's reproductive constraints, that is, strategies that essentially favor gene survival.

For example, Buss and Schmitt (1993) reported that men's tendencies to be more random and women's tendencies to be more selective have been observed to be universal across human societies. They conjectured that men tend to seek sexual variety and pursue a larger number of sexual relationships to ensure the replication of their genes in future generations. In attempting to identify which women were fertile, primitive man had to rely on cues indicating youth and physical health: "full lips, clear skin, smooth skin, clear eyes, lustrous hair, symmetry [breasts, waist and hips in proper proportions], good muscle tone, an absence of lesions . . . sprightly, youthful gait and high activity level" (p. 208).

In order to allocate their limited resources to the offspring that carried their genes, our male ancestors also needed assurance that they were the rightful parent. According to Buunk, Angleitner, Oubaid, and Buss (1996), "Over human evolutionary history, men have faced a profound adaptive problem that has not been faced by women: uncertainty in their parenthood of children" (p. 359). In modern times, men still tend to prefer "women who are young and physically attractive as indicators of reproductive value (see Buss, 1989b) and who are sexually loyal and likely to be faithful as indicators of paternity certainty" (Buss & Schmitt, 1993, p. 226).

These theorists (Buss & Schmitt, 1993) found that for the most part women are highly selective in choosing a mate. Their selectivity is partly a function of a biological imperative to find both the best genes for their children (Wilson, 1981) as well as the resources and parental interest necessary for assisting in the rearing of offspring to reproductive age. According to Buss and Schmitt, "*women in long-term mating contexts, more than men, will desire cues to a potential mate's ability to acquire resources, including ambition, good earning capacity, professional degrees, and wealth.* This prediction has been confirmed extensively across cultures" (p. 223). Although different groups value different characteristics, this general pattern appears to hold up across cultures.[19] According to evolutionary psychologists, men and women also have different strategies in relation to short-term partner selection and casual sex (Schmitt et al., 2003). For example, in "choosing partners for a sexual liaison, men reliably indicated lower criteria than did women" (Kenrick & Trost, 1993, p. 154).

The hypotheses set forth by evolutionary theorists are not without their critics, especially when the theory is applied to assumed differences in male and female mating strategies. Moore and Travis (2000) argued that,

> As applied to human culture, this view [that males benefit by mating with as many females as possible] supports the notion of promiscuous behavior in men as being adaptive, when in reality there is no evidence that promiscuous men have more offspring than men who invest heavily in the nurturing of their children. (p. 48)[20]

In our opinion, although certain evolved sexual or reproductive strategies and tendencies may still persist in individuals of both genders, other factors including cultural and psychological factors and the availability of potential partners probably have more influence in shaping people's sexual behavior and preferences (Hazan & Diamond, 2000). Gender researchers Eagly and Wood (1999) tend to agree with our point of view. They found that "a re-analysis of Buss's [1989] . . . study of sex differences in the attributes valued in potential mates in 37 cultures yielded cross-cultural variation that supports the social structural account of sex differences in male preferences" (p. 408). In a more general sense, rather than attributing sex differences in human behavior primarily to evolved dispositions that differ by sex, it may well be that these differences lie "mainly in the differing placement of women and men in the social structure" (p. 408).

More importantly, human beings are far from being passive recipients of certain inclinations that may have helped their ancestors survive. In other words, we have some choice in the matter, our destiny is not predetermined, and our behavior and propensities are continually being influenced by a myriad of other factors.

CONCLUSION

In most aspects of their psychological makeup, men and women cannot be easily categorized according to their gender identity. Their behavior should not be evaluated or judged by conventional criteria that stress gender differences. Clinically, it is important to work with clients to facilitate an understanding that they do not have to comply with these gender expectations and stereotypes. It is helpful to explore with them the similarities between women and men, describe their mutual strengths, and to demonstrate through attitude and action that it is possible to change destructive, traditional sexist attitudes.

Although considerable effort has gone into attempts to delineate early environmental influences on gender-role behaviors and different sexual attitudes and behaviors observed in men and women, it appears that many findings from gender research are ambiguous or inconclusive. In any case, these findings and popular interpretations of such findings should not be used to support destructive stereotypes that still exist in our culture.

On a social level, proponents in the men's and women's movements have contributed to the struggle to achieve personal freedom while developing a sense of kinship with members of the opposite sex. Yet, because sexist attitudes are internalized so early in the developmental sequence, people still face a difficult task in challenging and transcending sexual stereotyping, traditional gender roles, and the defensive behaviors embedded in these roles. This struggle requires boldness and determination when confronting internal conflicts and external social pressures that support conformity to rigidly defined sex roles.

We believe that women and men can develop themselves personally and become equal partners in all aspects of their relationships, including sexually. Women can take responsibility for their sexual desire and fulfillment and ask more directly for what they want sexually. Men can view their partners as equal and not take a paternalistic attitude toward them. Men can challenge their idealization of women especially in their role as mothers. Women can challenge their idealization of men as "rescuers" who should protect and take care of them. Women can break the negative aspects of their identification with their mothers and face the anxiety of living as separate individuals. Men can break the negative aspects of their identification with their fathers and overcome fears of achieving intimacy in their relationships, even if their fathers did not.

By becoming more aware of the sexism and the distortions of men and women still prevalent in Western culture, people can gradually move beyond these views and develop closer, more congenial relationships. As they relinquish defensive attitudes about themselves and their sexuality, they can achieve higher levels of self-differentiation and experience more fulfillment in their sexual lives.

NOTES

1. Aries (1997) noted that "Decades of research has shown widespread agreement among people about the characteristics of men and women" (p. 96).

   Men are characterized by a cluster of instrumental traits: they are seen to be leaders, to be dominant, aggressive, independent, objective, and competitive. Women, in contrast, are characterized by a cluster of affective traits: they are seen to be emotional, subjective, tactful, and aware of the feelings of others. Gender stereotypes have changed relatively little over the past twenty years despite considerable changes in women's status in society. (p. 96)

2. Pleck (1995) and Levant (1992) have discussed the effects of "gender-role strain" on males, that is, the inconsistent and contradictory roles they are supposed to fill. According to Walsh's (1997) description of this concept, "For example, men are expected to be independent and competitive at work and caring and cooperative at home. Failure to fulfill male role expectations can lead to 'low self-esteem and other negative consequences'" (pp. 399–400).

3. Silverstein et al. (2002) commented that

   Gender roles were seen as culturally defined on the basis of cultural stereotypes rather than as emanating from an intrinsic biological feminine or masculine essence. . . . Attempts to conform to these role norms, therefore, inevitably lead to psychological stress rather than to psychological well-being. (p. 362)

4. Although differences between men's and women's levels of sexual desire have been reported by a number of researchers and clinicians (H. Kaplan, 1995; Love & Robinson, 1994), it has also been shown that these differences appear to be a matter of degree and are influenced by a wide range of factors, including social, psychological, and biological influences.

5. Observing this pattern in the families he studied, Pollack (1998) attributed some of the father's difficulties to what he termed "gatekeeper mothers":

Gatekeeping is what happens when mothers, despite their very best intentions, unwittingly maintain so close a bond with their sons that there is simply little room left for the father to play a meaningful role—the emotional "gate" has been kept closed. (p. 125)

6. Currently, many feminists continue to focus on inequities between the sexes, both politically and economically. Others, particularly feminists in academia, have concentrated their efforts on altering stereotypic attitudes and beliefs about women, as well as developing a "relational" therapy approach. Notable among these are a group of clinicians and researchers at the Stone Center for Developmental Studies at Wellesley College (Jordan, Kaplan, Miller, Stiver, & Surrey, 1991; J. Miller & Stiver, 1994; Rogers, 1994).

7. According to Gilligan (1991), women's struggle to resist complying with restrictive, traditional patriarchal prescriptions is a psychological battle that begins in preadolescence. "Girls are pressed at adolescence to take on images of perfection as the model of the pure or perfectly good woman: the woman whom everyone will promote and value and want to be with" (p. 24).

8. In recent years there have been concerted efforts on the part of many women to move past "benevolent" stereotypic views. For example, Dowling (2000) documented a significant countertrend where women are refusing to accept these paternalistic, condescending views of themselves. In her book *The Frailty Myth*, she emphasized the strides made by many women to correct these sexist views of women as inherently weak, frail, or helpless in relation to men. Drawing on various studies in the sports world, including statistics from Women's Olympics, Dowling noted that "Women of all ages have begun trading in the crimped 'femininity' of the past for a bold new female bravado" (p. xxxi).

9. However, there are a few gender differences in other areas of sexual functioning. Smith (1998) found that 54% of men think about or fantasize about sex every day or several times a day, whereas only 19% of women think about sex with this same frequency. Results from the Laumann et al. (1994) large-scale survey indicated that 26.7% of men, compared with 7.6% of women, reported that they had masturbated at least once a week during the past year. According to Hyde and Oliver (2000), "Many other gender differences were moderate in magnitude . . . Males were more sexually permissive . . . and females reported more anxiety, fear, and guilt about sex. . . . Still other behaviors showed no gender difference" (p. 68).

10. Kindlon and Thompson (1999) have emphasized how important it is for fathers to be able to make an "emotional connection" with their sons. They noted that

Even though fathers in two-parent families today tend to be slightly more involved in child care than they were twenty years ago (a gain of about 15 percent), their involvement doesn't always translate into the kind of emotional connection that boys want. . . . We find that boys feel shortchanged, not only in terms of time but also in terms of affection, and this loss remains with them into adulthood. (p. 100)

11. According to G. Parker (1983),

> There are two broad types of overprotection: a caring form labeled "affectionate constraint," which is not clearly associated with psychiatric disorder; and a form in which there is an associated decrement in care, labeled "affectionateless control" which appears to be strongly associated with several psychiatric disorders and with several anomalies in psychosocial development. (pp. ix–x)

See also the study by Jain, Belsky, and Crnic (1996), in which four groups of fathers were identified by cluster analysis: caretakers, playmates-teachers, disciplinarians, and disengaged fathers.

12. See Westkott's (1997) critique of Stone Center's New Psychology of Women:

> The Stone Center writers do not question what they describe as "the mother's interest in being understood and cared for" by her daughter. . . . Instead, they accept it as a given . . . implying that it is "natural" or unproblematic. However, by doing so, they close off the possibility for interpreting it as a parent's *use* of her child, a practice which others . . . have argued has harmful developmental consequences. (p. 367)

13. Findings from a number of infant studies tend to support Levant's (1998) observations and hypotheses regarding emotional expressiveness in male infants. For example, Tronick (1980) reported that "When mothers held a frozen posture and a still face while looking toward their [2-month-old] infants, the babies looked away and eventually slumped away with a hopeless facial expression" (p. 7). According to Tronick and Weinberg (1997),

> Infant boys are more emotionally reactive than girls. They display more positive as well as negative affect, focus more on the mother, and display more signals expressing escape and distress and demand for contact than do girls. Girls show more interest in objects. (p. 61)

See also Lyons-Ruth and Zeanah (1993). However, in other observational studies, female infants and toddlers tended to surpass male infants and toddlers in maintaining eye contact with caregivers and peers, recognizing faces, and reacting with empathy to another infant's crying (Zahn-Waxler, Radke-Yarrow, Wagner, & Chapman, 1992; Zahn-Waxler, Robinson, & Emde, 1992).

14. Critics have argued that "outdated" psychoanalytic theories generally "ignore individual circumstances and assume an essentialist position (i.e., the belief that there exists a basic female nature that remains relatively impervious to contextual factors)" (Reid & Bing, 2000, p. 145). In particular, these critiques strongly disagree with approaches suggesting that daughters have "difficulty identifying with their mothers because they held sexual desires for their fathers" (p. 145). For example, Reid and Bing claimed that "In light of current incidents of family sexual abuse and reexaminations of Freud's notes, researchers now give less credence to the notion of female gender emanating from penis envy or childhood feelings of female inferiority" (p. 145). Similarly, in relation to

male development, Silverstein and Auerbach (1999), in criticizing the essential-ist assumption "that boys need a heterosexual male parent to establish a mascu-line gender identity" (p. 403), noted that "a significant amount of research on the children of lesbian and gay parents has shown that children raised by lesbian mothers (and gay fathers) are as likely as children raised in heterosexual, two-parent families to achieve a heterosexual gender orientation" (p. 403).

15. From a cross-cultural perspective, Morokoff (2000) has asserted that "women's sexual behavior is subject to social control in most if not all societies" (p. 308). Morokoff noted, however, that recent social changes have reduced the power exerted by some of these techniques, for example, "The advent of effective contraception has [led to] . . . a steadily increasing percentage of adolescent women [who] become sexually active with each new survey conducted" (p. 309).

16. According to Gilligan, only when girls reach preadolescence (sometime be-tween the ages of 9 through 13) do they become compliant, give up their opinions, and lose a sense of who they are and what they know. In comparing the different developmental crises that boys and girls must navigate, Gilligan (1991) emphasized that "The relational crisis of boys' early childhood and of girl's adolescence is marked by a struggle to stay in relationship—a healthy resistance to disconnections which are psychologically wounding (from the body, from feelings, from relationships, from reality)" (p. 24).

17. Benjamin (1995) further explained that

    Once core gender identity is established in the first twelve to eighteen months of life, the child proceeds to elaborate gender role identity in conjunction with separation-individuation issues, hence in a conflictual and variable context. . . . Children continue throughout the second and third years to identify with both parents, even though their roles are some-what differentiated and the father may assume special importance. (p. 127)

18. Classical psychoanalytic theories of male psychosexual development and the oedipal conflict have been articulated for more than 100 years; whereas theories of female psychosexual development were not explicated until the latter half of the 20th century.

19. Buss (1994) also asserted that "In evolutionary terms, men and women are identical in many or most domains, differing only in the limited areas in which they have faced recurrently different adaptive problems over human evolutionary history" (p. 18). Thus, men and women also evolved a number of similar personality characteristics and behaviors that they prefer in potential partners, such as intelligence, affection, generosity, and altruism. These traits can also be hypothesized to have evolved through the process of sexual selection, because in modern times these traits are among those that appear to be equally distributed statistically between the two genders. As Ridley (1993) put it, "Not everything is different; most things, in fact, are identical between the sexes. Much of the folklore about differences is merely convenient sexism" (p. 248).

20. Moore and Travis (2000) cite numerous examples of media "hype" surrounding supposedly scientific findings based on sociobiological or evolutionary princi-

ples. For example, in describing an ABC television news program on the reality of sex differences, they commented: "The message of the program was that men and women are 'just biologically hard-wired to be different,' and, accordingly, expectations of gender specific behaviors and attitudes should be different as well" (p. 49).

5

APPROACHES TO THE ETIOLOGY OF SEXUAL DYSFUNCTIONS AND PROBLEMS IN SEXUAL RELATING

In contrast to normal lovers, dysfunctional individuals focus on and expect unpleasant sensory input, which effectively decreases the experience of pleasurable, erotic sensations. In short, these patients engage in innumerable ploys and maneuvers to down-regulate their desire for sex, including such tactics as "turning off" their sexual partners by putting their "worst foot forward."

—H. Kaplan (1995, p. 23)

Since the publication of S. Freud's (1905/1953) *Three Essays on the Theory of Sexuality*, psychoanalytic approaches to the origins of sexual dysfunctions have gone through many transformations, and new conceptual models are continually being developed. Psychoanalytic theories regarding factors that predispose the development and maintenance of sexual disorders have decreased in popularity. At the same time, other approaches based on object-relations, attachment, cognitive–behavioral, and family systems theories, along with biomedical models explaining the etiology of these disorders, have become increasingly prominent.

Many mental health professionals attribute the current biomedical focus on dysfunctional sexual relating to the widespread acceptance of Masters and Johnson's models of sexual health and inadequacy set forth in *Human Sexual Response* (1966) and *Human Sexual Inadequacy* (1970). The work of these sex researchers has been criticized for its neglect of the emotional, relational, and spiritual aspects of sexuality. For example,

---

although H. Kaplan (1995) acknowledged Masters and Johnson's contributions to changes that have occurred in treating sexual dysfunctions, she also emphasized that "The oversight of sexual desire disorders created problems in that this left large numbers of patients and couples whose complaints center around *inadequate sexual motivation* out in the cold" (p. 2).

In this chapter, we discuss the definitions of the various sexual dysfunctions as delineated in the *Diagnostic and Statistical Manual of Mental Disorders, Fourth Edition* (DSM–IV; American Psychiatric Association, 1994). Biomedical factors clearly contribute to the development of sexual dysfunctions. However, our focus is primarily on the psychological factors involved in the etiology of disturbances in sexual relating. We first discuss our views regarding the origins of sexual dysfunctions and other sexual problems in intimate relationships. Next we briefly review several object-relations, attachment theory, social learning, cognitive–behavioral, and family systems approaches to the etiology of sexual dysfunctions. We discuss similarities between these approaches and our approach to the psychodynamics involved in the development of these dysfunctions and other problems in intimate relating.

DEFINITIONS OF SEXUAL DYSFUNCTIONS

Sexual disturbances and problems in sexual relating are widespread in Western society. According to the 1992 National Health and Social Life Survey conducted by Laumann, Paik, and Rosen (1999), 43% of women and 31% of men suffer from some form of sexual dysfunction. According to the *DSM–IV* (American Psychiatric Association, 1994): "A Sexual Dysfunction is characterized by a disturbance in the processes that characterize the sexual response cycle or by pain associated with sexual intercourse" (p. 493).

According to Rosen and Leiblum (1995), "Sexual desire disorders are among the most prevalent and challenging problems encountered in current sex therapy" (p. 19). Sexual desire disorders include hypoactive sexual desire disorder (HSP) and sexual aversion disorder. The other sexual dysfunctions, corresponding to the other three phases in the sexual response cycle, are the sexual arousal disorders, which include female sexual arousal disorder and male erectile disorder; the orgasmic disorders, which include female and male orgasmic disorders and premature ejaculation; and the sexual pain disorders, which include dyspareunia (pain during or after intercourse in both males and females) and vaginismus ("recurrent or persistent involuntary contraction of the perineal muscles . . . when vaginal penetration . . . is attempted") (American Psychiatric Association, 1994, p. 513).[1]

The diagnostic categories have been criticized by some clinicians and theorists (McConaghy, 2003; Weeks & Gambescia, 2002) who argued that the definitions of various sexual dysfunctions are confusing and "perplexing." For example, Weeks and Gambescia noted that the DSM–IV's definition of hyposexual desire disorder "raises a number of clinical and theoretical issues" (p. 2). Clinicians are left to determine whether the problem lies in one partner's subjective perception of low sexual desire in the other, which partner is experiencing interpersonal distress, and whether the problem is acquired, situational, or generalized.

As is the case with most emotional disturbances, the sexual dysfunctions delineated above are multidetermined. Genetic predispositions, biochemical factors, and environmental influences combine to contribute to the development and maintenance of various sexual dysfunctions in adult individuals. In some cases, biological predispositions may exert a greater influence, whereas in other cases, family, social and cultural factors are more important. For example, in certain cases, the cause of a specific sexual dysfunction may be traced to the direct effects of a general medical condition. "If psychological factors also play a role in the onset, severity, exacerbation, or maintenance of a sexual dysfunction, the diagnosis is the primary Sexual Dysfunction (with the subtype Due to Combined Factors)" (American Psychiatric Association, 1994, p. 517). In addition, a wide variety of pharmaceuticals have been found to be associated with the development of sexual dysfunctions or an intensification of their symptoms (Segraves & Balon, 2003).

OUR VIEWS ON THE ETIOLOGY OF SEXUAL DYSFUNCTIONS

All people exist in conflict between tendencies to pursue real gratification in their closest relationships, and tendencies to depend on internal sources of gratification, including fantasy, excessive use of substances, and inward, routinized behavior patterns. The major threat to physically and emotionally fulfilling sexual relations can be traced to the developmental history of each partner and to experiences that necessitated the formation of psychological defenses, as described in chapter 3.

The Oral Basis of Sexuality

We propose that an individual's sexuality may be represented on a continuum, ranging from total fantasized self-sufficiency, as in seriously disturbed or psychotic patients, to a healthy interdependence with another person in meeting one's needs (Firestone, 1985). This continuum can be conceptualized as ranging from the oral phase to mature genital sexuality. To understand where clients are on this continuum, it is valuable to examine their sexual life and sexual fantasies because they symbolically express attitudes toward the giving and receiving of love in relation to other people.[2]

Basic attitudes toward the giving and receiving inherent in sexual intercourse are closely related to feelings associated with early oral experiences and other reciprocal interactions with the mother or primary parenting figure that take place during the preverbal stage of development (Stern, 1985). Studies of early sexual development have also emphasized the preoedipal stage as being a critical period for establishing one's sexual identity as well as basic feelings of trust in attachment figures (H. Kaplan, 1979; Schoenewolf, 1989). Indeed, many problems in sexual relating may have their origins in the mother–infant dyad (Caplan, 1981; Chodorow, 1978; Genevie & Margolies, 1987; L. Kaplan, 1984; Park, 1995; Rheingold, 1967).

It is interesting that the only two direct exchanges of bodily fluids between human beings are breast-feeding in infancy and ejaculation in adulthood. In this conceptualization, sexual attitudes relate to the underlying oral symbolism, in that the penis symbolizes the breast, the vagina symbolizes the mouth, the semen symbolizes the milk, and the pregnancy the full belly (Firestone, 1957). The oral basis of sexuality and the symbolic confusion of sexual and feeding symbols are not restricted to serious psychopathological syndromes. We suggest that this conceptualization contributes to understanding sexuality in normal individuals.

People who avoid sex and closeness are, in effect, turning away from seeking gratification from the external world—from someone outside themselves. When there has been considerable anxiety and deprivation related to early feeding experiences, sexual relationships, physical touch, and bodily contact with other persons may become threatening. Sexual dysfunctions such as premature ejaculation, retarded ejaculation, or erectile difficulties in the male and hypoactive sexual desire disorders and arousal and orgasmic problems in the female may reflect a movement away from sex and a close, emotional exchange between two people and a movement toward relying on sex more as a means for self-gratification.

The prevalence of obesity and addictions in Western society may be indicative of a movement away from or an avoidance of sex on the part of many individuals (Brody, 2004). The compulsive eater, drug abuser, and alcoholic are all denying dependency needs and the natural drive to affiliate with other people. Through their addictive habit patterns, they appear to be expressing a belief that they are completely self-sufficient—a defiant, pseudoindependent attitude: "I can take care of myself. I don't need anything from anybody else."

In general, the way people relate in their intimate relationships reveals a great deal about where they are in their development psychologically. Their attitudes toward sex as well as their mode of sexual relating indicate the extent to which they are defending themselves against becoming fully autonomous adults. It has been our experience that healthy, mature sexual relating, in combination with feelings of friendship in an intimate relationship, tends to arouse anxiety because it represents a powerful intrusion into people's defensive posture and their illusions of self-sufficiency and pseudoindependence.

Developmental Factors That Interfere With Adult Sexual Functioning

We contend that the child's natural attraction to the mother grows out of the satisfaction of his or her need for proximity to the parent or caregiving adult. The drive to be physically close to the mother is one of the earliest determinants of an appropriate gender identification for both male and female offspring. However, if the child's natural attraction to the mother or primary caregiver is frustrated, healthy sexual functioning may be compromised in any number of ways.

As described in chapter 3, sexual abuse, incest, or inappropriate behaviors on the part of a seductive adult or adults are harmful to children's emerging sexuality and can also contribute to the development of sexual dysfunctions. The authors have found that the child's defensive reactions to these painful impingements may take one of two different forms: (a) sexual sensations may be heightened in parts of the body that were violated or inappropriately touched, that is, those parts become sexualized; or (b) those parts of the body may become deadened to sensation. As noted earlier, child sexual abuse can predispose either condition in adult males and females. (Herman, 1981; Purcell et al., 2004).

In the former cases, where sexual sensations have been intensified, pleasurable sex is often accompanied by intense guilt reactions. Even when the sexuality in a relationship is initially passionate, guilt reactions (in some cases, the guilt is associated with the emergence of long-forgotten memories of child sexual abuse or incest) are often eventually triggered in the abuse survivor, especially as he or she becomes more emotionally close to the partner. The stage is thus set for possible development of a hyposexual desire disorder or, in more severe cases, a sexual aversion disorder.

In cases of orgasmic disorders, a combination of painful affects and defenses, including those described above, may be operating in individual partners and in turn can have a detrimental effect on the couple's sexual interaction. For example, we found that in some cases, retarded ejaculation appears to be influenced by the man's awareness of his partner's escalating tension as she approaches orgasm or when he attempts penetration. In this case, the antecedents of the problem of retarded ejaculation may be complicated. On the one hand, it may be that the man was abused sexually as a child, or on the other, his partner may have been traumatized by such events and be selectively phobic in relation to penetration. In these instances, the intervening variables linking the original trauma experienced by the symptomatic partner to his or her current sexual problem need to be explored through extensive history-taking and depth psychotherapy. In addition, the therapist needs to examine the ways that the symptomatic partner's sexual disturbance affects the other's ability to respond sexually and to understand how the couple's sex life is affecting the relationship as a whole (Johnson, 2002).

Orgasmic disorders in women may be directly or indirectly related to environmental factors from childhood. Defensive behaviors developed in the aftermath of child sexual abuse are some of the mediating factors that contribute to an inability to experience orgasm in both males and females, although studies have shown that females are more at risk for this specific outcome (H. Kaplan, 1995).[3]

We have also described the role of shame and guilt in the development of disturbances in sexual relating (Firestone, 1990b). Shame and guilt represent the internalization of parental rejecting attitudes in relation to the body, to simple bodily needs and desires, as well as the need for affectionate contact and love. In many of the individuals we interviewed, it appeared that if they had developed feelings of shame about a particular part of their body as children, they often experienced destructive thoughts about that area in their present-day relationships. In some cases, they reported that this specific part became insensitive to physical touch or sexual caresses. Others appeared to have invested a certain symbolic meaning in one area of their body such that being touched sexually in this area often triggered feelings of shame. In addition, many people seemed to be able to pick up their partner's feelings of shame about the affected part or area (probably through projective identification) and felt hesitant about touching or caressing those areas.

Lastly, in considering the psychodynamics involved in other forms of sexual disturbances, we suggest that patients who manifest sadomasochistic fantasies or behaviors (Jureidini, 2001; Stoller, 1975) have strongly identified with an abusive, sadistic, or aggressive parent as a child, a defense first described by Ferenczi (1933/1955) and later by A. Freud (1966). Sexual activities can be accompanied by feelings of hostility toward oneself or one's partner, by aggressive, sadistic fantasies, or the feelings may be expressed through the acting out of behaviors that function to humiliate or degrade oneself and/or one's partner. The underlying dynamics are often a result of an internalization of parental sadism and aggression under conditions of extreme stress. In examining possible origins of sadomasochistic fantasies and behaviors, it is interesting to note that Ferenczi's original paper (1933/1955) dealt specifically with the consequences of incest or sexual child abuse. Ferenczi began his analysis of such cases as follows:

The real rape of girls who have hardly grown out of the age of infants, similar sexual acts of mature women with boys, and also enforced homosexual acts, are more frequent occurrences than has hitherto been assumed.

It is difficult to imagine the behaviour and the emotions of children after such violence. . . . These children feel physically and morally helpless, their personalities are not sufficiently consolidated in order to be able to protest. . . . *The same anxiety, however, if it reaches a certain maximum, compels them to subordinate themselves like automata to the will of the aggressor, to divine each one of his desires and to gratify these; completely oblivious of themselves they identify with the aggressor.*

The most important change, produced in the mind of the child by the anxiety-fear-ridden identification with the adult partner, is *the introjection of the guilt feelings of the adult.* . . . The misused child changes into a mechanical, obedient automaton or becomes defiant, but is unable to account for the reasons of his defiance. His sexual life remains undeveloped or assumes perverted forms. (pp. 161–163)

Ferenczi's germinal paper opened up the way for an alternative interpretation of Freud's oedipal complex. In other works, the first author (Firestone, 1994a, 1997a) has described this alternative perspective on the oedipal complex, which often predisposes a powerful identification with the aggressive parent. In more severe or pathological cases, the internalized hostility and sadism are often manifested in sexual fantasies containing aggressive or sadistic components or they may be expressed through the acting out of aggression toward self and partner. Silverstein (1994) identified still another costly consequence of this defense mechanism: "The child, identifying with the aggressor, satisfies his or her superego and fear of retaliation by channeling aggression into fantasy and/or by blocking sexual desire from consciousness" (p. 37). It is important to note here that less aggressive or less severe sadomasochistic behaviors are not considered pathological by many mental health professionals or by individuals who engage in these practices and find them enjoyable and pleasurable.

In other less severely disturbed individuals, such as a man who has an exclusive interest in young, postpubescent girls (as distinguished from pedophilia), the causative factors may include fears of being engulfed by an overly involved, seductive mother, avoidance of incestuous attraction to female siblings, or oedipal fears of retaliation from other males. Men who are attracted to adolescent girls often believe that being sexually involved with a younger, inexperienced woman rather than a mature, sexually experienced woman is essential to avoid feelings of humiliation and sexual inadequacy. Similarly, women who are exclusively attracted to adolescent boys may avoid full sexual relations with adult males for a variety of reasons:

they may fear penetration or they may have unresolved oedipal issues in relation to the father and thus fear retaliation from the mother.

A BRIEF REVIEW OF OTHER THEORETICAL APPROACHES TO SEXUAL DYSFUNCTIONS

A number of theories have evolved to explain the etiology of the various sexual disorders. Each conceptual model mirrored the social and political climate, the economic conditions, and the scientific and philosophical thinking of its particular era.[4] These distinctive theoretical approaches have different implications for how clinicians intervene with clients who are suffering from symptoms of a sexual dysfunction.

Psychoanalytic Perspectives

Briefly stated, in his theory of sexuality, S. Freud (1940/1964) proposed that disturbances in "normal" sexual functioning are largely caused by the failure to resolve the oedipal conflict. Remnants of the conflict are repressed, maintained in the unconscious, and continue to have an effect on an individual's sexual functioning throughout his or her life. S. Freud (1912/1957) hypothesized that in many cases, male erectile dysfunction or impotence was related to an inability to integrate sexual desire and love. In describing these patients, he commented that "Where they love, they have no desire, where they desire, they cannot love" (p. 183).

Other theorists (Fairbairn, 1952; Guntrip, 1971; Melanie Klein, 1975; Sullivan, 1953) place the origin of sexual conflicts in the preoedipal phase and in the relationship to the mother. For example, in a recent reworking of classical psychoanalytic views regarding the etiology of hysteria, Bollas (2000) emphasized the importance of the child's early love and attraction to the mother as well as the mother's acceptance of her infant, including his or her body and emerging sexuality.

The clinical work of psychoanalyst Kernberg (1980) supports our thinking regarding adult versus regressed modes of sexual expression. For example, Kernberg (1980, 1995) stressed the importance of individuation and self-differentiation in suggesting that mature or "genital" sex requires a leaving behind of the parental figure of the same sex. In addition, Kernberg (1980) conceptualized a continuum of sexual love that is largely determined by "the capacity—or rather, the incapacity—to fall and remain in love" (p. 278). At one extreme on Kernberg's continuum are "narcissistic personalities who are socially isolated and who express their sexual urges only in polymorphous perverse masturbatory fantasies" (p. 278; Level 1). At the other extreme

(Level 5) is "the normal person who has the capacity to integrate genitality with tenderness and a stable, mature object relation" (p. 278).

According to Kernberg (1980, 1995), Fromm (1956), and others, "immature" sexuality and love relations also reflect an individual's failure to extend "self-love" (primary narcissism) to the love object. In our terms, the criteria for "mature" sexuality and intimate relating would imply a transformation from self-gratifying forms of sexuality into a reliance on others for satisfaction in interpersonal relations.

Object Relations Perspectives

During the past five decades, a number of object relations therapists have begun to employ Fairbairn's (1952) and Guntrip's (1969) concept of split ego—the libidinal and antilibidinal ego—as a basis for understanding the etiology of patients' sexual problems. Object relations theorists emphasize the importance of experiences that occur during the preoedipal phases as formative influences on later sexual dysfunctions. According to Guntrip (1961), who interpreted Fairbairn's work, disturbances in libidinal (sexual) development begin in infancy:

> When the mother does not succeed in making the child feel she loves him for his own sake and as a person in his own right. . . . That is the factor that dominates all other and more detailed, particular issues such as oral deprivation, anal frustration, genital disapproval, negative and over-critical discipline and so on. (p. 284)

In a similar vein, we propose that when children suffer excessive frustration, deprivation, parental intrusiveness or rejection during the preoedipal stage of development, they develop defenses that may be often manifested in their adult lives in the form of sexual dysfunctions, aberrations, or other sexual inhibitions.

From Fairbairn's perspective, an individual is motivated from the beginning of life by the need to affiliate with other people, not as a means of reducing tension (related to hunger, sex, etc.), but for purposes of survival from an evolutionary standpoint. In describing his theoretical approach, Fairbairn (1952) asserted that when "the child comes to feel (a) that he is not really loved for himself as a person by his mother, and (b) that his own love for his mother is not really valued and accepted by her" (p. 17), there may be a regression to an earlier stage of development. The child tends to internalize the rejecting object (the mother) and repress the emotional pain of rejection.

Of particular note is Guntrip's (1969) interpretation of Fairbairn's view of the resultant split self: "We view the libidinal ego as in bondage to guilt or fear, that is imposed by an *antilibidinal ego* which in part represents the frightening or accusing parents who have themselves disturbed the child" (p. 202). According to Guntrip (1971), "Fairbairn treated sexual problems as . . . internal bad-object relationships with either the exciting object or the rejecting object" (p. 95).

Fairbairn's and Guntrip's theory is comparable to our concept of the self and the antiself systems described in chapter 6. In fact, there is a close relationship between the two theoretical positions. In our theory, the self system is composed, in part, of identification with and imitation of parents' positive traits and behaviors and is constructive and goal-directed. The antiself system is made up of identification with and incorporation of negative aspects of parents' personalities and behaviors. These "negative parental introjects" are manifested in the form of a destructive thought process or internal voice that is alien to an individual's aspirations and desires. However, from our perspective, the split ego is not only a function of parental abuses but is also a result of the child's defensive adaptation to existential concerns. Both interpersonal trauma and ontological issues foster the "antilibidinal ego" or, in our terms, the antiself system that leads to self-limiting aspects of the personality and predisposes inhibitions and disturbances in sexual relating.

Fairbairn's and Guntrip's theories are important because they represent significant contributions to contemporary models explaining the ways that individuals relate sexually in their intimate associations. For example, Guntrip (1971) emphasized the fact that, "Of all the appetites, sex is the only one that cannot be wholly divorced from object-relations" (p. 36). Guntrip also stressed the importance of using an object-relations perspective when treating individuals with sexual problems: "I have never yet met any patient whose overintense sexuality and/or aggression could not be understood in object-relational terms, as resulting from too great and too early deprivations of mothering and general frustration of healthy development in his childhood" (p. 40).

British psychoanalyst and family systems theorist Dicks (1967) expanded Fairbairn's (1952) concept of the "antilibidinal ego" in investigating the effects of aversive childhood experiences on adult sexual relationships. Dicks first outlined the inevitable conflicts that arise even during a healthy or "ideal" developmental sequence and went on to describe how defenses and ego-splitting can occur in less-than-ideal environments, with less-than-ideal objects (parents). According to Dicks, the effects of this defensive splitting can be observed in people who, although they are "intellectually and socially competent adults," remain "impoverished in their intimate object relations" (p. 42).

Dicks's clinical and theoretical work helps explain one phenomenon under consideration in this book—why sexual relating often becomes troublesome as a relationship matures and partners become emotionally closer and reach deeper, more profound levels of sexual intimacy. Dicks argued that

> [Fairbairn's theory] also explains why, when biological sexual maturation and cultural pressures stimulate the need of such a "well-adjusted" person for total sexual loving commitment and spontaneity, the result can be so inadequate; infantilely demanding, crude and ambivalent, hence sabotaged by the anti-libidinal ego. (p. 42)

Another major contribution of object relations theory, as articulated by Melanie Klein (1975), Fairbairn (1952), and Guntrip (1971) lies in its elucidation of the concept of "projective identification," which has added substantially to the pool of knowledge about mature sexual love. In Dicks's (1967) conceptualization of a "collusive marriage," each partner has projected elements of the "split-off, guilt-laden libidinal and anti-libidinal egos" (p. 118) into the other through projective identification, an unconscious process that adversely affects the couple's love relations. Scharff and Scharff (1991) explained the role of projective identification in marital relationships and applied the concept to treating couples' problems in sexual relating. These clinicians proposed that the medium for projection in the sexual encounter is the body rather than the mind. "Any body part of self or other can become identified with the disclaimed projection, but the erotic zones are particularly likely targets. . . . Penis, vagina, and the woman's breasts become the physical locus of the repressed rejecting and exciting object systems" (p. 55). Scharff and Scharff as well as Zinner (1976) suggested that through the process of projective identification, feelings of sexual inadequacy in one partner can be defensively and unconsciously transferred to the other.[5]

Kernberg (1991) has also emphasized that both unresolved preoedipal and oedipal conflicts are core issues that affect the couple's sexual relationship, especially as partners become closer emotionally and sexually: "With sexual intimacy comes further emotional intimacy, and with emotional intimacy, the unavoidable ambivalence of oedipal and pre-oedipal relations" (p. 156). Kernberg traced this ambivalence to the differential developmental tasks faced by men and women and the ways in which healthy sexual development may be compromised by faulty parent–child relations.

> The man's ambivalence toward the exciting and frustrating mother from early childhood on and his deep suspicion of the teasing and withholding nature of mother's sexuality become issues interfering with his erotic attachment, idealization, and dependency on the woman he loves. His unconscious oedipal guilt, his sense of inferiority to the idealized oedipal mother may result in sexual inhibition with or intolerance of a woman who becomes sexually free and is no longer a little girl-woman toward whom he may feel reassuringly protective. . . .

In the case of a woman who did not have an early satisfactory relationship with a mother who tolerated the little girl's sexuality, the unconscious experience of a hostile and rejecting mother who interfered with her early development of bodily sensuality and, later on, with her positive relationship to father may result in exaggerated unconscious guilt about sexual intimacy in conjunction with commitment in depth to a relationship with a man. Under these circumstances, the little girl's normal shift in object from mother to father is unconsciously distorted. (p. 156)

Kernberg's explanation of the dynamics underlying many types of sexual disturbance within the couple agree to a certain extent with our understanding of family influences on the sexual development of male and female offspring, as described in chapter 4. We also found that many women who had an unsatisfactory relationship with a hostile, rejecting mother not only suffer exaggerated unconscious guilt about sexual intimacy, but they are also fearful of disrupting the imagined connection (fantasy bond) with the mother. We further suggested that, in these cases, entering into a satisfying sexual relationship with a man symbolizes emotional separation from the mother and loss of the imagined safety and security provided by the fantasized fusion with her, which constitutes an anxiety-provoking situation.

Attachment Perspectives

According to Bowlby (1973), the tendency to seek proximity to the caregiving figure originally served to protect the infant from predators; it is not a secondary drive derived from hunger or sensual needs as Freud believed. Fear of potential danger or brief separations from the mother or parenting figure activate a built-in behavioral control system in the infant or toddler and stimulate actions (sucking, smiling, clinging, crying, and following) that (ideally) elicit appropriate maternal responses. Since the time Bowlby first introduced his ethnologically based theory, attachment researchers have investigated the relationship between an individual's early attachment history and his or her style of relating in an adult romantic relationship (Fraley & Shaver, 2000; Hazan & Shaver, 1987; Shaver & Clark, 1994; Shaver, Collins, & Clark, 1996; Shaver & Hazan, 1993). Others have studied proposed links between attachment styles and types of sexual behavior (Brennan & Shaver, 1995; Feeney, Noller, & Patty, 1993; Schachner & Shaver, 2004; Stephan & Bachman, 1999).

According to Shaver and Hazan (1993), approximately 55% of the people involved in romantic relationships have a secure attachment style. As children, these individuals were likely to have formed a secure attachment pattern with one or both parents. According to Schachner and Shaver

(2004), people who are categorized as securely attached "are open to sexual exploration and enjoy a variety of sexual activities, including mutual initiation of sexual activity and enjoyment of physical contact, usually in the context of a long-term relationship" (p. 180). In contrast, people who are categorized as "anxious/ambivalent" or "preoccupied" lovers (approximately 20%) "show a greater preference for the affectionate and intimate aspects of sexuality than for the genital aspects (e.g., vaginal or anal intercourse)" (p. 180). Avoidant or dismissing lovers, who make up approximately 25% of couples "are less likely than their less avoidant counterparts to fall in love . . . and their love style is characterized by game playing (Shaver & Hazan, 1988). . . . Avoidant adults express dislike for much of sexuality, especially its affectionate and intimate aspects" (p. 181).

In describing how these attachment types might play out in a relationship, Schachner and Shaver (2004) asserted that sexual encounters between "anxious and avoidant individuals seem especially troublesome, given that one partner may be inclined to seek approval and lasting affection [through sex] while the other is inclined to have short-term sex without intimacy or commitment" (p. 193).[6]

Attachment theorists Shaver, Collins, and Clark (1996) have provided descriptions of how "internal working models" mediate partners' styles of relating in adult romantic attachments. Internal working models are described by many theorists as representing children's beliefs about self, others, and relationship, and as mediating partners' styles of relating in an adult romantic attachment (Batgos & Leadbeater, 1994; Bretherton, 1996; Bretherton & Munholland, 1999; Fischer & Ayoub, 1996). According to Bretherton (1996) "insecure individuals develop working models of self and attachment figure in which some schemas or schema networks [cognitive processes] may be dissociated from others" (p. 14). Shaver and Clark (1994) suggested that children who grow up with a negative internal model of themselves and their attachment figure often become adults who have relatively low self-esteem and distrust relationship partners.

There are important similarities between the above descriptions of negative aspects of internal working models and our concept of the destructive thought process or the internalized "voice." We conceptualize the "voice" as a basic part of internal working models that can help explain the complex dynamics involved in interpersonal relationships (Firestone & Catlett, 1999). The voice is hypothesized as an intrapsychic mechanism that is primarily responsible for the perpetuation of negative parental attitudes, beliefs, and defenses in succeeding generations. It also influences the type and quality of attachments formed by adult individuals in their couple relationships. In describing Robert Firestone's theoretical model, Van Horn (1999)[7] noted

Firestone has made a convincing case that difficulties in intimate adult relationships can be traced to internal working models of self and other and to the thoughts about self and other that are inspired by those models. [His] clinical material . . . demonstrates clearly the ways that both positive and negative models of the self are transmitted from parent to child and the ways that the negative models are incorporated into defensive patterns that prevent true intimacy in adult relationships.

Attachment theory has also contributed substantially to the understanding, evaluation, and treatment of sexual dysfunctions in intimate partners and of marital distress in general (Johnson & Whiffen, 1999; Shaver & Hazan, 1993). According to Johnson and Whiffin (1999), in situations where an individual believes the partner is unavailable or unresponsive, anger and anxiety are aroused which, in turn, trigger that individual's internal working models of self in relation to the other person. These working models, which are derived from his or her past experiences in early attachment relationships, shape how the partner's "responses will be appraised and interpreted, and how an individual will then communicate and respond" (p. 369).

We would add to the above statement by stressing that even the way that a partner's personal qualities and behaviors are perceived is often strongly influenced or distorted by internal working models or destructive thought processes, which represent the internalization of negative aspects of one's early attachment relationship(s). As Johnson and Whiffen noted, the purpose of working models is to make predictions in attachment relationships. "Insecure models may predispose people to selectively attend to and defensively distort information. . . . An anxious partner [may think] . . . 'He is distant. He doesn't love me and I am unlovable'" (p. 373).

Johnson and Greenberg (1995) and Bader and Pearson (1988) have used aspects of attachment theory, in conjunction with some concepts from family systems theory, to formulate treatment strategies for couples with sexual dysfunctions and other problems. (See chap. 9.) According to Bader and Pearson (1988), one type of troubled sexual relationship, the "enmeshed" type,

Is characterized by merger, avoidance of conflict and the minimization of differences. The other type is almost the behavioral opposite. The hostile-dependent system is dominated by anger and conflict. Too terrified to end the relationship and not mature enough to end the battles, the couple remain locked in endless rounds of mutually inflicted pain. (p. 10)

This dynamic is similar in many respects to our descriptions of partners who form a fantasy bond or imagined connection with each other as the relationship evolves, who suffer from a deterioration in the quality of their sexual relating as a consequence and who may develop a secondary sexual dysfunction.

Social Learning and Cognitive–Behavioral Perspectives

Early social learning theorists, Bandura (1986) and Maccoby and Jacklin (1974), proposed that sexual attitudes and sexual behaviors, like all attitudes and behaviors, are learned both explicitly and implicitly through the processes of identification and imitation. A major tenet of social learning theory states that individuals tend to imitate the actions of a role model, that is, a person with whom they closely identify. In the process of assimilating attitudes about sex, children use as role models not only actual persons, especially parents, but also symbolic models, including people portrayed in the media.

Several clinicians and theorists have employed an integrated social-cognitive–behavioral approach in an effort to delineate familial and societal factors influencing the development of heterosexual, lesbian, gay, and bisexual gender identity (Crosbie-Burnett, Foster, Murray, & Bowen, 1996; Hogben & Byrne, 1998; Hyde & Oliver, 2000). H. Kaplan (1995), who expanded her original behavioral approach to include interpersonal and psychodynamic perspectives, joins Beck (1988; Beck, Rush, Shaw, & Emery, 1979) and other cognitive therapists in hypothesizing that sexual preferences, idiosyncratic sexual desires, and fantasies are also determined by the interaction of individual histories, learning, and experience. Based on clinical work with more than 7,000 patients, Kaplan (1995) concluded

> In terms of learning theory . . . it may be speculated that any and all experiences that are *sexually arousing to the child and occur during a critical period of development* . . . may become permanently and indelibly programmed into his or her "erotic software." . . .
>
> It may be further speculated that the continuous and repeated mutually pleasurable intimate physical and emotional contact that small children normally enjoy with their mothers, fathers, and other family members . . . are *inadvertently mildly erotically arousing to infants and young children, and sensuously pleasurable for their parents* . . . *and that these experiences form the psychologic origins of normal sexual fantasies and desires.* (p. 40–41)

Kaplan did not imply that these mutually pleasurable experiences harm children in the way that sexually abusive or incestuous experiences do. She did contend, however, that "this hypothetical normal sexual 'imprinting' process can go awry and result in linking sex with fear and/or in the acquisition of and fixation on atypical and possibly disadvantageous sexual fantasies and desires" (p. 42). In other words, sexual responses may be genetically "hardwired" into the brain before birth, yet learning and experience interact with predispositions to shape adult sexual desires, fantasies, and behaviors, and many of these experiences can interfere with this process.

In exploring the more complex causes of inhibited sexual desire (ISD), Kaplan (1979) described theories derived from learning theory and interpersonal orientations. Expanding on these systems of thought, Kaplan noted, "The child may learn to inhibit his sexuality, to sabotage his romantic success, and to be guilty about pleasure, if the emotional nonverbal and verbal responses of his family are destructive and not encouraging in these respects" (p. 89). In a subsequent work, *The Sexual Desire Disorders*, Kaplan (1995) emphasized the critical role played by "*selectively negative cognitive and perceptual processes . . . in the pathogenesis of HSD* [hypoactive sexual desire] disorders" (p. 117). She also called attention to specific negative thoughts her patients had reported:

> The sexual symptom protects against the evil eye of the harsh and irrational conscience which is evoked by this success [a gratifying sexual experience]. The unconscious injunction—"you are not entitled," "something will happen if things get too good," "who do you think you are?" "you can't have everything"—may be the underlying cause of sexual difficulties in such cases. (1979, p. 171)

Kaplan also observed that such negative beliefs caused many patients to be fearful about experiencing pleasure and finding fulfillment in an intimate relationship. Paradoxically, anticipating success in a sexual experience seemed to bring many of these negative cognitions to the surface. Many of Kaplan's patients reported that these destructive thoughts became more intense and were experienced more frequently as their relationship became more meaningful or after they made a commitment to the partner.

In exploring family dynamics that might be linked to inhibited (or hyposexual) desire disorders, Kaplan asserted that "I have come to believe that a good relationship with the same-sex parent confers considerable immunity against subsequent sexual psychopathology" (1995, p. 134). In describing the mother-daughter relationships of many of her female patients, Kaplan wrote,

> In our patient population, the great majority of women with HSD and sexual aversion disorders had not received proper encouragement from their mothers, and they had for the most part been unable to form healthy female identifications. The mother-daughter relationships of our female patients were poor for a variety of reasons, including the mother's unavailability, cruelty, alcoholism, narcissism, or her own emotional problems. . . . On the other side of the coin, the key to much of male sexual pathology lies in *faulty father-son relationships*. (pp. 134–135)

Kaplan's views regarding the etiological factors involved in these types of sexual dysfunction agree in substance with our perspective on negative aspects of the mother–daughter and father–son relationships, as described in chapter 4. Kaplan's focus on "negatively charged emotions and cognitions" is similar to our focus on destructive thought patterns and the associated anger that can block sexual desire and interfere with sexual arousal.

Kaplan (1995) has also suggested that the fear and emotional pain associated with sexual abuse or other trauma experienced in childhood may become sexualized and have a negative effect on adult sexual functioning. "On a psychological level the erotization of trauma and pain, which is especially devastating to a child when this occurs at the hands of parents, makes this psychic wound less overwhelming and easier to bear" (p. 45). However, the defense of identifying with the abusing parent and eroticizing the painful interactions with that parent can have additional costs in terms of the child's later adjustment. For example, Kaplan has pointed out that "As is true of all mechanisms of defense, the process of eroticizing the aggressor can backfire; when this happens, the person may have to pay a heavy price" (p. 45). One price, according to Kaplan, is that the individual may develop deviant sexual fantasies and behaviors. She noted that

> It is common for men who were hurt by rejecting, withholding, demanding, controlling, cruel, elusive, or sadistic mothers to eroticize the very same destructive qualities that caused them so much pain when they were children. When they grow up these men may feel attracted only to women who hurt them in similar ways, but they are unable to form attachments to decent women. (p. 137)

As noted earlier, a number of theorists have suggested that a direct relationship exists between shame, dysfunctional beliefs, and sexual dysfunctions, especially in cases of inhibited sexual desire (Goldberg, 1996; Kaufman, 1980; M. Lewis, 1992; Morrison, 1989). For example, in his treatment of symptoms of pathological shame in both neurotic and narcissistic patients, Goldberg (1996) noted, "If [the child] . . . is unable to express clearly her feelings of hurt and anguish, she develops a disparaging inner 'narrative voice' that constantly warns her away from situations in which she might again be hurt or painfully exposed" (p. 38).

Beck (1976), cognitive therapy, Ellis and Harper (1975), rational-emotive therapy, and Elliott (1999), anthetic therapy, among others, have discussed concepts such as "automatic thoughts," "irrational beliefs," and the "inner critic" hypothesized to contribute to depression, anxiety, and sexual disturbances. Others, including Kaufman (1980), Guidano and Liotti (1983), and Kaplan (1979, 1995) have investigated the psychodynamics underlying clients' negative beliefs about sex, men, women, and relationships.

Family Systems Theory

Schnarch's (1991) approach to the etiology of sexual dysfunctions (or problems in achieving one's sexual potential, as he would put it) integrates Bowenian family systems theory with aspects of existential psychology. In working with couples, Schnarch uses various techniques from sex and marital therapy to help individual partners increase their level of self-differentiation (Bowen, 1978; Kerr & Bowen, 1988).[8]

In explaining the basic tenets of family systems theory, Bowen (1978) argued that "In the average nuclear family . . . the spouses are emotionally 'fused' with each other and with the children, and it is difficult to get far beyond the fusion or to do more than react and counterreact emotionally" (p. 545). Bowen indicated that the degree of "emotional fusion" varied tremendously among families. Kerr and Bowen (1988) defined a major concept of family systems theory—"self-differentiation"—as

> The degree to which [people] . . . are able to distinguish between the feeling process and the intellectual process. Associated with the capacity to distinguish between feelings and thoughts is the ability to choose between having one's functioning guided by feeling or by thoughts. . . . People who have achieved the least amount of emotional separation from their families (the most entangled child in a poorly differentiated family) have the least ability to differentiate thinking from feeling. (pp. 97–98)

Bowen's treatment, based on his family systems theory, was primarily focused on helping patients differentiate from the "external" family, whereas the goal of our therapeutic approach is to achieve insight into the sources of low levels of self-differentiation and assist patients in the differentiation of self from the "internal" family, that is, separation from negative parental introjects or the voice process.

We suggest that Schnarch's (1991) adaptation of Bowen's approach neglects important contributions consolidated from findings in attachment research that have expanded our understanding of the diverse factors influencing the development of problems in sexual intimacy. In publications and lectures, Schnarch has overlooked important findings from these studies that explain how early attachment to caregivers can affect the quality of sexual relating in adult romantic attachments. Schnarch (1991) quoted a number of writers who tend to dismiss, to a certain extent, closeness as an important factor in intimate relationships. For example, Schnarch cited Malone and Malone (1987), who said "Closeness is certainly important and necessary, but it has become a neurotic, obsessive preoccupation, and a destructive overconcern in current human societies" (p. 3). In contrast, we contend that "Intimacy and mutual regard can only be achieved when couples struggle through the anxiety aroused in movement toward closeness and individuation" (Firestone & Firestone, 2004, p. 393).[9]

Overall, Schnarch (1991) appears to believe that raising individual partners' levels of self-differentiation is the only viable pathway to sexual intimacy, while ignoring other formative influences and aspects of partners' psychosexual development and attachment history. His view of "closeness" noted above, is in sharp contrast to Bowen's original thinking, exemplified by Bowen's statement that "Giving up some togetherness does not mean giving up emotional closeness" (Kerr & Bowen, 1988, p. 107). Schnarch's theoretical approach fails to take into account the fact that developing a secure attachment (earned security in an adult romantic attachment) and emotional closeness with an intimate partner is, in fact, a major aim of psychotherapy with couples. Movement toward that goal would of course be contingent on each partner achieving a higher level of self-differentiation.

Schnarch (1991) views the couple as a system and perceives sexual problems as reflecting interactional processes within the couple system rather than intrapsychic processes within the individual partners. Thus, the term "inhibited sexual desire" has a certain relativity to its meaning because "The actual level of the 'low sex drive' partner's desire might increase with a different partner and might well have been higher with the current partner at a prior time" (p. 225).

Schnarch emphasizes that low levels of self-differentiation in each partner contribute to a couple's troubled sex life. He asserts that partners involved in committed relationships have sexual difficulties because they are operating at relatively low levels of self-differentiation. We tend to agree with Schnarch's observation that partners with low levels of self-differentiation cling to a conventional form of "other-validated" intimacy, based on the need for fusion, rather than "self-validated" intimacy based on the ability to tolerate separateness and existential aloneness. Schnarch also argues that a committed sexual relationship provides the crucible in which partners can "grow up" by differentiating themselves emotionally from their family of origin. In treatment, Schnarch uses techniques aimed at eliciting "profound intimacy," acknowledging that anxiety will be aroused by an increase in intimacy during sex. We concur with Schnarch's emphasis on existential anxiety and his explanations regarding why partners with low levels of self-differentiation have boring, routine sex: "*People have boring, monotonous sex because intense sex and intimacy (and change itself) are more threatening than many people realize*" (Schnarch, 1991, p. 143).

CONCLUSION

In this chapter, we provided a brief summary of several theoretical perspectives, including our own, related to the etiology of sexual dysfunctions. According to these perspectives, there are many environmental factors that contribute to the development of disturbed sexual functioning in adults. Sexual dysfunctions and other problems in sexual relating have serious consequences in that they affect every aspect of the couple's relationship, including activities and pursuits far removed from sexual relating.

We propose that sexual dysfunctions, particularly inhibited sexual desire disorders, represent a denial of one's needs, whether these needs are oral or sexual or for love. The majority of problems in sexual relating clearly indicate a defensive posture in relation to the giving and receiving of products in an equal exchange with an intimate partner. To better understand this defensive posture as it is manifested in an individual's style of expressing his or her sexuality, it is necessary to develop a conceptual model of healthy sexual relating and to characterize the elements that enter into disturbed or dysfunctional modes of sexual relating.

We have concluded that people have a basic conflict between strong tendencies to pursue real sexual gratification in an intimate relationship, and powerful propensities to rely more on internal sources of gratification, including fantasy, substance abuse, inward habit patterns and impersonal modes of sexual relating. Most people, however, are unaware that they are trying to avoid love and sexual fulfillment. Their withdrawal from these experiences may become habitual and eventually lead to symptoms of a clinically diagnosable sexual dysfunction. The challenge for therapists is to help clients resolve this conflict by encouraging them to move toward a less defended, more vulnerable posture in relation to their loved ones.

An understanding of defense formation in early childhood, specifically the core defense—the fantasy bond (described in chap. 6)—is crucial to understanding why people find it difficult to move beyond low levels of self-differentiation, establish a secure base in their relationship, and achieve "profound intimate sex" as described by Schnarch (1991). In this regard, Bowen commented that "the concept of the fantasy bond provides an understanding of the intrapsychic processes operating within each individual that predispose the development of the 'emotional ego mass,' characterizing families in which members have low levels of self-differentiation" (personal communication, November 1986).

In our view, difficulties that arise during the course of a long-term sexual relationship clearly indicate each partner's respective levels of self-differentiation as well as reflecting the type of attachment they have formed with their partner, that is, preoccupied, dismissing, or fearfully avoidant.

Progress in therapy will be largely determined by the degree to which the individual can break free from destructive family ties on an external level, and from negative parental introjects (destructive thought processes or internalized voices) on an internal level, to form a secure attachment with his or her mate. The way people relate sexually reveals the extent to which they are still defending themselves against becoming separate, autonomous individuals capable of enjoying emotional closeness and sexual intimacy with a relationship partner. Mature, genital sexuality, combined with feelings of companionship in a long-lasting relationship, does indeed precipitate anxiety states because it represents a powerful intrusion into the fantasy bond—the imagined fusion with one's parent or parents.

NOTES

1. Other categories of sexual disturbance include the Paraphilias or sexual perversions, which are defined as being characterized by "recurrent, intense sexually arousing fantasies, sexual urges, or behaviors generally involving 1) nonhuman objects, 2) the suffering or humiliation of oneself or one's partner, or 3) children or other nonconsenting persons" (American Psychiatric Association, 1994, pp. 522–523). According to the *DSM–IV*, when perverse fantasies or behaviors lead to "clinically significant distress or impairment," for example, if they are compulsive and "require the participation of nonconsenting individuals, lead to legal complications, [or] interfere with social relationships" (p. 525), they may be defined as perversion. Stoller (1991) included the term "perversion" in his original definition of sexual aberration. "Sexual aberrations can be divided into two classes: variants (deviations) and perversions" (p. 37). Perversion is "a habitual, preferred aberration necessary for one's full satisfaction, primarily motivated by [unconscious] hostility" (p. 37).

2. Silverstein (1994) also suggested studying a client's sexual fantasies. She proposed a continuum of "eroticism that includes varying degrees of dominance and power. . . . The more powerless and helpless the child feels, the more likely he or she will develop dominance and control fantasies" (p. 34). "Both men and women channel power needs into sexual fantasies; both men and women wish to control the love object" (p. 36).

3. Research has shown that in some women, the physiological response indicates orgasm has occurred, yet they report having experiencing no orgasm (Basson, 2003). The subjective experience of orgasm appears to be damaged in these women; the underlying mechanisms for this phenomenon have yet to be determined (Everaerd, Laan, Both, & van der Velde, 2000).

4. The social and political conditions of each era, specifically the conservative "antisex" bias that has existed in America since the 1970s obviously influenced theory formation, treatment, and the direction of sex research (Melby, 2001; Richard, 2003). Also see feminist perspectives and critiques of S. Freud's

hypotheses regarding the origins of sexual dysfunctions in the female (Chodorow, 1999; Everaerd et al., 2000).

5. Zinner (1976) has also noted that many sexual disorders and distorted sexual attitudes have a historical basis in childhood. He found that the unconscious material that is projected onto the other person during sex contains "highly conflicted elements of the spouse's object relationships with his or her own family of origin" (p. 297).

6. In a related study, Feeney (1999) reported that "In a 6-week diary study . . . we . . . found that female avoidant and male ambivalent subjects were the least likely to report engaging in sexual intercourse. This finding suggests that gender and attachment style interact in their effects on sexual behavior" (p. 371). However, Bogaert and Sadava (2002) found that correlations between attachment style and variations in sexual behavior were less than .20. They proposed that "Perhaps attachment processes may strongly predict sexuality (e.g., frequency of sexual behavior, number of partners or affairs) only when a relationship is threatened, such as when a partner has an affair" (p. 201), that is, when the attachment behavioral system is activated by threat of loss.

7. Van Horn's work includes Lieberman, Compton, Van Horn, and Ippen (2003) and Lieberman and Van Horn (2004).

8. There are major differences between family systems theory and psychodynamic perspectives in terms of conceptualizing "causality" of emotional and sexual disturbances. Psychodynamic theories deal with unconscious motivations and cause-and-effect, linear explanations to understand their origins, which to Bowen and Schnarch's are generally inaccurate. According to Kerr and Bowen (1988), "Systems theory links all symptoms [of neurosis] to the emotional system, a system that is not equivalent to the psychoanalytic 'unconscious'" (p. 230).

9. We also agree with Bray's (1991) definition of intimacy "as voluntary closeness with distinct boundaries. . . . Closeness that lacks boundaries and is not perceived as voluntary reflects emotional fusion rather than intimacy" (p. 275).

III

THE DEFENSIVE PROCESS
AND SEXUALITY

6

THE ROLE OF THE FANTASY BOND, THE VOICE PROCESS, AND DEATH ANXIETY IN SEXUAL RELATIONSHIPS

Man is subject to a basic need that conceptually transcends and cannot be reduced to libido or aggression, the primary drives of psychoanalytic theory. . . . The individual is impelled throughout his life by [a] dual psychological phenomenon: the need for contact and the aversion to awareness of separateness. . . . The universal psychopathology is defined as the attempt to create in real life by behavior and communication the illusion of fusion.

—Fierman (1965, pp. 208–209)

The decline in sexual passion and quality of intimate relating that is so common in long-term relationships and marriages cannot be attributed to the reasons usually given: familiarity, gender differences, economic hardship, or other stressors. As a relationship matures, there is often a shift in its dynamics, fears of potential loss or rejection may surface, and painful feelings from childhood may emerge, which can cause partners to retreat to a more defended posture. Disturbances in sexual relating arise primarily because at a certain point the defensive processes that both individuals bring to the relationship come into play and limit their ability to continue to enjoy sexual intimacy.

Many men and women encounter difficulty in trying to maintain relationships that are both emotionally and sexually satisfying, because in their earliest relationships, hurt and frustration caused them to turn away from love and closeness and to become suspicious and self-protective. To varying degrees, children are forced to rely on a fantasy of connection and self-nourishing, self-soothing behaviors because of less than adequate parenting. As adults, they still seek to gratify themselves internally rather than trust or depend on external relationships. For example, some people replace emotional gratification with overeating, excessive drinking, using

135

drugs, working compulsively, or masturbating rather than depending on another person to gratify their wants or needs for affection and sex (Firestone, 1985).

During childhood, people internalize negative as well as positive views of themselves during the socialization process. Positive self-attitudes are easily assimilated into the personality while those that are negative are incorporated in the form of an alien aspect of the personality that cannot be fully integrated. These negative attitudes and fantasies eventually became a basic part of people's feelings toward themselves and adversely affect their lives. By the time they reach adulthood, most have developed a strong defense system, incorporated a critical view of themselves in the form of an internal thought process (the "voice"; Firestone, 1988) and achieved a psychological equilibrium compatible with this destructive view. The reality of being genuinely acknowledged or loved threatens to disturb this equilibrium, and people usually refuse to allow it to affect their basic defensive structure and negative self-concept (Firestone & Catlett, 1999).

Fears of sexual intimacy are not only related to the anxiety associated with closeness on an interpersonal level, they are also based on existential fears. Being intimate with another person in a loving sexual encounter makes one aware that life is precious, but must ultimately be surrendered. If one embraces life and love, one must also face death's inevitability (Firestone & Catlett, 1999).

Although we have touched on these concepts in previous chapters, in the following pages we will elaborate on the underlying psychological defenses that originate in childhood and that ultimately interfere with close sexual relating. We provide an in-depth perspective on the fantasy bond (the primary defense) and voice process (the secondary defense) and elucidate a conceptual model of sexuality that helps clarify why people retreat from sexual and emotional intimacy. In discussing this theoretical approach to sexual problems in the context of an intimate relationship, we show how defenses formed by each partner early in life in relation to interpersonal pain and death anxiety can have detrimental effects on his or her sexual functioning as an adult.

We delineate two modes of sexual expression that may be manifested by intimate partners and elucidate how manifestations of the fantasy bond, initially formed with a parent or parents, contribute to inward, self-gratifying modes of sexual relating as contrasted with genuine feelings and relating during the sex act. In exploring the factors that lead to disharmony in sexual relationships, we show how destructive thought processes or internalized "voices" of both partners interfere with achieving and sustaining a loving sexual relationship. Lastly, we describe how death anxiety and a heightened awareness of one's essential separateness are often precipitated as partners become closer and more intimate in their sexual relating.

PSYCHODYNAMICS

In this section, we explore the environmental factors that predispose defense formation and show how these defenses act as barriers to healthy sexuality.

The Formation of the Primary Defense—The Fantasy Bond

Early in the developmental sequence, the infant compensates for emotional deprivation and defends against separation anxiety by forming a primary defense, which we refer to as the *fantasy bond*. The fantasy bond is an imagined fusion with the mother or primary caregiver. It is an effective defense because a human being's capacity for imagination provides partial gratification of needs and reduces separation anxiety. For example, research has shown that fantasy processes are satisfying for people exposed to conditions of physical deprivation. In one study (Keys, Brozek, Henschel, Mickelsen, & Taylor, 1950), volunteer subjects deprived of food and kept on a minimum sustenance diet reported that they spent hours daydreaming about food, which partly alleviated their tension and reduced their physical pangs of hunger.

The fantasy bond helps individuals cope with the intolerable pain and anxiety that arise when the infant is faced with excessive separation anxiety or frustration. This type of anxiety can be far more devastating to the infant than the frustration itself, at times representing for the infant "a *threat of annihilation*. This ... is a very real primitive anxiety" (Winnicott, 1958, p. 303).

Infants have a natural ability to comfort themselves by using images and memories of past feeding experiences to ward off the anxiety caused by excessive frustration. When parents are generally unavailable or inconsistent in meeting their infant's needs, the infant increasingly relies on fantasies of imagined fusion with his or her parents. The fantasy bond now becomes a substitute for real gratification, and the child becomes progressively more dependent on this process as a means of comfort and security.

No child has the ideal environment. There are inevitable frustrations and separation experiences in the lives of all children (Briere, 1992; Felitti, 2002).[1] To varying degrees, all people depend on internal gratification from an imagined connection with the introjected parent or primary caregiver. However, the greater the frustration, pain, and anxiety and the greater the degree of reliance on this imagined connection, the more maladaptive the individual may become in his or her adult relationships (Firestone, 1984, 1985).

A number of theorists, beginning with Kaiser (Fierman, 1965) have described modes of relating based on fantasy processes or a delusion of fusion

(Karpel, 1976, 1994; Wexler & Steidl, 1978). In a discussion of Kaiser's work, Fierman (1965) noted that Kaiser focused on duplicitousness or indirect communication, which he identified as a major manifestation of the illusion of fusion. "To engage in indirect communication, the individual blunts and distorts his own awareness of separateness, creates the illusion of fusion, and is precariously gratified on an imaginary basis in a fusion relationship with the other person" (p. 209). Kaiser's hypothesis that this "delusion of fusion" is the universal psychopathology is analogous to Firestone's (1984) conceptualization of the fantasy bond as the primary defense mechanism in neurosis.

The development of the fantasy bond leads to a pseudoindependent posture, that is, an illusion that one can take care of oneself and needs nothing from the outside world. The more an individual comes to rely on fantasy, the less he or she will seek or be able to accept gratification from other people in real relationships (Firestone, 1985; Firestone & Catlett, 1999). Once a fantasy bond is formed, it predisposes inward behavior patterns, including a preference for fantasy gratification over real satisfaction, a reliance on substances as painkillers, asceticism or self-denial, patterns of holding back affection and sexual responses from one's partner (withholding), tendencies toward isolation and passivity, self-critical attitudes, and cynical, hostile views of self and others. All of these reflect negatively on a person's development and later sexual satisfaction.

The Self-Parenting Process

The core defense or fantasy bond takes the form of a self-parenting process that the child (and later the adult) uses to both nurture and punish him- or herself internally. The process involves self-nourishing thoughts and habit patterns as well as self-punishing ideation and behaviors. The fantasy of being merged with a parent, and the use of self-nourishing, self-soothing behaviors such as thumb-sucking or rubbing a favorite blanket, combine to alleviate the emotional pain of rejection and the fear of separation and aloneness.[2] The self-parenting process is maintained throughout one's childhood and persists into adult life, and in many people, it may come to be preferred to real relationships as a source of comfort and safety.

In parenting themselves, children experience a false sense of being totally self-sufficient because they have introjected or taken into themselves, the image of the "good and powerful" parent. The more pain and frustration the child experiences, the more that child will need to introject this positive parental image.[3] In describing the process of introjection, Erikson (1963) noted that "In introjection we feel and act as if an outer goodness had become an inner certainty" (pp. 248–249). Unfortunately, in so doing, the child also takes on the parent's hostile, rejecting attitudes toward him or her (Firestone, 1985). These internalized parental attitudes or negative parental introjects form the basis of his or her negative self-image (Guntrip, 1969).

In defending themselves against overwhelming frustration and emotional pain, children tend to depersonalize, fragment, lose feeling for themselves, and become hostile and suspicious of others. In denying their needs and wants in relation to other people, they become a complete system unto themselves. In an attempt to maintain some sense of ego intactness under stressful circumstances, the child merges with the powerful parent in fantasy, incorporates hostile parental attitudes, and, at the same time, retains painful, "primal" feelings of being the helpless "bad" child. This fragmentation leads to a confused self-concept in which one sees oneself as better or worse than others, and accounts for significant variations of mood (Firestone, 1997a).

Clearly, the degree of fragmentation and the subsequent effects on adult functioning exist along a continuum. The extent to which children defend themselves by becoming fragmented into elements of the parent–child system is generally proportional to the amount of damage they incur while growing up.[4] The more deprived, rejected, or exploited the child, the more he or she comes to rely on the fantasy bond as a compensation and then goes on to reject genuine closeness and affection in adult romantic attachments.

As adults, individuals continue to parent themselves—nurturing, soothing, and punishing themselves—in much the same way they were treated as children. Bollas (1987) has described his concept of the "self as object" in similar terms in his work: "Each person transfers elements of the parents' child care to his own handling of himself as an object" (p. 59). Kohut's (1977) concept of the "selfobject" is similar in some respects to the concept of the fantasy bond or self-parenting process, in particular the self-nurturing component. According to Elson's (1987) summary of Kohut's theoretical approach, Kohut proposed that

> With every denial from the parents, with every delay, which is a kind of denial, something is set up internally. The ego performs internally something that formerly was performed externally by the mother or father. . . . If the loss is traumatic, beyond what the psyche at a specific developmental moment can actually perform, or if it is done in too great a measure, then there will be a gross identification with the lost parent. (p. 103)

Self-nourishing tendencies are subsequently elaborated into more sophisticated means of self-gratification, such as praising and comforting oneself; vanity; eating disorders; addiction to cigarette smoking, alcohol, and other drugs; compulsive masturbation; and an impersonal, self-soothing style of sexual relating. Self-critical thoughts, guilt reactions, attacks on the self, and cynical views of other people are examples of the punitive element of the self-parenting process.

At some point in the developmental sequence, children gradually come to realize that the life they perceived as permanent is in fact temporary (Anthony, 1971/1973; Kastenbaum, 1974, 1995; Lester, 1970; Nagy, 1948/1959; Rochlin, 1967). Their secure world is turned upside down by the dawning awareness of first their parent's future death and then their own. After they develop an awareness of death, separation experiences, whether real or symbolic, tend to arouse death anxiety. The defenses that the child developed to deal with early interpersonal distress are then used and reinforced as he or she attempts to alleviate this existential pain. Thereafter, the fantasy bond of fusion with parents and other family members becomes the child's basic defense against the dread of separation and death.

Individuals who form a fantasy bond in an intimate relationship tend to externalize aspects of the internalized parent–child fused image or system into their sexual relating, and may alternatively act out either aspect in relation to their partner.[5] In general, people who are operating from the parent or child ego state tend to manifest self-gratifying modes of sexual relating. In particular, maintaining the stance of a child symbolizes the refusal to become an adult and grow older. In this way, the imagined fusion with the partner provides an illusion of immortality on an unconscious level.

The Formation of the Secondary Defense—The Voice Process

Self-nurturing and self-punishing behaviors are regulated by an internal thought process, antithetical toward self and cynical toward others, that we refer to as the "voice" (Firestone, 1988). All people suffer, to varying degrees, from internal conflict and a sense of alienation from themselves—dynamics that extend beyond such descriptive terms as ambivalence or dissonance. On the one hand, each individual has a point of view that reflects his or her natural wants, aspirations, and desires for affiliation with others, as well as the drive to be sexual, to reproduce, and to be creative. On the other hand, each individual has another point of view that reflects tendencies for self-limitation, self-destruction, and hostility toward other persons.

The voice can be defined as a systematized pattern of destructive thoughts and attitudes, accompanied by varying degrees of angry affect, that is at the core of an individual's maladaptive behavior (Firestone, 1988). It is an overlay on the personality that is not natural or harmonious but represents the incorporation of destructive parental thoughts, attitudes, and defenses. In essence, the voice can be conceptualized as the language of the defensive process. It functions as a secondary defense that supports the primary defense, the fantasy bond, and strongly influences self-parenting, inward behavior patterns. It takes the form of intrapsychic communication that ranges along a continuum from minor self-criticisms to major self-attacks. In addition, the voice supports self-soothing habit patterns, isolation, self-denial, self-destructive lifestyles, suicidal ideation, and, at the extreme end, actual suicide.

The conditions in childhood that predispose formation of negative thought processes that govern self-limiting, self-destructive behaviors include neglect, emotional deprivation, overt and/or covert rejection, and physical, emotional, and sexual abuse (Firestone, 1997a). To maintain the illusion of connection to the parent under these harsh circumstances, children idealize their parents at their own expense. At the same time children imitate the personality traits and behaviors of their parents, even if they perceive these traits as negative or undesirable. Imitation involves two other important psychological processes, *identification* and *introjection*, which are vital in the developmental sequence (Rapaport, 1951).

When children feel the most threatened and fearful, they generally identify with the aggressor (the person causing their suffering) in an attempt to possess that person's strength or power. Through this process of identification, children assume the qualities of the parents and, at the same time, assimilate or introject the hostile, critical attitudes their parents are expressing toward them (Bettelheim, 1943/1979; Ferenczi, 1933/1955; A. Freud, 1966). Unfortunately, children tend to incorporate the attitudes of the parent at his or her worst, that is, at times of extreme tension and abuse. Therefore, negative parental introjects (the voice process) may not be truly representative of parental attitudes on the whole.

In those moments of extreme distress or abuse, children disconnect from themselves and cease to exist as a real self, a separate entity. In this way, the process of introjection is responsible for the inclusion of a systematized "parental" point of view within the self (Firestone, 1988). This introjected view militates against the individual's unique personal aspirations and opposes his or her motivations to fulfill basic wants and needs, including desires for sexual gratification.

In previous works, Firestone (1988, 1997a, 1997b) described how negative parental introjects or "voices" internalized during the formative years lead to an essential dualism within the personality. He emphasized that a primary split exists within every individual between forces that are constructive and goal-directed (the self system) and a destructive thought process alien to his or her best interests (the antiself system).

The division of the psyche into the self and antiself systems occurs early in life, often during the preverbal stage of development. Both systems are dynamic and continually evolve and change over time (Firestone, 1984, 1985, 1988, 1997a, 1997b). (See Exhibit 6.1.)

Negative attitudes toward self and others based on this split can have a devastating effect on intimate relationships. This insight is crucial in

EXHIBIT 6.1
Division of the Mind

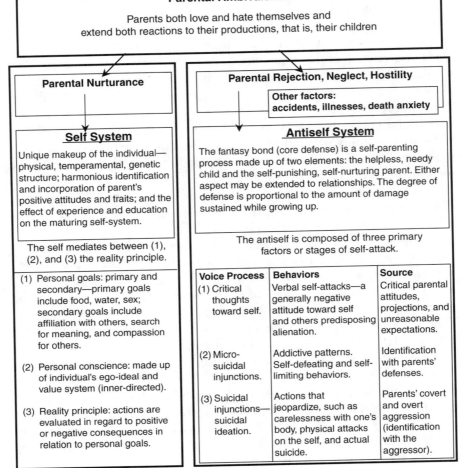

Parental Ambivalence

Parents both love and hate themselves and
extend both reactions to their productions, that is, their children

Parental Nurturance

Parental Rejection, Neglect, Hostility

Other factors:
accidents, illnesses, death anxiety

Self System

Unique makeup of the individual—
physical, temperamental, genetic
structure; harmonious identification
and incorporation of parent's
positive attitudes and traits; and the
effect of experience and education
on the maturing self-system.

The self mediates between (1),
(2), and (3) the reality principle.

(1) Personal goals: primary and
    secondary—primary goals
    include food, water, sex;
    secondary goals include
    affiliation with others, search
    for meaning, and compassion
    for others.

(2) Personal conscience: made up
    of individual's ego-ideal and
    value system (inner-directed).

(3) Reality principle: actions are
    evaluated in regard to positive
    or negative consequences in
    relation to personal goals.

Antiself System

The fantasy bond (core defense) is a self-parenting
process made up of two elements: the helpless, needy
child and the self-punishing, self-nurturing parent. Either
aspect may be extended to relationships. The degree of
defense is proportional to the amount of damage
sustained while growing up.

The antiself is composed of three primary
factors or stages of self-attack.

Voice Process	Behaviors	Source
(1) Critical thoughts toward self.	Verbal self-attacks—a generally negative attitude toward self and others predisposing alienation.	Critical parental attitudes, projections, and unreasonable expectations.
(2) Micro-suicidal injunctions.	Addictive patterns. Self-defeating and self-limiting behaviors.	Identification with parents' defenses.
(3) Suicidal injunctions—suicidal ideation.	Actions that jeopardize, such as carelessness with one's body, physical attacks on the self, and actual suicide.	Parents' covert and overt aggression (identification with the aggressor).

understanding the psychodynamics underlying the way individuals relate to
each other sexually, because destructive thought processes directed both
toward self and a significant other predispose alienation in an intimate
relationship (Firestone, 1990c). During those times when thoughts based
on the internalization of parents' harmful attitudes and defenses predominate
in one's thinking, serious distortions of oneself and one's partner are often
introduced into the sexual situation.

When people are under stress, there is a breakdown in the self system. When an individual is "not him- or herself," the self is fractured into parental and childlike behaviors that fit the model of transactional analysis.[6] These parental and childish elements (within the antiself system) are part of the self-parenting process. Paradoxically, the child's struggle to maintain some sense of intactness and ego integrity under conditions of extreme stress produces fragmentation and disintegration (Noyes, Hoenk, Kuperman, & Slymen, 1977). In forming an imagined fusion with his or her parents, the child becomes divided into being at once the weak, bad child and the nurturing/punishing parent (Firestone, 1997b).

These destructive thought processes (negative parental introjects) can be brought to the surface and identified through voice therapy, and when expressed, they reveal an unusual amount of aggression toward self. Writers from other disciplines have long been aware that people harbor considerable aggression toward themselves and have described destructive forces within the personality that create most of the misery in life. In 1621, Burton (1621/2001), in *The Anatomy of Melancholy*, captured the essence of the antiself system or internal enemy and its destructive effects on people's lives when he wrote,

> Every man [is] the greatest enemy unto himself. We study many times to undo ourselves, abusing those good gifts which God hath bestowed upon us, health, wealth, strength, wit, learning, art, memory to our own destruction: *Perditio tua ex te* (thy destruction is from thyself). . . . We arm ourselves to our own overthrows; and use reason, art, judgment, all that should help. us, as so many instruments to undo us. (p. 136)

Most people tend to underestimate the depth of this division within themselves as well as the pervasiveness of their tendencies to make self-limiting, self-destructive choices. They try to deny this fracture by identifying negative traits predisposed by the antiself system as their own. "That's just the way I am; I've always been like that." Unable to tolerate the lack of integration within themselves, they tend to compromise their wants and desires, which are a fundamental part of their identity, and move in the direction of the prescriptions of the voice. Freud's realization that unconscious motives determine much of human behavior was a threat to people's illusions of omnipotence, yet discoveries made in the course of investigating the voice are even more threatening because they make people painfully aware of the aggression toward themselves (Firestone, 1997b).

Several theorists and clinicians have described irrational beliefs, maladaptive core schemata, automatic thoughts, and other aspects of destructive thinking that are similar in some respects to our concept of the voice process. (A. Beck, Rush, Shaw, & Emery, 1979; Ellis, 1973; Epstein, 1973, 1993, 1994; Epstein, Lipson, Holstein, & Huh, 1992; Stiles, 1999). For example, according to cognitive-experiential self-theory, developed by Epstein et al. (1992), "individuals have 2 systems for processing information, a rational system and an experiential system" (p. 328). In Epstein's model, people develop basic schemata or implicit beliefs in the experiential system rather than the rational system. In addition, these beliefs "consist primarily of generalizations derived from emotionally significant past experience" (Epstein, 1994, p. 715).

Epstein (1994) further argued that

The main sources of maladjustment ... are disharmony (including dissociation) within the experiential system and a failure in need fulfillment, not a discrepancy between conscious and unconscious thinking. ... The task of therapy is to change the maladaptive schemata in the experiential system and to promote synergistic (rather than conflictual) need fulfillment. (p. 717)

In his approach, Stiles (1999) suggested that people can be "considered to be psychologically composed of multiple internal voices" (p. 268). One implication based on Stiles's conceptual model is that "the occurrence of dysphoric emotion reveals the presence of ... two discrepant voices within the person" (p. 270). According to Stiles, one voice represents "*continuity-benevolence assumptions*" or CBA voices that "arise from early positive experiences of nurturing and care" (p. 269) while other "voices" may be "derived from problematic (traumatic or threatening) experiences [which] are sometimes warded off or cast out" (p. 268).

TWO MODES OF SEXUAL RELATING

The fantasy bond plays a fundamental role in how people relate sexually. The way children learn to cope with pain in their earliest relationships, and the kind of defenses they adopt to deal first with separation anxiety and later with the awareness of death, are preserved intact within their personalities as adults. In particular, as one begins to invest meaning in an intimate relationship or becomes more committed to one's partner, the self-parenting process is seriously threatened and there is a strong tendency to revert to a more self-protective or defended style of sexual relating.

In general, one can conceptualize two distinct modes of sexual relating: (a) a personal, outward style of interaction that is a natural extension of affection, tenderness, and companionship between two people; and (b) an impersonal, self-gratifying expression in which sex is used primarily as a drug or painkiller. Sexual experiences can be viewed as existing on a continuum between the two modes of sexual expression, one in which there is a personal exchange between two people and the other in which sex is being used

EXHIBIT 6.2
The Continuum of Sexual Relating

Inward	Outward
Less personal, more "mechanical" style of sexual relating.	Close emotional contact and personal relating, not focused on techniques.
More masturbatory: use of partner as a means to gratify oneself, one's own needs for security, relief from stress, and to enhance self-esteem.	Relating to partner as a real person, not a sex object, concern for partner's well-being and satisfaction as well as for one's own. The sex act is viewed as an equal exchange, physically and emotionally.
Sexual withholding: holding back or inhibiting sexual desire, physical affection, attractiveness, sexual responsiveness.	Spontaneous expression of affection, free flow of feelings of excitement in which the sex act naturally proceeds to completion uninterrupted by inhibitions.
Control: attempts to control or manipulate aspects of the sexual relationship, for example, the frequency, time, place, and positions of the sex act.	Both partners allow the sex act to naturally flow from one phase to the next.
Relying on fantasy to increase excitement: fantasies are kept a secret from the partner.	Minimal use of fantasy: sexual fantasies shared with partner.
Voice attacks experienced before, during, and following the sex act are kept to oneself.	If voice attacks arise, they are shared with the partner.
Feelings of emptiness, irritability, and dissatisfaction are often experienced after the sex act.	Feelings of happiness, pleasure, satisfaction, and emotional closeness are often experienced after the sex act.

primarily to relieve tension, or feelings of emptiness and insecurity. (See Exhibit 6.2.)

We have proposed that the sex act may be conceptualized as a real, but temporary, physical connection or union followed by a sharp separation (Firestone, 1984). Thus, a satisfying sexual experience is capable of arousing separation anxiety in many individuals, who then attempt to protect themselves by retreating to a more inward, defended mode of sexual expression. At the same time, they revert to acting out parental or childish behaviors in relation to each other rather than continuing to maintain an adult ego state. It is important to emphasize that in most cases, people distance themselves emotionally from their sexual partner before their anxiety reaches the level of conscious awareness.

In our experience, we have found that most people are resistant to maintaining an adult ego state and often regress to childish or parental modes of interacting in the face of anxiety. It appears that any interaction symbolizing separateness, individuation, or lack of fusion is capable of arousing anxiety and can lead to a regressive trend. For some people, a defended or impersonal style of sexual relating is manifested in most or even all of their sexual encounters, and rarely, if ever, do they experience genuine sexual intimacy in their relationships. In other words, in contrast to many people who may regress to self-gratifying modes of sexual relating as a defense against intimacy, these individuals, who have been damaged in their ability to relate closely, are characteristically inward and self-gratifying in their style of relating. In fact, it could be said that the adult mode represents an ideal state of adjustment that most individuals are incapable of achieving to varying degrees. The ability to remain in an "adult ego state" (Berne, 1961; Firestone, 1988) appears to depend primarily on an individual's level of self-differentiation (separation from the fantasy bond with the family-of-origin; Bowen, 1978; Hellinger, 1998; Karpel, 1994; Kerr & Bowen, 1988; Schnarch, 1991; Willi, 1978/1984, 1999).

THE EXTENSION OF SELF-PARENTING INTO SELF-GRATIFYING MODES OF SEXUAL RELATING

As described earlier, children who parent themselves develop an illusion that they do not need to be gratified by another person. As they develop through adolescence and into adulthood, they extend this illusion and the self-parenting behaviors that support this fantasy process into self-gratifying modes of sexual relating. They also use other elaborate methods to comfort and soothe themselves, including promiscuous sexual relating, compulsive masturbation, or other addictive, repetitive sexual practices that relieve tension. The use of sex as a narcotic is directly analogous to addictions such as alcoholism and other forms of substance abuse, in that the sexual experience acts as a painkilling drug to cut off or inhibit feeling reactions. It represents a movement away from real sexual intimacy and emotional exchange between two people, and toward reliance on sex as a mechanism for self-gratification that may actually place a limitation on a mature, healthy, or loving relationship. In some cases, these disturbances in sexual relating can reach a clinical level and be manifested in symptoms of a specific sexual dysfunction.

Symptoms of a self-gratifying mode of sexual relating can be present, to varying degrees, in any sex act. One or both partners can revert to this mode of sexuality at any point before, during, or following lovemaking. After an especially satisfying sexual experience, many people become distant, preoccupied, or argumentative, or they become childlike, dependent, and/or punishing in expressing elements of the internalized parent–child system.

Understandably, this regressive process may be difficult to identify because people tend to retreat to an inward, defensive posture or revert to parental or childlike behaviors before the anxiety, sadness, and other painful emotions evoked by the experience reach the level of conscious awareness.

A shift during lovemaking from close emotional contact to a more self-gratifying style of relating is damaging to the well-being of the individuals involved. Many people report feelings of emptiness, a sense of dissatisfaction, boredom, and irritability following sexual experiences in which an inward or less personal mode of relating predominates. For example, in a discussion group, Grant talks about his reactions to this impersonal style of sexual relating.

> Grant: Some of the women I dated when I was in my early twenties were very seductive. They seemed really interested in being sexual with me, which intrigued me. They definitely pursued me, which was more comfortable for me. I would describe them as being very sexually energetic. Making love with them was usually fast, breathless, kind of a frenzied sexuality, like in some movie love scenes. But lots of times being sexual in this way didn't make me feel good even while it was going on. Afterwards I usually felt sort of let down and kind of empty because it wasn't personal in any way.

In another discussion group, Chuck reveals the difficulties he has being personal in a sexual relationship.

> Chuck: I always anticipate having a really passionate experience when I make love with my girlfriend. But I usually end up feeling empty and disappointed afterwards, even though everything works out fine technically. She always has an orgasm, or several of them, and I have no trouble coming, so things seem really okay. Yet the whole act is somehow unsatisfying to me. This one night, she even complained that she didn't feel very close to me when we made love, that it seemed more like a performance than like an exchange between us. This upset me even more and I thought about our typical sexual experience. I'm constantly planning different techniques and positions to use that I think will turn her on. Sometimes I visualize erotic pictures I've seen, so I can feel more excited. I realize I'm in my head thinking about sex a lot, but I feel I'm not very much in contact with her most of the time.

For both men and women, a pseudoindependent posture is central as they attempt to defend against the threats to their defense system that are inherent in intimacy. The quality of a couple's sexual relating is strongly influenced by each partner's mode of sexual expression, that is, whether it is based on a core defense of fantasized self-sufficiency or on the pursuit of a healthy interdependence with another person. Similarly, both partners' modes of sexual expression are largely determined by whether they are "being themselves," that is, operating from the adult ego state, or whether they have regressed to a more defended, parent–child state. Often as the relationship evolves and a fantasy bond develops, each partner tends to externalize the parental or childish ego state and, through the process of projective identification, relates to the other from this defended posture.

When threatened by the unique combination of an emotionally close and sexually fulfilling experience, people may unconsciously hold back one or the other aspect during lovemaking. As Hellinger (1998) pointed out, "The sexual expression of love is also our most humble action. Nowhere else do we expose ourselves so completely, uncovering our deepest vulnerability" (p. 32). Some people are more prone to retreating from being emotionally close to their partner, while others inhibit or withhold their physical sexual responses. Withdrawing from emotional contact with one's partner and dissociating one's feelings during the sex act itself can become habitual or can occur intermittently, leading to a more impersonal style of sexual expression.

DEFENSES AGAINST INTIMACY THAT ENCOURAGE THE FORMATION OF A FANTASY BOND

We use the term *fantasy bond* to describe both the original imaginary connection formed during childhood and the repetitive efforts of adult individuals to make fantasized connections in their intimate associations (Firestone, 1984). In their adult relationships, people unconsciously attempt to recapture the more familiar conditions within the family, the conditions under which they formed their defenses. Individuals accomplish this in three ways: through selection, distortion, and provocation. They tend to select partners who are similar in appearance, behavior, and defenses to one or another family member; they distort their perceptions of their partner in a direction that corresponds more closely to this family member; or, if these defensive maneuvers fail to recreate the past, they tend to manipulate their partner to elicit familiar parental responses. Through these three methods, individuals are able to externalize the fantasy bond and repeat the negative circumstances of the original family in their intimate relationships.

Selection

Selection is a defense mechanism whereby individuals choose their partners to replicate the early family situation. People are usually drawn to someone who is similar to a person who was a significant figure in their early life. They are attracted to a person whose style of relating feels comfortable and familiar. They select someone whose defenses mesh with their own. Initially, there is a great deal of sexual chemistry in these relationships.

Linda grew up with a domineering, punitive mother. Leaving home at an early age, she met and was drawn to Tom, who dominated and criticized her, treating her in a way that was negative, yet familiar, to her. Several years later, after breaking up with Tom, she moved to another state where she met Anthony, an attractive, seemingly gentle man, and immediately fell in love. However, as the relationship developed, Linda realized that she had once again chosen a man who expressed the same patronizing, yet judgmental attitudes toward her as Tom and her mother had. Linda's typical response to Anthony's disapproval and condescension was to feel victimized and sullen, as she had felt as a child when her mother criticized her. She found herself passively accepting his criticisms. In this way, she maintained the image of being unlovable and worthless that she had developed in her family. Yet these powerful, negative feelings about herself felt comfortable and familiar to her.

In other cases, people may select a partner with complementary personal qualities and behaviors in an attempt to compensate for perceived deficits in themselves. For example, a quiet, somewhat passive person will tend to be attracted to a gregarious, active person. These relationships are also often characterized, initially at least, by strong "sexual chemistry." Partners may experience a sense of wholeness from this union, when in reality, both partners are weakened as they come to depend on each other for these complementary functions and traits. Many people who form this type of relationship eventually come to resent or even hate the traits in the other person that they initially sought out. This sense of a merged identity in those relationships eventually leads to a decline in sexual attraction to one another.

Distortion

Individuals who use distortion as a defense modify their perceptions of a partner so as to see them as more similar to a parent or family member than they are in reality. When people choose a partner who is different from a parent or other family member, someone who loves or values them for who they really are, they often become self-conscious or anxious. In particular, at points where their partner's responses challenge the basic image of themselves formed within the family, individuals begin to distort their partner to relieve their anxiety and to recreate conditions that are more familiar, albeit negative. Both positive and negative qualities of one's partner may be exaggerated, but the distortion usually functions to make the new person more closely approximate an important person from the past.

When Tim fell in love with Barbara, one thing that particularly appealed to him was her excitement in sharing activities and projects with him. The couple spent hours playing tennis and working together on landscaping projects.

One day Barbara needed to run errands and was unavailable for a tennis match with Tim. Finding himself resentful and angry, but reluctant to express directly what seemed to him to be irrational feelings, Tim became sullen and silent. From that point on, whenever Barbara made plans with her friends that did not include him, Tim made subtle comments implying that she was self-centered and was neglecting their relationship. Sometimes, he went so far as to question her regarding her whereabouts. Over a period of time, Tim's complaints and suspicions began to affect Barbara negatively. They interfered with the closeness they had shared and their sexual relationship suffered. The deterioration continued and they eventually went their separate ways.

Much later in therapy, Tim recognized that he had seriously distorted Barbara's behavior and had come to attribute qualities to her that were more characteristic of his mother, who was narcissistic, emotionally unavailable, and indifferent to his wants and needs as a child. He realized that his mistreatment of Barbara, based on his distorted attributions, began when she expressed a desire for them to begin living together. Her desire to be with him in a more committed relationship challenged his basic image of himself as a burden, an identity he had formed as a result of his mother's neglect.

Provocation

If the first two defensive maneuvers fail to recreate the past and maintain the defense system, people tend to manipulate their partner to elicit familiar parental responses. They may behave in ways that provoke angry, critical, or harsh reactions from a mate. In the example above, Tim's sullen complaints and suspicious questioning served the purpose of dampening Barbara's excitement for sharing activities with him, including lovemaking. He was finally able to evoke the same response from Barbara that was familiar to him, the indifference and emotional unavailability that had characterized his mother's interactions with him throughout his childhood.

As previously noted, when a relationship challenges a person's essential image of him- or herself, the person often becomes anxious. Before developing a conscious awareness of this anxiety, one may begin to act in a way that changes the relationship in a manner that replicates one's early life experiences. Partners may begin to hold back their affectionate, loving, and sexual responses, which originally were so appealing to the other person. They may incite anger in each other with forgetfulness, intrusiveness, silence, and other insensitive behaviors that indicate an underlying hostility. Frequently, one or both partners are provoked to the point where they actually verbalize the internalized self-critical thoughts of the other person. Most people who provoke their partner are unaware that their actions are inducing aggression, hostility, or withdrawal in the other person. They feel innocent because they do not recognize that their behaviors have changed, only that their partner is changing. Many relationships fail because each partner is protecting him- or herself, maintaining a "safe" distance, thereby holding on to his or her primary fantasy bond with the parent.

All three maneuvers—selection, distortion, and provocation—operate to recapitulate the type of relationship people had originally with a parent or family member. In this way, partners transform the new relationship into one that more closely corresponds to the environment in which they developed their defenses, and they are thus able to reestablish their psychological equilibrium.

MANIFESTATIONS OF THE FANTASY BOND IN COUPLE RELATIONSHIPS

Men and women are most likely to become romantically involved at a time in their lives when they are breaking dependency ties and experiencing a sense of separateness and independence. In this state, they tend to attract others with their vitality and aliveness. They tend to lower their defenses to varying degrees and are more open and vulnerable than usual. The new lovers often report experiencing an enhanced sense of well-being and a heightened sense of joy and closeness.

Falling in love is an exciting time in people's lives. Being passionately in love brings out powerful emotions, such as elation and joy, that the lovers may never have experienced before. At the point where the partners begin to feel anxious, they often subtly withdraw or create distance in the relationship without being aware of altering their behavior, as noted earlier (Karpel, 1994).[7] They gradually give up the most valued aspects of their relationship, especially the eroticism and sexuality. They may also retreat from being close emotionally. These partners often substitute a fantasy bond for genuine personal contact. Conflict often develops as both individuals strive to preserve their defenses while at the same time they try to hold on to their initial feelings of sexual attraction, affection, and friendship. The two conditions tend to be mutually exclusive.

Following the initial phase of falling in love, many couples form a fantasy bond, particularly after making a significant commitment—to living together, to marriage, or to starting a family. They may revert to a more routinized, mechanical style of lovemaking, experience a diminution in their feelings of attraction for each other, or find themselves making love less often (Firestone, 1987; Orbach, 1999).[8] These are all signs that a fantasy bond has been formed. However, most people are unaware that the quality of their sexual relating has been adversely affected by this unconscious attempt to merge with their partner for purposes of security. Fenchel (2000) described this phenomenon as follows:

> Sustained intimacy requires that both partners are capable of giving and receiving love. Where intense unconscious wishes for merger and primitive omnipotence prevail, the ensuing discomfort can become unbearable and lead to withdrawal, frustrating the need for intimacy. (p. 172)

Clients in couples therapy commonly attribute the loss of attraction and diminished frequency of lovemaking to familiarity; yet, when they develop more independence or self-differentiation, they frequently recover many of their original feelings of attraction and sexual desire.

INDICATIONS OF THE FANTASY BOND IN COUPLE RELATIONSHIPS: A CASE EXAMPLE

Rick and Cecelia had been married for ten years. Their sexual relationship, passionate and loving during the early phases, had gradually deteriorated, particularly during the past five years. Both partners were dissatisfied with the quality and frequency of their lovemaking and the overall relationship as well. In the following sections, we discuss this couple's relationship and describe their sexual relating, examining specific behaviors that indicate how they formed a fantasy bond as their relationship evolved.

Background

Rick and Cecelia met when they were in their late twenties. At the time, Rick had recently finished college, received his architectural license, and was working in a well-respected firm as part of a team that designed low-income housing for the elderly and the poor. After years of schooling, he was gratified to finally be working in the field of architecture. Cecelia, who had grown up working in her family's drugstore, was managing a trendy restaurant. She was happy that she had broken away from the family business a few years earlier and was now her own boss in a business that she loved.

When they first became involved, Rick and Cecelia were strongly attracted to each other. Rick found Cecelia's optimistic, energetic personality especially appealing. In addition, he perceived her as being "very pretty" and especially enjoyed looking at her while making love. Cecelia perceived Rick as highly intelligent and responsible and was drawn to his fun-loving, spontaneous manner. The couple discovered that they were highly compatible and shared many common interests, values, and goals in life.

As children, Rick and Cecelia had both felt lonely and isolated. During the depression, Rick's father had struggled to make a living and the family had to make frequent moves. At each successive move, Rick found it increasingly difficult to make new friends and eventually gave up. Cecelia's parents had divorced when she was 5 years old, and her mother remarried. Cecelia spent the rest of her childhood feeling like an outsider in the new blended family and felt ostracized by her stepfather and step-siblings. Both Rick and Cecilia had led very inward, self-protective lives, and even though they were generally friendly and outgoing, neither had many close and meaningful relationships before they met each other.

Routinized, Impersonal Sexuality or a Decline in Sexual Relating

Shortly after they fell in love, Rick and Cecelia decided to move in together. At the time, they were thoroughly enjoying the sexual part of their relationship, which was free-wheeling, playful, and spontaneous. Soon they began to talk about getting married. During this period of time, Cecelia gradually stopped seeing her old friends and began to spend most of her time with Rick. Also, their sexual relationship seemed to "sort of flatten out," as Rick described it. Both partners revealed that they made love somewhat less frequently, and when they did, it was not as passionate or spontaneous as before. They still enjoyed being sexual; however, their sexual relations had become predictable: the same behaviors, same position, at the same time, in the same location.

In many couples, when one or both partners sacrifice their individuality to fuse with the other, their basic attraction to each other is jeopardized. People in a fantasy bond often treat each other as an appendage, which causes their feelings of sexual attraction to wane. The quality of their sexual relating continues deteriorating because of deadening habit patterns, exaggerated dependency, negative projections, and loss of independence.

Moreover, to maintain a comfortable distance, when they feel vulnerable, many people begin to withhold the desirable qualities in themselves that attracted the partner to them in the first place. This withholding leads to a sense of guilt and remorse in the person who is withholding. Many times, couples whose sexual feelings have decreased because of a fantasy bond find themselves making love out of a sense of obligation and responsibility rather than out of a genuine desire to be together.

Form Versus Substance

People who form a fantasy bond usually resist accepting the fact that they have lost much of their feelings of sexual attraction and friendship for each other and have, to some extent, become alienated. They attempt to cover up this reality with a fantasy of enduring love, substituting form for the substance of the relationship. The conventional form of relating consists of the convenient habits and superficial conversation that many partners come to rely on to preserve their fantasy of being in love. Everyday routines, customs, and role-determined behaviors provide the structure and form of the relationship, replacing the warmth, sexual attraction, affection, and companionship that characterized its early phases.

After their wedding, Rick and Cecelia threw themselves into "making a life together." They bought a new car and a house that they carefully decorated. Rick left his architectural firm and started his own company. Cecelia left her job to begin a part-time catering business from their home. For fun, she enjoyed throwing elaborate parties for family and friends, the highlight being an annual birthday celebration for Rick.

However, in spite of trying to set up a perfect life together, Rick and Cecelia's sexual relationship continued to deteriorate. They were making love less and less frequently, and when they did, the thrill and excitement were gone. On the evening of their fifth anniversary, Cecelia invited family and friends to their home for a dinner party. During the evening, Cecelia and Rick overate and drank too much wine. Afterward, when they went to bed, they were not affectionate and did not make love; they just climbed into bed and fell asleep.

Recognizing that people are able to use elements of reality to support their fantasies is crucial to understanding how the fantasy bond operates in many couple relationships. In a previous work (Firestone, 1993), we described a continuum of fantasy involvement arbitrarily divided into three categories: "(1) the person with extreme propensities for fantasy and isolation . . . ; (2) the person who utilizes elements of reality primarily to reinforce and support an ongoing fantasy process rather than really investing in relationships . . . and (3) the person who lives a realistic committed life whose actions match aspirations and capabilities" (p. 341).

> Individuals in Category Two merely give the impression or illusion of seeking satisfaction in reality. They use real events as a means of reinforcing or "feeding" their most prized fantasies, and value form over substance in interpersonal relationships. (p. 341)
>
> It is difficult to try to convince people who are trying desperately to preserve a fantasy of love that they are not in a loving relationship. They know that they *feel* love and attraction, they spend considerable

time *thinking about* it, yet their outward expressions of affection may be very limited or even contradicted by hostile or rejecting behavior toward their mates. (p. 342)

In couples who have formed a fantasy bond, partners use the conventional symbols of love to maintain the form of the relationship. They depend on certain routines and rituals to strengthen the illusion that they are still in love. For example, anniversary celebrations, the traditional Saturday night dinner out, family reunions, and other rituals become symbols of togetherness and romance, and these are used to reinforce the couple's mutual fantasy of closeness and love (Firestone & Catlett, 1999).

At the same time, any event that arouses an awareness of separateness threatens the partners' fantasies of fusion, precipitating anxiety states that predispose anger, hostility, and self-destructive tendencies, as well as a regression to childish, overly dependent, or parental, domineering behaviors. Sensing this threat on some level, most couples negotiate agreements regarding a wide range of rules and implicit contracts to reassure themselves that they are still in love. When analyzed, these rules can be seen to represent the "form" of a relationship; they include unspoken rules governing conventional and obligatory behaviors that replace partners' spontaneous acts of generosity and kindness that characterized the initial phases of their relationship (Boszormenyi-Nagy & Spark, 1984; Hellinger, 1998; Sager et al., 1971).[9]

A common pattern that we have observed is one derived from traditional gender role expectations and based on stereotypic views of women as weak, dependent, and helpless and men as strong, masterful, and dominant. For example, the implicit contract of a more traditional couple in which both partners hold such internalized stereotypes might contain the following unspoken rules: The man's rule, if made explicit, would be: "I'll take care of you because you need to be taken care of," and the woman's would be: "I'll continue to need to be taken care of, that is, I'll be dependent and will defer to your wishes and decisions."

In a chapter appropriately titled "Domestic Gulags" Kipnis (2003) lists a hundred (or more) of these rules, restrictions, or "interdictions," as she labels them. Her essay includes nine pages filled with examples of the implicit rules of "coupledom" that regulate each partner's behaviors in relation to the other. These interdictions, based on people's expectations regarding love and marriage, are automatically accepted because they provide protection against perceived threats to a couple's illusion of love and closeness.

> Sexual interdictions are, needless to say, standard. But it is the panoply of other interdictions that is actually far more revealing about the conditions of modern couplehood. From bathroom to bedroom, car to kitchen, no aspect of coupled life is not subject to scrutiny, negotiation, and rule formation . . . and love means voluntary adherence to them. . . .

What follows is a brief sample of answers to the simple question: "What can't you do because you're in a couple?"

You can't leave the house without saying where you're going. You can't not say what time you'll return. . . . You can't go to parties alone. You can't go out just to go out, because you can't not be considerate of the other person's worries about where you are, or their natural insecurities that you're not where you should be, or about where you could be instead. . . .

You can't sleep apart, you can't go to bed at different times, you can't fall asleep on the couch without getting woken up to go to bed. . . . You can't get out of bed right away after sex. . . .

You can't have friends who like one of you more than the other, or friends one of you likes more than the other. . . . You can't be too charming in public, especially to persons of the opposite sex (or same sex, where applicable). You can't spend more than X amount of time talking to such persons, with X measured in nanoseconds. . . .

Thus is love obtained. . . . What matters is the form. . . . Exchanging obedience for love comes naturally—we were all once children after all, whose survival depended on the caprices of love. And thus you have the template for future intimacies: If you love me, you'll do what I want or need or demand to make me feel secure and complete and I'll love you back. (pp. 82–94)

In a similar vein, Willi (1978/1984) pointed out that in many marriages and couple relationships, each partner adjusts his or her behaviors in adapting to the demands of the partnership. According to Willi (1999), unspoken rules representing such demands are part of "a collusion—an unconscious interplay between two partners based on corresponding relationship fears and deficits" (p. 94). Willi emphasized that collusions become destructive or "pathological when they commit the partners to restricting their interactive effectiveness to a particular form" (p. 94).

> This leads them to infringe upon each other's personal integrity and autonomy. The partners become unacknowledged accomplices in maintaining the collusion by accepting the destructive demands of the other without resistance, and by accepting behavior which hinders their personal development. (p. 94)

Karpel (1994) noted that relationships organized around these destructive rules may often lead to a pattern of distance and pursuit, which is only one among many patterns that emerge when couples adhere to relational rules learned in their family of origin. Hellinger (1998) emphasized that couples need to become aware of these types of unspoken rules before they can move past them, and then they need to face the resulting guilt:

When two people join in a partnership, each brings a model of partnership and for the roles and functions of men and women based on the
values of his or her family of origin, and they both follow these rules,
patterns, and norms out of habit. . . . For love to succeed, it is often
necessary for partners to rise above the dictates of the conscience binding
them to their reference groups. Thus, the price of love is often guilt.
(p. 47)

Mutual Self-Deception

In addition to implicit contracts that support the form of a relationship,
the capacity of human beings for self-deception enables partners to maintain
an internal image of closeness and intimacy, often while the frequency and
quality of their sexual relating is steadily decreasing. Yet eroticism, passion,
and the enjoyment of sex are important aspects of a loving relationship.
Genuine love includes affection, companionship, sexuality, honest communication, and shared activities; otherwise, love can become merely an ab-
straction in one's mind.

Over the years, Rick and Cecelia rationalized the decline in the quality
and frequency of their lovemaking. Rick believed that it was because he
was so distracted and stressed by starting his own business. Even though he
missed being sexual with Cecelia, Rick still enjoyed the feeling that there
was somebody to come home to at the end of a long day. Cecelia reasoned
that her low sexual drive was based on hormonal changes and probably had
something to do with her approaching age 40. Even though she could recall
the passion of their earlier lovemaking and enjoyed the memories, she also
felt that there was something comforting about just cuddling with Rick
at night.

For several years, they said nothing to each other about any concerns
they had regarding the deterioration in their sexual relationship. When
they finally talked about this change, they came to the conclusion that
nothing was really wrong. Articles in popular magazines, as well as what
they surmised from observing their friends' relationships, convinced them
that all sexual relationships naturally deteriorate with time, familiarity,
and maturity.

Polarization of Parental and Childish Ego States

As noted previously, when a couple forms a fantasy bond, each partner
tends to retreat to a defended posture and alternatively acts out either
parental or childish behaviors. During the sex act, both people may be
operating from the childish mode, and at the same time, projecting the

voice (the introjected parent) onto the other person. When they are in this defended state, both partners are subject to voice attacks regarding their sexual performance and their partner's and are fearful of losing control or surrendering themselves fully to the experience.

When Rick and Cecelia fell in love, they were two independent, highly competent adults. Each was attracted to the other's strength and maturity, and both participated in their sexual relationship as equal and active partners. However, after they were married, they began to polarize: Cecelia reverted to the role of child and Rick to that of parent. This dynamic became apparent in nearly every area of their relationship.

In particular, in their sexual relationship, Cecelia became more and more childish and passive. She no longer took an active role in pursuing sex and instead acted as though sex was something that Rick wanted. Rick became more and more parental, vacillating between "caretaking" (tending to Cecelia, coaxing, and helping her to feel sexual) and "scolding" (being patronizing, condescending, and at the same time angry at her for not wanting to be sexual).

In relationships characterized by a fantasy bond, the partners may polarize into a parental or childish posture, as Rick and Cecelia did. By regressing to childish styles of relating, people are capable of manipulating their partners into taking care of them. Behaviors that provoke parental reactions—worry, fear, anger—act to cement this externalization of the self-parenting process (Willi, 1975/1982, 1978/1984, 1999). In describing this polarization in *Couples in Collusion*, Willi (1975/1982) asserted: "*In the disturbed partner relationship we often observe that one partner has a need for over-compensatory progression while the other seeks satisfaction in regression. They reinforce this one-sided behavior in each other because they need each other as complements*" (p. 24).

The process of reverting to a childish mode of experience can also function as a defense against an awareness of death. Observing how people tend to seek a sense of immortality, albeit on an unconscious level, from a partner who is acting out the role of parent, expert, or "ultimate rescuer," Rank (1941) stated,

> As a rule, we find . . . in modern relationships . . . one person is made the god-like judge over good and bad in the other person. In the long run, such symbiotic relationship becomes demoralizing to both parties, for it is just as unbearable to be a God as it is to remain an utter slave. (p. 196)

In most relationships, this type of interaction persists with occasional role reversals, and so it is rare that either or both partners are relating from an adult ego-state, either sexually or in other areas of the relationship. Indeed, only those individuals who exist primarily in an adult ego state are capable of consistently enjoying a mature sexual experience or relationship—one that combines affection, love, and sex.

Idealization of the Partner

In order to preserve the fantasy bond, each partner must maintain a positive idealized image of the other. The most effective way to prevent reality from tarnishing that image is to exaggerate the other person's real strengths or admirable qualities. These are the same dynamics that existed in the original fantasy bond in which the child idealized his or her parents at his or her own expense.

Moreover, many people enter marriage with the expectation that all their needs will be met by the other, which places a heavy burden on their partner. Obviously, no one person can fulfill such unrealistic expectations or live up to such an idealized image of power and goodness. Often when a partner is made aware of the weaknesses, shortcomings, or simple human foibles of the other, he or she becomes angry and resentful because this idealization is threatened. Many people alternate between the extremes of distortion. At times they exaggerate their partner's strengths and desirable qualities, while at other times they severely criticize or focus on his or her perceived undesirable qualities or weaknesses.

When Rick fell in love with Cecelia, he was especially drawn to her looks and captivated by her liveliness and generosity. As the years went by, Cecelia gained 40 pounds. She complained of being tired and often went to bed early. Rick found himself taking over tasks and responsibilities that Cecelia had previously performed. However, Rick still referred to Cecelia as beautiful and spoke of how attractive she was to him. He thought of her as tireless, always ready to lend a hand, and generous to a fault. At the same time, he was angry at the money she spent on gifts for friends, for him, and for herself, and he continuously nagged her about living beyond their means and felt victimized by her spending habits.

When Cecelia first met Rick, she was especially drawn to him because he was competent and responsible. However, when Rick went into business on his own, his company did not do well, and the couple's finances suffered. Over time, he became withdrawn and irritable. It is ironic that Cecelia deferred to Rick about practical and financial matters because she was always able to successfully manage her own business. She told friends that she was lucky to have a man like Rick because he understood so much more than she did about such things. Her anger at him for putting them into financial straits was saved for private moments. At those times, she would lash out at Rick with nasty, sarcastic reminders about his lack of business sense and his "stupidity."

Loss of Independence and a Sense of Separate Identity

A significant sign that a fantasy bond has been formed is when one or both partners relinquish important areas of personal interest, their opinions, unique points of view, and their individuality, to become an imagined unit, a whole entity. Attempting to find security in an illusion of fusion with another person contributes to a progressive loss of identity in each person. The people involved increasingly depend on habitual contact, with less personal feeling and emotional closeness, and find life somewhat superficial or empty as they give up more aspects of their personalities.

After Rick and Cecelia were married, Cecelia quit her job managing the restaurant and started a part-time at-home business. Before making this change, Cecelia had enjoyed the challenge of running a full-time business, and she had especially liked meeting people and developing relationships with her clientele. She would talk to Rick about all the different experiences she encountered in her day. Cecelia thought that she would enjoy working at home but she found that it left her feeling understimulated. She realized that she did not have much to talk to Rick about.

When Cecelia spoke to Rick about these feelings, he suggested that she work for him. He told her that he could use someone to organize the office and keep his books. Cecelia readily accepted the offer. However, in working with Rick, Cecelia was unable to reexperience the excitement that had made her happy when she was working on her own. Instead Cecelia and Rick's identities became more fused and the negative behaviors that were symptomatic of their fantasy bond became more pronounced.

With less and less awareness of each other as separate people, Cecelia and Rick no longer felt sexually attracted to one another. To overcome this obstacle in their sexual relationship, they turned to an external source for sexual stimulation. They began to watch pornography to become aroused. Rick said, "It was strange—we were together but we were not really together."

Unfortunately, conventional beliefs and the myth of eternal love reinforce people's tendencies to give up their independence and individuality. Society's belief in unconditional, everlasting love supports people's resistance to understanding the sources of deterioration in their sexual relating. The false assumption that true love is unconditional reinforces both partners' tendencies to cling to illusions of connection and oneness, while remaining unaware that the real closeness and sexual intimacy between them have declined to a significant degree.

More often than not, when a couple has formed a fantasy bond, the individuals involved are following the dictates of their respective voices. Their communications are being filtered through a biased or alien point of view that distorts their partner's real image. Both parties tend to withdraw from expressing affection or sexual responses to the other and use various rationalizations promoted by the voice to justify their anger, provocations, and withdrawal. In addition, as described earlier, anything that arouses an awareness of separateness or an independent existence is anxiety-provoking and often leads to hostility. This anger is frequently experienced in the form of self-critical thoughts: *You're so boring, how could he(she) still want to be sexual with you?* and voice attacks against one's partner: *He's not really responding to you. She's not that attractive. He's (She's) not interested in sex— he(she) doesn't really care about you.* Or: *He's (She's) only interested in sex, he (she) doesn't really care about you.*

MANIFESTATIONS OF THE VOICE PROCESS IN SEXUAL RELATING

In this section, we explain how negative thoughts, internalized voices, or self-attacks and hostile attitudes toward one's partner can intrude into the sex act at any point, before, during, or after the experience, disrupting or seriously interfering with the natural flow of feelings of excitement and passion.

Problems in sexual relating and many symptoms of sexual dysfunctions are strongly influenced or controlled by negative thought processes that take away from the bodily experience and feelings before, during, or following a sexual encounter. Similarly, experiencing a sexual problem predisposes an increase in one's negative thinking, resulting in a kind of feedback loop.

Although the voice exists primarily on an unconscious level, many people are partially aware of its manifestations in the form of a running commentary or internal dialogue that criticizes and attacks them. During a sexual experience, these attacks often come to the foreground in one's thinking, reinforcing negative attitudes toward one's body, nudity, and sexuality. For example, *You're too fat. You should keep your body covered up and hidden. You'd better have an orgasm.* The voice also influences self-denying tendencies and causes many men and women to give up their natural sexual desires and wants by conforming to early programming and conditioning. *You don't need sex that often. You're just not a sexual person. You're too old for sex.*

Destructive thought processes or voices support the defense mechanisms of distortion and provocation described earlier. Tim's distortion of Barbara, in a previous example, was promoted and reinforced by destructive thoughts such as *You'd better watch out! She's really changed. She used to love doing things with you. But now she's more excited about having lunch with her friends than being with you. She's so selfish, all she thinks about is herself.* His pattern of distorting Barbara led to behaviors that eventually provoked distance in the relationship. In therapy, Tim reported that his complaints and accusations were influenced by increasingly intense voice attacks: *You'd better let her know that she's no fun to be with anymore. Show her how miserable you are, how she's hurting you.* His suspicions regarding her other activities were instigated by thoughts such as *Look, you just can't trust her. You can't trust women. They act interested, then they drop you. You'd better find out where she's really going. She's probably seeing someone else. That's why she doesn't want to be sexual with you anymore.*

Patterns of chronic misunderstanding often develop in a couple's sexual relating and can be traced to distorted perceptions of one's partner as well as critical thoughts about oneself. This type of distorted thinking may be manifested in two ways: (a) in negative attitudes toward oneself, one's body, and one's sexuality that often lead to feelings of being criticized or misjudged by one's sexual partner; or (b) in negative expectations, perceptions, or distortions of one's partner that can be used to feel misunderstood, unappreciated, or exploited sexually. Both types of attitudes, toward oneself or one's partner, lead to behaviors that create emotional distance between partners during lovemaking.

Marcia identifies negative thoughts she experiences while making love. (The contents of her self-attacks appear in italics.)

> When things start to get close sexually between Cody and me, I start to feel sad. But then I start thinking things about myself like, *You're not like other women. You don't feel things the way other women feel things, you don't feel anything.* Then things start to feel mechanical to me.
>
> When I'm feeling mechanical like that, and Cody touches me, I am actually thinking about my response, like, *You don't really feel right. You're not going to be able to relax and feel this. You're not going to be able to respond and really enjoy this,* and then it affects the way I am in the situation. It seems like the only way I can stop thinking these things is if I feel sad. That helps me. The thoughts quiet and then I feel like I'm able to be there, present in the situation.

It is worthwhile for individuals to identify and challenge their negative views of self and others in the context of a psychotherapy that exposes the core issues underlying sexual problems. Partners need to learn to free themselves of distortions and provoking or self-defeating behaviors that cause distress in their sexual relationships (Foley, Kope, & Sugrue, 2002).[10]

Recognizing the restrictions imposed by the introjected parent or voice process enables them to improve the quality of their lovemaking and maintain real closeness with their partner during the sex act.

THE ROLE OF DEATH ANXIETY IN THE DEVELOPMENT OF SEXUAL PROBLEMS

Disturbances in sexual functioning are not solely due to a client's residual fears related to painful experiences or trauma in childhood; they are also based on existential fears (Firestone & Catlett, 1999). In previous works (Firestone, 1994b; 1997a; Firestone, Firestone, & Catlett, 2003), we have delineated a number of defenses that individuals employ in an attempt to deny existential realities and their personal mortality. Observing how human beings are remarkably capable of denying death on an unconscious level, Zilboorg (1943) pointed out that, "In normal times we move about actually without ever believing in our own death, as if we fully believed in our own corporeal immortality" (p. 468).

The basic framework for denying death can be found in the system of defenses that children construct at a stage in the developmental sequence that precedes their understanding of death. As described earlier, when children become aware of death, they tend to regress to an earlier stage of nonawareness and strengthen the fantasy bond. Thereafter, individuals adapt, to varying degrees, to death anxiety through a process of depersonalization, self-denial, and withdrawal of libido (emotional investment) from other people and life-affirming activities. The denial of death often generalizes to an antifeeling, antisexual existence and supports the choice of addictive attachments over involvement in genuinely loving and sexually satisfying relationships.

Viewing problems in sexual relating from an existential perspective both challenges and expands on Freudian theoretical considerations. For example, empirical research from existentially based terror management theorists (TMT) has suggested a different way of looking at people's ambivalence toward sex. In discussing the theoretical implications of terror management research, Goldenberg et al. (2002) noted that

> Although social scientists from Freud on have viewed ambivalence about sex as a byproduct of cultural mores, the present research supports an opposite causal sequence. The findings suggest rather that rules and restrictions for sexual behavior protect individuals from confrontation with their underlying animal nature that frightens us because of our knowledge that all creatures must someday die. (Implications Regarding Sexual Regulation section, ¶ 1)

An understanding of how defenses function in relation to painful experiences within the family as well as to death anxiety helps explain many puzzling phenomena about human sexual behavior, including people's tendencies to retreat from loving sexual experiences and intimate relating in their adult associations. We have noted that when people have the closest, most intimate experiences, they frequently become acutely aware of their mortality and the pain and loss associated with it, and as a result, many retreat from such experiences. Indeed, in extreme cases, they may avoid sexual gratification altogether. On an unconscious level, they prefer not to be loved and valued because it makes them more vulnerable and aware of their own death. They often experience negative thoughts toward themselves and/or their partner that they believe represent their point of view. For example, many individuals have reported experiencing voice attacks such as *Why do you need anyone, anyway? You'll just be disappointed and hurt if you really get involved. You can't trust him or her. Even if you find someone who loves you, relationships don't last forever.*

Loving sexual contact in combination with feelings of friendship in a committed relationship arouses anxiety because it represents a powerful intrusion into one's sense of safety and security, albeit false, achieved by forming a fantasy bond. Moreover, experiencing the unique combination of love and sex often reminds people of the fragility of the physical body and of life itself.

We (Firestone et al., 2003) have called attention to people's tendencies to renounce sexual pleasure and deny themselves happiness in close sexual relationships because of the fact that sexual experiences are inextricably linked to the body, which is subject to deterioration and eventually, death. We have noted that "some individuals may become sexually withholding to escape an awareness of being connected to their body" (p.194). As Becker (1973/1997) put it, "The sexual conflict is thus a universal one because the body is a universal problem to a creature who must die. One feels guilty toward the body because the body is a bind, it overshadows our freedom" (p. 164). "Sex is of the body, and the body is of death" (p. 162).

Recent findings from research based on terror management theory have confirmed our views as well as Becker's hypotheses. Proponents of TMT (Goldenberg, Pyszczynski, McCoy, Greenberg, & Solomon, 1999; Solomon, Greenberg, & Pyszczynski, 1991) have argued that "sexual behavior is affected by mortality concerns, because sex is an activity that reminds us of our core animal nature" (Goldenberg et al., 1999, p. 1175).

Goldenberg et al. (1999) conducted empirical studies to test the following basic tenets of TMT theorists, which stated that "Sex is a ubiquitous human problem because the creaturely aspects of sex make apparent our animal nature, which reminds us of our vulnerability and mortality. People minimize this threat by investing in the symbolic meaning offered by the cultural worldview" (p. 1173).

One experimental study demonstrated that anxious individuals who ranked high in neuroticism "who are especially likely to find sex threatening, rated the physical aspects of sex [on a scale] as less appealing when reminded of their mortality" (Goldenberg et al., 2002, Introduction). Goldenberg et al. (1999) concluded that "high-neuroticism individuals are conflicted by sex and that the conflict is rooted in mortality concerns" (p. 1184). Because the human body is vulnerable to illness, deterioration, and death, many people also have a tendency to feel shame about their bodies and the pleasure potentially available through bodily sensations and feelings. There is a sense of betrayal in knowing that one is trapped in a body that will eventually deteriorate and die.

Involvement in a close, loving sexual relationship would mean, in effect, becoming reconnected to one's body, to one's deepest emotions, to one's sense of self as a unique individual. It would entail the reexperiencing of feelings of aloneness, separateness, and existential anxiety that may have been successfully repressed. We have found that often in therapy, when clients are relieved of a sexual symptom or problem (for example, a woman becomes orgasmic for the first time, or a man overcomes an habitual pattern of premature ejaculation), there is usually increased apprehension about death.

Existential psychologist May (1969) reported his observations of this phenomenon in his patients. He proposed that "The relationship between death and love is surely clear in the sex act" (p. 103). In a case analysis, he discussed a patient who illustrated this hypothesis:

> A patient, whose problem was sexual frigidity and who had never experienced an orgasm in intercourse, told me of a dream which dramatically illustrates this sex and death theme. In her dream, she experienced herself for the first time in her own identity as a woman. Then, still in the dream, she had the strange conviction that she would have to jump into the river and drown. The dream ended in great anxiety. That night, in sexual intercourse, she had an orgasm for the first time. (p. 103)

These dynamics can also be manifested in other sexual problems as in this personal account revealed by Simone during a seminar on sexuality:

> *Simone:* (to husband) When you and I first met, I so much enjoyed getting to know you, and I really fell in love with you. You were a different person from anyone I had ever known. I felt like it was an amazing time in my life. Being with you, I felt different sexually from the way I had felt before in any relationship. You really wanted to know me on a deep level, you wanted to know my body, my sexuality, and me, my personality. I learned so much about myself in being close to you in that way, whereas in previous relationships, I had mainly focused on the sex, on whether I was going to have an orgasm or not. But I think that in getting to know myself, I became aware of the amount I had to lose. I began to have thoughts and dreams about death.

I remember a recurring dream I had around that time. In the dream I'm on a train speeding across a long trestle bridge high over a bottomless canyon. The train is headed straight for a mountain, where the track abruptly comes to an end. Everybody knows the fate of the train and we're all running frantically through the cars, trying to get to the last car. I'm running fast, trying desperately to stay alive a few more minutes. I want to get to the last car before the engine crashes into the mountainside. While I'm running, I realize it's futile, that the situation is hopeless, there is really no escape. But I keep running anyway, frantically trying to reach the last car.

Usually I would wake up screaming. Obviously, in the dream, the train represents my body, which I can't escape and the train ride is my life. The mountainside we're crashing into is my death which I have no control over, no matter how hard I try.

Looking back, I realize that after a while, I turned our relationship into a source of comfort and I somehow stopped relating to you personally. My nightmares disappeared. At the same time, I was using you in that way to think you could save me somehow. Our relationship became very connected and I lost sight of what it really was in the first place.

In general, the more individuals become reconnected to the body and the more they become emotionally invested in a sexual partner or mate, the more anxiety and sadness they experience and the more they have to lose. People often respond to the resulting rise in anxiety and emotional pain on a preconscious or unconscious level by reverting to a defended posture with little or no awareness of any alteration in their behavior. Therapists can find it difficult to identify specific defenses against death anxiety for this reason: defense mechanisms are instituted before clients become aware of their anxiety on a conscious level.

Thus, it appears that the resistance, manifested by many individuals, to a biological drive and a desire for activities that provide so much pleasure is partly rooted in a powerful fear—the fear of deterioration, and death of the body. Becker (1973/1997) stressed the fact that most people "chafe at sex . . . [because] they resent being reduced to the body . . . sex to some degree terrifies them: it represents two levels of the negation of oneself. Resistance to sex is a resistance to fatality" (pp. 163–164).

> The sexual act represents a double negation: by physical death and of distinctive personal gifts. This point is crucial because it explains why sexual taboos have been at the heart of human society since the very beginning. They affirm the triumph of human personality over animal sameness. (p. 163)

The implications of this point of view for understanding and treating problems in sexual functioning are impressive. As Goldenberg et al. (2002) noted in their conclusion, "Recognizing the conflict between our animal and symbolic natures in the domain of human sexuality may shed light on a myriad of problems associated with this most pleasurable aspect of human existence" (Conclusion section, ¶ 1).

CONCLUSION

To sustain a loving sexual relationship, individuals must be willing to face the threats to the defense system that loving another person and being loved for oneself evoke. To be able to accept genuine affection, tenderness, love, and fulfilling sexual experiences as a part of an ongoing relationship, they must be willing to challenge their negative voices, modify the image of themselves formed in the family, and give up well-entrenched defenses, which would cause them a great deal of anxiety.

Many people come to prefer a fantasy bond or illusion of connection, where their psychological equilibrium is maintained, over genuine companionship and actual love. In forming a fantasy bond with their partner, each person recreates painful experiences from childhood in present-day relationships while maintaining an illusion of merged identity to cope with the anxiety of existing as a separate, distinct individual. Essentially, individuals face a fundamental dilemma when entering into an intimate relationship: whether to invest fully in the relationship and remain vulnerable to possible rejection and loss, or to attempt to protect themselves by retreating to a more inward, defensive posture and impersonal, self-gratifying modes of sexual relating.

People could choose to go against their voice attacks and retain their feelings of affection for each other. A couple could learn to share their feelings about existential realities inherent to the human condition. In recognizing that all human beings face the same existential crisis, they could approach each other with a sense of genuine compassion and empathy. Embracing life fully with minimal defenses would enable individuals to remain open and vulnerable to experiencing love and sexual intimacy in their relationships. As Coelho (2004) declared, "*Profound desire, true desire is the desire to be close to someone. . . . When desire is still in this pure state, the man and the woman fall in love with life, they live each moment reverently, consciously*" (p. 133).[11] People who have the courage and determination to achieve these goals are better able to maintain an equal adult relationship, personal closeness, and sexual fulfillment.

NOTES

1. These effects of cumulative Averse Childhood Experiences (ACE) on the physical and mental health of adults have been documented in a large population study by Felitti (2002). Briere (1992) also has asserted that "the majority of adults raised in North America regardless of gender, age, race, or social class, probably experienced some level of maltreatment as children" (p. xvii).

2. See Silverman, Lachmann, and Milich (1982) and Keys et al. (1950). See also Orbach, Shopen-Koffman, and Mikulincer (1994).

3. The idealization of the parents at the child's expense acts as a survival mechanism for the helpless, dependent child because recognizing the full impact of the negative characteristics of one's parents predisposes severe anxiety states and a sense of hopelessness in the child. In Bloch's (1978) book *So The Witch Won't Eat Me*, she asserted "That a distorted parental image may be essential to the psyche's defensive system has emerged with great clarity from both my work with children and my psychoanalytic treatment of adults" (p. 162).

4. Empirical studies conducted by Bocknek and Perna (1994) demonstrated how childhood trauma is internalized. In his research, Bornstein (1993) also investigated hypotheses stating that dysfunctional parental introjects predict an individual's risk for psychopathology.

5. The formation of the fantasy bond or self-parenting process leads to a split within the antiself system itself. The three ego states described in this chapter are similar in some respects to those depicted by transactional analysis (TA; Berne, 1961, 1964). Our analysis differs from TA analysts in terms of emphasis. "We tend to stress the underlying defensive processes determining the movement between the ego states, whereas TA clinicians generally concentrate more on phenomenological aspects" (Firestone, 1988, p. 127). Obviously, adult individuals do not exist exclusively in a childish or regressed state; rather they vacillate between the parental and the child mode of experience. As a result, they may spend only a small proportion of their time in the adult ego mode.

6. In *Voice Therapy*, Firestone (1988) described three modes of experience as described in transactional analysis, the parental, the childish or regressive, and the adult mode:

   > These modes of experience refer to *internal* ego states as well as to behaviors and feelings expressed *outwardly*. Each person is in transition between these modes, but he or she may become stabilized in one mode or another in relation to other people. (p. 113)

   The parental mode is reflected in self-attacks and other critical, superior attitudes toward others, whereas the childish mode is reflected in regressive trends and often in overly dramatic reactions to present-day events that are similar to painful experiences in childhood.

7. Karpel (1994) described how people often remain unaware that their interactions are defensive or negative when each partner's early attachments have not been "good-enough":

When early relationships have not been good-enough, these longings are likely to be *intensified*, by virtue of having been unmet, and to be accompanied by *fears* and *defenses* which have developed to cope with a range of negative feeling-states (such as frustration, rage, shame and guilt, fear of abandonment, grief, and despair) and which interfere with the natural development of the individual's capacity for intimacy. However, because these feeling-states are so distressing, they are likely to be repressed by the individual so that he or she has little conscious awareness of them, but instead expresses them unconsciously in the give-and-take of close relationship. (pp. 48–49)

8. Orbach (1999), in *The Impossibility of Sex*, described this process of deterioration in sexual relating as follows:

   Sexual intimacy, once irresistible and exciting—*the* way to connect and communicate—turns humdrum. Sex becomes less frequent, less urgent, and moves from being an opening up and exploration by two people of one another to becoming a block between them, an act surrounded by expectations, disappointment, worry or routine. (pp. 153–154)

9. The notion of implicit rules or contracts ("marriage contracts") was initially described by Sager et al. (1971) as unconscious elements in each partner that have an adverse effect on marital relationships. Other clinicians (Boszormenyi-Nagy & Spark, 1984; Hellinger, 1998; Karpel, 1994) have delineated various role expectations, family-of-origin "process" rules, and cultural prescriptions that partners bring to the relationship. Harper, Anderson, and Stevens (2004) investigated these rules in developing the Couple Implicit Rule Profile. They cited both positive and negative unspoken rules: "facilitative (e.g., 'Share your feelings,' 'Play, have fun together') and constraining rules (e.g., 'Don't feel or talk about feelings,' 'You are responsible for how your partner feels,' 'Rely on yourself, not your partner')" (p. 1).

10. See Foley, Kope, and Sugrue (2002, pp. 257–261) about challenging negative thoughts that affect sexuality.

11. Quotation from *Eleven Minutes* by Paulo Coelho. Copyright © 2004 by Paulo Coelho. Reprinted by permission of HarperCollins Publishers Inc.

7

SEXUAL WITHHOLDING

If the sexual desires of one of the partners aren't reciprocated, he or she is in a weak position because the other has the power to reject. (p. 34)

The fundamental balance of giving and taking that love requires is threatened when one partner habitually gives or takes more, or when what is given in love is not taken in love.

—Hellinger (1998, p. 46)

The phenomenon of sex-deprived marriages has become the focus of the popular media and mental health professionals as well (H. Kaplan, 1995; McCarthy, 1997a, 1999; Weiner-Davis, 2003). McCarthy (1997a) defined a nonsexual relationship as one in which partners have sex less than ten times a year. According to this definition, "approximately 20% of married couples and 40% of nonmarried couples who have been involved more than 2 years have a nonsexual relationship. This is a major mental health problem that poses a threat to marital satisfaction and viability" (p. 231).

Sex therapists tend to agree that the complaint of a majority of couples who seek professional help is that of low or inhibited sexual desire (H. Kaplan, 1995; McCarthy & McCarthy, 1998, 2003). McCarthy and McCarthy (2003) noted that "Research studies . . . find that 1 in 3 women and 1 in 7 men report inhibited sexual desire. Sometime in marriage more than 50 percent of couples experience inhibited desire or a desire discrepancy" (p. 5). H. Kaplan (1995) also emphasized that "The majority of our patients with sexual desire disorders reported that their problem was *acquired*, that is, that they lost their sexual desire after some period of normal functioning" (p. 56).[1]

Portions of Helen Singer Kaplan's *The Sexual Desire Disorders* were reprinted in this chapter. Copyright © 1995 from *The Sexual Desire Disorders: Dysfunctional Regulation of Sexual Motivation* by Helen Singer Kaplan, MD, PhD. Reproduced by permission of Routledge/Taylor & Francis Books, Inc.

There is confusion about the factors that are responsible for this trend. We propose that the decline that many couples experience in sexual desire and activity as their relationship matures is largely attributable to the tendencies of individuals to form a fantasy bond with their partner. Once a fantasy bond is formed, a person withdraws from intimacy to a self-protective illusion of being fused with the other. Underlying this withdrawal is a fear of needing anything from others and of having to give anything of oneself. These feelings manifest themselves in withholding behaviors.

In this chapter, we describe how sexual withholding—a major dimension of the defensive process—blocks the subjective experience of sexual desire, thereby contributing to the deterioration in sexual relating that many couples experience as their relationship matures. Next we delineate environmental factors that predispose the development of self-denying and withholding tendencies. These include parental withholding in relation to children's wants, fears of competing because of covert or overt sexual rivalry within the family, or parents who were unable to offer or accept affection in relation to each other or to their children. In addition, we discuss how the experience of incest and sexual abuse during childhood can lead to inhibited sexual desire in adulthood. Case studies illustrate how destructive thought processes or internalized voices regulate or control the withholding of affectionate and sexual responses.

Sexual withholding is one form of a more general pattern of withholding and self-denial that has not been fully explored in the psychological literature, with some exceptions (Bach & Deutsch, 1979; Carnes, 1997; Love & Shulkin, 1997; Mitchell, 2002). Holding back one's positive qualities and goal-directed behaviors represents a major dimension of an inward, defensive process that intrudes into all areas of one's life. Withholding is part of a self-destructive process that represents an attempt to gain control over potential hurt, loss, or separation. Such tendencies to avoid fear and pain are understandable and yet the very act of holding back to avoid being hurt can paradoxically exacerbate an individual's misery (Firestone, 1985; Firestone & Catlett, 1999).

Sexual withholding can be defined as an inhibition of expressions of sexual desire and interest, including physical affection, touching, attractiveness, and other aspects of healthy sexuality. People tend to withhold loving feelings and sexual responses from their partners as part of a basic defense against genuine closeness and sexual intimacy. This reduction of emotional transactions with one's partner is characterized by the reluctance to exchange psychonutritional products.[2] Thus, the withholding partner is able to maintain a comfortable distance in the relationship and keep his or her defenses intact.

Sexual withholding and denying oneself sexual pleasure, referred to by some clinicians as "sexual anorexia" (Carnes, 1997), can lead to a wide range of sexual disturbances in an intimate relationship.[3] Individuals who tend to be sexually withholding or chronically self-denying may have sex infrequently or not at all, experience discomfort in sexual situations, withdraw from being close emotionally to their partner during sex, or experience difficulties during the arousal phase, foreplay, or penetration. Clinically, they may manifest symptoms of inhibited sexual desire, psychogenic impotence, or female orgasmic disorder. Many individuals suffering from low sexual desire are hesitant about entering into intimate transactions because of their resistance to offering love and affection outwardly or to taking love in from an outside source.

We are not referring here to people who intentionally or consciously withhold as a calculated manipulation that is meant to be hurtful. Instead, the focus is on individuals for whom sexual withholding is largely unconscious and causes both partners pain and distress. Much of the suffering and conflict within relationships is due to one or both partners taking back the love, affection, and sexual responses they once felt and expressed.

WITHHOLDING BASED ON SELF-DENIAL

In an intimate relationship, sexual withholding may involve (a) a holding back from or distancing of oneself from one's partner, or (b) a holding back of pleasure from oneself, which incidentally hurts the other person as well. On some level, the partner who denies him- or herself sexual pleasure becomes increasingly more self-hating and guilty, which in turn leads to more self-denial, sexual inhibition, and avoidance of sexual situations. The individual who is being withheld from experiences considerable frustration and anger, which he or she often attempts to suppress.

The process of denying oneself sexual pleasure and fulfillment often becomes automatic and involuntary over time. Many cases of low sexual desire and lack of sexual responsiveness can be directly or indirectly attributed to habitual self-denial (Carnes, 1997; Firestone, 1985). Individuals who deny themselves gratification may also have strong needs to control other aspects of the sexual relationship. In terms of our theoretical approach, these individuals are attempting to regulate an inner world of fantasy and maintain psychological equilibrium. They tend to perceive spontaneous sexual responses and free-flowing sexual experiences as risky and potentially painful. In his book, *Can Love Last?*, psychoanalyst Mitchell (2002) provided a cogent explanation for people's need to control sexual passion in a long-term relationship:

> Erotic passion destabilizes one's sense of self. When we find someone intensely arousing who makes possible unfamiliar experiences of ourselves and an otherness we find captivating, we are drawn into the

disorienting loopiness of self/other. We tend to want to control these experiences and the others who inspire them. Thus, emotional connection tends to degrade into strategies for false security that suffocate desire. (p. 92)

Lori grew up feeling that she did not deserve much out of life. Whenever she hesitantly expressed a desire for something, her parents automatically denied her requests and told her she was selfish, needy, and demanding. As an adult, she gradually lost interest in sex and began working compulsively in her career in real estate. In her midtwenties, she met Scott and their relationship was fun and romantic for a brief period of time. However, troubled by her decreasing interest in being sexual, Lori entered psychotherapy. In the first session, she revealed that she had a self-denying approach to life:

Lori: I rarely allow myself to have fun, to go out to movies or dinner. But the main thing that bothers me is I'm not as excited or as interested in making love as I was, and things have started to feel bad between Scott and me.

In fact, anytime I start to feel happy, I feel incredibly guilty, like I shouldn't be having fun. I find myself thinking, Just wait until the ax falls. Things can't stay this good forever. I even start wondering why Scott still likes me, especially since I've been so rejecting of him. Why would he like me? I really get myself into a down mood thinking like that, and then I find myself wanting to avoid him even more.

I remember when I left home for college, my mother told me that I was going to regret going away and leaving them. My mother and father didn't get along, and I think she resented the fact that I was getting away and leaving her with him. She was so sarcastic and nasty the day I left: She practically yelled at me as I went out the door. I remember her exact words: "So you think you can just go off and have your own life, do you? Well, don't be so sure of yourself, Lori. You're nothing special. What have you ever done for your father and me? You're so ungrateful for all we've done for you. You don't deserve anything!"

Just remembering those words makes me realize more than ever before why I deny myself pleasure and hold back from Scott. Why I have to control myself and him so much. Why I won't simply be happy. Why I only let myself have little dibs and dabs of fun and happiness. It's pretty clear how I learned to deny myself everything, It's exactly like the way my parents denied me anything I wanted when I was a kid.

PASSIVE–AGGRESSIVE WITHHOLDING BASED ON SUPPRESSED ANGER

One common form of withholding is passive–aggression, which can be attributed to suppressed anger. H. Kaplan (1995) has noted that "anger at the partner is the most common and serious underlying cause of partner-specific loss of desire" (p. 142). Withholding behaviors based on hostility have the effect of provoking angry responses in a partner, thereby creating alienation and distance in the relationship.[4] In a sexual situation, hostility may be acted out in a disguised form in a number of ways. The partner who has suppressed hostile feelings toward his or her mate often pulls back unconsciously from being emotionally close during the sex act.

According to McCarthy and McCarthy (1998), one cause of inhibited sexual desire is "negative emotions, especially anxiety, depression, or anger. . . . Anxiety is the problem easiest to treat. . . . Anger is the most difficult emotion to deal with. . . . Anger usually involves nonsexual issues, but it poisons the sexual relationship" (p. 179).[5] H. Kaplan (1995) also emphasized that most patients have little awareness of the underlying anger and anxiety that fuel their avoidance of sexual relations with their mate: "It should be noted once again that patients with sexual motivation dysfunctions typically have *no insight* into the self-induced elements in their lack of sexual interest in the partners; they tend to blame this on 'poor chemistry'" (p. 117).

In a long-term relationship, if partners become withholding, they tend to perceive sexual intimacy as threatening to their defended, inward state and so try to avoid spontaneous sexual interactions. In some cases, one partner may attempt to control certain dimensions of the sexual encounter, including how often the couple makes love, the conditions under which they make love, as well as the techniques and positions they use. In general, by reducing both their responses of giving to and taking from a sexual partner, men and women effectively limit or control the emotional transactions in the relationship, which in turn contributes to a deterioration in the quality of their sexual relating.

WITHHOLDING AND MIXED MESSAGES

In relationships characterized by a fantasy bond, mixed messages play an important role in supporting the form of the relationship while negating the fact that love and sexual passion have declined. If partners are made aware of their withholding patterns and reveal the underlying hostility or grudges, this admission necessarily disrupts their illusion of closeness and connection. Mixed messages, combined with withdrawal and withholding, have been observed in videotaped interactions between partners as part of a research study conducted by Gottman and Krokoff (1989). Their studies demonstrated that when double messages are part of partners' customary ways of interacting, their negative emotions tend to be communicated nonverbally through their posture, tone of voice, and other bodily cues. A preponderance of negative nonverbal or latent messages, in conjunction with positive verbal messages, between partners more often than not is predictive of the eventual dissolution of the relationship.

Other clinicians have described mixed messages, communication styles, and actions that are used to cover over anger. Keeley and Hart (1994) asserted,

> Mixed messages may lead to uncertainty about the relationship or partner and very often are communicated with nonverbal cues. . . . These cues (e.g., eye blinking, increased self-touching, more speech hesitations) may send messages of distraction and reticence, which would be detrimental to the intimacy process. (pp. 156–157)

Passive–aggressive, withholding behaviors, together with positive verbal messages, create considerable confusion and conflict in intimate relationships. Bach and Deutsch's (1979) book, *Stop! You're Driving Me Crazy*, examines the myriad ways that people in everyday life attempt to disguise their aggression through double messages, resulting in what they termed "crazymaking" (CM). Citing cases from their clinical research, Bach and Deutsch reported, "From thousands of stress reports during individual and group psychotherapy sessions, a linkage emerged between pathogenic communication patterns and indirect, so-called passive aggression" (p. v).

According to Bach and Deutsch, CM "derives from the obscure portion of a double message" (p. 20).

> The open half of the message is always clear and understandable. . . . It is invariably a message of goodwill, acceptance, agreement, love, concern, loyalty. But the second half of the double message is always foggy. It is indirect. And it is always especially hard for us to hear and understand, because it is something we don't want to hear. In many cases, it suggests a conflict in the relationship. . . . That contradiction is what is so maddening. (p. 20)

Bach and Deutsch suggested that double messages and passive-aggressive or withholding behaviors are particularly detrimental to a couple's sexual life. "Sexuality can encompass CM behaviors at their most impactful" (p. 270). One CM pattern they described ("your wish is my wish") represents a "false kind of accommodation" (p. 152).

He: Gee, it feels good to be close to you. I know you've had a tough day, with the kids being sick and all. But wouldn't you like to roll over and come closer?

She: [*Exhausted but accommodating even though she feels little or no sexual interest*] You know I *always* like to be close to you. [*And she rolls over. But note that she does not answer his question about what she wants.*]

He: [*Touching*] Does this feel good?

She: [*Again not really answering*] You know I always like it when you touch me.

He: [*After some minutes of touching*] I want to be inside you. Do you want me inside you?

She: Have I ever said no, dear?

But there comes a time when the accommodator's partner realizes that *yes* did not really mean genuine and willing assent—only submission. When he tries to enter her, he finds that she is really not prepared for him to do so. (p. 153)

Withholding behaviors are the nonverbal manifestations of anger that partners are afraid to express through direct communication. Often this anger has been suppressed and exists on an unconscious level. For example, a man told his fiancee that he loved her long hair; the next day she had it cut short and permed and could not understand his shock and angry reaction. A woman who repeatedly asked her husband to leave the keys to the family car for her whenever he went on a business trip felt provoked each time he "forgot" and took the keys with him. In both cases, the CM partner was "innocent" in one sense, in that the anger driving the withholding behavior was mostly unconscious.

In many cases, individuals use subtle patterns of withdrawal and withholding to disguise rejection. Intimate partners may not wish to acknowledge, either to themselves or to the other, the fact that they are rejecting the other person. For example, Joshua and Lynn had been dating for several months. From the beginning of their relationship, Joshua had been open in expressing his love for Lynn. Lynn, who was somewhat reserved, was more cautious in communicating her feelings toward Joshua. Although he was satisfied for the most part with the way the relationship was evolving, Joshua told Lynn that his fantasy was for her to fall in love with him as he had with her. Specifically, he longed for her to verbally state her love for him.

One evening, after their lovemaking had been especially passionate and close, Lynn found herself spontaneously saying the words of love that Joshua had been waiting to hear. She realized that she valued the relationship and was willing to take a chance and invest more emotionally than before. After she shared her feelings with Joshua, the couple talked at length about themselves and their relationship. Then Lynn fell asleep in Joshua's arms. Waking several times during the night, she continued to be physically affectionate and close to him.

The next morning, Joshua woke up irritable and sullen. He accused Lynn of keeping him awake all night and complained of being "sleep-deprived" because her affectionate embraces had disturbed his sleep. During the next several weeks, Joshua became less affectionate and avoided opportunities to be sexual, while continuing to tell Lynn that he loved her. In an interview six months later, Lynn revealed that she and Joshua had ended their relationship. After the breakup, Joshua entered individual psychotherapy. In his sessions, he identified the negative attitudes he had toward women and his belief that no woman would ever love him. Desperate to hold on to Lynn, he had tried to deny the anger and anxiety that were aroused when her statement that she loved him contradicted his negative attitudes and expectations. Unable to face his angry feelings, Joshua had struggled to suppress them, yet his underlying hostility had been expressed in his behavior toward Lynn.

PREDISPOSING FACTORS IN FAMILY RELATIONSHIPS

In growing up, children experience a number of events and circumstances that predispose the development of withholding behaviors. Examples of these are parents who are disrespectful of the boundaries of their children and continually intrude on their lives; immature parents who use their children's achievements to enhance their own self-image or to live through them; parents who are withholding themselves and therefore are incapable of accepting or offering love and affection to each other or to their children; or an environment that is characterized by neglect, rejection, or outright abuse.

In his work, Barber (2002) called attention to a particular form of parental intrusiveness that some research has shown to be detrimental to the developing autonomy of children and adolescents. He referred to this type of negative parental behavior as "psychological control" and has explored the correlations between this type of parental control and outcomes in adolescence, in particular in teens who are aggressive in their peer relationships.

In a series of research studies investigating the components of psychological control, Nelson and Crick (2002) elaborated on Barber's (1996) earlier conceptualization. Their findings tended to support Barber's initial construct and his descriptions of the types of parental behaviors that make up psychological control, including parental withdrawal of love, guilt and shame induction, criticism, and excessive control of a child's life through possessiveness and overprotection. Nelson and Crick conducted studies to explore their hypothesis that "relationally aggressive children, within the context of exclusive, enmeshed relationships with parents, may learn that close, intimate relationships are highly valued and, perhaps, that the manipulation of such relationships is an effective means for achieving one's goals" (p. 168).

Our descriptions of parental intrusiveness, possessiveness, and emotional hunger are similar in many respects to Barber's concept of psychological control. We have observed that children growing up in an environment in which their feelings are manipulated through guilt and shame, where their wants and needs are invalidated or disappointed, and where there is no respect for personal boundaries, often begin to withhold from their parents to protect themselves. Unfortunately, this protective behavior on the child's part can persist into adult life.

When children suffer emotional pain and frustration in family interactions, they tend to withdraw their emotional investment in parents or other caretakers, that is, a process of decathexis occurs. They learn to stop wanting real affection and become self-denying. At the same time, they give up their natural feelings of love and affection toward others and learn to withhold. They restrict the expression of their natural feelings and gradually substitute fantasy and a defensive, inward posture toward life that keeps real experiences manageable and helps maintain psychological equilibrium. In addition, as described in chapter 3, emotionally hungry parents exert a pull on children that leaves them drained of their own resources. Later, as adults, they may self-protectively turn away from potential sources of gratification, including being fulfilled in an intimate sexual relationship. Many adults who were hurt as children also indicate fears of being drained that persist into adult life, and interfere with relationship satisfaction.

Factors Predisposing Withholding Based on Self-Denial

One environmental factor strongly related to the child's developing a posture of self-denial is the parents' inability to accept expressions of love and affection from their offspring. Many well-meaning parents unconsciously discourage loving responses from their infant or young child because these responses threaten their defenses and emotional equilibrium. When parents find it difficult to accept expressions of love from their offspring, their children learn to gradually disengage from themselves and suppress their positive feelings.[6] Many come to believe that there is something wrong with their loving feelings and that their affection or their physical nature is somehow unacceptable. The resultant shame they experience causes them to unconsciously resolve to hold back their warmth, tenderness, and affection in future interactions.

Children are also injured psychologically when parents vacillate between being self-protective or inward and being in a more emotionally responsive state. When parents are in a feeling state, they are more sensitive to their offspring and may be able to feel and express the love they characteristically withhold. The child, in turn, naturally responds to his or her parents with love and affection. However, when parents revert to a more defended state and a more impersonal mode of relating, they are blocked in their sensitivity and concern for their child. Their withdrawal causes considerable hurt particularly when it occurs following unusually close times with their offspring (Ainsworth, Blehar, Waters, & Wall, 1978; Bowlby, 1973; Weinfield, Sroufe, Egeland, & Carlson, 1999).

As the child matures, other parental behaviors contribute to the tendency to be self-denying. Parents encourage this self-denial by responding with rejection to their children's wants and by humiliating them for expressing their wants and needs, as Lori's parents did. Parental withholding of affection instills a deep sense of shame in the child, which later in life is transformed into feelings of embarrassment, self-consciousness, and a sense of degradation about having sexual wants and desires. In addition, mothers and fathers who are self-denying and hold back affection from each other serve as poor role models for their daughters and sons. Children observe, and later imitate in their adult relationships, the withholding behaviors they saw acted out between their parents.

Fears of Competition

In some cases, sexual withholding can be motivated by a fear of competing because of covert or overt sexual rivalry within the family. As noted in chapter 3, children of both genders often feel threatened by retribution from their parent of the same sex. As adults they tend to retreat from expressions of mature sexuality and hold back their natural responses of affection and love. In many cases, they project onto their present-day rivals the fears of retaliation they originally experienced in relation to a parent. We suggest that many men and women retreat from competitive situations because they anticipate that either winning or losing will arouse destructive thoughts and angry self-attacks. The dynamics discussed here contribute to an understanding of one important outcome resulting from unresolved oedipal issues (Firestone, 1997a; Firestone & Catlett, 1999).

Other clinicians have noted this phenomenon. For example, in summarizing her clinical work, H. Kaplan (1995) concluded that the etiology of inhibited sexual desire lay in early childhood experiences. She asserted that "The family histories of patients with intimacy-passion splits often reveal one of two types of 'deeper' causes: 1) the *reawakening of the incest taboo,* and 2) *painful early emotional attachments*" (p. 146). In describing these patients, Kaplan noted that they "find nice partners, but always manage to destroy their relationships" (p. 146). Kaplan observed that these patients manifested "the *inability to sustain passionate feelings within a close committed relationship*" (p. 146).

> These men and women experience normal feelings of desire and passion in the early stages of a relationship. However, if the partner looks for more of a commitment or a greater degree of intimacy, at a certain point, a point that exceeds these individuals' psychic "safety zones," they shift into a critical, countersexual mode, and lose their erotic interest in the partner. (p. 146)

From our perspective, at this point people's defense systems ("safety zones") are threatened by the experience of being loved and especially valued, and they may begin to act out patterns of sexual withholding with little or no conscious awareness.

Factors Predisposing Withholding Based on Passive–Aggression

Children have limited outlets for expressing pain and frustration in the family. They find it safer and more acceptable to express their anger indirectly by holding back behaviors and responses that their parents request or demand from them. They also learn that they have some leverage over their parents by acting out passive–aggressive behaviors, including noncompliance, incompetence, and dawdling. The acting out of anger indirectly is an attempt to avert the retaliation they imagine they would receive for more direct acts of anger and provides a measure of release. Some children eventually become so accustomed to withholding that they come to believe that they are unable to perform certain tasks that are, in reality, within their capabilities.

Men and women who have grown up with the automatic response of saying "no" to themselves and others are resistant to changing these patterns. Because this form of holding back is largely an unconscious process and is manifested primarily in passive behaviors, it is difficult to confront this defense directly or to pinpoint which specific behaviors are being withheld. The person who is made aware of his or her negativism or hostility tends to act wounded and misunderstood and becomes defensive when passive-aggressive techniques are exposed. This is particularly evident in intimate relationships where people are often the most angry and defensive when their withholding patterns are pointed out by a mate or therapist.

Child Sexual Abuse

The effects of child sexual abuse are often manifested in symptoms of inhibited sexual desire disorders in adult individuals. In their work, M. Lewis (1992) and Fried (1960) have also suggested a direct link between shame and the inhibition of sexual responses. Moving in and out of physical closeness is intolerable to individuals who have acquired a sense of shame about their bodies or their sexuality during their formative years or who have become cut off or removed, to varying degrees, from themselves and their feelings. As adults, these individuals may unconsciously hold back a full sexual response to avoid reawakening these painful feelings or memories and reconnecting with their authentic self.

Findings by Kinzl et al. (1995) have shown that "Women who experienced multiple sexual abuse often reported intimacy disturbances (i.e., impairment of shame and a sense of guilt, disgust, anxiety), and impairment of sexual pleasure" (p. 790).[7] In many cases of child sexual abuse, dissociation is the basic defensive response (Courtois, 2000). During a close sexual experience, women with histories of child sexual abuse may become anxious, which can precipitate a number of defensive reactions, including the defense of dissociation. M. Lewis (1992) conjectured that "dissociation occurs as a consequence of early and severe childhood trauma, usually of a sexual nature" (p. 172).

> It appears reasonable to conclude that abuse, sexual or otherwise, leads to shame. The shame produced is too powerful and painful and needs to be transformed. During the shame-avoidance process the dissociation occurs. . . . When shamed, the self attempts to remove itself from the shamed self. One can remove oneself in a variety of ways. . . . The most intense way may be the splitting of the self. (p. 172)

Rothschild (2000) noted that for many people who suffer from posttraumatic stress disorder as a result of childhood sexual abuse, their symptoms—"accelerated heart rate, cold sweating, rapid breathing, heart palpitations, hypervigilance, and hyperstartle response (jumpiness)—[may become chronic]. When chronic, these symptoms can lead to sleep disturbances, loss of appetite, sexual dysfunction, and difficulties in concentrating" (p. 7).

Andrews (2002) also emphasized the fact that child sexual abuse has a profound effect on a woman's body image. She noted that "At a cognitive and emotional level, abuse survivors often report a deep shame and hatred of their bodies that goes far beyond the normative discontent experienced by the majority of women in Western societies" (p. 257).

In her clinical work, H. Kaplan (1974, 1995) described many cases of inhibited sexual desire and sexual aversion disorders that were related to child sexual abuse and trauma. Kaplan (1995) suggested one reason why feelings associated with child sexual abuse might be reawakened as partners became closer emotionally:

> The inability to meld emotional closeness with sexual passion is hardly surprising in persons who sustained substantial emotional damage in early life. These individuals simply feel safer reserving their erotic feelings and desires for strangers who cannot get close enough to hurt them. (p. 147)

We are familiar with many cases similar to those described by Kaplan (1995). In one case, Olivia, 25, found herself holding back her affection and sexual responses at times during sex. Olivia and Greg had been married a year when these problems began to surface. In one session, Olivia described the tumultuous emotions she experienced while making love. According to Olivia, these emotions usually emerged just as she was beginning to relax and enjoy Greg's affection and sexual caresses.

> Olivia: I don't feel like there are any words exactly when Greg and I are being sexual. It's more like a very strong feeling that I want him to stop.

> Therapist: If you could say something at the time, what would you say?

> Olivia: Well, in that situation, I really feel like saying to him, "Don't touch me there. It hurts. Leave me alone. Don't push my face like that. Leave me alone! I don't want to be with you. Don't touch me like that. I hate the way you touch me. Don't put your face on my face. Oh, I can't breathe, I can't breathe. Don't put your face there. I hate your face. I hate your breath in my face. Oh, it makes me not be able to breath. Don't come to me. I don't want to be with you. It hurts. [crying] You're so big and so heavy. It just hurts too much." [crying]

> Therapist: What are some of your thoughts about this?

> Olivia: I have clear thoughts about it, and it definitely relates to my father. I feel like I have flashes, like little pictures in my head of things that happened. I remember hearing him knock on my mother's door and then she would reject him and not want to be with him. Then for some reason, I remember him coming to me and that's when I felt those feelings. I feel like a kid sometimes now in the sexual situation. I feel like a small child. I feel like things hurt that wouldn't hurt if I could just relax and be myself, but I can't. It hurts in a way where it doesn't feel like I'm a woman. It feels old to me. It feels more like memories.

> Therapist: A repetition?

Olivia: Exactly. I think it was about three weeks ago that Greg and I were starting to make love and his face at one point was very close to mine. It felt like it was almost pushing a little bit and fury just overwhelmed me. I tried not to act it out or anything, but the feelings overwhelmed me. The feelings that I felt were that same thing, "Don't push on my face. It hurts. Don't push on my face!" But the feeling was that this huge face, this big face was near my face and the breath was on my face and I didn't want to be there. That was the feeling. All of a sudden this one little thing, his face being close to mine, reminded me of something from the past, and I completely lost any desire I might have had for making love. I just wanted to get away. And now it's been weeks since we last made love.

In other cases, where the sexual contact between adult and child was nonaggressive, the perpetrator may have been the only source of affectionate contact available in the family. Many clients, both men and women, have revealed that they found certain aspects of the sexual contact pleasurable, yet experienced considerable guilt regarding these reactions. For example, during the course of therapy, a woman remembered that as a child of five, she eagerly anticipated weekend visits with her father. Her parents were divorced, and the young girl lived with a cold, punishing mother. The affection and attention she received from her father on these occasions made her feel cared for, despite the fact that the affection included sexual fondling. On some level, she knew these activities were wrong and felt guilty for keeping them secret from her mother. Later, she revealed that she was resistant to telling her husband about what she liked to do sexually. On an intellectual level, she knew that her reluctance to talk with her husband about sexual issues was irrational, yet she found it impossible to break her silence and became increasingly more inhibited in her ability to experience pleasure during sex. As her therapy progressed, she was able to trace the origins of this withholding pattern to the guilt and secretiveness she had felt as a child in relation to the sexual activities with her father.

In cases of males who had been sexually abused as children, Gartner (1999) found that "Sexual dysfunctions are common among these men, including lowered or excessive sexual desire, sexual aversion, erectile disorder, inhibited orgasm, and premature ejaculation" (p. 201). H. Kaplan (1995) has noted that boys who are victims of childhood sexual abuse and incest often manifest symptoms of sexual dysfunctions as adults: "When they grew up, men who had been abused . . . developed a variety of severe and disabling sexual, as well as post-traumatic, emotional symptoms" (p. 125).

Alex, 26, grew up in an extremely dysfunctional family. Throughout his childhood, Alex, his father, mother, and five siblings had lived in his grandfather's home, where his uncle had been a frequent visitor. Both his grandfather and his uncle sexually abused Alex from the time he was nine until he left home at 17. Alex reported that his brothers and sisters had also been sexually abused by the two men.

During therapy, Alex had to face the fact that his parents could be considered criminally neglectful in that they had failed to notice the abuse that was "going on right under their noses," as Alex put it. He revealed that his mother, who was addicted to prescription drugs, was "totally out of it," while his father, who was rarely at home, was generally indifferent to his wife and children and, at times, explosive and violent.

Alex disclosed that in his relationships with women, he craved affection and tenderness. He enjoyed "cuddling," saying that he simply wanted to sleep with a woman, have her hold him in her arms, but was not drawn to being sexual. He tended to pursue women who were highly sexualized but then felt used by them and tended to withdraw and feel depressed after these encounters. Meanwhile, Alex had a fantasy of meeting the "perfect woman and settling down in a house with a white picket fence," where he would feel comforted, soothed and safe. It was understandable that Alex had intense fears of men and strong homophobic feelings, which he tried to disguise with a tough, macho facade.

The incident that motivated Alex to come to therapy occurred when his girlfriend had an affair. According to Alex, their relationship was going well until she began really liking him and indicated that she wanted to be with him more often. Frightened by what he perceived to be a demand for more frequent sexual relations, Alex pulled away sharply and did not contact her for two weeks. In the meantime, she began the affair out of hurt and anger. Alex felt devastated, even though he recognized that his rejection had precipitated the infidelity.

It became clear in the course of therapy that Alex's feelings and attitudes toward sex were closely related to the sexual abuse he suffered during his formative years. The connection between his current sexual inhibitions and his early abuse was particularly evident when he described the ways he felt sexually with women. For example, in one session, he said, "Whenever a woman has sex with me, I feel so empty and used afterward. I absolutely can't stand those feelings."

DESTRUCTIVE THOUGHT PROCESSES UNDERLYING SEXUAL WITHHOLDING

The voice process regulates patterns of sexual withholding and self-denial that are at the core of inhibited sexual desire disorders and many other sexual dysfunctions. Self-critical attitudes as well as thoughts reflecting animosity toward one's partner can erupt into consciousness at any time during a sexual experience, decreasing feelings of sexual desire and increasing performance anxiety and feelings of self-consciousness. In responding to these negative prescriptions, men and women may inhibit their spontaneous, natural responses before, during, and/or following a sexual experience. As a result, they often shift their focus to concerns about performance and concentrate on the technical aspects of sex in an effort to circumvent these inhibitions and complete the act of sexual intercourse.

Self-attacks and the accompanying angry affect relate to people's basic feelings about themselves, their bodies, their sexual identity, and their ability to both give and receive sexual pleasure and gratification. Even the mildest voice attack can interfere with an individual's ability to take pleasure in making love (Firestone, 1990c). Internalized voices also reinforce feelings of shame and guilt that, in turn, effectively tone down or dampen sexual desire and arousal (Firestone, 1988, 1997a).

Other clinicians have called attention to dysfunctional attitudes and beliefs that are experienced by self-denying men and women. For example, in *Sexual Anorexia*, Carnes (1997) delineated a number of core beliefs subscribed to by men and women who deny themselves sexual pleasure and fulfillment; dysfunctional beliefs that can be translated into the form of voice attacks:

> Anorexics believe: that they are unworthy and unloveable, that they cannot depend on others, that they will have to take care of themselves; that relationships make them vulnerable to abuse and exploitation, that sex is terrifying, that sex must be controlled and repressed, [and] that intimacy and sex cannot be combined. (p. 92)

On the basis of extensive clinical and empirical research with 2,109 patients and couples "with chief complaints of deficient sexual desire," H. Kaplan (1995) concluded that

> *The pathological decrease of these patients' libido is essentially an expression of the normal regulation of sexual motivation gone awry....*
>
> Further, my observations of patients with "sexual anorexia" or HSD indicate that the psychogenic form of this syndrome is caused by their active, albeit unconscious selectively negative cognitions and perceptual processes by means of which they literally "turn themselves off." (p. 3)

Before a sexual encounter, these negative cognitions may take the form of self-protective warnings against becoming involved sexually and emotionally with another person, which can effectively destroy one's sexual interest, excitement, and desire. According to Kaplan, "The negative feelings of desire disorder patients typically surface *before* they enter the bedroom, thereby destroying any possibility of a normal build-up of their sexual desires" (p. 118). For example,

> You've had such a stressful day. You're too tired to have sex.
> He (She) was such a creep at dinner. Why would you want to make love to him (her)?
> Why all the fuss about sex? There are other, more important things to think about in life.

Men and women who are seeking a new partner or relationship often experience cynical attitudes and thoughts that take away from the excitement of a first date or meeting with a potential partner, thoughts such as,

> Why would he (she) like you, anyway?
> He (She) has no real interest in you.
> What are you so excited about? He (she) is only interested in what he (she) can get.
> Keep it casual. Don't get too attached.
> What do you need a relationship for anyway? You're okay on your own.

To add to these original difficulties, the acquired immune deficiency syndrome (AIDS) epidemic has become a destructive issue in people's sexual lives; those contemplating a new sexual involvement often experience voices warning them about the possibility of contracting AIDS or other sexually transmitted diseases. These thoughts contribute to feelings of distrust and hostility toward a potential partner. Clearly, these voice attacks are capable of extinguishing erotic feelings and sexual desire at a critical juncture prior to having sex.

> What if he (she) isn't telling the truth about being tested?
> How do you know he (she) is telling you the truth about his (her) sexual history?

When people fail to subject these pessimistic injunctions to reality-testing, their feelings of sexual desire are considerably diminished. This line of thinking can also contribute to hesitancy and nervousness during subsequent phases of the sex act.

People's angry, cynical attitudes toward their sexual partners have been identified as crucial factors in the development and maintenance of HSD in one or both partners. H. Kaplan (1995) has stressed this causative factor in her work:

> The major HSD theme . . . [is] the *selective focus on the negative aspects of the partner, with simultaneous denial of positive qualities.* To put it more graphically, when they are with the right person in the right place, instead of getting into gear and stepping on the gas, patients with HSD

keep their foot on the brake or shift into reverse, so that they never get anywhere, sexually speaking. (pp. 115–117)

Sexual withholding is prevalent in many long-term relationships and obviously contributes to the phenomena of "sex-deprived" marriages. Married couples often find themselves drifting into a pattern of habitually avoiding sex. A decrease in the frequency of having sex and deterioration in the quality of sexual relating may occur at certain points in the marriage. At each of these crucial periods of time, the voice can provide seemingly rational reasons for partners' gradual loss of interest in sex or it can effectively stifle erotic feelings that may still arise.

For example, after being married for a while,

The honeymoon is over. You should just settle down to the responsibilities of marriage.

He (She) is so familiar by now, there's nothing new or exciting to look forward to in making love.

After having a baby,

He's (She's) so unrealistic to want sex when he/she knows that you've been up all night with the baby.

She's (He's) so involved with the new baby. She (He) never wants to make love with you anymore.

When both partners are focused on their careers and/or children,

She's (He's) always distracted by work. She (He) never wants to make love.

All he (she) thinks about is the kids. He's (She's) never as interested in sex as you are.

As a person ages,

You won't be able to get an erection and you won't be able to feel as much anyway.

You'll just be dry and turn him off. Besides, people your age don't need sex.

Personal Examples

The following excerpts from a women's group exemplify the issues that contribute to withholding. The participants focused on identifying, revealing, and challenging behaviors that they believed were causing distress in their sexual lives and in their intimate relationships.

Carla: A few weeks ago, I told Ross that I really loved it when he was affectionate, touching my hair or coming up behind me and hugging me, and I wished he would do more. I also wanted to act in a way that would make him feel affectionate toward me. After that, he was really affectionate for the next couple of days in the way I wanted, but then I noticed I didn't like it. After a couple of days like that, I felt like it was too much, which was stupid because it was what I really wanted. He noticed it too—like sitting together, he would touch my leg and I didn't respond, and he would feel hurt.

Therapist: You found it difficult to tolerate getting what you wanted?

Carla: I feel like I can't stand it. Such a small thing would make me pull away. So that went on for a while, and I noticed I started thinking things like I used to think about him like. *Maybe he doesn't like being affectionate. Maybe he just wants sex,* or about myself, *When was the last time you showered?* I don't think those ways as much as I used to, but right at the moment we started kissing, I was thinking "Oh my God, can I do this?" [*sad, cries*] "I don't know if I can do this, if I can stand him touching me."

So that time I said to myself, "Just let yourself enjoy it, just let go." I did, and I really felt different. I felt turned on, I felt the kissing was nice. I wasn't thinking *Oh, this is gross.* But it was a struggle before we got fully into it. It felt good, but it's been a long time since we made love.

Therapist: So you avoided it for a while.

Carla: Yes, it's been a problem for about a year. Otherwise Ross feels good with me; our friendship is nice, and all the other things that were problems aren't anymore. So it's a painful thing because I'd feel better for a while sexually and felt I was making progress, but he still feels bad when things are off.

Therapist: What made you cry?

Carla: Picturing him touching me and my not liking it. The actual physical contact.

Therapist: How does it connect to just being touched? What agony is in that cry?

Carla: The feeling is that I'm doing it with a stranger, like this nasty man. That's the feeling, like I'm some thing that's being used by a stranger.

Therapist: By a dirty, ugly, nasty person?

Carla: Yes, that's the feeling.

Therapist:	How do you turn someone that you're attracted to into that?
Carla:	I distort him into that sort of a person.
Therapist:	But how do you make him look that disgusting to you?
Carla:	It's almost like a voice telling me, *He's repulsive*, or *He's disgusting right now. What does he want from you?"* It's like somebody talking to me, telling me things.
Therapist:	It's worthwhile to recognize it as a voice.
Carla:	I feel that I could go out with another person and it would probably be fine.
Therapist:	Why would it be different?
Carla:	I don't know, because there's no promise or guarantee [crying] because I could walk away and not worry about being with him again. I could drop him if I wanted to.
Ashley:	(another participant) I know what you mean. As soon as I feel that my boyfriend is expecting something from me, I start feeling trapped. So I don't want to be touched because it was like he was expecting something from me. I don't want to give that to him. It's like you're giving yourself away. It was like a voice telling me bad stuff about him.
Therapist:	So the thing that alters the situation from what would naturally be sexual is what the voice is telling you.
Rose:	With me, it's like all of a sudden, I'm not feeling right, but there's no real reason for me not to feel good. With me, I think there's such a projection of my father onto my husband in the way I think he's critical of me, in the way I think he picks me apart, in the way I'm critical of him. It's very much like the relationship with my father. And then all of a sudden, in the sexual situation, it's my father. I'm distorting him, like you said, you're distorting even his looks.
Carla:	How do you stop distorting?
Therapist:	By recognizing that these voices are distorting your partner. That you're seeing your father, not your boyfriend or husband. And by recognizing all the elements that go into it: what you owe him—what he owes you, and placing the hatred, the anger, the disappointment, all these feelings from your childhood, where they belong, and not letting anything spill over into the current relationship.

Excerpts from a therapy session with a young man who was experiencing sexual problems in relation to his girlfriend illustrate the dynamics involved in emotional incest and the important link to patterns of sexual withholding in many adults. As a young adult, Luke was popular and had many girlfriends, yet he rarely stayed involved with a woman for longer than a few months. Before this session, Luke had felt humiliated when he was unable to complete the sex act with his new girlfriend.

Luke: I've been thinking about this woman I started seeing recently. I've only seen her for about three weeks or so, but in the beginning, I really liked her and I liked being sexual with her, which was a huge thing for me because I had felt really bad about my sexuality until very recently.

Then we had a conversation where she said I was a really nice guy and she thought I was really special. The next couple of days she kept asking if I was okay because I wasn't as friendly as I had been, or as she wanted me to be. I got really uncomfortable. It was the night before I left to go skiing—this is very embarrassing—I actually couldn't be sexual with her. It was something about that wanting on her part that made me feel suffocated. I felt like she wanted too much from me. Also she likes being on top when we're sexual and there's something about that that's so uncomfortable. I mean, I had almost a panic attack while we were being sexual. I felt suffocated.

Finally I was able to leave town and get away from her. I actually was happy and relieved to be going on the ski trip, because I wouldn't have to see her. [long pause] I feel more relaxed from saying this.

Therapist: It's sad what happened in the story you told about shying away from your girlfriend when she was really liking you.

Luke: I was looking forward to going skiing anyway, but part of why I wanted to go was so I could get away from her. She wanted too much. It was okay when it was on my terms more. [sad, tearful] I feel embarrassed to say this, but I feel really screwed up. I feel very confused about my own reactions to her because they feel physical and I don't have a clear thought about what's happening. I feel so creepy. I hate to say this, but there are very few sexual situations where I come away feeling closer or better. I only feel that I'm screwed up, like I'm insensitive, or I'm a little boy, and I can't satisfy a woman. Like I should just be alone.

Therapist: Can you say those as voices?

Luke: I don't know. They feel so angry. They'd go something like this: *You're right. You should just be alone. You are a creep! You're weird. You don't belong in a man's world. You're small. You're incompetent. You can't satisfy a woman. Why is she so interested in you anyway? There's probably something weird about her.*

Why go after her? You'd be better off alone. Stay away from her! [angrier] *You can't have her! She can't have you! You belong to me! You're mine! You'd better stay with me. You're my special boy, she can't have you!* [tearful]

God, that's my mother's voice. It feels so embarrassing to hear those words coming out of my mouth. But she was so clinging, sticky, and so dependent on me, even though she was neglectful. I remember that she always kept me at her side. By the time I was a teenager, I couldn't stand being in the same room with her.

Since she died, other people, even some of her friends, have said that they couldn't stand being alone with her for very long because she was so all-consuming. They said that they felt drained after being with her, and I felt exactly the same way. I'm starting to understand more about this from saying these voices. It makes sense that I'm afraid when I feel a woman wanting to be closer to me. I immediately think that she wants more from me, that she's going to drain me dry.

THE DYNAMICS OF SEXUAL WITHHOLDING IN ONGOING COUPLE RELATIONSHIPS

The dynamics underlying the patterns of sexual withholding that are operating within each member of the couple create a feedback system of reaction and counterreaction that is often difficult to interrupt. McCarthy and McCarthy (1998) contended that "More than any other sexual difficulty, ISD [inhibited sexual desire] involves the couple's relationship" (p. 183). People who have been hurt emotionally become increasingly intolerant of closeness, affection, and passion as their relationship becomes more meaningful. They begin to hold back their responses either sexually or emotionally, trying to avoid the special combination of love, sexuality, and tenderness that can be the most satisfying.

Withholding patterns also are acted out in areas of a couple's relationship that are far removed from their sexual relating. In addition to withholding in the sexual situation, people may gradually start holding back the very qualities that originally attracted their mates, their unique way of expressing themselves, their looks, friendliness, simple acts of consideration and kindness, and their enjoyment in each other's company. Feelings of anger, resentment, or disappointment stemming from everyday interactions can have a detrimental effect on the couple's lovemaking. Both parties become more inward and defended against each other as the withholding patterns become well established.

In the first stages of a romance, people usually feel sexually attracted to each other, but later, one or the other may withdraw sexually and lose enthusiasm for sex. The process of first being responded to sexually, then having it held back, bewilders the other person, at which point he or she begins to lose self-confidence and the sex act starts to feel less natural or spontaneous. This withholding makes the person being withheld from feel increasingly inadequate and inferior and often reawakens suppressed anger from childhood experiences of being withheld from or rejected (Firestone, 1985). H. Kaplan's (1995) analysis of the course that many long-term couple relationships take is congenial with our understanding of the ways in which sexual withholding (in one or both partners) leads to anger and guilt, which in turn, contributes to diminished sexual desire or motivation in each partner with the consequent avoidance of sexual relations. Kaplan asserted that,

> Rather than assuming that a couple's lust for each other normally disappears after a while, one can make a case that the erotic bond may simply lie dormant . . . Thus, while some decrease of passion is normal, I regard a marked or complete loss of sexual desire in a long-term relationship as pathological. Such declines are often due to the corrosive effect of marital hostility and disillusionment, and *not* to familiarity. (p. 38)

CONCLUSION

Sexual withholding is a defense characterized by holding back positive responses from one's partner and denying oneself pleasure and fulfillment. It plays a significant role in the development of many sexual problems, particularly disorders of low sexual desire. Sexual withholding is often manifested in passive-aggressive behaviors and in duplicitous communications and mixed messages.

Patterns of sexual withholding are predisposed by experiences during an individual's formative years. Parental behaviors such as intrusiveness, possessiveness, and attempts to live through their offspring lead children to hold back from others and to deny their own wants and desires. These patterns are often carried into adult relationships and interfere with the achievement of real intimacy. Sexual withholding may also stem from fears of competing with the same-sex parent as a child, especially when that parent was jealous of the attention shown by the opposite-sex parent. Child sexual abuse can also be a contributing factor in that adult sexual relations come to be feared, avoided, or defended against. Feelings of being exploited as a child tend to be projected on to one's adult partner, leading to a holding back of warmth, affection, and sexual responses. In addition, feeling close emotionally and sexually to one's partner may trigger memories of the earlier abuse, which in turn can interfere with one's ability to enjoy the sexual experience.

Destructive thoughts play a major role in sexual withholding. Self-critical thoughts as well as thoughts reflecting animosity and anger toward one's partner can erupt into consciousness at any time during a sexual encounter. Voice attacks often function to increase performance anxiety and feelings of self-consciousness in sexual situations. Thoughts that one doesn't deserve to be happy or to be close to a partner may lead to self-denial. Depreciating thoughts about one's partner or thoughts exacerbating feelings of distrust can predispose holding back from one's partner.

When withholding patterns become well-established they can contribute to the development of symptoms of hyposexual desire disorders, or in some cases, they may lead to a complete shutting down of all feelings of sexual desire. On a broader level, holding back personal qualities and behaviors that are especially loved and admired by a loved one also interferes with the achievement of sexual and emotional intimacy in couple relationships.

Progress in therapy requires that clients become more aware of their customary methods of manipulating their partner through withholding their positive responses. They need to further develop their ability to be loving and sexually responsive, as well as increase their tolerance for accepting love. Therapeutic interventions that are directed toward the personal development and increased individuation of each partner can help break patterns of sexual withholding, enabling both individuals to restore the intimacy, sexual passion, and companionship that characterized the early stages of their relationship.

NOTES

1. Schmidt and Arentewicz (1983) asserted that "[sexual] dysfunctions are the expression of sexual inhibition, whether they manifest themselves as lack of desire, erectile, ejaculatory, arousal, or orgasmic disturbances or as vaginismus" (p. 40). Regarding inhibited sexual desire, McCarthy and McCarthy (1998) raised an important question:

   But isn't sexual desire a problem solely for women? . . . The reality is ISD occurs on occasion for almost every man. For ten to fifteen percent of men it is a chronic problem, becoming more frequent and severe with age. . . . In fact, one of the most thought-provoking statistics is when couples stop having sex, in over ninety percent of the cases it is the man's decision. This is conveyed indirectly and nonverbally. (pp. 177–178)

2. Psychonutritional products include expressions of affection and sexuality; acts of kindness, generosity, and empathy; open communication and self-disclosure, interest in one's partner, eye contact, making an effort to be physically attractive, having a pleasant facial expression, smiling, humor, and numerous other positive behaviors.

3. H. Kaplan (1995) noted that

   Patients with the global form of HSD [Hypoactive Sexual Desire] may be described as *sexually anorexic* because they have simply lost their appetite for sex under any circumstances; in the language of the "dysfunctional control" model, their sexual motivation is down-regulated across the board. (p. 67)

4. Passive–aggression is related to "pseudoaggression," which is different from genuine anger because it is not necessarily a response to frustration; instead it is often a reaction to positive gratification or acknowledgment. Unusually positive experiences frequently arouse painful feelings of deep sadness as well as anger, which people try to shut off by manipulating or pushing away the person offering acknowledgment, affection, or love (Firestone et al., 2003).

5. McCarthy and McCarthy (1998, 2003) also suggested that inhibited sexual desire has numerous causes, especially "sexual secrets and hidden agendas" (2003, p. 13). In their book *Rekindling Desire* (2003), they posed an important question regarding the psychodynamics in inhibited sexual desire: "Do desire problems cause sexual dysfunction, or does sexual dysfunction cause desire problems?" They found that for the majority of their male patients, it appeared that "the causation is clear—sexual dysfunction results in desire problems" (p. 51).

6. See Schore (1994), Beebe (1986), and Tronick and Weinberg (1997). Also see Mitchell (2002) who emphasized

   Because clinicians see the problems and can easily trace them back to developmental causes, they tend to imagine a healthy child-parent love that would only facilitate adult love and leave no problems. But it may be that childhood love is always fraught with areas of overstimulation and areas of understimulation, too much in some ways and too little in others. It may be that "just right" is found only in fairy tales. (p. 102)

7. Kaufman (1980), Morrison (1989), Goldberg (1996), and M. Lewis (1992) identified guilt as self-critical feelings experienced in relation to one's actions, whereas shame is a primary affect. Both shame and guilt are mediated or controlled by the voice.

8

COUPLE RELATIONSHIPS:
JEALOUSY AND SEXUAL RIVALS

Jealousy is a complex reaction to a perceived threat to a valued relationship or to its quality.
                                                                    —Pines (1998, p. 3)

In all of us there still lives the child's unregarding possessiveness—the longing for an absolute, certain, and exclusive love.
                                                                    —Downing (1977, p. 74)

Jealousy, sexual rivalry, and competitiveness arise naturally in interpersonal relationships. In fact, one of the primary reasons people seek therapy is because of the extreme distress they experience upon discovering that their mate is sexually involved with another person (Glass, 2003; Glass & Wright, 1997). The feelings aroused by this crisis are often even more distressful and emotionally painful than those experienced by people facing rejection or loss when a third party is not involved.

There are a number of reasons why feelings of jealousy are among the most disturbing emotions that people can experience in an intimate relationship. Even the suspicion that a mate is sexually involved with someone else disrupts the illusion that one is exclusively chosen and preferred above all others. Also, in relationships characterized by a fantasy bond, infidelity jeopardizes the delusion of fusion that has functioned as a symbol of safety, security, and eternal happiness for each partner. The threat of losing one's mate or lover to a rival often precipitates self-destructive thoughts and profound feelings of shame and humiliation that, under extreme conditions, can lead to thoughts of self-harm or suicide. On occasion, sexual infidelity can trigger vicious thoughts against one's mate and/or rival including a strong desire for revenge that may lead to violent acting-out behavior or even homicide (Felson, 2002).

In this chapter, we address the many facets of jealousy as it occurs in couple relationships, including (a) distinctions between competitiveness and jealousy; (b) the subjective experience of jealousy; (c) psychoanalytic, attachment, and evolutionary psychological perspectives on jealousy; (d) manifestations of jealousy in relationships characterized by a fantasy bond; (e) destructive thoughts or voices that intensify feelings of sexual jealousy and contribute to self-defeating responses; and (f) the relationship between sexual withholding and jealousy. In addition, we discuss the role that deception plays in exacerbating jealous reactions and explore social factors that influence jealous reactions in different cultures. Lastly, we offer their views regarding advantages and disadvantages of open, nonexclusive relationships versus the benefits and costs of closed or exclusive sexual relationships.

COMPETITIVENESS AND JEALOUSY

Competition and jealousy are both dimensions of sexual rivalry in intimate relationships. Competitive feelings are based on a natural desire for attention, affection, love, and sex. On the one hand, competitive feelings may be considered "irrational" in the sense that everyone has unrealistic fantasies and desires to be the center of attention, to always be admired, chosen, preferred, or unconditionally loved. On the other hand, competitive feelings can be conceptualized as "rational" in situations where two people are pursuing the same goal, because the outcome has actual consequences for both winner and loser. For example, when two people are applying for the same job or position or pursuing the same love object, there are obviously real issues involved, and winning becomes vitally important to both individuals. As people achieve more of their career and personal goals, and especially as they feel increasingly fulfilled in an intimate relationship, their competitive feelings tend to diminish in intensity.

Feelings of competitiveness, like the other primary emotions of sadness, anger, fear, envy, shame, joy, happiness, and exhilaration, are inextricably tied to one's wants, needs, and desires (Firestone et al., 2003). Competitiveness involves the desire to triumph over one's rival as well as to denigrate or bring one's rival down. Both of these motives can function to increase feelings of competitiveness and intensify efforts to win the competition. People who accept these motives and desires as natural are more likely to be straightforward in pursuing their goals in life. In a sexually rivalrous situation, for example, they attempt to "put their best foot forward" and expend considerable effort trying to defeat their rival. In these cases, the competition is secondary; the people involved are not competitive merely for the sake of "winning" in itself, but for the sake of achieving a real goal—achieving, maintaining, or regaining closeness and sexual intimacy with the person they love.

It is important to recognize and uncritically accept competitive feelings as simply being a part of our psychological makeup, just as anger is a natural response to frustration. However, if people are not accepting of anger or "irrational" feelings in themselves, or if they are afraid of competing, they tend to avoid rivalrous situations and feel ashamed and guilty about their competitive thoughts and feelings.

Important distinctions can be made between feelings of jealousy and competitiveness. According to *Webster's Dictionary* (Random House, 1998), jealousy is defined as

> 1. jealous resentment against a rival, a person enjoying success or advantage. . . . 2. mental uneasiness from suspicion or fear of rivalry, unfaithfulness, etc., as in love. . . . 3. vigilance in maintaining or guarding something. . . . 4. a jealous feeling, disposition, state, or mood. (p. 1025)

Whereas competitiveness or competition is defined as

> 1. Rivalry for supremacy, a prize, etc. . . . 2. a contest for some prize, honor, or advantage. . . . 3. the rivalry offered by a competitor. . . . 4. a competitor or competitors. . . . 5. . . . rivalry between two or more persons or groups for an object desired in common, usually resulting in a victor and a loser but not necessarily involving the destruction of the latter. 6. The struggle among organisms, both of the same and of different species, for food, space, and other vital requirements. (p. 417)

One significant difference between these two feelings or moods is that jealousy is fueled by self-critical thoughts and hostile attitudes toward the love object and rival, whereas competitiveness is generally characterized by the relative absence of voice attacks.[1]

A certain amount of jealousy is normal in everyday life simply because if people are unable to achieve their goals, they are jealous and envious of those who achieve more than they do (Pines, 1998).[2] Jealousy is inevitable to the extent that someone else has attained what one desires for oneself—love, attention, affection, or a love object. The fact that jealousy necessarily involves a rival is self-evident. In defining jealousy, DeSteno and Salovey (1996) stated, "Concern over the possible termination of a relationship, in and of itself, is not a sufficient condition to evoke jealousy; rather, the presence of a rival is a necessary and defining condition for this emotion" (p. 920).

The primary problem in sexual rivalries does not lie in people's competitiveness or even in their jealous reactions; rather the problem lies in the fear and guilt that cause many men and women to deny their competitive feelings and retreat from pursuing their goals in rivalrous situations. It is important to emphasize that feelings of jealousy are intensified when one retreats from one's natural competitiveness. People who experienced a parent's rivalrous feelings during their formative years often retreat from competing as adults in a rivalrous situation. As noted in chapter 3, rivalrous feelings exist in many families and are particularly strong in parents who are overly possessive and jealous. Individuals who have been raised in such a family constellation often experience considerable fear and guilt when faced with either winning or losing in competing with a sexual rival.

THE SUBJECTIVE EXPERIENCE OF JEALOUSY

When men and women describe their subjective experience of sexual jealousy, they usually indicate feelings of fear, anger, or depression. Often they tend to imagine or compare themselves unfavorably with their rivals to their own detriment, especially when their rivals are unknown. The various ways in which jealousy is experienced and the myriad behavioral expressions associated with feelings of jealousy have been described by a number of researchers (Buunk et al., 1996; Buunk & Hupka, 1987; Pines & Aronson, 1983; Salovey, 1991).

According to Pines and Aronson (1983), intense jealousy is an extremely painful emotional state that is associated with physical sensations, such as "feeling hot, nervous, and shaky; and experiencing fast heartbeat, and emptiness in the stomach" (p. 131). Pines and Aronson noted that participants in her study on jealousy reported that "the emotional reactions felt most strongly were anxiety, fear of loss, pain, anger, vulnerability, and hopelessness" (p. 131). In summarizing findings from a phenomenological study of the ways that people experience jealousy, White and Mullen (1989) concluded,

> When studying large samples of jealous people, we may find that thoughts about personal inferiority, feelings of sadness and despair, and demands on the beloved for commitment are inter-correlated. Another cluster of reactions may consist of thoughts of revenge and comparison to the rival, feelings of anger and rage, and behaviors intended to damage the rival. (p. 13)

Another distinction between jealousy and competitiveness lies in the consequences of behaviors based on these emotions. Feelings of jealousy are natural, yet behaviors based on jealous feelings (acting out anger, resentment, and suspiciousness toward the love object or rival, and even violent behavior) are often unacceptable. These behaviors must be subject to a moral consideration with respect to the harmful effects these actions could have on oneself and others. Feelings of competitiveness are also natural but, in contrast, it is acceptable to behave competitively in a rivalrous situation, that is, to attempt to win the competition.

In investigating jealousy and competitiveness, we interviewed men and women about the ways they experienced these emotions in sexually rivalrous situations. Several of their responses are listed below:

Trish: For me jealousy is a threatened feeling. A very threatened, insecure feeling. Competitiveness is different, it comes up in situations where I still can feel confident. When I feel jealous, it's from a very scared, desperate, hurt place, like something very precious is being taken away from me, or I'm being rejected for someone much better than I am.

Jack: Last week, my girlfriend told me that she was thinking of going out to dinner with an old friend of hers who was in town. He's a guy she used to date in college. Even though both of us had decided not to have an exclusive relationship, and I've dated other women sometimes, when she told me she was considering going out with someone else, I was furious and blew up at her. But underneath my anger, I felt like a nobody, completely worthless, like a little kid having a temper tantrum, not like a man.

Darlene: If I even picture the man I'm involved with being in another relationship, I have a totally panicked feeling, which makes me want to drop him and run. It's almost a physical feeling of coming apart. I feel that I would be nothing, I would be forgotten and it would change completely what exists between us.

Dustin: If I notice my wife paying attention to another man at a party, I feel desperate and angry at the same time. I start thinking, is she more interested in him than in me? Should I try to join in their conversation? But I feel that would be too obvious. Such a paralyzing feeling comes over me that I can't move. I just stand there and sweat and look awkward, but I rarely take any action on my own behalf. The things I'm thinking in that situation are really irrational because we've been married for five years and she's been totally faithful, but I still feel insecure and jealous.

Anita: I used to feel that if I even thought "my guy" was with somebody else, I would die. Many years ago, I suspected my boyfriend of having another girlfriend, and I tried to figure out the times when they might be together, like when he said he was going out with friends to a football game or bowling. During those times, I felt like I was going to explode out of my own skin. I felt I couldn't control my feelings. I'd go out to a bar and have some drinks, smoke cigarettes, I would do anything to contain that feeling of being totally out of control.

Kristen: I used to have so much self-hatred that I felt like I couldn't compete. I remember one time in college. I was with my boyfriend and this girl was walking across the street from us and he looked at her and I could tell he thought she was pretty, and I was so jealous. I remember it crossed my mind that this was so absurd. If I was going to be jealous on this level, about somebody across the street, it was insane. That's the first time it occurred to me that I could ruin my life over this.

Jared: When I'm jealous, I get really angry. I feel very insecure and anxious and stirred up inside. The feelings are very specific to the situation, and lots of questions come up in my mind: Is this someone who's a real threat? Is this a rival I'm going to lose to? How attractive am I to my partner? Sometimes I try to think about the situation more philosophically. Even if she rejects me, what would it really mean? Would it mean that I'm less attractive or less desirable than he is? Then I answer my own questions: Not necessarily. He might not be the better man. Or she might be making a bad choice because maybe she's afraid of being close to me. There could be lots of reasons. I find that I usually feel less anxious when I think about the situation more objectively. But I have to admit that it's really hard to talk myself out of feeling threatened and like I'm going to lose her.

Generally speaking, people rarely know why they are rejected for someone else. In these painful circumstances, they tend to feel confused, experience intense self-attacks, and ruminate about the reasons they were rejected. In most cases, their conclusions or explanations are not based on reality, nor are their self-criticisms necessarily valid for the reasons noted above. In other instances, men and women desperately search for answers by interrogating the rejecting mate. However, the reasons a mate prefers someone else are often unconscious and thus unavailable, even if he or she has a sincere desire to provide an explanation.

Researchers studying the phenomenon of jealousy have noted the similarity between acute jealous reactions and the symptoms of posttraumatic stress disorder (PTSD; Glass, 2003; Glass & Wright, 1997; Lusterman, 1995). When jealousy is extreme, people tend to have exaggerated, dramatic emotional responses, which they themselves often perceive as abnormal. They may feel overwhelmed by torturous images of their mate and their rival in a sexual situation; or they may obsessively ruminate about the whereabouts of their mate, suffer severe constriction of thought and emotion, avoid situations where their jealousy might be intensified, lose interest in other people and activities, become hypervigilant, or suffer from insomnia, all of which are symptoms of PTSD as described in *Diagnostic and Statistical Manual of Mental Disorders, Fourth Edition* (DSM–IV; American Psychiatric Association, 1994).

Lastly, feelings of jealousy can sometimes serve a positive function in an intimate relationship. For example, an individual's jealousy in relation to the threat of a partner's infidelity may act as an incentive, providing the impetus to develop oneself, change negative characteristics and be more attractive, interesting, and sexually appealing than a rival (Person, 1988). Jealousy can also make a person more aware and appreciative of the value their partner has for them.

PSYCHOANALYTIC AND ATTACHMENT THEORISTS' PERSPECTIVES ON JEALOUSY

Jealousy appears to be a universal phenomenon. According to White and Mullen (1989) "Although cultures differ in the frequency and forms of their jealousy, there are no reports of jealousy-free societies" (p. 1). It is noteworthy that in spite of the apparent ubiquity of this profoundly troubling emotion, many researchers who in the past studied emotional processes in interpersonal relationships (Plutchik, 2000) considered jealousy to be a secondary emotion, derived from the more basic, central, primary emotions (Buunk et al., 1996).

In recent years, however, a number of clinicians and researchers have turned their attention to the emotions associated with jealousy, envy, and competitiveness as manifested in interpersonal relationships. Taking note of this trend, Salovey (1991) declared, "After decades of banishment to popular magazines and advice columns, jealousy and envy, as complex interpersonal emotions, have certainly emerged as legitimate topics of scientific inquiry" (p. xi). Social psychologist Shaver (1989) has argued that "Far from being expunged, jealousy—along with love, loneliness, caring, and sympathy—is as prevalent and insistent as ever" (p. v). In fact, in contemporary society, jealousy appears to be on the increase as social and economic changes "continue to have profound impacts on the nature of romantic relationships and marriage" in every culture (White & Mullen, 1989, p. vii).

Theorists, clinicians, and researchers have employed a number of approaches in attempting to explicate the complicated emotional state that we refer to as jealousy. Psychoanalysts view jealousy as closely related to earlier triangles within the nuclear family, to specific childhood events, and to the way that the child resolved the Oedipal or Electra conflict. S. Freud (1922/1955) conceptualized jealousy as being either "normal" or pathological and included projected and delusional forms of jealousy in the pathological category. According to Freud,

> Although we may call it normal, this jealousy is by no means completely rational, that is, derived from the actual situation, proportionate to the real circumstances and under the complete control of the conscious ego; for it is rooted deep in the unconscious, it is a continuation of the earliest stirrings of the child's affective life, and it originates in the Oedipus or brother-and-sister complex of the first sexual period. (p. 223)

Ellis (1996) clarified and expanded on S. Freud's distinction between "normal" and "abnormal" jealousy:

> Jealousy can be seen as rational or undisturbed when people strongly desire love and affection from others but do not dogmatically insist that they *absolutely must* have it. When they are irrationally or self-defeatingly jealous, they usually have a number of irrational beliefs leading to their feelings of insecurity, rage, and low frustration tolerance. (p. 23)

S. Freud proposed that jealousy originates sometime between the ages of 2 and 3, when children direct their emerging sexual urges toward the parent of the opposite sex. Obviously, boys and girls face competitors who have all the advantages; boys inevitably lose out to the father, while girls are defeated by the mother. Later, as adults, whenever a rival presents a threat to a valued romantic relationship, they reexperience abandonment anxiety as well as the painful longing, despair, hopelessness, rage, and grief they felt at the time of the original loss.

In a discussion of "morbid jealousy," Dutton (1995a) described "cyclical/ emotionally volatile abusers [who] experience a constellation of feelings involving rage and jealousy" (p. 34). These feelings are characteristic of the men in Dutton's study who had assaulted their partners or wives. In assessing symptoms manifested by these men, Dutton found a strong relationship between behaviors manifested by patients with Borderline Personality Disorder and "scores and the associated features of cyclical abusiveness. Those strongly related to borderline scores included anger, jealousy, and tendencies to blame women for negative events in the relationship" (p. 153). In another work, Dutton (1995b) stressed that abandonment anxiety played a prominent role in the reactions of these men to perceived threats of losing their partner.

> Abandonment anxiety could be produced by . . . sexual threat or any other instance of the female moving emotionally further away (or re-

investing her energy outside the primary relationship). . . . Sexual jealousy, especially to the extent that it involves delusions or distortions, may represent a form of chronic abandonment anxiety. Jealousy is mentioned frequently by battered women as an issue that incited violence. . . . Jealousy produces a range of behavioral responses (including aggression and increased vigilance) and affective reactions (including rage and depression). (pp. 67–68)

Attachment theorists have suggested that jealousy varies in intensity and chronicity according to the type of attachment pattern that one originally formed with the parent or caregiver during the formative years. In an adult relationship, this pattern of attachment, whether secure, anxious/avoidant (dismissing), or anxious/ambivalent (preoccupied), is replicated in the form of a particular style of relating to one's romantic partner. Holtzworth-Munroe, Stuart, and Hutchinson (1997) cited a study that found that securely attached participants "reported more positive beliefs about relationships, longer romantic relationships, and less jealousy in romantic relationships" (p. 315) than adults classified as insecurely attached. They also noted that individuals with anxious or preoccupied attachment patterns have been described as "emotionally dependent, 'clinging,' romantically obsessive, and jealous" (p. 316). In their research, Sharpsteen and Kirkpatrick (1997) noted that avoidantly attached individuals

> Were relatively more likely to turn their anger and blame against the interloper [rather than the partner; whereas] . . . anxiously attached [preoccupied] people focused on the implications of the situation for themselves. . . . Despite this, though, they were relatively unlikely to take steps to maintain their self-esteem. (pp. 636–637)

In extending attachment theory to other aspects of romantic relationships, Downey, Feldman, and Ayduk (2000) suggested that *rejection sensitivity*, which they define as "the disposition to anxiously expect, readily perceive, and intensely react to rejection by significant others" (p. 45) is a factor to be considered in attempting to understand individuals' differential reactions to sexual rivalry.

Other approaches have viewed jealousy as a "learned response that when inappropriate can be unlearned" (Pines, 1998, p. x).[3] In describing her findings from an extensive study on jealousy, Pines concluded that "jealousy is both a social phenomenon and a product of an individual's mind" (p. 131). In working with couples, we have focused on the thought processes in "an individual's mind," self-depreciating thoughts that intensify jealous reactions. In coping with feelings of jealousy, it is helpful for individuals to identify the underlying self-critical thoughts and cynical, distrustful attitudes toward their mates, to develop insight as to the sources of these thoughts, and to counter them by learning to pursue their goals more directly.

EVOLUTIONARY FACTORS THAT INFLUENCE JEALOUSY

Evolutionary psychologists propose that jealousy is an innate emotion and the result of evolutionary forces that endowed "our jealous ancestors" with a selective advantage over their less jealous or more tolerant peers and rivals. Buss (2000), in delineating many of the adaptive benefits of sexual jealousy, stated

> Jealousy [is] . . . a supremely important passion that helped our ancestors, and most likely continues to help us today, to cope with a host of real reproductive threats. Jealousy, for example, motivates us to ward off rivals with verbal threats and cold primate stares. It drives us to keep partners from straying with tactics such as escalating vigilance or showering a partner with affection. And it communicates commitment to a partner who may be wavering, serving an important purpose in the maintenance of love. Sexual jealousy is often a successful, although sometimes explosive, solution to persistent predicaments that each one of our ancestors was forced to confront. (pp. 5–6)

It is interesting to note that women tend to feel more threatened if their mate develops a close, emotionally intimate relation with another woman than if he becomes involved in a sexual liaison. On the other hand, men appear to feel more threatened when their partners are sexually unfaithful (Glass & Wright, 1997; Pines, 1998).[4] Evolutionary psychologists have conjectured that these gender-specific threatening scenarios have their basis in the differential sexual strategies developed by men and women throughout the centuries (Buss, 1994, 2000; Daly & Wilson, 1983).

According to Buss (2000), during the course of evolutionary history, women risked the loss of a mate's time, energy, resources, and commitment if he invested these attentions in a rival. "The most reliable indicator that a man would divert his investment was not in having sex with another woman per se, but rather in becoming *emotionally involved* with another woman" (p. 53).

On the other hand, males who were betrayed by their partners risked expending their energy and resources on a rival's genetic children in the mistaken belief that they were his own. Therefore a "sexual infidelity by the woman, more than any other form of infidelity, imposed the greatest costs on ancestral men" (pp. 52–53). In addition, in the past and in the present, a man's reputation can be seriously damaged by his mate's sexual infidelity, because "cuckolds are universally ridiculed in the eyes of others" (p. 52).

Buss also documented the more dire behavioral consequences of the jealousy, humiliation and ridicule experienced by "cuckolded" males: "Jealousy can be emotional acid that corrodes marriages, undermines self-esteem, triggers battering, and leads to the ultimate crime of murder. . . . A full 13 percent of all homicides are spousal murders, and jealousy is overwhelmingly the leading cause" (pp. 7–8). According to Felson (2002), for women who are murdered, more than 50% are killed by an intimate partner or friend or acquaintance. Felson identified

> 192 cases in which a male offender killed his female partner and 115 cases in which a female offender killed her male partner. The percentage of incidents in which the homicide stemmed from jealousy or love triangles was about the same for male and female offenders (19.3% for men vs. 18.3% for women). (p. 110)

However, Barash and Lipton (2001) observed significant gender differences related to whether or not sexual infidelity leads to retribution against the unfaithful partner. They noted, "Compared with the high probability of male retribution after female infidelity, it is quite rare for male infidelity to trigger female retribution" (p. 159).

Buss (2000) has conducted numerous studies using self-report questionnaires, hypothetical situations, and physiological measures to test his evolutionary hypotheses about gender differences in the experience of jealousy. One study showed that

> 63 percent of the men, but only 13 percent of the women, found the sexual aspect of the infidelity to be most upsetting; in contrast, 87 percent of the women, but only 37 percent of the men, found the emotional aspect of the infidelity to be most upsetting. (p. 59)

In a number of related studies with gay and lesbian participants, Buss found that "Homosexual men appear to express less sexual jealousy than heterosexual men. . . . Lesbians appear to be more sexually jealous than their heterosexual counterparts, who overwhelmingly express more distress at emotional infidelity" (p. 65).

Terror management theorists (Goldenberg et al., 2003) proposed that gender differences with respect to sexual and emotional infidelity can be further explicated by considering the role played by self-esteem as a defense against the terror aroused by an acute awareness of one's personal mortality. These researchers found that "Mortality salience (MS) [being made acutely aware of one's personal mortality] increased distress in response to sexual infidelity for men and emotional infidelity for women" (p. 1585). Goldenberg et al. (2003) explained their findings as follows: "Men derive relatively more self-esteem from their sex lives, whereas women's self-esteem is more contingent on romantic commitment" (p. 1585). Becoming more aware of death through the experimenters' manipulation of mortality salience threatened both men's and women's self-esteem in different domains, that is, in the specific areas that each gender tends to rely on to enhance (defensive) self-esteem.

The personality characteristics of a rival that trigger the most intense feelings of jealousy are also determined by evolutionary forces, according to Buss (2000), who has noted that "Jealousy in each sex has evolved to mirror the mate preferences of the other sex" (p. 67). Historically, women prefer men who have resources that they can invest in protecting the woman and helping her raise her children to a reproductive age. "Since women desire professionally successful men, for example, men's jealousy should have evolved in tandem to be activated by a rival who excels professionally" (p. 67). Men prefer women who have a youthful and healthy physical appearance because these attributes signify fertility, the ability to bear children carrying his genes. Therefore, "women's jealousy should have evolved to be especially sensitive to rivals who are younger [because they are at a child-bearing age] or more physically alluring" (p. 67).

JEALOUSY AND THE FANTASY BOND

The way in which jealously is experienced by individuals is affected by several factors, including their personal qualities, the defenses they developed to cope with early interpersonal rivalries, and the quality of relating in their intimate associations. As noted in chapter 6, in a relationship characterized by a fantasy bond, partners have generally surrendered their autonomy, become overly dependent on each other, and are not necessarily kind or loving in their actions. The imaginary fusion functions to perpetuate feelings of distrust, self-hating thought processes, and the inward, defensive behavior patterns that each individual brings to the relationship. This illusory merger, while providing a certain sense of safety and security, nonetheless leads to an unconscious belief in both partners that they could not exist without each other. If one partner breaks this fantasized connection by becoming sexually involved with a third party, powerful feelings of anger, fear, and anxiety are likely to be aroused in the other.

Although initially pledges of fidelity may be based on a real desire or mutual agreement, these vows can become part of a destructive bond in a couple. This is most likely when the vows are based on the false premise that people have proprietary rights over each other, particularly over each other's bodies and sexuality. Within a relationship, monogamy imposed by external social mores routinely assumed or expected by partners is different from sexual fidelity based on freedom of choice, genuine personal commitment, and the desire to share one's life with another person (Firestone, 1985).

Feelings of jealousy experienced by partners who have developed a fantasy bond in their relationship are often intense and can become chronic. The "betrayed" partner may experience a resurgence of painful emotions repressed during childhood, as well as feelings of aloneness and vulnerability.

As a result of relinquishing certain areas of independent functioning to maintain this illusion of fusion, partners feel increasingly inadequate and insecure as well as more dependent on the other for their sense of self-worth. The degree of dependency may be closely related to the intensity and duration of jealousy experienced by partners when there is a threat to the imagined connection brought about by sexual infidelity. In describing their studies on infidelity, Glass and Wright (1988) observed that feelings of jealousy tend to be more intense in someone who has depended on a mate for their feelings of self-worth or "positive self-regard" (p. 341). In other words, the degree of dependency rather than the degree of love felt by the rejected partner is the more significant determinant of the intensity of his or her jealous reactions.

In relationships characterized by a fantasy bond, each partner has an exaggerated need for reassurance that he or she is always the first and only choice of the other. As one or both partners sacrifices their individuality, their basic attraction to each other is diminished. The quality of the couple's sexual relating often deteriorates and sex becomes routine and unexciting. These conditions can lead to sexual dissatisfaction and contribute to a partner seeking gratification in another relationship.

In general, one partner's sexual involvement with a third party disrupts the illusion of fusion operating within the couple and shatters the false sense of security both partners derived from their merged identity. We suggest that the feelings of anxiety, anger, and grief experienced by the betrayed party are often due more to the destruction of the fantasy bond with the partner than to the threat of the relationship actually ending or the loss of the partner to the rival. Person (1988) emphasized this point when discussing people's profoundly debilitating reactions to rejection and betrayal by an intimate partner:

> Not only is the love object lost, and the "I" (previously valued so highly by the beloved) cheapened, but also the "we." To the extent that the lover defines his identity through being part of a couple, he will be denuded of an identity when he is forced back upon a single state. (p. 305)

Personal Example

Alexis and Todd had been living together for two years when Alexis became involved with Peter. Before her affair with Peter, both Todd and Alexis had gradually slipped into routine, habitual ways of treating each other. As a result, the passion and excitement that had characterized the first months of their relationship had diminished to a considerable extent. Alexis had begun to exert more and more control over Todd's activities and at times made cutting, depreciating remarks about him in front of friends. However, Todd had seemed oblivious to these remarks and submitted to Alexis's control.

When Alexis admitted to Todd that she was having an affair, he felt as if his world had been turned upside down. After several arguments filled with anger and mutual recriminations, Todd and Alexis went their separate ways, and Alexis continued to date Peter. Within two months of the breakup, Todd began dating another woman. The sadness, anger, and rage that he had felt seemed to dissipate overnight and he appeared happier than he had been in years.

One evening, Alexis and Peter were having dinner at a nightclub when Alexis spotted Todd on the dance floor with his new girlfriend. Alexis's immediate reaction was one of shock, then anger and disbelief. Humiliated, she quickly left the club without speaking to Todd. The next few nights were torturous for her. Suffering from panic attacks, Alexis was unable to sleep and tormented herself with images of Todd and his new girlfriend. She could not understand why she felt so distraught, anxious, and hopeless. After all, she thought, "I am the one who left him!" Finally, Alexis decided to record her thoughts and feelings.

"Shattered Illusions"

When I saw this woman dancing with Todd, running her hand through his hair, looking into his eyes, I thought That used to be me—the woman of his dreams, the center of his world. I was the one, the one he wanted to have a deep relationship with, the one he courted, treated well, idealized, never criticized, the one he shared all of his thoughts, feelings, and life with. The only special one.

What I had thought was real love was shattered that night because I saw it being re-created before my very eyes. Then I understood what lies I had been living. Back then, I was the one who made him feel saved, made him feel like a whole man. And now she does that for him. She'll go home with him tonight and make love to him and she will think she is saved too, and maybe she is, saved from a life of emptiness, like me.

I believed and I still believe that a man gives me value, gives me safety in a world of the unknown. Even though I had survived alone before I met Todd, he felt like a savior because I became again a woman in a man's life. I was the one and he was only thinking of me. As long as he was wanting me, I didn't have to worry.

Todd said that he would always love me, and now he is offering all of that to her. I see it more clearly than ever, so much so that it keeps me up at night, so much so that the anxiety makes my stomach turn, a nausea in my throat, I feel crazy.

Then my thoughts turn to Peter—maybe I could be his special one. I can make him feel like a man, but he isn't consistent the way that Todd was. Or maybe I could even try to be friends with Todd again, just be with him every once in a while, just to keep that safe feeling alive, or else I might end up alone and without anyone.

I feel the fear and anxiety lessen when I realize what my anxiety is truly about: aloneness and death. But that's not all of it. Why do I wake up in the night these past days, startled, anxious, with images of them gazing into each other's eyes being played before me? Why is this happening? Logically I know it is not Todd who I want gazing at me, really. I left the relationship months ago.

Then it hits me, in the middle of my chest, in my heart! It's my mother who I once wanted that gaze from, who I still somehow want it from, even when I think I don't, and act like I don't. I still imagine and fantasize her looking at me, today, and saying she is proud to have me as her child, that I am beautiful and lovable. It is that bond with her that I grieve, that loss that I truly fear—the loss brought about by the realization that I am not her and that she is not me, that I became my own person a long time ago and now it's time to grow up.

VOICES THAT INTENSIFY FEELINGS OF JEALOUSY

In relationships characterized by a fantasy bond, indications of infidelity in one partner generally evoke a barrage of self-destructive attacks and vindictive attitudes toward the other. For some, it triggers deep-seated feelings of insecurity, low self-worth, shame, and unlovability. Losing a valued partner can give rise to extremely self-destructive thinking and rage toward self, the partner, and the rival. The process of identifying and challenging destructive thought processes underlying intense jealous reactions is valuable in learning how to better cope with these disturbing affects.

Negative voices range along a continuum of intensity from mild self-criticism to angry self-attacks and suicidal ideation. Voices at each level of intensity can be triggered in rivalrous situations whenever there is a threat (real or imagined) of losing a valued person to a rival. Destructive thoughts against the self and others can be brought into conscious awareness by asking clients to put their thoughts in the second person "you," as though another person were addressing them. In this way, clients are able to identify the contents of their voice attacks, separate them from a more realistic and congenial view of themselves and others, and challenge those thoughts that are creating irrational feelings of rage, despair, and hopelessness. Methods to elicit and counter these destructive thoughts and attitudes are described in depth in chapter 9.

Voices Promoting Low Self-Esteem and Feelings of Being Unlovable

Feelings of sexual jealousy are especially prevalent in individuals who perceive themselves as inadequate or deficient. These men and women have strong tendencies to compare themselves negatively with potential or actual rivals. Their negative self-evaluations are often based on deep-seated beliefs of being unlovable and undeserving of love. In competitive situations, their lack of self-esteem triggers feelings of desperation, panic, and depression. Their possessiveness and fear over a potential loss can be traced to an overwhelming sense of insecurity and low self-worth. Individuals with poor self-esteem may experience some of the following self-attacks in relation to perceived threats from a sexual rival:

> *You're not a real man (woman)!*
> *You're unlovable. No one could love you!*
> *You're so ugly; men (women) are repulsed by you.*
> *You can't compete with him (her). You'll lose for sure.*
> *You're so boring and uninteresting.*
> *What makes you think you can attract him (her)?*
> *He (She) is more sexy, more attractive, more interesting than you.*
> *You better hang on to him (her). You'll never have another relationship.*

Voices That Evoke Feelings of Shame and Humiliation

One of the more painful aspects of jealousy involves the feelings of humiliation and shame that sexual infidelity evokes in the "betrayed" party. These feelings may be traced to early childhood experiences of humiliation.[5] Many people develop a compensatory image of exaggerated self-importance to ward off these painful feelings. This adaptation leaves them especially vulnerable in rivalrous situations. Their shame and humiliation are intensified in relation to others finding out about their partner's affair. They may experience negative thoughts such as the following:

> *Now everyone knows that no one wants you.*
> *You're a shameful, pitiful person.*
> *Your friends think you're a pathetic loser.*
> *People have lost all respect for you.*
> *Now everyone will know that you can't satisfy a man (woman) sexually.*

Voice Attacks Triggered by Potential Loss or by Winning Over a Sexual Rival

The anticipation of potentially losing a partner to a rival can trigger self-destructive voices, feelings of intense anxiety, and antagonism toward oneself and one's partner. Often the mere thought of losing to a potential competitor evokes powerful voice attacks.

You'd better watch out! You're going to lose him (her).
What is he (she) doing! Where is he (she) going? You'd better find out.
What if he (she) meets someone else there?
You can't compete with that man/woman.
You won't be able to stand it!
You won't ever be able to meet anyone else.
Your life will be over.

It is important to note that fears of losing to a rival do not preclude fears of winning. Men and women fear both potential outcomes, that of being rejected and, paradoxically, that of being preferred. Winning may arouse an anticipation of attack from competitors or may arouse guilt feelings because the fact of winning causes real or symbolic pain or hurt to one's rival:

Look at all the heartache you caused!
You ruined their marriage! How can you live with yourself?
Her husband (His wife) is going to get even, just wait and see.
You don't deserve to be happy. How can you be happy now in
    your new relationship, knowing that you destroyed someone
    else's happiness?
One of these days you're going to get yours! He (She) will dump you
    for somebody else.

Both situations may precipitate intense voice attacks, causing people to retreat from actively pursuing relationships and eventually to progressively give up their individuality and sense of identity (Firestone, 1990a). As noted earlier, these self-destructive thoughts are internal representations of parental aggression that was directed toward them in rivalrous situations. Later, as adults, when they find themselves in competitive situations, their self-attacks tend to surface causing them to retreat or withdraw from competition.

Voices Promoting a Victimized Orientation

In a rivalrous situation, people who fear their anger and are unable to acknowledge their aggression often descend into feelings of being victimized or treated unjustly. Victimized feelings are an appropriate response for the child who actually does lack power, but for the adult focusing on these feelings is maladaptive.

People who have a victimized orientation toward life tend to be self-righteous and believe that they are entitled to good treatment from others. They issue judgments and evaluations of others, insist on authoritarian methods of punishment for those who make mistakes, and disclaim any personal responsibility for events not going right (Firestone & Catlett, 1989). In competitive situations, they focus on the unfairness of the situation and the injustices perpetuated on them and feel morally justified in their dramatic reactions to imagined or actual acts of infidelity on the part of a partner. The negative thoughts they experience may take the following form:

How could he (she) do this to you?
Doesn't he (she) care about how much you love him (her)?
You don't deserve to be treated like this!
After all you've done for him (her), this is what you get in return!
He (She) said that he (she) loved you! He (She) lied!
This isn't fair!
This always happens to you!
Men (Women) are no damn good!

It is detrimental to one's mental health to perceive oneself as a helpless victim of circumstances, even when faced with the infidelity of a partner. Rather than focusing on the injustice of the other's infidelity and what should or should not be happening, it is more adaptive to deal with the reality of the painful situation, feel the appropriate anger or sadness, and decide what constructive action one wishes to take in one's self-interest.

Voices Instigating Interpersonal Hostility or Violence in Response to Perceived Infidelity

Sexual jealousy is one of the major factors associated with interpersonal violence. Although angry feelings are often directed toward one's rival, in many cases the betrayed lover's anger is translated into aggressive behaviors directed toward the unfaithful spouse. Daly and Wilson (1988) asserted that "Sexual jealousy and rivalry have been prominent in virtually every study of homicide motives" (p. 186). According to Person (1988),

If the lover has been rejected in favor of another, he may be consumed by a jealous frenzy, tortured by the image of his lover and the rival together, causing him to focus his rage primarily on the rival. By venting all rage at the rival, the lover exonerates the beloved. Part of the mechanism involved here is Oedipal: The rival parent is deemed the villain. This allows rage to be discharged while preserving the goodness of the beloved. (p. 304)

The factors that determine a violent outcome for jealousy include an individual's personality characteristics, attachment history, belief system, and societal influences.[6] For example, attachment researchers have compared the tendencies toward violent behaviors in men who have secure versus insecure attachment styles. Findings from one comprehensive study (Holtzworth-Munroe et al., 1997) showed that "violent husbands are more likely to be classified as having preoccupied, ambivalent-anxious and disorganized attachment strategies and as being more jealous and less trusting" (p. 327) than nonviolent husbands. In one of the few studies of jealousy and female aggression, deWeerth and Kalma (1993) found that males reported that they would most likely get drunk, demand an explanation, or feign indifference in a hypothetical competitive situation, whereas females reported that they would most likely cry, verbally and physically abuse their mates, or try to look attractive and unruffled. In competitive situations, these individuals may experience the following hostile thoughts toward themselves and their partner.

> *How could she (he) do that to you? You'd better put her (him) in her (his) place!*
>
> *You should get even with that bitch(bastard). She (He) thought she (he) could get away with it. Maybe next time she'll (he'll) think twice before she (he) fools around.*
>
> *You can never trust a woman (man).*
>
> *Everybody knows he (she) cheated on you, and they're not telling you. Just look at what he (she) did to you!*
>
> *He (She) deserves everything he's (she's) going to get from you!.*
>
> *You idiot! You were faithful to him (her). Now look at what he's (she's) done to you.*
>
> *You're a fool! You trusted him (her) and he (she) doesn't care about you at all.*
>
> *Why don't you just fix things once and for all?*

These self-destructive thoughts and aggressive attitudes toward an intimate partner or rival are often exacerbated by other factors, including anxieties about abandonment, panic related to the potential loss of the partner, and narcissistic rage resulting from public exposure with the associated shame and humiliation.

THE RELATIONSHIP BETWEEN SEXUAL WITHHOLDING AND JEALOUSY

Fear of being close to another person in an intimate relationship predisposes provocative negative behaviors and withholding of one's positive qualities to ward off closeness. Sexual withholding in particular heightens feelings of possessiveness as well as jealousy. It leads to self-critical thoughts and cynical, distrustful attitudes toward one's partner. When men and women unconsciously inhibit their sexual desires or hold back sexual responses, they come to feel that they are at a disadvantage as competitors. Their sense of being unable to compete causes them to focus on their rival's advantages and they feel victimized and cheated. Sexual withholding exacerbates people's feelings of envy and jealousy. In pulling back from a competitive situation, they imagine their rivals as more attractive, powerful, better than they are. Individuals who are sexually withholding tend to experience vicious self-attacks, such as

> *Just look at him (her)! He's (She's) much more sexy, good-looking, interesting, and lively than you.*
> *You're not interested in sex much anymore. No wonder he (she) enjoys being with someone else.*
> *You don't stand a chance. You'd just as well give up.*

In general, people who are self-denying and withholding are inclined toward morbid, jealous brooding over imagined losses instead of actively competing (Firestone & Catlett, 1999). When these emotions are examined, it often becomes evident that the jealousy merely disguised the fact that it was the person's withholding that prevented him or her from succeeding in a romantic relationship, not the presence of a rival or competitor. In this sense, the person arranged for his or her own disappointment and defeat.

DECEPTION AND JEALOUSY

Deception may be the most damaging aspect of infidelity. Deception and lies shatter the reality of others, eroding their belief in the veracity of their perceptions and subjective experience (Bader & Pearson, 2000). The betrayal of trust brought about by a partner's secret involvement with another person leads to a shocking and painful realization on the part of the deceived party that the person he or she has been involved with has a secret life and that there is an aspect of his or her partner that he or she had no knowledge of.

Many men and women who originally commit to a monogamous relationship later violate the agreement. In these cases, the violation of trust can have a more damaging effect on the relationship than the "sexual infidelity" itself (Glass & Wright, 1997). In her book, *Not "Just Friends,"* Glass (2003) emphasized the point that lies, dishonesty, and deception in personal relationships invariably destroy the trust between partners. She asserted that

> relationships are contingent on honesty and openness. They are built and maintained through our faith that we can believe what we are being told. However painful it is for a betrayed spouse to discover a trail of sexual encounters or emotional attachments, the lying and deception are the most appalling violations. (p. 60)

In light of the damage to a person's feelings and sense of reality caused by lies and deception, honesty in personal relationships becomes a moral imperative. Therefore it is essential for partners who claim to love and respect one another to agree to maintain an open and honest dialogue about their feelings and behaviors in relation to sexual fidelity.

CULTURAL INFLUENCES ON JEALOUSY

Social scientists have proposed that the ways in which jealousy is experienced are determined largely by cultural forces operating within a given society (Daly & Wilson, 1983; Davis, 1977). Buunk and Hupka (1987) have suggested that "cultures differ in the behaviors that are viewed as a violation of the exclusivity of intimate relationships" (p. 21). According to Barash and Lipton (2001), "about 75 percent of societies permit male infidelity, whereas only about 10 percent permit female infidelity—and even in these cases, it is not guaranteed that males will actually be tolerant of such behavior" (p. 159).

In an essay entitled, "Jealousy and Sexual Property," Davis (1977) declared that, "A popular fallacy has been to conceive the jealousy situation as a 'triangle.' Actually it is a quadrangle because the public, or community, is always an interested element in the situation" (p. 129). Indeed, as noted in chapter 3, the pooled beliefs and defenses of each member of a society combine to form social mores, societal institutions, and community standards. In turn, conventional attitudes regarding the exclusivity of marriage and sanctions regulating the proprietary rights of one partner over the other tend to exacerbate the "normal" feelings of jealousy that individuals usually experience in a competitive setting.

In writing about manifestations of jealousy observed in diverse societies, Sluzki (1989) stressed the fact that

> Both the linguistic practice we call jealousy as well as its subjective experience are culture bound. Some cultures lend themselves better than others to creating a narrative of jealousy, contingent upon whether they value individual or collective rights, favor proprietary or non-proprietary relationships, or emphasize the differences in rights and privileges attached to gender. (p. 54)

Sluzki concluded that within couples living in a society that focuses on

> Proprietary rights, mistrust, and belief that the other is violating mutual agreements about intimacy . . . even denial or argument [about infidelity] implies consensual behavior patterns of jealousy. There is no escape from this closed circle, except perhaps, through an escalation severe enough to destroy the relationship. (p. 54)

In a relationship such as the one portrayed by Sluzki, each partner experiences powerful feelings of jealousy whenever there is a breach or even an imagined breach in the couple's mutually agreed-on contract about sexual fidelity. As Sluzki stressed, a society that affirms proprietary rights of one person over another and that supports the exclusivity of the dyad or marriage contributes to both partners' feelings of possessiveness and distrust. This type of social order reinforces anticipatory fears of being betrayed or rejected in favor of the rival and supports destructive self-attacks, cynicism toward loved ones, victimized feelings of rage, and justifications for retaliating against a rival. For individuals living in this type of social order, these disturbing thoughts and feelings add a negative loading to feelings that might well be considered as natural competitiveness by individuals living in a different social order. In commenting on the meaning assigned to extramarital sex throughout most industrialized and primitive societies, Gilmartin (1977) argued that "As long as jealousy is justified by our cultural norms, as long as the 'wronged party' is seen as a 'cuckold,' as long as individuals are excused for 'crimes of passion,' we may expect jealousy to pervade our interpersonal relations" (p. 158).

However, there have been a few exceptions to this seemingly universal prohibition against "infidelity." For example, according to Mazur (1973/2000), a small Quaker group in England published an essay (*Toward a Quaker View of Sex*) in 1964 in which they proposed that extramarital relationships might be a constructive force in the lives of some men and women:

> "We recognize," the group maintains, "that while most examples of the 'eternal triangle' are produced by boredom and primitive misconduct, others may arise from the fact that the very experience of loving one person with depth and perception may sensitize a man or a woman to the lovable qualities in others. . . . The man who swallows the words, 'I love you,' when he meets another woman, may in that moment and for that reason begin to resent his wife's existence." (cited in Mazur, 1973/2000, p. 5)

Adding his comments to the Quakers' declaration, Mazur wrote, "We assume also that the wife has the capacity to resent her husband's existence when she is constrained from acknowledging or confessing love for another man" (p. 5).

OUR POINT OF VIEW IN RELATION TO EXCLUSIVE VERSUS NONEXCLUSIVE RELATIONSHIPS

In Western societies, monogamous relationships are seen as providing more security, certainty, and a greater possibility for long-lasting love than nonexclusive relationships. In their style of coupling, many men and women take a proprietary interest in each other's activities and are overly possessive and controlling in their efforts to compensate for feelings of inadequacy and fears of competition. They subscribe to the conventional belief that married couples or people who are committed to a long-term relationship essentially belong to each other. As children, they were taught that they "belonged" to their families, and as adults they lack a sense of belonging to themselves. In failing to view themselves or their mates as autonomous human beings, they make themselves vulnerable to manipulations that play on their guilt and sense of obligation.

People who have formed a fantasy bond are often unaware that by limiting their partner's freedom, they are essentially limiting or entrapping themselves. When one's partner is not free to pursue other relationships, one never knows for certain if one has really been chosen or is really preferred. There is always the possibility that if one were not imposing restrictions on a partner's freedom, one would lose out in an openly competitive situation.

In previous works, we have given this question of open versus closed relationships considerable attention (Firestone & Catlett, 1999; Firestone et al., 2003). In general, we feel that it is unwise for people to place restrictions on each other in an intimate relationship, because eventually one or both partners may come to resent such limitations. At the same time, we have observed that most people are unable to cope with a partner's sexual freedom without suffering considerable distress As Buss (2000) noted in his study of jealousy, "Few marriages can endure third-party intruders" (p. 221).

Many couples struggle with the dilemma of whether to have an exclusive or nonexclusive sexual relationship. The issue is complicated, although not necessarily in the early stages of a relationship, when a person initially falls in love and tends to be focused exclusively on the other. As the relationship matures, some partners begin to question what type of arrangement they wish to have during the long term—open or monogamous. In trying to resolve this dilemma, it is beneficial for partners to fully discuss their attitudes, thoughts, beliefs, and feelings about the type of commitment they wish to make to each other. A primary goal of these communications would be to come to an agreement that would respect each other's feelings and desires. This agreement should not be violated or, at least, the partners should enter into new negotiations with each other before making any changes in the conditions.

One potential negative effect of pledging fidelity is that a person can come to feel that he or she has assigned his or her sexuality to another. As this person loses a sense of owning his or her sexuality, he or she often experiences a decrease in sexual desire and a declination in the quality of his or her sexual relationship. In addition, in many marriages, partners begin to take each other for granted and stop seeing each other as separate individuals, whereas in an affair, the lovers usually see each other as two separate people. They tend to have a more equalitarian relationship, that is, they relate to each other as equal participants with equal value and responsibilities. For example, Glass (2003) has observed that "Unfaithful spouses perceived more equity in their affairs than in their marriages. Understanding was considered to be equal in 47 percent of marriages and in 70 percent of affairs" (p. 226). However, when an affair replaces the marriage or the primary relationship, these patterns—for example, feeling obligated, taking each other for granted—gradually come to be manifested in the new relationship as well.

Within a society where serial monogamy is practically the norm, people often feel little motivation to develop themselves personally or to "work" on their relationship. They seem less interested in changing behaviors in themselves that are hurtful to the other person or that are causing distress in the relationship. Instead, they often blame their partner for their unhappiness and move on to an ostensibly "better choice," only to repeat the pattern with their new partner.

In addition, many people have an unconscious belief that love is available only in limited quantities, that it is impossible to love more than one person at a time, and that one can find everything one needs in one relationship. They tend to live by these beliefs rather than to subject them to scrutiny or reality-testing. In terms of honesty, it is psychologically impossible for people to commit their feelings of love or sexual attraction to a certain person for a lifetime, whereas individuals are perfectly capable of controlling their actions in this regard. There is a basic dishonesty involved when one attempts to block out or deny feelings of love or attraction for a person other than one's mate.

We have observed that as people achieve more emotional maturity in their relationships, they tend to evolve to higher levels of self-differentiation, which in turn enables them to better cope with primal elements inherent in jealous reactions and to handle competitive situations more constructively. Often there is a concomitant maturation in people's views of conventional marital arrangements, and they may choose to be more inclusive in relating, both emotionally and sexually, to other people outside the relationship or marriage. They come to recognize the impossibility and impracticality of gratifying all of their wants and needs in a relationship with one person. This evolved attitude toward love and marriage has been described by Person (1988) in her book *Dreams of Love and Fateful Encounters:*

> We must learn both to acknowledge the centrality of romantic love to our lives, and to maintain other relationships, other avenues to meaning.

For, perhaps most important of all for the survival of love, we must not ask it to bear the weight of all meaning. (p. 321)

As Kernberg (1995) wrote in *Love Relations,*

I think there is an irreducible conflict between conventional morality and the private morality that each couple has to construct as part of its total sexual life and that always implies a nonconventional degree of freedom the couple has to achieve for itself. The delicate balance of sexual freedom, emotional depth, and a value system reflecting mature superego functioning is a complex human achievement that provides the basis for a relation that is deep, passionate, conflicted, and satisfying and potentially lasting. (pp. 187–188)

In his book, *The New Intimacy,* Mazur (1973/2000) described a woman, a 30-year-old librarian, who had a nonexclusive relationship with her husband. In her interview, she spoke about her sense of accomplishment as well as about her doubts and fears:

I didn't plan on having an open-ended marriage. It simply began to develop that way when I discovered that my husband loves other women besides me; that he's not monogamous in a traditional way. This realization freed me from the obscenity of possessiveness. Some of my extramarital relationships have been fruitful to me. . . . I do wonder about the future—there's a measure of risk and uncertainty in the way we've now chosen, but I'm learning not to be afraid to be a person, a woman with worthwhile contributions to make to human society. As a matter of fact, there is a continual excitement about our marital relationship and mutual growing—anything else would be emotional death for us. (p. 10)

In *Eleven Minutes,* Paulo Coelho (2004) declared: "I am convinced that no one loses anyone, because no one owns anyone. That is the true experience of freedom: having the most important thing in the world without owning it" (p. 90).[7]

Our views regarding sexual freedom are similar to those expressed by the woman that Mazur interviewed, as well as the sentiments articulated by Person, Kernberg, and Coelho. We feel that the best situation for individuals in a couple relationship is to sustain each partner's freedom of choice and not limit the other by imposing unnecessary rules and restrictions. When partners agree to respect and support each other's freedom, it extends to every aspect of their lives and would logically apply to their sexual freedom. It is our point of view that attitudes of possessiveness and ownership of another human being, whether friend, mate, or child, combined with actions of manipulation and control, constitute a form of human rights violation. Intimate relationships tend to be the most meaningful and satisfying when they are not based on imposing limitation and restrictions on one another.

However, we recognize that many people find it difficult to develop the trust necessary to have an emotionally close relationship without a guarantee of monogamy. For example, Rob and Cathy had lived together for several years, and although they did not date other people, each believed in sexual freedom as an ideal. Yet when they faced the issue in reality, it turned out to be more difficult to live up to than either of them realized.

When Rob communicated that he was interested in another woman, Cathy became extremely upset. She experienced intense anxiety and emotional distress and found herself ruminating about and visualizing Rob becoming sexually involved with this other woman. In the weeks that followed, she withdrew from Rob and lost interest in being sexual with him. Sensitive to Cathy's struggle and the impact this was having on his relationship with her, Rob reassured her that their relationship was far more important to him than his sexual freedom. The couple talked at length about how much they valued each other and about the type of relationship they really wanted to have. Both agreed to be monogamous. After the conversation, Cathy felt relieved and was appreciative to Rob for taking her feelings seriously. The couple's relationship improved significantly, and both partners felt an increased emotional intimacy.

When personal contracts concerning exclusive relationships, such as the one described in the example above, are agreed on, it is essential to honor that commitment; otherwise, the deception often takes a tragic toll on the relationship. Thus, although giving up any personal freedom, by definition, constitutes a restriction, in some cases this sacrifice may be worth the price. If people are aware that having another sexual relationship would be excessively painful for their mate, they might want to remain monogamous out of consideration for the other's feelings.

CONCLUSION

Individuals' jealous responses, whether to sexual or emotional infidelities, are wide-ranging and vary according to their childhood experiences, the degree to which they have formed a fantasy bond with their partner, and the culture in which they live. Jealousy has been conceptualized by many theorists and researchers as a powerful emotion that can have both negative and positive consequences. Jealousy has been portrayed as the "dangerous passion," as a triggering mechanism for domestic violence, as a defense to safeguard love and help partners not take each other for granted, and as the predictable outcome of the oedipal triangle of early life, among many others. In elucidating the defensive function that jealousy has served throughout the ages, Buss (2000) argued that

> It's unlikely that love, with the tremendous psychological investment it entails, could have evolved without a defense that shielded it from the constant threat from rivals and the possibility of betrayal from a partner. Jealousy evolved to fill that void, motivating vigilance as the first line of defense and violence as the last. (p. 223)

Progress can be made in overcoming those aspects of jealousy that are damaging to couple relationships. In conceptualizing intense or chronic jealousy as a defense, we suggest challenging destructive thought processes that govern self-defeating, self-destructive behavioral responses in competitive settings. We encourage an exploration of residual feelings from childhood that are evoked in competitive settings as well as an identification of the self-attacks and hostile attitudes toward a rival that magnify natural feelings of jealousy, competitiveness, and envy.

In giving up illusions of connection, individuals would necessarily relinquish their sense of ownership over their respective partners. In becoming less withholding or self-denying in pursuing their love interests, they would find the intensity of their jealous reactions diminished to a considerable extent. By challenging the patriarchal assumption that women are the property of men, they might find the incidence of domestic violence significantly reduced. In disputing the false conventional assumption that love is constant and invariant, they would understand the ebb and flow of loving feelings that naturally occur in relationships and would feel less threatened by indications of a partner's interest in another person.

Being aware of and challenging any discrepancy between words and actions when communicating about these issues enables partners to build a sense of trust in each other. In attempting to establish and preserve trust in each other, partners need to learn how to communicate their desires and wishes more directly. They need to understand how important it is not to give double messages, particularly regarding competitive situations that inevitably arise during the course of a relationship.

Our goal in working with couples is to inspire the development of more mature forms of love that allow for ambiguity and uncertainty, and to help individuals remain open and vulnerable to all of inevitable vicissitudes of love. Mature love involves an appreciation and respect for the uniqueness of the other person. It goes beyond having an interest in the other person only as he or she fulfills one's own wants and needs. It entails seeing the other person as a separate individual with rights to an independent and free existence.

Ideally, society would encourage the development of intimate couple relationships where each partner would allow the other to live and flourish.

The goal would not be to reject or depreciate marriage as an institution, but to develop constructive long-term associations that would meet the needs of each individual and support his or her personal development.

NOTES

1. Sometimes partners are competitive with each other in the absence of sexual rivals. For example, Mazur (1973/2000) described this form of competitiveness within the couple: "Negative forms of competition stem from a lack of self-confidence or self-esteem leading to jealousy of the partner's achievements, attractiveness, friends, or sexual performance" (p. 107).

2. The terms "jealousy" and "envy" are sometimes confused in terms of describing the ways in which the two emotions are experienced and the behaviors they inspire. According to Friday (1985), jealousy is an emotional state based on a fear of losing what one already has, whereas envy is based on a condition of not having. One reason for the confusion is because, as Pines (1998) put it,

   > The jealous response includes, in many cases, a component of envy. A man who is jealous because his wife is having an affair with his best friend, for example, is likely to feel envious of his friend's success with his wife. (p. 9)

3. Regarding other approaches to jealousy, social psychologists DeSteno and Salovey (1996) proposed that the intensity of jealous feelings experienced by an individual is related to efforts to maintain positive self-esteem, a perspective that is based on self-evaluation maintenance (SEM) theory. Therefore, according to the SEM approach, the characteristics and attributes of one's rival "may be one variable that moderates the intensity of experienced jealousy" (p. 921). Also see Mathes (1991) who applied Lazarus's cognitive–phenomenological theory of emotions in his research on jealousy.

4. More recent studies (Becker, Sagarin, Guadagno, Millevoi, & Nicastle, 2004) found that the degree of commitment to the relationship tended to confound these gender differences between reactions to sexual infidelity and emotional infidelity. When emotions other than jealousy were considered, "Both women and men reported more anger and disgust to the sexual aspect of the infidelity. And both sexes reported more hurt to the emotional aspect of the infidelity" (p. 537).

5. Individuals whose voice attacks tended to arouse feelings of shame endorsed many items on the English version of the Swedish EMBU (Swedish acronym for *Egna Minnen Betraffande Uppfostran*, "Our Memories of Parental Rearing Experiences in Childhood") inventory (Perris, Jacobsson, Lindstrom, van Knorring, & Perris, 1980) that assesses, among other parental behaviors, those that generate shame and guilt in children.

6. In developing a scale to assess violence potential, the Firestone Assessment of Violent Thoughts (FAVT), we were able to identify four factors associated with criminal violence in our preliminary study: Factor 1, Social Mistrust—

Stereotypic Characteristics; Factor 2, Thoughts of Being Disregarded/ Disrespected by Others; Factor 3, Negative Critical Thoughts about Self and Others; and Factor 4, Thoughts/Expressions of Overt Aggression. In applying this model to domestic or interpersonal violence, we hypothesized that specific thoughts are triggered by infidelity and provide rationalizations for taking violent action against a spouse.

7. Quotation from *Eleven Minutes* by Paulo Coelho. Copyright © 2004 Paulo Coelho. Reprinted by permission of HarperCollins Publishers Inc.

IV

THERAPEUTIC APPROACHES TO PROBLEMS IN SEXUAL RELATING

9

VOICE THERAPY APPLIED TO PROBLEMS IN SEXUAL RELATING

[In sex therapy] much therapy time is spent in attempts to change negative attitudes toward sexuality. These attitudes are usually the result of societal or parental injunctions against sexuality, which are internalized during childhood and adolescence. Although the patient often has intellectually rejected these prohibitions, their emotional components are not so easily changed.

—LoPiccolo (1978, pp. 513–514)

Voice therapy is a cognitive–affective–behavioral methodology. It is cognitive because it helps clients access and identify destructive thoughts and attitudes toward themselves as well as hostile and cynical attitudes toward others. It is affective because it brings these thoughts into consciousness together with the associated feelings of anger and sadness. It is behavioral because there is a focus on modifying behaviors based on the voice that predispose alienation in personal relationships.

This chapter explains the methodology used to elicit and identify the self-critical thought process or voice. We have found that the techniques of voice therapy are effective for gaining access to people's core defenses and for facilitating changes in their maladaptive behaviors. Voice therapy helps individuals achieve insight into the origins of their distress and assists them in gradually altering behaviors in the direction of their stated goals. The overall purpose of the therapeutic approach is to identify and separate out those elements in the personality that are opposed to the self and that predispose hostility toward others (Firestone, 1997a).

When using voice therapy techniques as a treatment approach for sexual problems, we suggest that clinicians develop a case conceptualization regarding factors that affect the overall functioning of the client, taking into consideration the relevant biomedical, environmental, social, and cultural components. In all cases, the focus of therapy should be directed toward (a) helping clients identify their therapeutic goals and (b) helping facilitate their movement toward achieving these goals. As always, the therapist must approach the therapeutic relationship from a position free of bias and value judgments. In working with members of sexual minorities, the American Psychological Association *Guidelines for Psychotherapy With Lesbian, Gay, and Bisexual Clients* (American Psychological Association, 2000) provide a valuable resource. The guidelines recommend that clinicians familiarize themselves with the various ways that social prejudice "may affect the client's presentation in treatment and the therapeutic process" (p. 1). They also encourage clinicians to explore the ways that their attitudes toward sexual minorities might impact their work with these clients, and to "seek consultation or make appropriate referrals when indicated" (p. 4).[1]

In this chapter, we first describe how voice therapy is used as a psychotherapeutic technique to help clients overcome problems in their intimate relationships and improve the quality of their sexual relating. Next, we delineate the five steps involved in the application of the technique to problems with sexual desire and for other sexual dysfunctions in the context of couples therapy. We provide two case studies to illustrate the steps and discuss the impact of voice therapy. Lastly, we review methods that a number of sex and marital therapists have developed that are congenial with our approach.

As noted in chapter 3, there are a number of biological, psychological, and social factors that interact to interfere with an individual's ability to achieve emotional and sexual fulfillment in a close, personal association. In Western society, the extent of dissatisfaction experienced by people in their sexual relationships is noteworthy. For example, in a survey of more than 7,000 couples, 53% of the men and 59% of the women interviewed said they were not physically satisfied in their sexual relationship, while 59% of the men and 63% of the women said they were not emotionally satisfied (Laumann et al., 1994). A major barrier to a healthy or satisfying sexual relationship can be found in the psychological defenses and negative thought processes that the partners bring to the relationship and that support distorted views of sexuality.

VOICES THAT DISRUPT SEXUAL RELATIONS

The goal of voice therapy with couples is to help each partner access and identify the destructive thoughts that interrupt the smooth progression of feelings that naturally occur during a fulfilling sexual experience. The intrusion of these negative thoughts and attitudes can lead to a number of sexual symptoms. When clients learn to talk openly about their relationships and disclose specific voice attacks that they experience regarding sex, there are often significant positive changes in their sexual relations.

Voice therapy procedures have been used to identify a wide range of self-attacks in individuals who reported a variety of difficulties in achieving sexually fulfilling relationships. The presence of negative thoughts during sex has an adverse effect on people's physiological responses and, at times, on their ability to complete the sex act. For example, one man revealed that as soon as he begins making love, he often finds himself thinking, *You're not going to be able to keep your erection.* At that point, he usually does have difficulty and his nervousness increases with each subsequent failure. A woman reported thinking to herself, *You're not going to be able to have an orgasm,* and she experienced considerable tension and a corresponding diminution in feelings of excitement. The process of anticipating a negative sexual experience takes lovemaking out of the realm of affectionate and pleasurable feelings and transforms it into an anxiety-provoking activity in which men and women continually evaluate their performance.

Voices Prior to Sex

Voice attacks occur not only during sexual intercourse, but they can also be triggered far in advance of a sexual experience, as noted in chapter 7. Self-attacks are activated in relation to men's and women's basic feelings about themselves, their sexual identity, and their ability to both give and receive sexual gratification and pleasure. Self-protective thoughts warning against becoming involved with another person, both sexually and emotionally, are among the most common voices reported. Other negative, anticipatory thoughts emphasize the "dangers" of being hurt or taken advantage of in sexual situations.

Both men and women often have cynical thoughts that stifle their excitement upon first meeting a potential sexual partner, such as

> *Why should he like you?*
> *Why would she want to go out with you?*
> *He has no real interest in you. Why get so excited?*
> *He is just interested in what he can get.*
> *She's going to pressure you for some kind of a commitment.*

Today, with the threat of AIDS and other STDs, many people have voices discouraging them from pursuing sexual relationships at all: *This whole safe sex thing is such a hassle. Why even bother to get involved?*

People often feel anxious and experience voice attacks when a relationship transitions from a flirtation to a fully sexual relationship:

What makes you think she's interested in more?
Why do you think he wants to be with you?
How do you know you're reading the signals right?

Voices During Sex

Individuals often experience intrusive thoughts during sex that can detract from their feeling of excitement.

Negative Thoughts About One's Body

Self-depreciating thoughts about one's physical appearance and body, especially the sexual areas, can interrupt the progression of sexual feelings. Many men and women have negative views about nudity and critical feelings about their bodies that cause them considerable embarrassment in sexual situations.

Many women have self-conscious thoughts about their breasts:

Your breasts are small, they're not like other women's, and so forth.

Or about the genital area:

Your vagina is too large, or *You're too tight.*
Don't let him touch you there! You might not be clean.
Don't have oral sex, he'll be repulsed.

Similarly, many men feel inadequate in relation to the size of their penis:

Your penis is too small.
You won't be able to satisfy her.
You're not going to last.
You're not like other men.

Negative Evaluations of One's Sexual Performance

Feelings of affection and attraction that lead to a couple's mutual desire to express their feelings sexually are easily dispelled by negative thoughts about their sexual performance. Often, when the transition has been made from an affectionate embrace to a sexual caress, people's voices gain in ascendancy and can ultimately obliterate sexual desire. Both men and women have a tendency to find fault with every aspect of their lovemaking, including their level of excitement:

You're not excited enough.
You're not wet enough.
You're not erect enough.
You're not going to be able to come.

They criticize their movements:

You're moving too much.
He'll think you're a slut.
You're hurting her.
You're entering her too soon.
She's not ready.

They doubt their ability to please their partner:

You're not touching her right.
You're not sensitive about what he (she) likes.

Critical Voices About One's Partner

People often anticipate rejection based not only on their self-critical thoughts, but also on hostile, critical views they have of their partner. In voice therapy sessions, clients often verbalize negative attitudes toward their partner, such as

She's too needy.
He just doesn't understand you.
She's not reliable.
You can't trust him.

Voice attacks against one's partner often include many of the sexist attitudes and stereotypes described in chapter 4. Many women have negative attitudes toward men: *All men want is sex. They don't want commitment or marriage. They are afraid of getting emotionally involved.* Similarly, many men hold cynical attitudes toward women that act to cut off their feelings of sexual attraction and emotional closeness during sex: *Women are unreliable, jealous, erratic, and overemotional. They'll trap you into marriage.*

Negative Thoughts Following Sex

Many people have negative thoughts after a sexual experience. Some people even appear to change character immediately afterward, for example, becoming cool and aloof or argumentative. When a sexual experience has been particularly gratifying and emotionally meaningful, self-protective voices predicting negative outcomes may come into play. These thoughts are degrading to both partners and tend to devalue the sexual act. People have reported thoughts such as

What did you really get from this?
You think you felt really good. So what? He doesn't really care
about you.
You always give in—you have no dignity.
She didn't look happy afterward.
How do you know she had an orgasm?
You'd better make sure she's happy. That's your responsibility.

APPLICATION OF VOICE THERAPY PROCEDURES
TO COUPLES THERAPY

Voice therapy involves an individual verbalizing his or her self-critical thoughts in the second-person format, that is, in the form of statements *toward* him- or herself. For example, "You're unattractive. You're unlovable," rather than "I'm unattractive. I'm unlovable." When asked to verbalize their negative thoughts in the second person, people often spontaneously begin to speak louder and with more intensity of feeling. With this release of emotions, valuable material that the client was previously unaware of comes to the surface.

Hostile, cynical thoughts toward one's partner are verbalized in the third-person format, as though someone else were imparting negative information to the individual about his or her partner. For example, "*She's so cold and rejecting. She doesn't really care about you.*" "*He's so immature and clingy. Why would you want to get involved with him?*" rather than "*She's really cold and rejecting toward me,*" or "*I wouldn't want to get seriously involved with him because he's so immature.*"

The therapist who wants to deepen the level of emotion that the client is experiencing while verbalizing voice attacks encourages the client to "say it louder" or "say it how you're hearing it in your head." If the therapist observes that the client is holding back feeling or is on the brink of feeling, he or she may encourage the client to "really feel that," or "let go and say anything that comes to mind."

In the context of couples therapy, in sessions where both partners are present, each reveals the negative thoughts and attitudes toward him- or herself and the other. Clients are encouraged to understand that their voices are the cause of their overreactions, dramatic hostile thoughts, and grudges, even when these critical views have some basis in reality. When verbalizing hostile attitudes toward the other, partners often express the critical accusations their voices are making about traits and behaviors in the other person. During this process, they often become aware that their voice has taken on a sarcastic, snide tone and that these attacks are exaggerating their partner's characteristics. Disclosing their angry, judgmental views in the form of the voice helps people separate these views from a more realistic view of their mate.

In tracing the source of their self-attacks and hostile attitudes to early family interactions, the partners gain perspective into each other's problems and feel more compassion for their mates as well as for themselves. In this sense, they are sharing each other's individual psychotherapy. Recognizing that the effect of voice attacks is to create distance and alienation within the relationship has a powerful effect on improving partners' attitudes toward each other as well as on enhancing each individual's personal growth. Each partner learns to accommodate to the anxiety associated with breaking inward, self-protective defenses and is gradually able to tolerate more love and intimacy in his or her life.

Lastly, it is important to emphasize that voice therapy techniques are not used as a rigid system of psychotherapy but are applied as necessary to the specific client or couple. In using these techniques, people can begin to counteract the dictates of the voice and achieve greater emotional and sexual fulfillment in their closest associations.

Steps in the Therapeutic Process

In individual as well as conjoint and couples group sessions, clients generally progress through the following steps during the course of treatment:

1. Each partner formulates the problem that he or she believes is limiting the sexual relationship, while learning not to attribute blame to the other. It is important for therapists to identify any medical condition that could also be contributing to sexual dysfunction in one or both of the partners. They should consult the appropriate medical experts—in urology, gynecology, internal medicine, psychiatry, and pharmacology—to determine whether organic factors or certain medications (e.g., antidepressants, selective serotonin re-uptake inhibitors, anxiety-reducing drugs) are involved in a couple's problem and to refer for treatment physical components that could be contributing to the sexual dysfunction (H. Kaplan, 1995; Kellett, 2000; Phillips, 2000). Moreover, in cases where there is a physical component, clients often feel ashamed or critical of themselves for what they perceive as a disability. In these cases, the therapy needs to address the destructive thoughts and attitudes that clients experience regarding medication or a physical illness.
2. Partners learn to verbalize self-critical thoughts and negative perceptions of the other, in the form of the voice.[2] They release

the deep anger and sadness associated with the verbalization of the voice. It is important for the therapist not only to encourage the expression of these emotions but also to remain silent during any pause in the client's verbalizations. Following these pauses, deeper material in the form of core negative beliefs about self as well as intense feelings of rage and grief often emerge.

Each partner strives to "give away" the specific content of his or her cynical thoughts and beliefs toward the other. Both attempt to relinquish these hypercritical views and give up their grudges even when these views have some basis in reality. Partners are rarely surprised by their mate's voices about them. Rather than feeling hurt, victimized, angry or defensive, the partner frequently feels relieved because the other person has usually been acting out specific behaviors based on these voices in the couple's interactions.

3. Partners develop insight into the origins of negative cognitions that interrupt their feelings during sex and relate past experiences to present conflicts. In addition, they attempt to understand the relationship between their voice attacks and their self-limiting, self-destructive behavior patterns. The therapist encourages clients to make this connection by asking questions such as "Where do you think these attitudes come from?" or "Where have you heard them before?" Clients develop an awareness of the limitations they impose on themselves in their everyday life and in their relationships. In becoming aware that much of their distress is caused by restrictions they place on themselves, people tend to attribute less blame to their partner.

4. In collaboration with the therapist, clients plan ways to change behaviors and communications in a direction that counteracts the dictates of their voice and that helps them move in the direction of their stated goals. The therapist alerts clients to the possibility that anxiety and increased voice attacks may accompany positive changes in one's behavior or self-image. The new circumstances, including increased feelings of closeness and more fulfilling sex, although more positive, are unfamiliar and may initially cause anxiety as well. Many clients have reported that, although there often were strong voice attacks after taking action based on a corrective suggestion, these self-attacks gradually diminished after the new behavior had been maintained over a period of time.

5. After couples have learned the process of saying their voices in the therapy setting, they are encouraged to reveal their negative thoughts to each other when they occur during the sex act. They can discuss the results in subsequent sessions and deal with the emotions that arise. Steps 4 and 5 will be described in more detail in chapter 10.

The example that follows illustrates the application of the five steps in a session with a couple who had been in therapy for 6 weeks.

CASE EXAMPLE NUMBER ONE

Valerie and Mark had been married two years when they began to experience problems in their sexual relationship. Valerie revealed that she usually had difficulties during foreplay; she would start to worry about having an orgasm or feel distracted by thoughts that had nothing to do with the sexual situation. As a result, her level of arousal would immediately diminish and she would no longer feel excited. Mark disclosed that each time Valerie experienced any difficulty in becoming excited or if she failed to have an orgasm, he would blame himself. Often he had trouble getting an erection or completing the sex act. Afterward, he would feel confused, torn between hating himself and feeling angry and resentful toward Valerie. Believing that his anger was irrational in the situation, he would attempt to suppress it. After this pattern had repeated itself a number of times, he felt hesitant to approach Valerie even when he felt sexually drawn to her because he anticipated a negative experience. As a result, the frequency of the couple's lovemaking had decreased significantly. Both partners were strongly motivated to seek professional help. They hoped to recapture the initial feelings of attraction and passion that they had experienced throughout their courtship and in the early months of their marriage.

1. Formulating the Problem

Mark: When we first got together, it was really great. It was like a fantasy come true for me. And I remember that when we were first married, we had a very, very active sexual relationship. I felt very experimental with you. I felt very active with you. I enjoyed just doing whatever I felt like, and I got a great deal of pleasure out of that. And then as time went on, it seemed like I began to feel less that way, less experimental, less active—sex sort of became more routine—stylized, almost, and it lost a lot of the feeling for me that I had enjoyed so much.

Valerie: That's how it seemed to me, too. I know even recently what's happened is that I've been reluctant to show my excitement or embarrassed to do certain things sexually. And I think what I've done is to slowly stop doing everything. Once I got self-conscious, I think I gradually dulled my excitement down and then I would start wondering if I was going to be able to have an orgasm.

2. Verbalizing the Voice and Releasing the Associated Affect

In the first part of the session, Valerie articulated her voice attacks:

Therapist: What kinds of things make you feel embarrassed? What are you thinking at the time?

Valerie: It's hard to say, but one thing I noticed about myself is that very often before we start to make love I have an affectionate feeling toward you, Mark, but it doesn't last into the sexual situation. If I were really myself at the time, I'd be really affectionate and really sweet and responsive, but these days I rarely am. It's rare.

Therapist: What are you telling yourself at the time? Try to say it in the form of a voice.

Valerie: It's a little hard for me to put a voice to that, but as we start to be sexual it's like, *Don't touch him there. That's disgusting!* [pauses for a few seconds] I'm really embarrassed by what I'm thinking right now.

Therapist: It's okay. Just try to say what you're feeling.

Valerie: I know I feel critical of myself for being excited or making sounds. I start thinking things like, *You're moving too much. You're too excited. You're making too much noise. You're acting like a slut!* It seems like it's an attack on me for simply wanting to be sexual.

Therapist: Try to say that attack. Say it in the tone of voice that you're hearing inside your head.

Valerie: It's confusing. But I know that it makes me more passive. It's really angry.

Therapist: Let the anger out.

Valerie: It's like, *You slut, you dirty disgusting slut. What do you want to do, eat him up? Girls don't do that, girls don't do that, you slut!* [angry tone, then long pause followed by sobbing] [to Mark] Then it doesn't feel equal any more, the affection isn't equal. It's like you're being loving to me and I'm kind of holding back. You know, last night it started out sweet. I started off feeling like myself and feeling affectionate toward you and it made me feel great. It made me feel like I was a nice person. I felt like a sweet person. It's so rare.

Therapist: Do you have any voices about being a sweet person?

Valerie: [cries] It made me sad when you asked that.

Therapist: What are the voices about being sweet?

Valerie: The voice would be something like, *There's nothing sweet about you! Who would see you as sweet? I know who you really are!* [sad]

Therapist: Try to really get into it.

Valerie: [louder, angry] *This isn't you, this isn't you! This isn't how you are. You're not a sweet person.*

3. Developing Insights

Therapist: Does this voice sound familiar to you? Have you heard it before?

Valerie: It sounds just like my mother. That's how she really saw me. Somehow the way she saw me made me feel that if other people saw me as sweet or attractive, it was because I had been manipulative or seductive. Also the way she acted toward my father, so cold, there was no affection toward him. That really stood out to me as a child. I know they didn't make love, they slept in separate beds. So now if I start to feel excited or good sexually, I feel very different from how she was and I start to get anxious. The next thing I know, I'm attacking myself for feeling excited.

Next Mark identified what he considered to be a major problem in the relationship and responded to the voice attacks expressed by Valerie.

1. Formulating the Problem

Mark: When I first came here this morning, I wanted to urge you to talk, Valerie. I thought you should talk about our relationship, because in talking to you last night, I could see that you were sort of panicked. You saw that we were growing distant, especially sexually, and then I was going to be away on a business trip and you blew it up into a really dramatic thing in your head. But after you said your voices just now, I felt differently, I had a lot of feeling for you. And I wanted to try to say what my own thoughts were about our relationship.

There are a number of things I was thinking about along these lines. I'm aware that I've been defended in my relationships with women. With you, in the beginning I felt very open and I wanted to approach our relationship differently than any other relationship I had been in. But at some point, I know I started to have some of the same kinds of feelings that I'd had before. I felt quiet, held back, and sort of self-protective.

Therapist: [to Mark] How have you felt recently, over the past few weeks?

Mark: [to Valerie] I felt you pushing me away, like you said. For example, I came home the other night and you were happy to see me, you were sweet and appealing to me. I felt really good toward you. Then we went into the bedroom and I thought we were going to make love, but you started talking about how you had been feeling at work and I felt very pushed away by the change of your mood. Instead of being angry, I started sort of analyzing you. I know that when I don't admit that I'm angry, I get parental or I try to be helpful.

Therapist: What were you telling yourself in that situation?

2. Verbalizing the Voice and Releasing the Associated Affect

Mark: I don't know exactly, that's why I wanted to explore that here, but it's hard to get any feeling about it. I think the biggest problem that I have in my life is that I'm quiet. I'm kept quiet by my voices in some way. I'm kept under control by these voices.

Therapist: What would those voices be?

Mark: Be quiet. I can't get any emotion behind it. You know that saying about not waking the sleeping giant? I feel like that's what I'm avoiding, crossing that border that will wake that sleeping giant. That gives me a feeling of what those attacks are. I started to have an image of me as a little kid—[pauses]

Therapist: [waits a moment then responds] What kind of image?

Mark: It's sort of like a memory. I'm standing in front of my mother and she's yelling at me, "Look, just stay out of the fucking way. [snide, angry tone] Get out of my way. Don't make any noise. Do not call attention to yourself. Keep quiet!" [pauses for several seconds]

Therapist: [leans forward waiting, then says] Try saying that louder. You don't have to hold anything back.

Mark: It's just like, but there's shaking, you know—[loud voice, gesturing with his hands] "Stop crying. Shut the fuck up. God damn you! Keep quiet. You're bothering me. You bother me, you little shit! Don't make a sound. I don't want to hear a peep out of you. Get the fuck out of my way! [rapid, loud yelling] You little piece of shit. Do not touch anything. Stay still. God damn you! Do not make any sound, do you understand? Keep quiet. Stop crying. *Do you understand?*" [long pause] God, I had no idea that I would say anything like that. [sad]

Therapist: [after a few moments] What voices do you have about your sexual relationship?

Mark: I think I have a lot of voices about being sexual. They distract me sometimes when we're making love. They're like: *You'd better make her feel good. You're not a real man. Can't you see she doesn't want you!*

Therapist: Really get into those voices.

Mark: *Don't bother her. You're a creep. Why would she love you? Why would she want you? You're so pathetic. You're so little and disgusting!* [snide, angry tone of voice] *Of course nobody loves you. Of course, nobody wants you to touch them. Nobody wants that from you!*

It's funny, those voices are related to the first things I said. It all goes back to those old feelings of being pathetic and a bother for wanting anything.

Valerie: I felt so much when you were talking. I felt so sad for you and for the way you were treated and I felt like I love you a lot. I can really see that you're a sweet person, and I felt a lot of pain for you. I felt good to look at you and to love you. I wanted to be sweet to you. I really just wanted to hold you or just kiss your face. That was how I felt.

3. Developing Insight

Mark: I've had a mental block against seeing how I've been in the relationship. I've sort of understood it intellectually, but I haven't been able to see it operating until just now. It's being afraid to confront any of my issues directly and instead seeing you as the only one who has shortcomings, and then trying to help you out of whatever problems you're having. But it's so condescending.

Therapist: So you focus on her problems instead.

Mark: Yeah, if I see problems in you and tend to them, I avoid looking at my own problems and feelings.

Therapist: It's valuable to identify these negative thoughts and the emotions. If both of you challenge the prescriptions of your voices, you will be able to have more in your life. So you have to go against the old defensive patterns and the behaviors that are influenced by the voice. That's the biggest part of the therapy, in a sense, to actually counteract the effects of the voice by taking risks, being more vulnerable to each other, and hanging in there until you can tolerate more closeness. This is the more difficult part and it takes a certain amount of self-discipline to maintain the corrective experience of taking a chance again on loving and being loved.

4. Changing Behaviors to Counteract the Voice

In later sessions, Mark and Valerie, in collaboration with their therapist, formulated plans to change specific behaviors that were based on their respective voices. To counter his voices about being quiet, Mark set a goal for himself to be more direct and forthright in communicating with Valerie. He described his plans for speaking up on his behalf, which involved directly expressing his wants to Valerie and avoiding authoritarian or condescending pronouncements.

In a similar spirit, Valerie made a concerted effort to outwardly express the loving feelings she had for Mark by being more affectionate, tender, and generous in her interactions with him. These actions went against the specific voices telling her that she was not a sweet person, that she was seductive or a "slut." In addition, in order to overcome the voices that inhibited them during the sex act, they decided to reveal any negative or destructive thoughts toward each other.

5. Revealing the Voice During Lovemaking

In the intervals between sessions, Valerie and Mark revealed their negative voices or self-critical thoughts if either felt cut off emotionally or distracted during sex. They learned to describe their self-doubts and negative thoughts to each other while maintaining affectionate contact. It helped them to stay close and often they were able to recover their sexual feelings in the situation.

A few weeks later

Valerie: I've felt so different since we started talking about this subject. When we make love, if I start having voices about getting too excited or if I notice that I'm not feeling very much, the most important thing is to talk with you about what's going on. This past week, I haven't had as many voices as I used to have, especially the really critical ones. Sex doesn't feel like something I want to avoid anymore. When we run into trouble, we'll stop and talk. That's made me feel good and also much closer to you.

Mark: About two weeks ago when I said my voices about feeling pathetic and not like a real man, I felt such a relief from letting out the anger I was feeling against myself. Since then I think I've been more open and vulnerable to you. When I stopped focusing on you and on problems you might be having, I was more relaxed and could feel my own feelings. After I talked with you more honestly about my own doubts, I think I was able to express more of my affectionate feelings toward you while we were making love. And that's what makes me the happiest, when I'm able to express those feelings.

CASE EXAMPLE NUMBER TWO

In the following case, voice therapy was a helpful adjunct for a couple who had recently started psychotherapy. This was a difficult case in that both partners were involved in an escalating cycle of conflict and hostility. Early in the therapy, the couple's ongoing therapist requested a consultation with a clinician who had experience with voice therapy methodology and was familiar with the theoretical approach on which it is based.

Owen (53) and Corinne (46) sought marital therapy because of serious communication problems and lack of satisfaction in their relationship. This was the second marriage for both partners. The couple met 8 years prior to entering therapy and had been married for 6 years. Their mutual complaint was the lack of closeness in the relationship. In the intake interview, they revealed that it had been nearly a year since they had been sexual. According to Corinne, her husband simply refused to talk to her and would only answer her questions with a perfunctory yes or no. She expressed feelings of hopelessness about the possibility that their relationship could be improved by psychotherapy. Owen had recently sought treatment for depression and had begun a course of antidepressants.

Before this consultation, the clinician gave both partners the Firestone Voice Scale for Couples (FVSC; see Exhibit 9.1), the Behavioral Checklist

EXHIBIT 9.1
Page 1 of Firestone Voice Scale for Couples

FVSC

Instructions

All people experience thoughts that are critical toward themselves and others. For example, when a person is worried about his (her) relationship, he (she) might think:
"You'd better hang on to him (her). This may be your last chance. You may never get anybody again."

Or a person might have critical thoughts about a potential partner:
"Don't get involved. You might get hurt because he (she) is so unreliable."

Negative thoughts are a part of everyone's thinking process. Please indicate the frequency with which you experience the following thoughts by circling the corresponding number.

1 – Never   2 – Rarely   3 – Once in a while   4 – Frequently   5 – Most of the time
For example, you think or say to yourself:

1   2   ③   4   5   "You're unattractive. Why should she (he) want to go out with you?"

1.	You'd better put on a good front. Put your best foot forward or he (she) won't be interested.	1	2	3	4	5
2.	You'd be better off on your own.	1	2	3	4	5
3.	He (she) doesn't give a damn about you. If he (she) did he (she) would remember to do what he (she) promised.	1	2	3	4	5
4.	He (she) never spends time with you. He (she) is always with his (her) friends.	1	2	3	4	5
5.	He (she) doesn't want to hear your opinions, so keep them to yourself.	1	2	3	4	5
6.	You've got to be careful of what you say to a man (woman).	1	2	3	4	5
7.	What you feel and think isn't important to him (her).	1	2	3	4	5
8.	Even if your marriage isn't romantic anymore, it's better than most couples have.	1	2	3	4	5
9.	You've got to keep him (her) interested.	1	2	3	4	5
10.	He (she) can be such a jerk (bitch)!	1	2	3	4	5

for Partners (BCP; Firestone & Catlettt, 1999; see Exhibit 9.2), and the Experiences in Close Relationships Inventory (ECR–R; Fraley, Waller, & Brennan, 2000).[3] (See Exhibit 9.3 for an analysis of scores from the BCP.) The results showed that Owen and Corinne disagreed about his being satisfied with their sex life. (She thought he was satisfied, he expressed that he was not.) Owen perceived both Corinne and himself as deficient in terms of the positive qualities delineated on the Behavioral Checklist. Corinne saw herself in a more positive light and her husband as being deficient in most of the positive qualities. In other words, for the most part, the partners disagreed in their perceptions of themselves and of each other.

EXHIBIT 9.2
Behavioral Checklist for Partners (BCP)

How would you describe yourself and your partner along these dimensions (on a scale of 1 to 5)?

1. Does not describe me/does not describe partner at this time.
2. Describes me on infrequent occasions/describes partner on infrequent occasions.
3. Describes how I am some of the time/describes how my partner is some of the time.
4. Describes how I frequently am/describes how my partner frequently is.
5. Describes me most or all of the time/describes my partner most or all of the time.

Nondefensive and open (able to listen to feedback without overreacting/open to new experiences):

    Self 1 2 3 4 5 / Partner 1 2 3 4 5

Respectful of other's boundaries:

    Self 1 2 3 4 5 / Partner 1 2 3 4 5

Vulnerable (willing to feel sad, acknowledge hurt feelings, etc.):

    Self 1 2 3 4 5 / Partner 1 2 3 4 5

Honest (straightforward, nondeceptive):

    Self 1 2 3 4 5 / Partner 1 2 3 4 5

Physically affectionate:

    Self 1 2 3 4 5 / Partner 1 2 3 4 5

Sexuality (satisfied with sexual relationship):

    Self 1 2 3 4 5 / Partner 1 2 3 4 5

Empathic and understanding (lack of distortion of the other):

    Self 1 2 3 4 5 / Partner 1 2 3 4 5

Communicative (sense of shared meaning, feel understood):

    Self 1 2 3 4 5 / Partner 1 2 3 4 5

Noncontrolling, nonmanipulative, and nonthreatening:

    Self 1 2 3 4 5 / Partner 1 2 3 4 5

How would you rate yourself along these dimensions?

Sense of well-being 1 2 3 4 5

Self-confident   1 2 3 4 5

Optimistic   1 2 3 4 5

EXHIBIT 9.3
Corinne's and Owen's scores on the Behavioral Checklist for Partners (BCP)

	Corinne		Owen	
	Rating herself	Owen's rating of Corinne	Rating himself	Corinne's rating of Owen
Nondefensive	5	2	2	1
Respectful	5	3	3	3
Vulnerable	5	3	3	4
Honest	5	5	5	3
Affectionate	5	1	1	1
Sexually satisfied	1	1	1	5
Empathic	4	1	1	1
Communicative	—	1	1	—
Noncontrolling	4	2	2	2

On the FVSC, Corinne endorsed a number of seemingly positive thoughts indicating vanity or feelings of exaggerated self-importance:

"You can do anything you set your mind to."
"You're strong."
"You deserve better."

She also endorsed a number of hostile thoughts regarding her husband, including

"He doesn't give a damn about you."
"He's a jerk, embarrassing, critical, cold, insensitive."

In addition, she endorsed thoughts indicating a pseudoindependent orientation:

"You don't need anyone."
"You're better off on your own."

In general, Corinne reported thoughts about needing to protect herself against being hurt by her husband and beliefs that her husband was solely responsible for their sexual problems.

Owen endorsed a number of critical thoughts about his wife, although there were considerably fewer than she endorsed in relation to him, for example

"She's not practical."
"She's insensitive and critical."
"She doesn't pay attention to you."
"She always has to be right."

Owen also reported beliefs that his wife was better, smarter, friendlier, and had more knowledge than he. In relation to himself, Owen endorsed such thoughts as

"Hang on to her, you need her."
"Treat her special or she'll leave you."
"You need to take care of a woman and make her feel special."
"You're not a real man."

He also endorsed thoughts indicating low self-esteem, dissatisfaction with his performance at work, and frustration in relating and communicating with his wife. On the ECR–R, Owen's attachment pattern fell in the avoidant or dismissing quadrant, whereas Corinne scored as being anxiously attached or preoccupied with relationship issues.

The Consultation

Therapist: What are some of the things that create distance between you two?

Corinne: He never wants to socialize or go out with our friends, he just wants to sit at home and watch TV. We used to have a good time doing things together, but during the last few months, he doesn't want to do anything. He won't even talk to me. He acts like he doesn't hear me. I can't get him to talk to me.

Therapist: Was there a time in your relationship where you talked more?

Owen and Corinne: Oh, yes.

Therapist: How long ago was that?

Corinne: About 3 or 4 years ago.

Owen: I remember that when we first got together and before we got married, we used to talk a lot. We'd go for long drives in the country. We didn't care where we were going, we just went different places, and we'd stop and have lunch or go walking in the woods or along the beach.

Corinne: We were very adventuresome. It was fun. We would joke a lot—he was very funny.

Owen: We'd hold hands—we don't do that any more.

Therapist: How would you like it to be now?

Owen:	I'd like it to be the way it was.
Therapist:	So there was a lot of hand-holding? Was there affection?
Owen:	Oh, yes. I used to show her a lot of affection.
Corinne:	I was always a very affectionate person. But then everything just stopped dead.
Therapist:	When did it stop?
Owen:	It seems like a long time ago.
Therapist:	One year, two years?
Corinne:	As far as sex is concerned, it's been at least a year, or more.
Therapist:	But when you started out how was the sex?
Owen and Corinne:	[in unison] It was great!
Therapist:	So you both were really happy with that; you were having fun, you were joking around, talking more and you were having sex. Did you like being sexual?
Corinne:	Yes. But even before we got married, it slowed down a little, and I would do anything to get it going again. I'd wear sexy nightgowns. But he was less interested than me. We'd talk about that because I wanted more and he didn't want anything.
Therapist:	This was a long time ago, you're talking about now?
Corinne:	As time went on it got less and less. First it was down to once a month, then once every six months, then nothing lately.
Therapist:	What do you think happened?
Owen:	My desire just went away for whatever reason, I don't know why.
Therapist:	You don't know where it went. Do you want it back?
Owen:	I'd like to have it back.
Therapist:	You'd like to feel that way again?
Owen:	Yes, I would. I miss it.
Corinne:	That's surprising! [angry tone]

Owen: I'd like it more.

Corinne: Yeah, but you can't rely on magic or wishes.

Therapist: But he said he missed it, that was a good first thing to admit. That's a good first thing because that means he wants it.

Owen: Yes, I do.

Therapist: You'd like to have that back. Did it go completely? I mean, it just doesn't occur to you at all?

Owen: Well, it occurs to me every once in a while, but it just seems like the desire is not there.

Therapist: So you've thought about it, but the desire that gets you from point A to point B doesn't happen.

Owen: Yes, that's right. I don't know what it is. It's frustrating for me. When I'm depressed, I end up thinking what's the use? I'm going to fail anyway.

Therapist: I'm going to ask you to do something that may feel odd at first, but take those thoughts that you just said about failing and put them in the second person, like another person was saying them to you.

Owen: Okay. *What's the use? You're going to fail anyway.*

Therapist: Yes, that's right. What else are you telling yourself?

Owen: *It's never going to be the way it was. You're old and not attractive any more. You're lucky to have her.* [angry, long pause]

Therapist: [waits for several seconds, then says] Try to say more. Don't hold back.

Owen: It goes something like this, *When you're depressed you're so needy and dependent, no wonder she doesn't like you any more. You're not very much fun when you're depressed. You never have anything to talk about. You're so boring. No one could be attracted to you!* [pause]

Therapist: With all these voices about yourself, no wonder you've found it hard to feel sexual.

Owen: Yeah, yeah, but now I feel more interested in trying to deal with that situation.

Corinne: Yeah, but I'd still like him to initiate something.

Therapist: One interesting dynamic I've noticed is that he starts to reach out a little bit, but you attack. That's counterproductive. You're missing an opportunity to fulfill your real goal to get closer, especially closer sexually. It's like this little opening, and there haven't been this many openings.

Corinne: Not any!

Therapist: Well, you've got to decide whether you want to take those openings. You could leave it just the way it is. But it doesn't sound like you're happy with it the way it is.

Corinne: This sounds funny, but I'm almost afraid.

Therapist: It doesn't sound strange and I'm not surprised. You've gotten used to it the way it is.

Corinne: I'm afraid for him to just come and say, "Here I am, everything is okay." Do I trust him again, do I believe him?

Therapist: When he makes one of these offerings, what goes on in your mind? What are your thoughts when you hear that? Your fears or whatever is on your mind.

Corinne: I'm afraid to trust him. I'm afraid he's going to disappoint me again.

Therapist: Say your thoughts about not trusting him the way your husband expressed his thoughts earlier. How do the thoughts go? What are you telling yourself in your mind?

Corinne: I don't know. Something like, *How can you trust him again? Watch out, you're just going to get put in your place. You're going to be disappointed all over again. Why get your hopes up? Besides, he really doesn't give a damn about you. If he did, he would want to have sex with you.*

Therapist: I thought it was important for you to admit that you were afraid, that you had fear, because as much as you want it, you're kind of afraid to take a chance on it too.

Corinne: I've never really talked to anybody about this. It's even hard to talk to him about it, so I feel I have no one to talk to.

Therapist:	So you two haven't been talking about sex for a long time?
Both:	No.
Therapist:	So this makes it kind of a hot topic. You even started feeling a little bit open to having those kinds of feelings again.
Corinne:	Yes, I did, a little.
Owen:	It's just that we need to sit down and open up and talk about it.
Corinne:	I tried. You have to do your part, too.
Therapist:	He's talking to you right now.
Owen:	See! I do move my lips every now and then. [both laugh; Owen reaches out to hold Corinne's hand, and she responds in kind]

The consulting therapist, aware of Corinne's resistance to the possibility of making changes in the relationship, attempted to elicit the feelings of fear and trepidation that the therapist sensed might be responsible for much of the resistance. As Corinne verbalized the voices associated with her distrust and anger toward Owen, she uncovered fears about being hurt again if she were to make herself vulnerable.

Listening to Owen articulate his self-critical thoughts aroused empathic feelings in Corinne. It had the positive effect of dispelling a good deal of her anger and softening her feelings of bitterness regarding her husband's sexual rejection of her. Because this session was a consultation, follow-up data was difficult to obtain. However, at the end of the session, both partners expressed optimism about their future together. They indicated a determination to work closely with their ongoing therapist to recapture a part of their life that they had previously enjoyed.

IMPACT OF VOICE THERAPY

Partners using the procedures of voice therapy have found that it facilitates the separation of the hostile attacking part of the self from a more rational or realistic view of self and others. We have observed that during voice therapy sessions, clients tend to become more aware of the voice as an alien, antagonistic part of the personality. Furthermore, the techniques expose the important link between negative thought processes, repressed childhood pain, and negative parental attitudes, as in the case of Mark and Valerie. Articulating self-attacks as though they were coming from another person recapitulates those moment in childhood when clients incorporated hostile parental attitudes, whether spoken or unspoken, in the form of the voice. The techniques function to reconnect clients with the real self, and they are able to experience themselves again as separate individuals with their own motives, wants, and priorities (Firestone & Catlett, 1999). By regaining a sense of themselves and their desires, and by developing an understanding of the sources of their sexual problems, they can free themselves of many self-defeating sexual inhibitions and significantly improve their sexual relationships.

Individuals in voice therapy also become cognizant of the way they negatively perceive or distort events and significant people in their lives. They learn that it is not the negative or unpleasant event itself that is the primary cause of their distress, misery, and depression, but rather the way they are internally processing these events or perceiving other people. Clients are able to generalize the understanding they develop in voice therapy sessions to their everyday lives and relationships. They learn to deduce from their behavior or change in mood the fact that, on some level, they must be experiencing self-attacks or hostile thoughts about their partner. Subsequently, they are able to identify the specific voices motivating their behavior. The process of challenging the dictates of the voice by changing behaviors based on its negative prescriptions helps people overcome powerful defenses that had limited their sexual lives and relationships.

VOICE THERAPY METHODS AS AN ADJUNCT TO COUPLES AND SEX THERAPY

Voice therapy procedures can be of significant value to psychotherapists whose treatment is based on other theoretical approaches. It is possible to use the techniques as an adjunct to cognitive–behavioral approaches, emotionally focused couples therapy, family systems interventions, and psychodynamic couples therapy, which are described later in this chapter. Even for clinicians using these other treatment modalities, the theory and methodology contribute to understanding the core of resistance to constructive behavioral change.

We suggest that voice therapy procedures can help prevent the reliving and reenactment of the same dynamics that existed in the client's family-of-origin. Because the techniques gain access to significant unconscious processes in the personality, they have the added potential for becoming a valuable research tool for elucidating the causal relationship between destructive cognitive processes, their associated affect, and each partner's problems in sexual functioning. Moreover, the methods facilitate an understanding of the origins of the voice in early family interactions.

THE PERSONALITY OF THE THERAPIST

The therapist's personality sets the tone and the emotional quality of the therapy process and therefore cannot be divorced from interactions or techniques (Beutler, 1997; Horvath & Luborsky, 1993). Clients' neuroses and disturbances in their sexuality have developed within the context of a faulty family relationship and can only be changed or ameliorated within the context of another, more constructive relationship. According to Strupp (1989),

> The cumulative effects of interpersonal relationships . . . typically in childhood—has made the patient "ill" and . . . another human relationship, with a professionally trained person and under particularly benign circumstances, can provide corrections in the patient's self-esteem and in the quality of his or her interpersonal relationships with significant others. (pp. 717–718)

The characteristics and responses of the therapist are crucial in creating the "benign circumstances" to which Strupp referred and the type of relationship that could achieve this end (Firestone, 2002). For example, therapists using voice therapy techniques must be comfortable with the release of intense emotions and encourage their full expression rather than making interpretations that would cause the client to withdraw from feeling. In addition, because voice therapy methods deal with core defenses, it is vital that therapists have a complete understanding of the underlying theory of defense formation in order to effectively help clients through crucial phases in the therapy process.[4]

A BRIEF REVIEW OF APPROACHES TO SEXUAL PROBLEMS IN COUPLES THERAPY

Despite the fact that today many sex therapists remain technique-oriented in their interventions, others have integrated concepts from specific theoretical models (psychoanalytic, attachment, interpersonal, object relations, family systems) to help clients achieve insight into possible origins of their sexual difficulties.[5] During the 1980s, for example, Bishay (1988), Araoz (1982), and Segraves (1982) suggested integrating cognitive–behavioral techniques with an exploration of family dynamics assumed to be correlated with specific sexual disturbances or dysfunctions. In his review of the state of the art in sex therapy during this period, Bishay (1988) emphasized the need for further research "to identify the [distorted] cognitions present in different psychosexual dysfunctions . . . in order to establish a manual of practice for cognitive therapy in psychosexual problems" (p. 89).

Currently, there are a wide array of treatment approaches to couples who are experiencing sexual problems in their relationships. Bader and Pearson (1988) have employed aspects of Mahler's (Mahler, Pine, & Bergman, 1975) developmental model (symbiotic, separation/differentiation, rapprochement) to delineate types as well as stages of couple relationships and to formulate treatment strategies. In their work, they begin by using structured diagnostic tools, including questionnaires about self-differentiation, attunement, relationship history, and individual histories to determine the particular "stage" of the couple relationship. One technique they have employed in their therapy is the "short script" exercise derived from Gestalt therapy. This exercise identifies "the chronic negative feelings underlying the problem" and traces them "back to the original childhood traumas that spawned them" (p. 37).

Bader and Pearson have also emphasized the importance of identifying intrapsychic conflicts and making partners responsible for autonomous change. In cases where there is conflict caused, for example, by a discrepancy in sexual desire, they may teach partners "a technique in which one partner is the *initiator* and the other is the *responder*" (p. 130) in their communications within the session. "As partners alternate back and forth between each role in different sessions, a situation is created that enhances the development of object relations" (p. 133).

Cognitive–behavioral therapists (A. Beck, 1976; Ellis & Harper, 1975) have stressed the importance of accessing "automatic thoughts" and "dysfunctional beliefs" in their treatment of couples. These concepts are similar to our concept of the voice. However, their focus is primarily on refuting the illogic of the client's dysfunctional beliefs while neglecting to explore the origins of destructive thought processes in negative interactions within the family, parental abuses, or other environmental conditions (Firestone, 1990b).

Cognitive therapist J. Beck (1995) has emphasized that gaining access to emotions helps in identifying the "hot cognitions"—the core schema or previously unconscious beliefs about self, others, and the world. Because the techniques of voice therapy bring destructive thoughts to the surface together with their associated feelings of anger and sadness, the methodology can be useful as an adjunct in many of the therapies described below.[6] In his book, *Love Is Never Enough*, A. Beck (1988) attempted to convey to couples with sexual problems that "A first step in reducing the mutual anger in your relationship . . . [is to] determine to what degree your own mental workings contribute to the problem" (p. 261). He suggested that partners should then look at their automatic thoughts, note their response, and look for errors in their thinking. Next he recommends that partners reframe their image of the other person and attempt to see the other person from his or her perspective.

In treating patients presenting with inhibited sexual desire, H. Kaplan (1979, 1995) found that behavioral therapies aimed at simply reducing the level of sexual anxieties failed to ameliorate the problems for many couples. As noted in chapter 5, she suggested an in-depth approach in which partners could "attain insight into the immediate antecedent of the symptom. For many of these patients this is the involuntary and automatic focus on negatively charged thoughts, which produces a suppression of sexual feelings" (1979, p. 103). H. Kaplan (1995) used both individual and conjoint sessions in working with couples. She recommended sex education, sexual skills training, including masturbation, communication skills training, and "very gradual exposure" for highly anxious clients. In dealing with a couple's or client's resistance to homework assignments, Kaplan suggested

> An orderly and systematic sequence of gradually intensifying behavioral and cognitive interventions that are aimed at progressively "deeper" psychic levels. These progress from simple *repetition of the assignment*, to *reduction of its intensity*, to *the cognitive reframing of the problem*, to *confrontation*, and finally to *insight into the patient's underlying conflicts*. (p. 179)

During the past three decades, clinicians have increasingly employed techniques that help facilitate the release of feelings (Bianchi-Demicheli & Zutter, 2005; Greenberg, 2002; Johnson, 1999; Johnson & Denton, 2002; Solomon, 2001). In a chapter titled "Coaching for Emotional Wisdom in Couples," Greenberg (2002) provided examples of negative "voices" that support cycles of escalating anger and hurt in many couple relationships. He asserted that "closeness can occur only when people overcome their fear and shame and change the negative beliefs that appear to protect them but in reality prevent them from achieving intimacy" (p. 261). In his work, he tries to "help partners present their feelings and needs as honestly and openly as possible, in such a way that their partners are most likely to hear and see them" (p. 271).

Emotionally focused therapy (EFT) is based in part on attachment theory and has been effectively used to treat distressed couples and partners reporting low sexual desire and sexual arousal disorders (Johnson, 2002; Johnson & Greenberg, 1995). Two important goals of EFT, similar to those of voice therapy, are (a) accessing "negative" emotions, such as fear, anxiety, and anger, that trigger defensive maneuvers, and (b) exploring their possible sources in a person's developmental history.

Johnson, Hunsley, Greenberg, and Schindler (1999) delineated the nine steps of EFT as follows:

> Step 1. Assessment—creating an alliance and explicating the core issues in the couple's conflict using an attachment perspective. Step 2. Identifying the problem interactional cycle that maintains attachment insecurity

and relationship distress. Step 3. Accessing the unacknowledged emotions. . . . Step 4. Reframing the problem in terms of the cycle, the underlying emotions, and attachment needs. . . . Step 5. Promoting identification with disowned needs and aspects of self and integrating these into relationship interactions. Step 6. Promoting acceptance of the partner's new construction of experience. . . . Step 7. Facilitating the expression of specific needs and wants and creating emotional engagement. . . . Step 8. Facilitating the emergence of new solutions. . . . Step 9. Consolidating new positions and new cycles of attachment behavior. (p. 70)

Johnson (2004) also makes extensive use of what she terms "enactments," in which partners, in turn, are encouraged through the therapist's evocative, yet gentle questioning, to directly communicate their fears, anxieties, hurts, disappointments, desires, and requests to the other person. Johnson (2004) elaborated on the major change that occurs during the therapeutic process:

> In the process of EFT, emotions are processed and regulated differently, resulting in more adaptive responses. . . . For example, when a partner can acknowledge to self and other the panic that arises during close physical contact, this often evokes compassion and comforting behavior from the other spouse, allowing new healing emotional experiences to occur. (p. 69)

In her work with survivors of child sexual abuse and relationship trauma, Johnson (2002) follows many of the steps described above. She begins by creating a safe context—a "secure base" in the sessions "where partners can confront the ways in which trauma has defined their relationship and, often, their sense of self" (p. 87). To create such an alliance and sense of safety, Johnson emphasizes the importance of the survivor having "a sense of control over the pace and direction of therapy. . . . The therapist must be prepared . . . to help clients deal with traumatic experiences that emerge in therapy sessions and must know how to help clients manage and contain their distress" (p. 83).

In describing the complex tasks required of therapists working with survivors of child sexual abuse and their partners, Johnson (2002) emphasized that, "In particular, incest survivors and their partners usually have to craft their own detailed concept of pleasurable touch and safe sexuality to a much greater extent than nontraumatized couples" (p. 198).

Object-relations theory has been applied by Scharff and Scharff (1991) in their treatment of couples with sexual problems. In their clinical work, the Scharffs found that the conflicts and sexual difficulties experienced by couples may be functioning to exacerbate or magnify "the object relations difficulties in their internal worlds" (p. 34). According to the Scharffs, in these cases, the process of projective identification operates to maintain and intensify the problem.

The goal of object relations therapy with couples is similar in some respects to that of voice therapy, that is, to encourage the reinternalization of projected material, or, in our terms, encourage the taking back of negative projections based on the voice.

In *Object Relations Couple Therapy*, the Scharffs describe the use of sex therapy in conjunction with object relations marital therapy.

> The partners are assigned the first of the series of graded home exercises that have the aim of reducing their sexual interaction, beginning with a nonthreatening, nongenital level. When they have mastered each step, a new component is added. . . . Unlike more behavioral approaches, sex therapy from an object relations perspective tends not to shortcut the program, because of its focus on the totality of the couple's interaction, not only on the physical parts of their sexual life. (1991, p. 167)[7]

Willi's (1975/1982, 1999) approach to couples has changed during the past 20 years from a psychodynamic focus on "collusive" couples to an approach that incorporates some features of family systems thinking. Willi (1999) himself has noted that "I see couples less as a unitary system and more as a coevolutive process which raises questions that focus on the individual" (p. 50). His ecological brief therapy helps "improve patients' interactive effectiveness" (p. 236) in three spheres, including their "intrapersonal spheres: the constructs (schemata, beliefs, and 'internal objects') that form the basis of their intentions, plans, and actions" (p. 236), and "the intrapersonal spheres of the people they interact with" (p. 236), as well as "the interactional sphere: the interactions between patients and the people in their niches, the real effects patients produce, and the real responses they provoke from their partners" (p. 236).

There are similarities between several aspects of voice therapy and Willi's (1975/1982; 1999) coevolution approach to couple therapy, described by Berg-Cross (1997) as the "Willi Model." According to Berg-Cross' depiction of Willi's treatment approach, at a certain point in the therapeutic process, the therapist may intervene by asking a client to verbalize his or her thoughts and feelings in terms of "inner voices" and then may encourage an answer back by asking the client to verbalize any "different or competing thoughts." In describing this process, Berg-Cross explained that the therapist encourages the client to articulate what his or her feelings are as if the feelings could talk. Next, the therapist encourages the client to "expand on the inner voices and themes . . . not only the first thought or verbalization that he chose to share" (pp. 219–220).

In concluding his discussion of his goals for therapy with couples, Willi (1975/1982) asserted: "[Therapy] should enable . . . [people] to find a dialectical equilibrium between the need to develop their own personalities and the yearning for a way of life together, as a balance between 'self-realization within marriage' and 'self-realization through marriage'" (p. 253).

In his practice of the "sexual crucible" model, Schnarch (1991) combines a variety of sex and marital therapy techniques with helping partners attain higher levels of self-differentiation and increased tolerance for eroticism and intimate sexuality. (See chap. 5.) Perhaps the most important part of Schnarch's overall approach to treatment is contained in the following statement:

> The orientation of the sexual crucible is contained in the phrase "relationship with self in the context of relationship with partner." The therapist aligns with each spouse as a separate individual, reinforcing development of *self*-control and obviating the need to control the partner to control one's emotionality. (p. 404)

One aspect of the "sexual crucible" treatment model is described by Schnarch as "wall-socket" sex, which he states *"is a distinctly adult-only event"* (p. 465). According to Schnarch, when couples progress through treatment and reach higher levels of self-differentiation, they may begin to have "wall-socket" sex. This term refers to the shock that partners may experience after having a passionate, erotic sexual encounter following years of boring, mediocre sex, that is, "The shock of an *intense* erotic and intimate personal experience that seemly arises out of 'nowhere'" (p. 464). Another shock that partners often experience is "The shock of observing one's own intolerance and spontaneous withdrawal from such experiences" (p. 464).

In treating couples who have "no-sex" marriages, McCarthy (1997a, 1997b) uses bibliotherapy, psychosexual skills training, relaxation, pleasuring exercises, and relapse prevention strategies. In addition, he addresses the cognitive dimensions underlying sexual dysfunctions in the context of couple therapy (McCarthy, 1997a, 1997b; Metz & McCarthy, 2004). For example, in treating men who have problems with premature ejaculation, McCarthy assesses the patient's beliefs and expectations, which helps "identify distortions (e.g., 'sex should be unregulated and spontaneous' . . .)" or "unrealistic beliefs such as the need to bring the partner to orgasm by intercourse alone" (Metz & McCarthy, 2004, p. iv). McCarthy's (1995) therapy approach also incorporates exercises to help clients relax and enjoy nondemand pleasuring. As McCarthy (1995) puts it, "This is an active therapy that emphasizes *in vivo* learning 'homework assignments.' Reading and cognitive restructuring are important, but the crucial element is sexual exercises organized in a semistructured manner to build comfort and skill" (p. 150).[8]

CONCLUSION

Voice therapy procedures uncover major defenses against closeness and intimacy. In analyzing material gathered in voice therapy sessions, we found that most people have voices attacks, and these thoughts are often manifested during lovemaking. When expressed in voice therapy sessions, these attacks are usually accompanied by considerable sadness and rage toward self and others.

We also observed that clients, especially those who have formed a fantasy bond in their relationship, are "listening to" or following the dictates of their respective voices. In a sense, they filter their communications through a biased, alien point of view that distorts the other's real image. Both partners ward off loving, sexual responses from the other, using rationalizations promoted by the voice to justify their anger and withholding behavior. In many couples, fault-finding, hypercritical thoughts and misperceptions of the other person were often more intense following times when the partners had been especially close, both sexually and emotionally.

The goal of voice therapy with couples who have sexual difficulties is to help individual partners identify voice attacks that diminish sexual desire or interfere with sexual fulfillment and emotional intimacy in the relationship. By first eliciting and then challenging specific self-attacks as well as judgmental, cynical thoughts about the other, each partner is able to relate more closely during sex. Releasing the affect underlying voice attacks allows clients to again experience feelings of sexual desire and pleasurable sensations and increases sexual satisfaction and fulfillment.

Our approach to eliciting and identifying the contents of the voice is not didactic; that is, we do not directly persuade clients to think or behave rationally or point out the illogic of their thinking. Instead, we help them discover what they are telling themselves, in a negative sense, about their body, their sexual performance, their sexuality as a whole, and about their partner and their relationship, and attempt to assist them in moving away from these negative attitudes and prohibitions.

In an effort to achieve a sense of internal integration, many clients side with the alien point of view represented by the voice and come to accept this negative point of view as their own. Helping clients externalize their negative thoughts enables them to separate from these destructive elements of the antiself system, thereby strengthening the self system and their point of view. This process, in turn, enables them to cope more effectively with self-defeating, self-limiting sexual inhibitions and withholding tendencies.

Finally, by identifying the destructive effects of internalized voices, discovering their source, and understanding the role they play in restricting sexual fulfillment, an individual can separate from the dictates of the voice and move on to Step 4, planning and carrying out corrective suggestions for behavioral change. Before this phase in the therapeutic process, members of a couple have generally identified the voice attacks that operate to inhibit their expressions of affection and sexual responses. The first three steps in voice therapy facilitate changes in attitudes that allow them to challenge the fears underlying these inhibitions. By understanding the origins of their fears, individuals can develop the courage to initiate corrective suggestions that move them toward situations that they previously found too threatening.

NOTES

1. *Guidelines for Psychotherapy With Lesbian, Gay, and Bisexual Clients* can be found at http://www.apa.org. The first four guidelines delineate suggestions for developing nonbiased attitudes toward homosexuality and bisexuality. The second four encourage the acquisition of knowledge about relationships and families of sexual minority clients. The next five guidelines encourage therapists to understand the specific problems faced by sexual minorities from diverse ethnic groups, age groups, and those with cognitive challenges. The last three guidelines encourage education and training in relevant mental health resources available for these populations.

   See also Ritter and Terndrup (2002).

2. It should be noted that, at times, clients may feel moved to directly challenge the voice during a conjoint session. In attempting to counteract the effect of the destructive thoughts and voices on their sexual relating, they may elect to answer the voice dramatically with strong anger. "Yelling back," even at symbolic parental figures, unleashes feelings of rage and hatred for which people may feel considerable guilt. We have observed that some clients in couples therapy, after responding angrily to their voice attacks and differentiating themselves from their parents, for example, saying "I'm not like you," or "I'm different," later reverted to the very behaviors they were challenging.

   In other cases, it is important for clients to answer back to their voice attacks and assert their point of view regarding their sexuality, their partners, and their relationships. When clients feel so motivated during the session, it is valuable to set aside some portions of subsequent sessions for the client to further verbalize his or her "answers" to the voice. The process of repeatedly "standing up for oneself" against voice attacks habituates the client to the guilt and anxiety precipitated during the process of answering the voice. Eventually, these feelings of guilt and anxiety are diminished to a considerable degree.

3. The Behavioral Checklist for Partners (Firestone & Catlett, 1999) was composed of items derived from dimensions of "Interactions in the Ideal Couple" (Figure 4 in Firestone & Catlett, 1999).

   The Firestone Voice Scale for Couples (FVSC) assesses the frequency of destructive thoughts the subject is currently experiencing toward self, toward his or her partner, and about relationships in general. The initial version of the FVSC consists of 96 items reflecting destructive thought patterns that are associated with intimate interpersonal relationships. These items were derived from clinical material, discussion groups with couples, and from graduate students studying psychology. (See Exhibit 9.1.)

Each partner endorsed the frequency with which he or she currently experienced destructive thoughts on a Likert-type scale ranging from 0 to 4 (0 = never, 1 = rarely, 2 = once in a while, 3 = frequently, and 4 = most of the time). Mean scores were calculated for the three item groupings: toward self, toward partner, and toward relationships. The mean is used because there are different numbers of items in each grouping, and additive scores would attribute more weight to those groups with more items and make comparisons between the different categories difficult. Reliability and validity have not yet been established for this instrument.

The ECR–R (Fraley et al., 2000) is a 36-item self-report attachment measure and is derived from four categories or regions (secure, preoccupied, dismissing, and fearful) represented in a two-dimensional (low anxiety to high anxiety and low avoidance to high avoidance).

4. It is recommended that therapists wishing to incorporate the techniques of voice therapy into their practice seek training in the concepts and methodology. A basic resource for more information about voice therapy can be found in Firestone (1988).

5. In discussing current trends in the field of sex therapy, Leiblum and Rosen (2000) noted there were four major trends: "(1) a trend toward greater 'medicalization,' (2) increasing emphasis on pharmacological intervention, (3) greater attention to desire disorders, and (4) more treatment utilizing interpersonal and object-relations theories" (p. 5). They also observed that constraints imposed by managed care (HMOs) have necessitated increasingly briefer interventions focused on ameliorating specific sexual problems. As a result, there has been an increasing use of short-term treatments, for example, behavioral techniques and pharmaceuticals (Kleinplatz, 2001; Segraves & Balon, 2003).

Goren (2003) also observed that during the 1990s, "sex therapists jumped on the medication bandwagon" (p. 496). This trend was precipitated in part by the introduction of sildenafil citrate (Viagra) in 1998 as a treatment for erectile dysfunction. Leiblum and Rosen (2000) warn that "With the success of new pharmacological agents, there is an inevitable focus on biological causes for sexual dysfunction and a tendency to seek simple medical solutions for more complex individual or couples' problems" (p. 11). Bancroft (1999) and Kleinplatz (2001) contend that for the most part, contemporary sexual science and sex therapy is essentially atheoretical, noting that "Until recently, in the more traditional field of sexual science, theory has been notable by its absence" (Bancroft, 1999, p. 226). Kleinplatz argued that "Few sex therapists . . . are known to struggle with these basic theoretical questions," such as "What is sexuality? What turns on people and why? . . . What is the basis/origin of sexual desire?" (pp. xv–xvi).

6. As one example, in emotionally focused therapy (EFT), asking clients to put their negative, angry thoughts about the partner into the third person: *He*

won't let you be close to him. She doesn't understand you, can help them separate the destructive point of view from a more rational or congenial point of view. As noted, saying one's hostile thoughts toward oneself and one's partner elicits strong emotions and leads to insights regarding their origins. We suggest that voice therapy techniques could be used to enhance emotional expression and understanding of the sources of partners' fears and distress, specifically during Steps 5 and 6 in EFT (Johnson, 2004). According to Johnson, these steps "also involve the accessing of core self-concepts or models, which are associated with the intense emotions that arise here" (p. 164). In a case example, Johnson's client explained how he negatively defines himself: "So I say to myself, *what do you expect? You're not good at this love stuff.* I feel about this big (making a small space between thumb and forefinger). I can't even ask her anymore" (p. 164).

Johnson noted that this reprocessing of primary emotions related to the client's perception of him- or herself in relation to the other allows key wishes and longings inherent in the emotions to "emerge and to be articulated" (p. 164).

7. Scharff and Scharff (1991) described the treatment strategy used with a couple in which both partners had histories of child sexual abuse and dysfunctional family relations. They delineated the steps in the sequence of sex therapy exercises including nongenital sensate focus, self-pleasuring and masturbation and genital sensate focus but not to orgasm, among others. The Scharffs emphasized that this last exercise "allows full intimacy and expanded cooperative object relating, still without the threats of penetration and interpenetration. Safety and lowered anxiety are maintained" (p. 171). They provided an extended case example of this couple, allowing readers to "examine the process of an unusually extensive and integrated treatment, from which we can learn about the interlocking of individual, couple, and family processes, and the mutual influence of the three treatment approaches" (p. 179).

8. Other therapeutic methodologies dealing with negative thought processes as well as accessing negative affects which are hypothesized to be contributing factors in the development of sexual dysfunctions and other sexual disturbances are described in Beck (1988); Johnson (1999, 2002, 2004); H. Kaplan (1979, 1995); Wile (1995); and Waring (1988). Several psychoanalytically oriented clinicians have focused, to some extent, on destructive thoughts influencing sexual difficulties. See Scharff and Scharff (1991) and Scharff (1995). Also see Solomon's (1997) chapter, "On Love and Lust in Therapeutic Treatment," and Johnson's (2003) report on the effectiveness of couple therapy, including therapies dealing with couples' sexual problems. Emotionally focused couple therapy, behavioral approaches, and the restructuring of attributions were among the approaches found to be effective by empirical research studies.

10

SUGGESTIONS FOR ENHANCING SEXUAL INTIMACY

The challenge of the conscious or mature person is to live through the terror of being loved and touched and held.

—Love and Brown (1999, p. 64)

Corrective suggestions that initiate change in an individual's behavior and affect his or her everyday life are a vital part of an effective therapy. Therapeutic progress involves more than identifying destructive thoughts, releasing repressed feelings, and achieving insight; it also requires changing specific behaviors that will create a new interpersonal environment.

The suggestions and methods described in this chapter are focused on helping individuals develop personally in the context of their most intimate associations. They are an integral part of voice therapy and act as catalysts to move people toward new, unfamiliar situations that will challenge their customary defenses. The ideas and recommendations often lead directly to a corrective emotional experience.[1] For instance, when one stops engaging in withholding behaviors that have provoked distance in the relationship, a new set of circumstances is generated, which in turn creates an unfamiliar, albeit more positive, emotional climate. At this point, the dynamics of the relationship shift to a certain extent, which necessitates a different response from the other.

Some suggestions are directed toward helping people alter negative attitudes and core beliefs about themselves and their partner that have interfered with their sustaining a fulfilling sexual relationship. Others are focused more directly on behavioral change. The rationale underlying these suggestions is that each person gradually modifies his or her behavior toward his or her stated goals in opposition to the dictates of critical inner voices. The process also involves breaking habitual ways of relating sexually and disrupting routines that support a fantasy bond.

Corrective experiences are directly related to maladaptive behavior patterns that are influenced or controlled by destructive thought processes. As noted in the previous chapter, these negative thoughts and attitudes affect people's feelings about themselves as men and women, restrict their ability to both give and receive sexual gratification and pleasure, and create tension in the sexual situation. Thus, recognizing their irrationality, understanding their sources, and changing the actions they dictate are worthwhile steps in helping couples achieve a more satisfying sexual relationship.

TEACHING CORE ATTITUDES ABOUT LOVE AND SEXUALITY

Ideally, in working with couples and individuals, the clinician strives to inspire a better understanding of a tender, respectful, and empathic way of being with another person. Clients are encouraged to develop a noncritical, accepting attitude toward themselves and their partner and to be sensitive to the heightened vulnerability associated with experiencing more closeness and sexual intimacy in their relationship. They learn to develop a more empathic understanding of the other person, particularly in situations where they encounter roadblocks in striving to develop their capacity to give and receive love. The following are several attributes that a therapist could inspire.

Compassion and Empathy

It is valuable for men and women to develop a compassionate understanding of themselves and how they function in an intimate relationship. It also is important that they come to realize that their problems in relating sexually and being close emotionally are not unusual in our culture. Clients can benefit from learning that much of the hurt that people in general experience in close relationships is due to an unwillingness to allow the reality of being loved to affect their basic defensive structure.

Both men and women have a tendency to punish others who love them in order to preserve their negative self-image, which is a fundamental part of their defense system. The man who perceives himself as cold or harsh is likely to be cynical toward a woman who indicates an interest in him and eventually he may push her away. Similarly, the woman who sees herself as unattractive or unlovable is likely to find fault with the man who offers her love. Because most people are defended to varying degrees, their intimate relationships, which offer the most potential for happiness and joy, also have the potential for generating considerable pain and distress.

In a sexual relationship, both individuals are often functioning in ways that prohibit the free exchange of psychonutritional products. In other words, they find it difficult to express their feelings of love, affection, and sexuality and to accept loving responses from the other. The intolerance of eroticism and love represents a basic dynamic in couple relationships and is far more common than most believe. Facing the truth about the sources of the emotional pain inherent in being close allows clients to develop more compassion for themselves, empathy for the other person, and a sense of kinship based on an awareness of the hurt that both of them experienced in their formative years.

Generosity

As people become more compassionate and understanding toward one another on a feeling level, they begin to spontaneously express these emotions in numerous acts of kindness. They seek opportunities where they can extend themselves to the other person through sensitive acts of generosity. They discover that giving more freely of themselves, their time and their energy, counteracts self-protective defenses, increases feelings of self-esteem, and makes them feel worthwhile.

The generous acts described here are different in some sense from "exchange agreements" or "contracts" that couples may negotiate in some forms of marital therapy. They are not performed quid pro quo, nor are they performed to gain points, to soothe a nagging spouse, to elevate one's status, or to make one feel superior to one's mate. Acts of this nature are not representative of a genuine giving attitude and can be damaging to both the giver and the receiver. Generosity, in this context, is a sensitive, feeling response to another person's wants and needs. Acts of generosity and altruism that are an outgrowth of a partner's understanding of the other's uniqueness are the most appreciated by the recipient and bring the most satisfaction to the giver.

Essentially, there are three aspects of a healthy response to a generous act on the part of one's mate. The first involves being open to accepting what is offered, allowing the other to meet one's needs; the second involves verbally expressing appreciation; and the third entails reciprocal actions—offering generosity and kindness in return. These actions would not necessarily be the same as what was given. The recipient would simply return the favor by offering something of him- or herself in a way that is sensitive to the other's unique wants, preferences, and needs.

A therapist's philosophical approach in conveying these attitudes helps clients learn that personal happiness and sexual fulfillment are by-products of extending themselves in love and generosity. Sexual intimacy is an outgrowth of each placing the other's well-being and happiness on an equal level with his or her own desires, wants, and priorities.

Individuality

Another attitude to convey to couples is the importance of acknowledging each other as separate individuals and of developing respect for the other's boundaries, wants, and goals. Sustaining a satisfying sexual relationship presupposes a nonintrusive posture in relation to the other's values, interests, and behaviors. Ideally, the individuals become more willing to feel their own emotional pain without implicating the other in their inner conflicts and they relinquish efforts to fix or change the other person.

In being sensitive to each other's wants and needs, it is also important that people do not compromise their integrity in an attempt to maintain harmony. Each person needs to be cautious about demanding fundamental concessions from the other through complaints or other efforts to control the relationship. These compromises often lead to a sense of obligation, resentment, and disharmony. It is also important for each to strive to attain a higher level of self-differentiation, which involves freeing oneself from destructive ties or fantasy bonds with members of one's family-of-origin.

Overcoming Stereotypes

The development of mature sexual attitudes involves challenging and overcoming conventional stereotypes that define men and women as essentially different and basically enemies or, at the very least, as alien to each other. It is important for couples to recognize that much of the tension and pain that has contaminated their sexual relating stems from stereotypes learned throughout life. By becoming more aware of the sexism and distortions of men and women typical in Western society, both people can gradually move beyond these biases to develop empathy for the other, based on a sense of kinship and commonality with members of the opposite sex. During the course of an effective couple therapy, individuals gradually alter the distorted attitudes toward sexuality that they acquired during the process of socialization. They learn to conceptualize sex as a shared pleasure rather than as a conquest, obligation, or submission to a domineering partner.

OVERVIEW OF CORRECTIVE SUGGESTIONS

The fourth step in voice therapy involves formulating corrective suggestions for behavioral change. By the time a couple has reached this phase of therapy, each partner's personal goals for the relationship have become clear and self-evident. Both individuals have developed an awareness of behaviors that limit the relationship and alienate the other person, have developed more compassion for each other and themselves, and have made a concerted effort to focus on constructive behavioral changes.

Both work closely with the therapist and collaborate to interrupt maladaptive behavior patterns by planning corrective experiences that are in accord with each individual's personal goals. Plans for changing behavior tend to fall into two categories: corrective suggestions that help control or interrupt self-nurturing habit patterns and other defensive behaviors; and those that expand people's boundaries by helping them overcome fears.

The first category includes suggestions for challenging and disrupting manifestations of the fantasy bond, which encompass giving up destructive behaviors that predispose alienation as well as altering role-determined habit patterns that support the form rather than the substance of the relationship.

The second category includes suggestions for expanding personal boundaries and enhancing sexual relations, learning to set goals for the relationship, revealing voice attacks while making love, journaling, and composing an imaginary dialogue with one's parent regarding one's sexuality.

Corrective Suggestions for Challenging the Fantasy Bond

Suggestions challenging habitual routines that cut off feeling are important for partners who have become alienated or impersonal in their interactions. Seemingly innocuous alterations in routines and schedules can be a first step in effecting change in an individual's overall defensive posture. Even minor modifications can break into a person's inward, self-protective state and increase his or her energy level and vitality.

One way to break into a habitual behavior pattern is to encourage clients to step out of the traditional roles they have become accustomed to enacting in their relationships. For example, in one couple, the wife characteristically made the decisions, and her husband tended to passively follow her lead. The suggestion was made to switch roles for a certain time period. He was to decide where to go to dinner and which movie they would see, while she was encouraged to avoid giving her opinions regarding his decisions.

Implementing a suggestion that breaks an addictive or compulsive behavior also allows feelings to reemerge that often have been suppressed for years. The use of addictive substances numbs people's feelings of pain, anxiety, and sadness, and unfortunately functions to dull other, more positive emotions as well. There are other self-nurturing activities that are not associated with substance abuse that serve to cut people off from their feelings and isolate them from other people. For example, compulsive work, excessive reading, computer game-playing, television watching, and Internet-surfing are painkillers in that they dull a person's sensitivity to experiences in the interpersonal environment. Even sexuality can be used to cut off feeling. For example, compulsive masturbation, sexual addiction, and routine, mechanical sex without emotional contact can serve the same function as any other addiction.

In one case, a male client indicated that he wanted to have a closer sexual relationship with his wife. When describing this goal to the therapist, he realized that he habitually watched television late at night in spite of his wife's entreaties to come to bed. After identifying the contents of a voice that supported his avoidant behavior, he developed a plan that he hoped would interrupt this pattern. He decided that each night he would turn off the television by 10 p.m. However, he was surprised by the internal resistance he encountered when trying to carry out a plan that he himself had initiated.

In the course of investigating his resistance, the client first remarked that he never would have known that his wife would be so responsive to what he considered to be a slight change in his schedule. On the one hand, he said that he was grateful for the opportunity to compare his wife's positive response to her previous complaints and irritability. On the other hand, he revealed that he felt extremely anxious. He expressed uncertainty about changing other habitual patterns that he knew were interfering with the couple's sexual relationship.

In a subsequent session, the client disclosed that he was now engaging in other compulsive activities such as checking and responding to his e-mails late at night. He recognized that this new activity had taken the edge off his anxiety. He also realized that the feelings of anxiety he had experienced indicated that a strong defense was being disrupted. This understanding motivated him to redouble his efforts to adhere to the schedule he had set and to drop other compulsive activities. The following week, he reported feeling "the best I've felt in years." He attributed his sense of well-being and happiness to the renewed closeness he felt with his wife.

In another case, a woman who was self-centered and domineering provoked her husband by constantly talking. As a result, he felt progressively more distant from her and guilty for feeling angry. In their conjoint sessions, the therapist observed that she attempted to manipulate the conversation to her advantage and interrupted her husband whenever he spoke. After identifying these toxic behaviors and the underlying voices, she and her therapist together formulated a plan to counteract them. She decided to listen to her husband when he spoke without interrupting him. In addition, she would monitor how much time she spent talking as opposed to listening.

Initially, the woman found this plan difficult to follow because it made her anxious and she experienced voice attacks warning her that she was giving up a basic part of her "naturally outgoing" identity. At the same time, she felt relieved as her husband gradually became more relaxed and opened up to her. Describing her reactions in a subsequent session, she reported that she now knew that by talking constantly she had been cutting off a multitude of feelings, both for herself and her husband. She said, "When I'm quiet, just listening to him talk, and really looking at him, I see him as a person separate from me, as vulnerable and lovable. I think it also takes my focus off myself in some way to stop talking and just experience the moment. It also makes me deeply sad. It's interesting though that during those quiet times, I don't have any voice attacks."

There are a number of ways that therapists and clients can plan corrective experiences to disrupt the fantasy bond. People can recognize that their actions are no longer loving, reveal feelings of anger and withholding patterns, and face the pain and sadness involved in trying to resume intimacy. Both partners can expose their fears of individuation, separation, loss, and death, move toward a more independent existence, and develop genuine respect for each other's goals and priorities. They can strive to develop a nondefensive posture toward feedback and work toward establishing an open, honest style of communication. We have found that as manifestations of the fantasy bond are understood and relinquished, partners experience new energy and self-confidence and feel closer to each other, both sexually and emotionally.

Corrective Suggestions for Expanding Personal Boundaries

Suggestions for expanding personal boundaries are valuable for couples who want to enhance their sexual relating. First, they discuss goals for the relationship that each partner feels would enhance the quality of their sexual relating; second, they plan, with the therapist, means of supporting or moving toward these goals; and, then as they move toward a new level of vulnerability, they learn to tolerate the anxiety involved in making positive changes in the relationship. The overall process has an experimental flavor and is undertaken in a cooperative spirit.

Clients may plan suggestions that would increase their tolerance for giving and accepting tender expressions of affection during lovemaking. For example, if one partner realizes that he or she wards off the other person, who typically initiates sexual contact, the couple might plan for that partner to take the initiative in terms of expressing affection, touching, kissing, and sexual caressing. The other person might agree to be the recipient of his or her caresses during lovemaking instead of feeling pressured or expected to always take the initiative.

Couples are encouraged to carry out these types of exercises slowly, with tenderness and sensitivity. Those whose love life has become routine can plan to be more experimental during sex, make arrangements to spend a romantic evening together, or set aside a special time to devote to lovemaking. Many have reported that as a result of participating in these exercises, they have felt a sense of permission that allowed them to go further in their sexual expressiveness and spontaneity.

If clients put into practice the corrective suggestions they plan with the therapist, there will be substantial changes in the overall emotional climate within the couple. As a person modifies behaviors that have created distance during lovemaking or in other areas of the relationship, he or she is generally responded to with more warmth and affection. For example, a female client who engaged in the corrective suggestion to be more expressive of her affectionate feelings to her husband was gratified as he became more communicative and open to her in their daily interactions. As a result, she found herself responding more spontaneously during their lovemaking.

Learning to Set Goals for One's Sexual Relationship

When partners are planning behavioral changes they want to make in their sexual relationship, it is important for each person to focus on setting goals and identifying specific actions that move him or her closer to these goals. Next, the client examines his or her behaviors to determine whether or not they correspond to his or her stated goals. Although people have no power to change another person, they do have the power and ability to change themselves. Changing undesirable behaviors in themselves has the effect of modifying the dynamics and interactions in their relationship.

For example, in therapy, William had decided that a major goal for him was to be closer to his wife, Monica, both during lovemaking and in their daily interactions. In an earlier session, Monica had told William that she wished he would talk with her more about the things he was interested in. In response, William began to spend some time each evening talking with Monica about the events of her day as well as sharing his thoughts and feelings about various aspects of his life.

Returning to his office from a week-long business trip, William received a phone call from Monica who suggested that they go out to dinner to celebrate his homecoming. Feeling that his wife was being inconsiderate of the fact that he was exhausted from traveling and wanted to get home, he started to respond angrily to her request, but quickly stopped himself. As they continued to talk on the phone, William was aware of a series of hostile thoughts about Monica: *If she really cared about you, she would know how you feel. If she was sensitive, she would know that you don't want to go out after spending a week away from home. She's so inconsiderate!*

William realized that if he followed his first impulse to be angry, he would be acting according to the dictates of his hostile voices and against his goal to be closer emotionally to his wife. He decided to make a conscious effort to change his mood of irritation and resentment and to be more open about his feelings based on his real point of view. As the conversation went on, William first admitted that he was tired from traveling. He then told Monica how much he had missed her and said he preferred to spend a romantic evening at home. She responded enthusiastically and that evening, the couple enjoyed dinner and conversation at home, and their lovemaking was especially tender. William was struck by the realization that had he not chosen to directly communicate his real feelings and preferences to Monica, their evening might have been very different.

Clients in individual therapy who wish to become involved in a romantic relationship can also use corrective suggestions. In these instances, clients often think of ideas that will move them in the direction of meeting a potential partner or initiating a conversation with someone they are interested in. Individuals need to identify the voices underlying their hesitancy and awkwardness in approaching others and set reasonable goals toward which they can steadily move.

Encouraging Partners to Reveal Voice Attacks During Sex

As described in chapter 9, partners can use the techniques they have learned during sessions to share or "give away" their destructive thoughts and attitudes while making love. This fifth step in voice therapy is particularly important if partners begin to notice a decrease in sexual desire or arousal or become more involved in thinking rather than feeling. The term "giving away" implies revealing that one is experiencing negative thoughts about oneself or one's partner, taking responsibility for these thoughts, acknowledging that they are not being "caused" by the other, and reassuring the other that these thoughts do not represent one's real point of view.

Instead of trying to ignore intrusive thoughts while concentrating on completing the sex act, people are encouraged to stop and talk about their thoughts and feelings. Even though the couple has actively stopped making love for the moment, it is important that they maintain physical contact while revealing their critical thoughts to each other.

The person experiencing the voice attacks expresses his or her negative thoughts in the second person, as in a therapy session. The other person listens, allowing the partner sufficient time to verbalize all of the voices and express the feelings that accompany them. The focus of this exercise is on maintaining emotional contact and not on necessarily completing the sex act. Couples who have done this exercise report that they experienced a resurgence of affectionate feelings and felt closer rather than more distant.

Case Example

Elaine and Donald were married for 10 years when they began experiencing difficulties in their sexual relating. In couples therapy, they had learned to give away their self-critical thoughts and cynical attitudes to each other. One night while being sexual, Elaine noticed that she had started to feel cut off from her feelings of excitement during foreplay. After some initial hesitation, she decided to apply what she had learned in voice therapy and disclosed her concerns to Donald.

> *Elaine:* It's so strange, but until a minute ago I was feeling really excited and very sexual when you were touching me, but suddenly I started feeling distracted. Then I noticed I wasn't feeling any sensations or feelings. I was thinking of other things, like all the things I have to do tomorrow. So I wanted to stop a minute and talk.
>
> As soon as I became aware of being distracted, I got very critical of myself, thinking, *What's the matter with you? Why can't you just relax? See, now you're not feeling anything. He's going to notice.*
>
> Then I started thinking things about you. I know this sounds weird but I was asking myself if you really wanted to make love with me tonight. I know I'm probably crazy to think something like that, but I wanted to be honest and give it away. As soon as I got cut off, I started thinking, *He doesn't really want to be sexual tonight. You're the one who suggested going to bed early. He just went along with it because he didn't want to hurt your feelings. Can't you see he's preoccupied with other things and doesn't feel that close to you anyway.* That last thought is so much the opposite of how I believe you really feel that it's uncomfortable to say it out loud. [sad]

After listening to Elaine, Donald told her that he was grateful that she had suggested talking because he had started to feel cut off himself.

> *Donald:* It did seem like you started to pull away from me. I hardly noticed it. But then I got nervous and started thinking things like: *What's going on here? She seems excited, She really wanted to be sexual. It must be you. You should touch her more gently, more sensitively, You don't know how to touch a woman. Don't let her know that something's wrong.*

After Donald and Elaine had disclosed their respective voices and shared their feelings, they felt closer to each other and resumed their lovemaking. By taking time to share their thoughts and express their fears, they were able to regain a level of feeling and closeness rather than remaining cut off from their feelings.

Journaling Exercises

As an adjunct to voice therapy sessions, clients can maintain a journal to help them recognize events that precipitate self-attacks and hostile attitudes toward each other as well as to identify the content of such thoughts. Writing down destructive thoughts and attitudes that interfere with the expression of sexual feelings and desires helps individuals challenge their fears of sexual intimacy and make constructive changes in their relationship.

In this journaling process, individuals record their destructive thoughts and attitudes in a specific format: On the left-hand side of the page, they write down self-critical thoughts they have experienced during the day about their sexuality, their partner, and the relationship. They record these thoughts in the second person "you"—the way they verbalize the voices in their sessions. They attempt to allow the thoughts to flow freely, to not censor them, and to write them down as they are "hearing" them in their minds. In other words, they try to capture in writing the snide, sarcastic, or vicious tone of the thoughts they have experienced that day. Next, on the right-hand side of the page, they try to generate a more realistic view of themselves. (See example in Exhibit 10.1.)

Clients then repeat the journaling process, using the same format to write down critical thoughts they have about their mate. These voices may be irrational distortions, but they generally reflect exaggerations of real objectionable traits in their partner. On the left-hand side of the page, they record their negative thoughts in the third person, "he/she" format. Next, they write down a more realistic or rational view on the right side of the paper. (See example in Exhibit 10.2.)

Composing an Imaginary Dialogue With One's Parent

The authors have found it helpful for couples to describe in writing what they believe to be their parents' point of view toward them, their sexuality, their partner, and their relationships. Next, they describe their own point of view on the same subjects. (See Exhibit 10.3.) The purpose of this exercise is to facilitate separation from negative parental introjects and to strengthen aspects of the self system. Afterward, many people seem to be better able to make a clear distinction between attitudes that reflect their parent's point of view and those that represent their own wants, desires, and aspirations.

EXHIBIT 10.1
Negative Thoughts Toward Oneself in a Relationship

Self-critical thoughts	Rational thoughts
Examples: *You're not as sexy as other women. Your breasts are too small. Your hips are too large. You're too fat, too thin. You're not going to feel anything. You're not going to be able to feel excited.*	Examples: *I have a lot of features that are attractive to men. I'm also an interesting person with a good sense of humor. My figure is OK the way it is. When I'm relaxed, I'm very passionate.*
You're not good-looking like the other guys. You're not athletic looking. Your penis is too small. You can't satisfy a woman. You're insensitive and unfeeling.	*Women are attracted to a lot of other qualities in me besides my looks. Most men think their penises are too small. I'm sensitive to women, I feel a lot making love to my girlfriend, and she seems to feel a lot, too.*

EXHIBIT 10.2
Negative Thoughts Toward One's Partner

Hostile attitudes toward partner	Rational attitudes toward partner
Example: *All he/she is interested in is sex.*	Example: *Of course he/she is attracted to me, but he/she is interested in me in many other ways, too.*

EXHIBIT 10.3
An Imaginary Conversation About Sex

What would your mother/father say about your sexuality, your partner, and your sexual relationship?

What my mother/father would say:

_____

_____

_____

_____

_____

_____

_____

_____

_____

_____

_____

What I would say back to my mother/father:

_____

_____

_____

_____

_____

_____

_____

_____

_____

_____

Case Example

Glenn and Claire met at a college dance, started dating, and had been together for six months. They spent nearly every available night making love and were very affectionate. For both, it was the best relationship they had ever experienced. One night, Glenn spoke lightly of the possibility of getting married some day. Soon after, Claire became increasingly critical of Glenn, was preoccupied during sex, and the relationship started to deteriorate. Claire was upset that she was ruining this relationship in much the same way as she had ruined several others, and she was experiencing considerable anxiety. As a result, she sought counseling.

After a few sessions of voice therapy, Claire was asked to say her critical thoughts toward herself and Glenn. As a result of verbalizing her voice and releasing her feelings, she began to recognize her pattern in relationships. In addition, it was suggested that she write an account of her mother's point of view toward her relationship, followed by her own point of view. This was her imaginary dialogue:

> My mother's point of view:
> I agree that Glenn is a nice boy, good-looking and fun to be with. And I can understand that you like sex with him, but darling, think of your future. He has no money, his family is nothing, and besides, he's Jewish. That alone makes it impossible. You know how your father feels about that sort of thing. You know, you were always the rebel, always causing trouble. It's about time you outgrow it. Why can't you be like me, do the right things and live a good and decent life? I stayed with your father even though he was boring. At least he came from a good family.
> My point of view:
> I really love Glenn and I like being with him more than anything I ever did before. I don't give a damn if he has money or not, or where he comes from. He's strong and sensitive and affectionate and we have fun together. You've always been critical of my boyfriends. You don't want me to be happy. You only want things to look right.

After writing her imaginary dialogue, Claire had a clearer understanding and insight about why her relationship had changed when Glenn had talked of marriage and why she felt so anxious. She realized that a serious commitment to Glenn would lead to conflict with her family and, in particular, with her mother. She felt alone and like an outcast, a feeling that was all too familiar. In addition, she recognized that she was very angry at her mother and had always felt hurt and rejected by her. These insights helped her to improve the relationship with Glenn and reduced her level of anxiety.

Resistance to Corrective Suggestions

Resistance occurs in all forms of psychotherapy and is indicative of an underlying fear of and aversion to change (Blatt & Erlich, 1982; Ghent, 1990/1999; Leahy, 2001; Neborsky & Solomon, 2001; Rank, 1941, quoted in Kramer, 1996; Wachtel, 1982). Many couples who seek professional help because they are dissatisfied with their sexual relationship are strongly invested in an inward, defended mode of relating that precludes sexual intimacy. Movement toward fulfilling their sexual potential and increasing their capacity for giving and receiving love is threatening and arouses considerable guilt and anxiety.

Resistance to corrective suggestions can take numerous forms: individuals can continue to act out hostile behaviors while blaming the other for their dissatisfaction, they may be reluctant to carry out a previously agreed-on exercise, or they may be resistant to changing negative perceptions of themselves and cynical views of the other person. When resistance is viewed in terms of protecting the primary defense or fantasy bond from intrusion, it is easier to predict the points at which anxiety will be aroused. Negative reactions can be anticipated whenever there is any change in an individual's cognitive, behavioral, or affective state that threatens either the self-nourishing process or object dependency.

People who engage in corrective suggestions often report that initially they experience increased voice attacks; however, if they maintain the new behavior over an extended period of time, these destructive thoughts gradually diminish. In fact, the anticipatory anxiety aroused prior to instituting changes is often more intense than the actual emotional responses to changing the target behavior. Only by dealing with the anxiety created by positive changes can people hold on to the psychological territory they have gained. Through corrective suggestions individuals realize, on a deep emotional level, that they can gradually increase their tolerance for intimate sexuality without being overwhelmed by primitive fears and anxiety states.

CONCLUSION

Voice therapy techniques, used in conjunction with corrective suggestions in the context of couple or sex therapy, help people challenge negative thought processes, establish important personal goals for their relationship, and develop core attitudes of empathy, compassion, and respect for one another. Corrective suggestions act to challenge the voice process and help clients expand their boundaries. They stimulate changes in each person's actions that are consistent with changes in his or her self-concept. The process of carrying out corrective suggestions teaches people on a deep emotional level that they can apply rational thought and insight to control their distancing behaviors in an intimate relationship.

The suggestions described in this chapter are based on our views about how people could ideally affiliate with one another and express their affection, sexuality, and love.

These recommendations are not based on authoritarian prescriptions from the therapist, nor are they imposed on clients on the basis of a predetermined plan. Just as clients are encouraged to take a strong role in separating the alien point of view represented by the voice from their own point of view, they are encouraged to explore alternatives and possibilities as equal participants in the therapy process. Through candid discussions about aspects of their sexuality and intimate relating that disturb them, each individual, together with the therapist, contributes ideas that apply to his or her unique circumstances. The suggestions and ideas are in accord with an individual's personal goals and focus on the areas of the relationship he or she wishes to change.

Proper timing, rapport, and a strong therapeutic alliance are essential in this phase of therapy. It is important to be aware that these suggestions can lead to serious anxiety states and even regression. Movement toward individuation in a direction away from fantasy bonds and negative parental introjects (the voice) needs to be undertaken with care and diligence and a deep understanding of personality dynamics (Firestone, 1988).

By using self-discipline to overcome defensive behaviors, each person is moving away from compulsively repeating painful experiences from the past. In order to move in that direction, people must take risks at certain crucial points, risks that arouse anxiety. When clients manage to sweat through the anxiety that is inherent in positive change, it gradually diminishes and there is generally substantial therapeutic progress.

NOTE

1. The term "corrective emotional experience" was suggested by Alexander (cited in Arlow, 1989). Alexander believed that the patient needed to have a "corrective emotional experience" to overcome the effects of his or her original traumatic experience.

EPILOGUE

This epilogue reflects our summary views regarding sex and love. As noted throughout the book, people's sexual identity, their love life and sexual practices, are at the core of their existence. Indeed, life is the most satisfying when one's sexuality is combined with love in a close personal relationship. Yet one must not exclude the importance of sexuality, even when it fails to meet these criteria.

The tragedy is that for many people, their sense of self and their sex lives have been damaged in their earliest associations. This interpersonal damage, combined with destructive cultural influences, acts to prevent most people from fulfilling their true potential for sexual comfort and gratification.

The following are excerpts from interviews with each of the authors about their views on sexuality:

Interviewer: As a clinician dealing with the manifestations in adults of what happens to them as children, what's your opinion of the institutionalized, societal attitudes that we have concerning sex, nudity, and the human body?

Robert Firestone: Attitudes toward sex, if you really look at them with any intelligence or perspective, are totally bizarre as people experience them in our culture. Sex is a natural human function, as natural as eating. It's not a separate function. It is not a bizarre activity that people need to do secretly and hide. There's nothing essentially ugly or sinful or bad about a human being, about their body, about their genitals. When a man and a woman are together and they are holding each other and feeling loving, they touch and caress each other. It is a tender moment. The sexual touching is a natural extension of those feelings. It's a natural extension to go from caressing an arm, holding hands, to touching a breast or a vagina or a penis. The sexual touching is no different than any other touching. But you learn early in life to suppress the impulse to touch a penis, to look at it. You're taught that it's bad or wrong to touch a vagina or that you will hurt a woman if you do.

Why are these actions singled out? Why are these parts of the body wrong? They are no different from any other parts of the human body. A strange feeling is attached to them and they come to take on a shame and secrecy. Anything below the waist is bad. Often the genitals are confused with anal functions because both regions are located in the same area. It is just as natural to touch a penis as to touch a hand or a face. It is natural to touch a breast and to hold it. These are not actions to be ashamed of. Why wouldn't people feel easy touching each other? There is nothing wrong with this.

On a simpler level, many women in Europe go topless on the beaches. They feel wonderful, they feel fine. No one is leaping on anybody or attacking anybody. There is no increase in rape. Men are not walking around with giant erections and desperately longing and lurching. There is no chaos. It's just part of a pretty scene, a natural scene. It feels good, it looks good, it's natural.

Interviewer: The socialization process that goes on in every family with their children seems to have inherent within that process the concept that the body is dirty.

Robert Firestone: Within most families, a complete socialization process is imposed on a natural system, foolishly and stupidly. And in a way that damages people seriously. This is why we are concerned with this subject in this book. We see people who are seriously damaged in their attitudes toward their bodies and their sexuality, and it affects them in other areas of their functioning. In fact, the crazy limitations and perverse attitudes against sexuality which make it unclean or peculiar or different from other natural functions lead to serious states of hostility. These states often culminate in vicious acts, such as man against man, which are totally unnecessary. And they are primarily based on this bizarre frustration of a very natural and simple human function.

Interviewer: That being the case, I wonder why it started and why it's maintained.

Robert Firestone: What I think is really operating here is related to death anxiety. In some sense, death can be viewed, or may have been viewed, as a punishment. Because each person who is born is living with a death sentence, we view death as a punishment. There are a lot of powerful emotions surrounding death: fear, anxiety, guilt, shame, fear of the unknown. I think that these negative emotions turned us against our basic nature, our physical nature, which we know cannot ultimately survive.

So we postulate and pray for a soul, a future, an afterlife potential. We hope for something more in us than the body. Unfortunately, along with the postulation of a soul, we turn against life, against the body, and against natural activities and sexual activities. It is a trade-off—the body for the soul. The historical roots for this no-win situation lie in the desperation to avoid death anxiety and the terror of the unknown.

Interviewer: What can be done about this?

Robert Firestone: It is important to bring the subject of sexuality out in to the open, as we have done in this book. I think an open discussion of all the feelings and attitudes and dynamics involved in sexuality help bring the subject out in the open, allowing people to be less ashamed of their sexual nature. I think this type of education is important. The possibility of this education in the public schools would be important. More books, articles, and educational films should be disseminated on this subject. This is why we have written this book.

It is often clear that certain restrictions and taboos about sexuality are unnecessary or destructive or damaging to people. There is an obvious implication that different actions should be taken. People can learn not to act on these negative attitudes. Parents can be educated to not be reactive to behaviors that children engage in, such as masturbation or sex play with peers. Parents can't learn not to have an emotional reaction that has been ingrained in them and has been part of their upbringing, but they can learn to control the destructive urge to suppress or even attack the innocent behavior of children in regard to their sexuality.

Interviewer: It is your opinion that nearly every individual in our society suffers personally in some aspect of his or her sexuality. Why is this so?

Joyce Catlett: Everyone is damaged in his or her sexuality, whether it takes the form of excessive guilt or inhibited sexual drive or perversion or shame about the body or performance anxiety or feelings about themselves as men and women. We are all hurt. As we have discussed in this book, these symptoms are the result of destructive attitudes that are expressed as critical voices that are directed toward both one's self and one's partner. The effects of these attitudes and attacks on a person's sexuality go beyond the sexual area of one's life.

In addition, restrictive societal influences on natural sexuality, such as fanatical religious beliefs, promote shameful attitudes about the body and negative attitudes about sexuality and masturbation and sex play among children. These restrictive teachings can contribute to an increase in adult aggression and hostile behaviors. It is our contention that the immature and puritanical and sexist and suppressive attitudes toward sex that permeate our culture could actually be considered a form of sexual abuse because they cause so much harm.

We contend that beliefs that postulate a soul and an afterlife to counter death anxiety and assure salvation involve a trade-off that requires turning against the body and the core of a person's sexuality. Our work agrees with Terror Management theorists in their understanding that the fear of death causes humans to emphasize differentiation from their animal heritage. In other words, knowing that animals die, people divorce themselves from their animal nature. This defensive reaction has far-reaching consequences for people's sexual development. Many sexual problems reflect this defended adaptation to death anxiety.

Interviewer: Then how can a person have a healthy attitude about sex?

Joyce Catlett:	To have a healthy and natural attitude toward sexuality, a person would have to accept their animal nature and have a positive attitude toward his or her body and nudity and sexual urges. Sex would be seen as a simple and pleasurable act. It would be a high level priority in life. Unfortunately, for many people today sex is a low priority in their lives. Many couples have severely impoverished sexual lives. While many people are avoiding sex and starving themselves sexually, they are finding other sources of gratification. They are substituting addictive behaviors for sex: eating, drinking, smoking, TV watching, internet surfing. You just have to look around you to see examples of these types of behaviors. When a person's sexuality is restricted, it not only has a damaging effect on their personal relationships but it negatively impacts every aspect of their being.
Interviewer:	What would your advice be to people?
Joyce Catlett:	A healthy principle would be to embrace sex as an important aspect of life, to give value to one's sexuality, and strive to improve one's capability to give and receive sexual pleasures. Erich Fromm has described the art of loving, and there is an art to making love as well. There is much that a person can learn. A person can actually benefit from viewing sexuality as a continuous learning process. It is necessary for people to develop the capacity to be sensitive and tender and loving to one another in order to touch someone, and feel for them, and sense what they want, and remain close and compatible. It is important to be comfortable and easy in the sexual situation rather than agitated or hurried. It is important to enjoy each other, and to know each other, and really be with the person you are with. Performance anxiety and self-consciousness have a negative effect on sexual feelings and cause people to lose their focus and disconnect from their partner and can actually disrupt the sex act.
Interviewer:	Sexual attraction is so indefinable and obscure. What would you say makes a person sexually attractive?
Lisa Firestone:	True wanting is at the core of a person being sexually attractive. When you are truly wanting, you are asking an implicit question of the person you are interested in to be responsive to you. Everyone, men

and women alike, benefits from being acknowledged sexually. This is true even when they don't necessarily feel attracted to the other person or they don't plan on being sexual. On the other hand, when people retreat from their sexuality, they do not look as alive or vital. An essential part of sexuality is looking attractive. Ideally, a person's sexuality should be apparent in their everyday life apart from the bedroom. Sex should be openly talked about, and personal feelings and preferences should be discussed in an adult fashion.

Interviewer: How do you think people can develop sexually?

Lisa Firestone: In order to develop sexually, a person must first overcome emotional problems stemming from childhood. These limitations pertain to the early interpersonal environment—to the way people were treated as children. If they grew up in an environment that was not loving or trusting or open to feelings, they necessarily shut down and defended themselves. When children are damaged and hurt they pull inward to cut themselves off from their feelings. Feelings are in the body, not in the head. Therefore, in defending themselves, these children cut themselves off from their bodies. They are subject to self-attacks and destructive voices. They turn away from wanting as a basic defensive reaction and become emotionally and physically deadened.

People who are defended need to maintain control of their feelings and of their expression. Being in control is the enemy of healthy sexuality. Fear of being vulnerable and of being out of control are serious impediments to enjoying sex. Many people are afraid of sex or frightened of being fully responsive because they fear that painful emotions or memories might surface. These people are often more responsive in sexual situations that are distant or more anonymous. Often, after a close and personal and successful sexual experience with someone they love, they defend themselves even more. This explains why some people are so resistant to developing sexually.

People can overcome basic limitations in their sexual lives even though there are powerful resistances, but they must have the courage and persistence to break with core defenses. In order to be free themselves, they must cope with painful emotions and sometimes revive traumatic memories from the past. Accepting the challenge allows for increased sexual pleasure and fulfillment in life.

REFERENCES

Aanstoos, C. M. (2001). Phenomenology of sexuality. In P. J. Kleinplatz (Ed.), *New directions in sex therapy: Innovations and alternatives* (pp. 69–90). Philadelphia: Brunner-Routledge.

Ainsworth, M. D. S., Blehar, M. C., Waters, E., & Wall, S. (1978). *Patterns of attachment: A psychological study of the Strange situation.* Hillsdale, NJ: Erlbaum.

Allen, M. (1997). We've come a long way, too, baby: And we've still got a ways to go: So give us a break! In M. R. Walsh (Ed.), *Women, men, and gender: Ongoing debates* (pp. 402–405). New Haven, CT: Yale University Press.

American Academy of Pediatrics. (2001). Sexuality, contraception, and the media [Electronic version]. *Pediatrics, 107,* 191–194.

American Association of Marriage and Family Therapy Staff. (2002, July/August). The men's movement and beyond: Thoughts from Sam Keen. *Family Therapy Magazine, 1*(4), 32–35.

American Psychiatric Association. (1994). *Diagnostic and statistical manual of mental disorders* (4th ed.). Washington, DC: Author.

American Psychological Association. (2000). *Guidelines for psychotherapy with lesbian, gay, and bisexual clients.* Washington, DC: Author.

Anderson-Fye, E. P. (2003). Never leave yourself: Ethnopsychology as mediator of psychological globalization among Belizean schoolgirls. *Ethos, 31,* 59–94.

Andrews, B. (2002). Body shame and abuse in childhood. In P. Gilbert & J. Miles (Eds.), *Body shame: Conceptualisation, research and treatment* (pp. 256–266). Hove, England: Brunner-Routledge.

Anthony, S. (1973). *The discovery of death in childhood and after.* Harmondsworth, England: Penguin Education. (Original work published 1971)

Araoz, D. L. (1982). *Hypnosis and sex therapy.* New York: Brunner/Mazel.

Aries, E. (1997). Women and men talking: Are they worlds apart? In M. R. Walsh (Ed.), *Women, men, and gender: Ongoing debates* (pp. 91–100). New Haven, CT: Yale University Press.

Arlow, J. A. (1989). Psychoanalysis. In R. J. Corsini & D. Wedding (Eds.), *Current psychotherapies* (4th ed., pp. 19–62). Itasca, IL: Peacock.

Bach, G. R., & Deutsch, R. M. (1979). *Stop! You're driving me crazy.* New York: Berkley Books.

Bader, E., & Pearson, P. T. (1988). *In search of the mythical mate: A developmental approach to diagnosis and treatment in couples therapy.* New York: Brunner/Mazel.

Bader, E., & Pearson, P. T. (with J. D. Schwartz). (2000). *Tell me no lies: How to face the truth and build a loving marriage.* New York: St. Martin's Press.

Bader, M. J. (2002). *Arousal: The secret logic of sexual fantasies.* New York: St. Martin's Press.

Bancroft, J. (1999). Sexual science in 21st century: Where are we going? A personal note. *Journal of Sex Research, 36,* 226–229.

Bancroft, J. (2002). Biological factors in human sexuality. *Journal of Sex Research, 39,* 15–21.

Bandura, A. (1986). *Social foundations of thought and action: A social cognitive theory.* Englewood Cliffs, NJ: Prentice-Hall.

Bandura, A., Ross, D., & Ross, S. A. (1961). Transmission of aggression through imitation of aggressive models. *Journal of Abnormal and Social Psychology, 63,* 575–582.

Barash, D. P., & Lipton, J. E. (2001). *The myth of monogamy: Fidelity and infidelity in animals and people.* New York: Freeman.

Barber, B. K. (1996). Parental psychological control: Revisiting a neglected construct. *Child Development, 67,* 3296–3319.

Barber, B. K. (2002). Reintroducing parental psychological control. In B. K. Barber (Ed.), *Intrusive parenting: How psychological control affects children and adolescents* (pp. 3–13). Washington, DC: American Psychological Association.

Barber, B. K., & Harmon, E. L. (2002). Violating the self: Parental psychological control of children and adolescents. In B. K. Barber (Ed.), *Intrusive parenting: How psychological control affects children and adolescents* (pp. 15–52). Washington, DC: American Psychological Association.

Barrett, L. F., Robin, L., Pietromonaco, P. R., & Eyssell, K. M. (1998). Are women the "more emotional" sex? Evidence from emotional experiences in social context. *Cognition and Emotion, 12,* 555–578.

Basson, R. (2003). Women's difficulties with low sexual desire and sexual avoidance. In S. B. Levine, C. B. Risen, & S. E. Althof (Eds.), *Handbook of clinical sexuality for mental health professionals* (pp. 111–130). New York: Brunner-Routledge.

Batgos, J., & Leadbeater, B. J. (1994). Parental attachment, peer relations, and dysphoria in adolescence. In M. B. Sperling & W. H. Berman (Eds.), *Attachment in adults: Clinical and developmental perspectives* (pp. 155–178). New York: Guilford Press.

Beavers, W. R., & Hampson, R. B. (1990). *Successful families: Assessment and intervention.* New York: Norton.

Beck, A. T. (1976). *Cognitive therapy and the emotional disorders.* New York: New American Library.

Beck, A. T. (1988). *Love is never enough: How couples can overcome misunderstandings, resolve conflicts, and solve relationship problems through cognitive therapy.* New York: Harper & Row.

Beck, A. T., Rush, A. J., Shaw, B. F., & Emery, G. (1979). *Cognitive therapy of depression.* New York: Guilford Press.

Beck, J. S. (1995). *Cognitive therapy: Basics and beyond.* New York: Guilford Press.

Becker, D. V., Sagarin, B. J., Guadagno, R. E., Millevoi, A., & Nicastle, L. D. (2004). When the sexes need not differ: Emotional responses to the sexual and emotional aspects of infidelity. *Personal Relationships, 11,* 529–538.

Becker, E. (1997). *The denial of death.* New York: Free Press. (Original work published 1973)

Beebe, B. (1986). Mother–infant mutual influence and precursors of self and object representations. In J. Masling (Ed.), *Empirical studies of psychoanalytic theories* (Vol. 2, pp. 27–48). Hillsdale, NJ: Analytic Press.

Beebe, B., & Lachmann, L. M. (2002). *Infant research and adult treatment: Co-constructing interactions.* Hillsdale, NJ: Analytic Press.

Belsky, J. (1980). Child maltreatment: An ecological integration. *American Psychologist, 35,* 320–335.

Benjamin, J. (1995). *Like subjects, love objects: Essays on recognition and sexual difference.* New Haven, CT: Yale University Press.

Benjamin, J. (1999). Women's Oedipal conflicts and boys' Oedipal ideology. In D. Bassin (Ed.), *Female sexuality: Contemporary engagements* (pp. 87–95). Northvale, NJ: Jason Aronson.

Berg-Cross, L. (1997). *Couples therapy.* Thousand Oaks, CA: Sage.

Bergen, H. A., Martin, G., Richardson, A. S., Allison, S., & Roeger, L. (2003). Sexual abuse and suicidal behavior: A model constructed from a large community sample of adolescents. *Journal of the American Academy of Child and Adolescent Psychiatry, 42,* 1301–1309.

Berne, E. (1961). *Transactional analysis in psychotherapy: A systematic individual and social psychiatry.* New York: Grove Press.

Berne, E. (1964). *Games people play: The psychology of human relationships.* New York: Grove Press.

Bettelheim, B. (1979). Individual and mass behavior in extreme situations. In *Surviving and other essays* (pp. 48–83). New York: Knopf. (Original work published 1943)

Beutler, L. E. (1997). The psychotherapist as a neglected variable in psychotherapy: An illustration by reference to the role of therapist experience and training. *Clinical Psychology: Science and Practice, 4,* 44–52.

Beyer, S., & Finnegan, A. (1997, August). *The accuracy of gender stereotypes regarding occupations.* Paper presented at the 105th annual meeting of the American Psychological Association, Chicago.

Bianchi-Demicheli, F., & Zutter, A. (2005). Intensive short-term dynamic sex therapy: A proposal. *Journal of Sex and Marital Therapy, 31,* 57–72.

Bigler, R. S. (1999). Psychological interventions designed to counter sexism in children: Empirical limitations and theoretical foundations. In W. B. Swann, Jr., J. H. Langlois, & L. A. Gilbert (Eds.), *Sexism and stereotypes in modern society: The gender science of Janet Taylor Spence* (pp. 129–151). Washington, DC: American Psychological Association.

Billig, M. (1987). *Arguing and thinking: A rhetorical approach to social psychology.* Cambridge, England: Cambridge University Press.

Billig, M., Condor, S., Edwards, D., Gane, M., Middleton, D., & Radley, A. (1988). *Ideological dilemmas: A social psychology of everyday thinking.* London: Sage.

Bishay, N. R. (1988). Cognitive therapy in psychosexual dysfunctions: A preliminary report. *Sex and Marital Therapy, 3,* 83–90.

Blatt, S. J., & Erlich, H. S. (1982). Levels of resistance in the psychotherapeutic process. In P. L. Wachtel (Ed.), *Resistance: Psychodynamic and behavioral approaches* (pp. 69–91). New York: Plenum Press.

Bloch, D. (1978). *"So the witch won't eat me": Fantasy and the child's fear of infanticide.* New York: Grove.

Bloch, D. (1985). The child's fear of infanticide and the primary motive force of defense. *Psychoanalytic Review, 72,* 573–588.

Bly, R. (1990). *Iron John: A book about men.* Reading, MA: Addison-Wesley.

Bocknek, G., & Perna, F. (1994). Studies in self-representation beyond childhood. In J. M. Masling & R. F. Bornstein (Eds.), *Empirical perspectives on object relations theory* (pp. 29–58). Washington, DC: American Psychological Association.

Bogaert, A. F., & Sadava, S. (2002). Adult attachment and sexual behavior. *Personal Relationships, 9,* 191–204.

Bollas, C. (1987). *The shadow of the object: Psychoanalysis of the unthought known.* New York: Columbia University Press.

Bollas, C. (2000). *Hysteria.* New York: Routledge.

Bolton, F. G., Jr. (1983). *When bonding fails: Clinical assessment of high-risk families.* Beverly Hills, CA: Sage.

Bolton, F. G., Jr., Morris, L. A., & MacEahron, A. E. (1989). *Males at risk: The other side of child sexual abuse.* Newbury Park, CA: Sage.

Bonner, B. L. (2001). Normal and abnormal sexual behavior in children. *Psychotherapy Bulletin, 36*(4), 16–19.

Bornstein, R. F. (1993). Parental representations and psychopathology: A critical review of the empirical literature. In J. M. Masling & R. F. Bornstein (Eds.), *Psychoanalytic perspectives on psychopathology* (pp. 1–41). Washington, DC: American Psychological Association.

Boszormenyi-Nagy, I., & Spark, G. M. (1984). *Invisible loyalties: Reciprocity in intergenerational family therapy.* New York: Brunner/Mazel.

Bowen, M. (1978). *Family therapy in clinical practice.* New York: Jason Aronson.

Bowlby, J. (1973). *Attachment and loss: Vol. II. Separation: Anxiety and anger.* New York: Basic Books.

Bray, J. H. (1991). The Personal Authority in the Family System Questionnaire: Assessment of intergenerational family relationships. In D. S. Williamson (Ed.), *The intimacy paradox: Personal authority in the family system* (pp. 273–286). New York: Guilford Press.

Brennan, K. A., & Shaver, P. R. (1995). Dimensions of adult attachment, affect regulation, and romantic relationship functioning. *Personality and Social Psychology Bulletin, 21,* 267–283.

Bretherton, I. (1996). Internal working models of attachment relationships as related to resilient coping. In G. G. Noam & K. W. Fischer (Eds.), *Development and vulnerability in close relationships* (pp. 3–27). Mahwah, NJ: Erlbaum.

Bretherton, I., & Munholland, K. A. (1999). Internal working models in attachment relationships: A construct revisited. In J. Cassidy & P. R. Shaver (Eds.), *Handbook of attachment: Theory, research, and clinical applications* (pp. 89–111). New York: Guilford Press.

Briere, J. N. (1992). *Child abuse trauma: Theory and treatment of the lasting effects.* Newbury Park, CA: Sage.

Briere, J., & Elliott, D. M. (2003). Prevalence and psychological sequelae of self-reported childhood physical and sexual abuse in a general population sample of men and women. *Child Abuse and Neglect, 27,* 1205–1222.

Brody, S. (2004). Slimness is associated with greater intercourse and lesser masturbation frequency. *Journal of Sex and Marital Therapy, 30,* 251–261.

Brooks, D. (2003, November 8). Love, internet style. *New York Times* [Electronic version]. Retrieved November 8, 2003, from http://www.nytimes.com/2003/11/08/opinion/08Broo.html

Burleson, B. R., Kunkel, A. W., Samter, W., & Werking, J. (1996). Men's and women's evaluations of communication skills in personal relationships: When sex differences make a difference—and when they don't. *Journal of Social and Personal Relationships, 13,* 201–224.

Burn, S. M. (1996). *The social psychology of gender.* New York: McGraw-Hill.

Burton, R. (2001). *The anatomy of melancholy.* New York: New York Review Books. (Original work published 1621)

Buss, D. M. (1994). *The evolution of desire: Strategies of human mating.* New York: Basic Books.

Buss, D. M. (2000). *The dangerous passion: Why jealousy is as necessary as love and sex.* New York: Free Press.

Buss, D. M., & Barnes, M. (1996). Preferences in human mate selection. *Journal of Personality and Social Psychology, 50,* 559–570.

Buss, D. M., & Schmitt, D. P. (1993). Sexual strategies theory: An evolutionary perspective on human mating. *Psychological Review, 100,* 204–232.

Bussey, K., & Bandura, A. (1984). Influence of gender constancy and social power on sex-linked modeling. *Journal of Personality and Social Psychology, 47,* 1292–1302.

Buunk, B. P., Angleitner, A., Oubaid, V., & Buss, D. M. (1996). Sex differences in jealousy in evolutionary and cultural perspective: Tests from the Netherlands, Germany, and the United States. *Psychological Science, 7,* 359–363.

Buunk, B., & Hupka, R. B. (1987). Cross-cultural differences in the elicitation of sexual jealousy. *Journal of Sex Research, 23,* 12–22.

Calderone, M. S., & Johnson, E. W. (1989). *The family book about sexuality* (Rev. ed.). New York: Harper & Row.

Canary, D. J., Cupach, W. R., & Messman, S. J. (1995). *Relationship conflict: Conflict in parent–child, friendship, and romantic relationships.* Thousand Oaks, CA: Sage.

Caplan, P. J. (1981). *Between women: Lowering the barriers.* Toronto, Canada: Personal Library.

Carnes, P. (1997). *Sexual anorexia: Overcoming sexual self-hatred*. Center City, MN: Hazelden.

Carpenter, K. M., & Addis, M. E. (2000). Alexithymia, gender, and responses to depressive symptoms. *Sex Roles, 43*, 629–644.

Chen, Z., & Kaplan, H. B. (2001). Intergenerational transmission of constructive parenting. *Journal of Marriage and Family, 63*, 17–31.

Chesler, P. (2001). *Woman's inhumanity to woman*. New York: Thunder's Mouth Press/Nation Books.

Chessick, R. D. (1992). On falling in love and creativity. *Journal of the American Academy of Psychoanalysis, 20*, 347–373.

Chiland, C. (2004). Gender and sexual difference. In I. Matthis (Ed.), *Dialogues on sexuality, gender, and psychoanalysis* (pp. 79–91). London: Karnac.

Chodorow, N. (1978). *The reproduction of mothering: Psychoanalysis and the sociology of gender*. Berkeley: University of California Press.

Chodorow, N. J. (1989). *Feminism and psychoanalytic theory*. New Haven, CT: Yale University Press.

Chodorow, N. J. (1999). *The power of feelings: Personal meaning in psychoanalysis, gender, and culture*. New Haven, CT: Yale University Press.

Cobia, D. C., Sobansky, R. R., & Ingram, M. (2004). Female survivors of childhood sexual abuse: Implications for couples' therapists. *Family Journal, 12*, 312–318.

Coelho, P. (2004). *Eleven minutes* (M. J. Costa, Trans.). New York: HarperCollins.

Cole, P. M., & Putnam, F. W. (1992). Effect of incest on self and social functioning: A developmental psychopathology perspective. *Journal of Consulting and Clinical Psychology, 60*, 174–184.

Conte, J. R. (1988). The effects of sexual abuse on children: Results of a research project. In R. A. Prentky & V. L. Quinsey (Eds.), *Human sexual aggression: Current perspectives* (pp. 310–326). New York: New York Academy of Sciences.

Conway, M. (2000). On sex roles and representations of emotional experience: Masculinity, femininity, and emotional awareness. *Sex Roles, 43*, 687–698.

Courtois, C. A. (1999). *Recollections of sexual abuse: Treatment principles and guidelines*. New York: Norton.

Courtois, C. A. (2000). The aftermath of child sexual abuse: The treatment of complex posttraumatic stress reactions. In L. T. Szuchman & F. Muscarella (Eds.), *Psychological perspectives on human sexuality* (pp. 549–572). New York: Wiley.

Cramer, B. (1997). The transmission of womanhood from mother to daughter. In B. S. Mark & J. A. Incorvaia (Eds.), *The handbook of infant, child, and adolescent psychotherapy: Vol. 2. New directions in integrative treatment* (pp. 373–391). Northvale, NJ: Jason Aronson.

Crosbie-Burnett, M., Foster, T. L., Murray, C. L., & Bowen, G. L. (1996). Gays' and lesbians' families-of-origin: A social–cognitive–behavioral model of adjustment. *Family Relations, 45*, 397–403.

Cummings, E. M., Goeke-Morey, M. C., & Raymond, J. (2004). Fathers in family context: Effects of marital quality and marital conflict. In M. E. Lamb (Ed.), *The role of the father in child development* (4th ed., pp. 196–221). New York: Wiley.

Daly, M., & Wilson, M. (1983). *Sex, evolution, and behavior* (2nd ed.). Belmont, CA: Wadsworth.

Daly, M., & Wilson, M. (1988). *Homicide.* New York: Aldine De Gruyter.

D'Angelo, L. L., Weinberger, D. A., & Feldman, S. S. (1995). Like father, like son? Predicting male adolescents' adjustment from parents' distress and self-restraint. *Developmental Psychology, 31,* 883–896.

Davidson, J. K., & Darling, C. A. (1993). Masturbatory guilt and sexual responsiveness among post–college-age women: Sexual satisfaction revisited. *Journal of Sex and Marital Therapy, 19,* 289–300.

Davis, K. (1977). Jealousy and sexual property. In G. Clanton & L. G. Smith (Eds.), *Jealousy* (pp. 129–134). New York: Lanham.

Deaux, K. (1999). An overview of research on gender: Four themes from 3 decades. In W. B. Swann Jr., J. H. Langlois, & L. A. Gilbert (Eds.), *Sexism and stereotypes in modern society: The gender science of Janet Taylor Spence* (pp. 11–33). Washington, DC: American Psychological Association.

DeMause, L. (1991). The universality of incest. *Journal of Psychohistory, 19,* 123–164.

DeSteno, D. A., & Salovey, P. (1996). Jealousy and the characteristics of one's rival: A self-evaluation maintenance perspective. *Personality and Social Psychology Bulletin, 22,* 920–932.

deWeerth, C., & Kalma, A. P. (1993). Female aggression as a response to sexual jealousy: A sex role perversion? *Aggressive Behavior, 19,* 265–279.

Dicks, H. V. (1967). *Marital tensions: Clinical studies towards a psychological theory of interaction.* London: Karnac Books.

Dindia, K., & Allen, M. (1992). Sex differences in self-disclosure: A meta-analysis. *Psychological Bulletin, 112,* 106–124.

Dittmann, M. (2004). Women like women more than men like men. *Monitor on Psychology, 35*(11), 11.

Dix, C. (1985). *The new mother syndrome: Coping with postpartum stress and depression.* New York: Pocket Books.

Doll, L. S., Koenig, L. J., & Purcell, D. W. (2004). Child sexual abuse and adult sexual risk: Where are we now? In L. J. Koenig, L. S. Doll, A. O'Leary, & W. Pequegnat (Eds.), *From child sexual abuse to adult sexual risk: Trauma, revictimization, and intervention* (pp. 3–10). Washington, DC: American Psychological Association.

Dorais, M. (2002). *Don't tell: The sexual abuse of boys* (I. D. Meyer, Trans.). Montreal, Canada: McGill-Queen's University Press.

Dowling, C. (2000). *The frailty myth: Redefining the physical potential of women and girls.* New York: Random House.

Downey, G., Feldman, S., & Ayduk, O. (2000). Rejection sensitivity and male violence in romantic relationships. *Personal Relationships, 7,* 45–61.

Downing, C. (1977). Jealousy: A depth–psychological perspective. In G. Clanton & L. G. Smith (Eds.), *Jealousy* (pp. 72–79). New York: Lanham.

Duck, S. (1994). *Meaningful relationships: Talking, sense, and relating.* Thousand Oaks, CA: Sage.

Dutton, D. G. (1995a). *The batterer: A psychological profile.* New York: Basic Books.

Dutton, D. G. (1995b). *The domestic assault of women: Psychological and criminal justice perspectives* (Rev. ed.). Vancouver, Canada: UBC Press.

Dutton, D. G., & Aron, A. P. (1974). Some evidence for heightened sexual attraction under conditions of high anxiety. *Journal of Personality and Social Psychology, 30,* 510–517.

Eagle, M., & Wolitzky, D. L. (1997). Empathy: A psychoanalytic perspective. In A. C. Bohart & L. S. Greenberg (Eds.), *Empathy reconsidered: New directions in psychotherapy* (pp. 217–244). Washington, DC: American Psychological Association.

Eagly, A. H., & Crowley, M. (1986). Gender and helping behavior: A meta-analytic review of the social psychological literature. *Psychological Bulletin, 100,* 283–308.

Eagly, A. H., & Wood, W. (1999). The origins of sex differences in human behavior: Evolved dispositions versus social roles. *American Psychologist, 54,* 408–423.

Edwards, W. M., & Coleman, E. (2004). Defining sexual health: A descriptive overview. *Archives of Sexual Behavior, 33,* 189–195.

Elliott, K. J. (1999). The "inner critic" as a key element in working with adults who have experienced childhood sexual abuse. *Bulletin of the Menninger Clinic, 63,* 240–253.

Ellis, A. (1973). *Humanistic psychotherapy: The rational–emotive approach.* New York: Julian.

Ellis, A. (1996). The treatment of morbid jealousy: A rational–emotive behavior therapy approach. *Journal of Cognitive Psychotherapy, 10,* 23–33.

Ellis, A., & Harper, R. A. (1975). *A new guide to rational living.* North Hollywood, CA: Wilshire Books.

Ellis, B. J., Bates, J. E., Dodge, K. A., Fergusson, D. M., Horwood, L. J., Pettit, G. S., et al. (2003). Does father absence place daughters at special risk for early sexual activity and teenage pregnancy? *Child Development, 74,* 801–821.

Elson, M. (Ed.). (1987). *The Kohut seminars on self psychology and psychotherapy with adolescents and young adults.* New York: Norton.

Epstein, S. (1973). The self-concept revisited or a theory of a theory. *American Psychologist, 28,* 404–416.

Epstein, S. (1993). Implications of cognitive–experiential self-theory for personality and developmental psychology. In D. C. Funder, R. D. Parke, C. Tomlinson-Keasey, & K. Widaman (Eds.), *Studying lives through time: Personality and development* (pp. 399–438). Washington, DC: American Psychological Association.

Epstein, S. (1994). Integration of the cognitive and the psychodynamic unconscious. *American Psychologist, 49,* 709–724.

Epstein, S., Lipson, A., Holstein, C., & Huh, E. (1992). Irrational reactions to negative outcomes: Evidence for two conceptual systems. *Journal of Personality and Social Psychology, 62,* 328–339.

Erikson, E. H. (1963). *Childhood and society* (2nd ed.). New York: Norton.

Everaerd, W., Laan, E. T. M., Both, S., & van der Velde, J. (2000). Female sexuality. In L. T. Szuchman & F. Muscarella (Eds.), *Psychological perspectives on human sexuality* (pp. 101–146). New York: Wiley.

Everaerd, W., Laan, E. T. M., & Spiering, M. (2000). Male sexuality. In L. T. Szuchman & F. Muscarella (Eds.), *Psychological perspectives on human sexuality* (pp. 60–100). New York: Wiley.

Fagot, B. I., & Hagan, R. (1991). Observations of parent reactions to sex-stereotyped behaviors: Age and sex effects. *Child Development, 62,* 617–628.

Fairbairn, W. R. D. (1952). *Psychoanalytic studies of the personality.* London: Routledge & Kegan Paul.

Faller, K. C. (1999). Child maltreatment and protection in the United States. In K. C. Faller (Ed.), *Maltreatment in early childhood: Tools for research-based intervention* (pp. 1–12). New York: Haworth Press.

Fausto-Sterling, A. (2000). *Sexing the body: Gender politics and the construction of sexuality.* New York: Basic Books.

Feeney, J. A. (1999). Adult romantic attachment and couple relationships. In J. Cassidy & P. R. Shaver (Eds.), *Handbook of attachment: Theory, research, and clinical applications* (pp. 355–377). New York: Guilford Press.

Feeney, J. A., Noller, P., & Patty, J. (1993). Adolescents' interactions with the opposite sex: Influence of attachment style and gender. *Journal of Adolescence, 16,* 169–186.

Fehr, B., & Broughton, R. (2001). Gender and personality differences in conceptions of love: An interpersonal theory analysis. *Personal Relationships, 8,* 115–136.

Felitti, V. J. (2002). The relation between adverse childhood experiences and adult health: Turning gold into lead. *Permanente Journal, 6*(1), 44–47.

Felitti, V. J., Anda, R. F., Nordenberg, D., Williamson, D. F., Spitz, A. M., Edwards, V., et al. (1998). Relationship of childhood abuse and household dysfunction to many of the leading causes of death in adults: The Adverse Childhood Experiences (ACE) study. *American Journal of Preventive Medicine, 14,* 245–258.

Felson, R. B. (2002). *Violence and gender reexamined.* Washington, DC: American Psychological Association.

Fenchel, G. H. (1986). Maternal unavailability as intergenerational trauma. *Issues in Ego Psychology, 9,* 25–31.

Fenchel, G. H. (Ed.). (1998). *The mother–daughter relationship: Echoes through time.* Northvale, NJ: Jason Aronson.

Fenchel, G. H. (2000). Eroticism and the conventional. *Journal of the American Academy of Psychoanalysis, 28*, 163–173.

Ferenczi, S. (1955). Confusion of tongues between adults and the child. In M. Balint (Ed.), *Final contributions to the problems and methods of psycho-analysis* (M. Balint & E. Mosbacher, Trans., pp. 156–167). New York: Basic Books. (Original work published 1933)

Fergusson, D. M., Horwood, L. J., & Lynskey, M. T. (1996). Childhood sexual abuse and psychiatric disorder in young adulthood: II. Psychiatric outcomes of childhood sexual abuse. *Journal of the American Academy of Child and Adolescent Psychiatry, 10*, 1365–1374.

Fierman, L. B. (Ed.). (1965). *Effective psychotherapy: The contribution of Hellmuth Kaiser.* New York: Free Press.

Firestone, R. W. (1957). *A concept of the schizophrenic process.* Unpublished doctoral dissertation, University of Denver, CO.

Firestone, R. W. (1984). A concept of the primary fantasy bond: A developmental perspective. *Psychotherapy, 21*, 218–225.

Firestone, R. W. (1985). *The fantasy bond: Structure of psychological defenses.* Santa Barbara, CA: Glendon Association.

Firestone, R. W. (1987). Destructive effects of the fantasy bond in couple and family relationships. *Psychotherapy, 24*, 233–239.

Firestone, R. W. (1988). *Voice therapy: A psychotherapeutic approach to self-destructive behavior.* Santa Barbara, CA: Glendon Association.

Firestone, R. W. (1990a). The bipolar causality of regression. *American Journal of Psychoanalysis, 50*, 121–135.

Firestone, R. W. (1990b). *Compassionate child-rearing: An in-depth approach to optimal parenting.* Santa Barbara, CA: Glendon Association.

Firestone, R. W. (1990c). Voices during sex: Application of voice therapy to sexuality. *Journal of Sex and Marital Therapy, 16*, 258–274.

Firestone, R. W. (1993). The psychodynamics of fantasy, addiction, and addictive attachments. *American Journal of Psychoanalysis, 53*, 335–352.

Firestone, R. W. (1994a). A new perspective on the Oedipal complex: A voice therapy session. *Psychotherapy, 31*, 342–351.

Firestone, R. W. (1994b). Psychological defenses against death anxiety. In R. A. Neimeyer (Ed.), *Death anxiety handbook: Research, instrumentation, and application* (pp. 217–241). Washington, DC: Taylor & Francis.

Firestone, R. W. (1997a). *Combating destructive thought processes: Voice therapy and separation theory.* Thousand Oaks, CA: Sage.

Firestone, R. W. (1997b). *Suicide and the inner voice: Risk assessment, treatment, and case management.* Thousand Oaks, CA: Sage.

Firestone, R. W. (2002). The death of psychoanalysis and depth therapy. *Psychotherapy, 39*, 223–232.

Firestone, R. W., & Catlett, J. (1989). *Psychological defenses in everyday life.* Santa Barbara, CA: Glendon Association.

Firestone, R. W., & Catlett, J. (1999). *Fear of intimacy.* Washington, DC: American Psychological Association.

Firestone, R. W., & Firestone, L. (2004). Methods for overcoming the fear of intimacy. In D. J. Mashek & A. Aron (Eds.), *Handbook of closeness and intimacy* (pp. 375–395). Mahwah, NJ: Erlbaum.

Firestone, R. W., Firestone, L., & Catlett, J. (2003). *Creating a life of meaning and compassion: The wisdom of psychotherapy.* Washington, DC: American Psychological Association.

Fischer, K. W., & Ayoub, C. (1996). Analyzing development of working models of close relationships: Illustration with a case of vulnerability and violence. In G. G. Noam & K. W. Fischer (Eds.), *Development and vulnerability in close relationships* (pp. 173–199). Mahwah, NJ: Erlbaum.

Fisher, H. (1992). *Anatomy of love: A natural history of mating, marriage, and why we stray.* New York: Fawcett Columbine.

Fisher, H. (2000). Lust, attraction, attachment: Biology and evolution of the three primary emotion systems for mating, reproduction, and parenting. *Journal of Sex Education and Therapy, 25,* 96–104.

Fisher, H. (2004). *Why we love: The nature and chemistry of romantic love.* New York: Henry Holt.

Fisher, H. E., Aron, A., Mashek, D., Li, H., & Brown, L. L. (2002). Defining the brain systems of lust, romantic attraction, and attachment. *Archives of Sexual Behavior, 31,* 413–419.

Fisher, S., & Fisher, R. L. (1986). *What we really know about child-rearing: Science in support of effective parenting.* Northvale, NJ: Jason Aronson.

Fiske, S. T., Bersoff, D. N., Borgida, E., Deaux, K., & Heilman, M. E. (1997). What constitutes a scientific review? A majority retort to Barrett and Morris. In M. R. Walsh (Ed.), *Women, men, and gender: Ongoing debates* (pp. 321–333). New Haven, CT: Yale University Press.

Foley, S., Kope, S. A., & Sugrue, D. P. (2002). *Sex matters for women: A complete guide to taking care of your sexual self.* New York: Guilford Press.

Fosha, D. (2000). *The transforming power of affect: A model for accelerated change.* New York: Basic Books.

Fox, R. (1993). The lamp at the end of the tunnel. In D. N. Suggs & A. W. Miracle (Eds.), *Culture and human sexuality: A reader* (pp. 213–216). Pacific Grove, CA: Brooks/Cole. (Original work published 1983)

Fraley, R. C., & Shaver, P. R. (2000). Adult romantic attachment: Theoretical developments, emerging controversies, and unanswered questions. *Review of General Psychology, 4,* 132–154.

Fraley, R. C., Waller, N. G., & Brennan, K. A. (2000). An item–response theory analysis of self-report measures of adult attachment. *Journal of Personality and Social Psychology, 78,* 350–365.

Francoeur, R. T. (2001). Challenging collective religious/social beliefs about sex, marriage, and family. *Journal of Sex Education and Therapy, 26,* 281–290.

Freud, A. (1966). *The ego and the mechanisms of defense* (Rev. ed.). Madison, CT: International Universities Press.

Freud, S. (1953). Three essays on the theory of sexuality. In J. Strachey (Ed. & Trans.), *The standard edition of the complete psychological works of Sigmund Freud* (Vol. 7, pp. 125–243). London: Hogarth Press. (Original work published 1905)

Freud, S. (1955). Some neurotic mechanisms in jealousy, paranoia and homosexuality. In J. Strachey (Ed. & Trans.), *The standard edition of the complete psychological works of Sigmund Freud* (Vol. 8, pp. 221–232). London: Hogarth Press. (Original work published 1922)

Freud, S. (1957). Five lectures on psycho-analysis. In J. Strachey (Ed. & Trans.), *The standard edition of the complete psychological works of Sigmund Freud* (Vol. 11, pp. 1–56). London: Hogarth Press. (Original work published 1909)

Freud, S. (1957). On the universal tendency to debasement in the sphere in love: Contributions to the psychology of love II. In J. Strachey (Ed. & Trans.), *The standard edition of the complete psychological works of Sigmund Freud* (Vol. 11, pp. 179–190). London: Hogarth Press. (Original work published 1912)

Freud, S. (1964). An outline of psycho-analysis. In J. Strachey (Ed. & Trans.), *The standard edition of the complete psychological works of Sigmund Freud* (Vol. 23, pp. 144–207). London: Hogarth Press. (Original work published 1940)

Freyd, J. J. (1996). *Betrayal trauma: The logic of forgetting childhood abuse.* Cambridge, MA: Harvard University Press.

Friday, N. (1977). *My mother/my self: The daughter's search for identity.* New York: Delacorte Press.

Friday, N. (1985). *Jealousy.* New York: William Morrow.

Fried, E. (1960). *The ego in love and sexuality.* New York: Grune & Stratton.

Friedman, R. C., & Downey, J. I. (2002). *Sexual orientation and psychoanalysis: Sexual science and clinical practice.* New York: Columbia University Press.

Fromm, E. (1956). *The art of loving.* New York: Bantam Books.

Gage, R. L. (Ed.). (1976). *Choose life: A dialogue: Arnold Toynbee and Daisaku Ikeda.* Oxford, England: Oxford University Press.

Gagnon, J. H. (1985). Attitudes and responses of parents to pre-adolescent masturbation. *Archives of Sexual Behavior, 14,* 451–466.

Galinsky, E. (1981). *Between generations.* New York: Times Books.

Gartner, R. B. (1999). *Betrayed as boys: Psychodynamic treatment of sexually abused men.* New York: Guilford Press.

Geary, D. C. (1998). *Male, female: The evolution of human sex differences.* Washington, DC: American Psychological Association.

Geis, F. L. (1993). Self-fulfilling prophecies: A social psychological view of gender. In A. E. Beall & R. J. Sternberg (Eds.), *The psychology of gender* (pp. 9–54). New York: Guilford Press.

Genevie, L., & Margolies, E. (1987). *The motherhood report: How women feel about being mothers.* New York: Macmillan.

Gentzler, A. L., & Kerns, K. A. (2004). Associations between insecure attachment and sexual experiences. *Personal Relationships, 11*, 249–265.

Gerson, R. (1995). The family life cycle: Phases, stages, and crises. In R. H. Mikesell, D. Lusterman, & S. H. McDaniel (Eds.), *Integrating family therapy: Handbook of family psychology and systems theory* (pp. 91–111). Washington, DC: American Psychological Association.

Gewirtz, J. L., & Hollenbeck, A. R. (1990). Effects on parents of contact/touch in the first postpartum hour. In N. Gunzenhauser (Ed.), *Advances in touch: New implications in human development* (pp. 62–71). Skillman, NJ: Johnson & Johnson Consumer Products.

Ghent, E. (1999). Masochism, submission, surrender: Masochism as a perversion of surrender. In S. A. Mitchell & L. Aron (Eds.), *Relational psychoanalysis: The emergence of a tradition* (pp. 211–242). Hillsdale, NJ: Analytic Press. (Original work published 1990)

Giddens, A. (1992). *The transformation of intimacy: Sexuality, love and eroticism in modern societies.* Stanford, CA: Stanford University Press.

Gilligan, C. (1982). *In a different voice: Psychological theory and women's development.* Cambridge, MA: Harvard University Press.

Gilligan, C. (1991). Women's psychological development: Implications for psychotherapy. In C. Gilligan, A. G. Rogers, & D. L. Tolman (Eds.), *Women, girls and psychotherapy: Reframing resistance* (pp. 5–31). New York: Haworth Press.

Gilligan, C. (1996). The centrality of relationship in human development: A puzzle, some evidence, and a theory. In G. G. Noam & K. W. Fischer (Eds.), *Development and vulnerability in close relationships* (pp. 237–261). Mahwah, NJ: Erlbaum.

Gilmartin, B. F. (1977). Jealousy among the swingers. In G. Clanton & L. G. Smith (Eds.), *Jealousy* (pp. 152–158). New York: Lanham.

Glass, S. P. (with J. C. Staeheli). (2003). *Not "just friends:" Protect your relationship from infidelity and heal the trauma of betrayal.* New York: Free Press.

Glass, S. P., & Wright, T. L. (1988). Clinical implications of research on extramarital involvement. In R. A. Brown & J. R. Field (Eds.), *Treatment of sexual problems in individual and couples therapy* (pp. 301–346). Costa Mesa, CA: PMA.

Glass, S. P., & Wright, T. L. (1997). Reconstructing marriages after the trauma of infidelity. In W. K. Halford & H. J. Markman (Eds.), *Clinical handbook of marriage and couples interventions* (pp. 471–507). New York: Wiley.

Glick, P., & Fiske, S. T. (2001). An ambivalent alliance: Hostile and benevolent sexism as complementary justifications for gender inequality. *American Psychologist, 56*, 109–118.

Gold, S. N., Lucenko, B. A., Elhai, J. D., Swingle, J. M., & Sellers, A. H. (1999). A comparison of psychological/psychiatric symptomatology of women and men sexually abused as children. *Child Abuse and Neglect, 23*, 683–692.

Goldberg, C. (1996). *Speaking with the devil: A dialogue with evil.* New York: Viking.

Goldenberg, J. L., Cox, C. R., Pyszczynski, T., Greenberg, J., & Solomon, S. (2002). Understanding human ambivalence about sex: The effects of stripping sex of meaning [Electronic version]. *Journal of Sex Research, 39,* 310–320.

Goldenberg, J. L., Landau, M. J., Pyszczynski, T., Cox, C. R., Greenberg, J., Solomon, S., et al. (2003). Gender-typical responses to sexual and emotional infidelity as a function of mortality salience induced self-esteem striving. *Personality and Social Psychology Bulletin, 29,* 1585–1595.

Goldenberg, J. L., Pyszczynski, T., Greenberg, J., & Solomon, S. (2000). Fleeing the body: A terror management perspective on the problem of human corporeality. *Personality and Social Psychology Review, 4,* 200–218.

Goldenberg, J. L., Pyszczynski, T., McCoy, S. K., Greenberg, J., & Solomon, S. (1999). Death, sex, love, and neuroticism: Why is sex such a problem? *Journal of Personality and Social Psychology, 77,* 1173–1187.

Goren, E. (2003). America's love affair with technology: The transformation of sexuality and the self over the 20th century. *Psychoanalytic Psychology, 20,* 487–508.

Gottman, J. M. (1979). *Marital interaction: Experimental investigations.* New York: Academic Press.

Gottman, J. M., & Krokoff, L. J. (1989). Marital interaction and satisfaction: A longitudinal view. *Journal of Consulting and Clinical Psychology, 57,* 47–52.

Greenberg, L. S. (2002). *Emotion-focused therapy: Coaching clients to work through their feelings.* Washington, DC: American Psychological Association.

Greenberg, L. S., & Safran, J. D. (1987). *Emotion in psychotherapy: Affect, cognition, and the process of change.* New York: Guilford Press.

Grossman, M., & Wood, W. (1993). Sex differences in intensity of emotional experience: A social role interpretation. *Journal of Personality and Social Psychology, 65,* 1010–1022.

Guidano, V. F., & Liotti, G. (1983). *Cognitive processes and emotional disorders: A structural approach to psychotherapy.* New York: Guilford Press.

Gunderson, M. P., & McCary, J. L. (1979). Sexual guilt and religion. *Family Coordinator, 28,* 353–357.

Guntrip, H. (1961). *Personality structure and human interaction: The developing synthesis of psycho-dynamic theory.* New York: International Universities Press.

Guntrip, H. (1969). *Schizoid phenomena: Object relations and the self.* New York: International Universities Press.

Guntrip, H. (1971). *Psychoanalytic theory, therapy, and the self: A basic guide to the human personality in Freud, Erikson, Klein, Sullivan, Fairbairn, Hartmann, Jacobson, and Winnicott.* New York: Basic Books.

Harding, C. (2001). Introduction. In C. Harding (Ed.), *Sexuality: Psychoanalytic perspectives* (pp. 1–17). East Sussex, England: Brunner-Routledge.

Harlow, H. F. (1958). The nature of love. *American Psychologist, 13,* 673–685.

Harlow, H. F., Harlow, M. K., & Suomi, S. J. (1971). From thought to therapy: Lessons from a primate laboratory. *American Scientist, 59,* 538–549.

Harper, J. M., Anderson, R., & Stevens, N. A. (2004, September 10). *Development of the Couple Implicit Rule Profile (CIRP)*. Poster session presented at the American Association for Marriage and Family Therapy Conference, Atlanta, GA.

Harvey, J. H., & Weber, A. L. (2002). *Odyssey of the heart: Close relationships in the 21st century* (2nd ed.). Mahwah, NJ: Erlbaum.

Hatfield, E. (1988). Passionate and companionate love. In R. J. Sternberg & M. L. Barnes (Eds.), *The psychology of love* (pp. 191–217). New Haven, CT: Yale University Press.

Hatfield, E., & Rapson, R. L. (1993). *Love, sex, and intimacy: Their psychology, biology, and history*. New York: HarperCollins.

Hazan, C., & Diamond, L. M. (2000). The place of attachment in human mating. *Review of General Psychology, 4*, 186–204.

Hazan, C., & Shaver, P. R. (1987). Romantic love conceptualized as an attachment process. *Journal of Personality and Social Psychology, 52*, 511–524.

He, Z. (2001). Pornography, perceptions of sex, and sexual callousness: A cross-cultural comparison. In Y. R. Kamalipour & K. R. Rampal (Eds.), *Media, sex, violence, and drugs in the global village* (pp. 131–152). Lanham, MD: Rowman & Littlefield.

Heiman, J. R., & Heard-Davison, A. R. (2004). Child sexual abuse and adult sexual relationships: Review and perspective. In L. J. Koenig, L. S. Doll, A. O'Leary, & W. Pequegnat (Eds.), *From child sexual abuse to adult sexual risk: Trauma, revictimization, and intervention* (pp. 13–47). Washington, DC: American Psychological Association.

Hellinger, B. (with G. Weber & H. Beaumont). (1998). *Love's hidden symmetry: What makes love work in relationships*. Phoenix, AZ: Zeig, Tucker.

Herdt, G. (2004). Sexual development, social oppression, and local culture. *Sexuality Research and Social Policy, 1*, 39–62.

Herman, J. (with L. Hirschman). (1981). *Father–daughter incest*. Cambridge, MA: Harvard University Press.

Herman, J. (1992). *Trauma and recovery*. New York: Basic Books.

Hogben, M., & Byrne, D. (1998). Using social learning theory to explain individual differences in human sexuality [Electronic version]. *Journal of Sex Research, 35*, 58–71.

Holtzworth-Munroe, A., Stuart, G. L., & Hutchinson, G. (1997). Violent versus nonviolent husbands: Differences in attachment patterns, dependency, and jealousy. *Journal of Family Psychology, 11*, 314–331.

Hook, M. K., Gerstein, L. H., Detterich, L., & Gridley, B. (2003). How close are we? Measuring intimacy and examining gender differences. *Journal of Counseling and Development, 81*, 462–472.

hooks, b. (2001). Men: Comrades in struggle. In M. S. Kimmel & M. A. Messner (Eds.), *Men's lives* (5th ed., pp. 527–535). Boston: Allyn & Bacon. (Original work published 1984)

Horney, K. (1967). *Feminine psychology*, New York: Norton.

Horvath, A. O., & Luborsky, L. (1993). The role of the therapeutic alliance in psychotherapy. *Journal of Consulting and Clinical Psychology, 61,* 561–573.

Hudson, L., & Jacot, B. (1995). *Intimate relations: The natural history of desire.* New Haven, CT: Yale University Press.

Hyde, J. S., & Oliver, M. B. (2000). Gender differences in sexuality: Results from meta-analysis. In C. B. Travis & J. W. White (Eds.), *Sexuality, society, and feminism* (pp. 57–77). Washington, DC: American Psychological Association.

Hyun, M., Friedman, S. D., & Dunner, D. L. (2000). Relationship of childhood physical and sexual abuse to adult bipolar disorder. *Bipolar Disorders, 2,* 131–135.

Ickes, W. (1993). Traditional gender roles: Do they make, and then break, our relationships? *Journal of Social Issues, 49,* 71–85.

Insel, T. R. (2002). Implications for the neurobiology of love. In S. G. Post, L. G. Underwood, J. P. Schloss, & W. B. Hurlbut (Eds.), *Altruism and altruistic love: Science, philosophy, and religion in dialogue* (pp. 254–263). New York: Oxford University Press.

Jain, A., Belsky, J., & Crnic, K. (1996). Beyond fathering behaviors: Types of dads. *Journal of Family Psychology, 10,* 431–442.

Johnson, S. M. (1999). Emotionally focused couple therapy: Straight to the heart. In J. M. Donovan (Ed.), *Short-term couple therapy* (pp. 13–42). New York: Guilford Press.

Johnson, S. M. (2002). *Emotionally focused couple therapy with trauma survivors: Strengthening attachment bonds.* New York: Guilford Press.

Johnson, S. M. (2003). The revolution in couple therapy: A practitioner–scientist perspective. *Journal of Marital and Family Therapy, 29,* 365–384.

Johnson, S. M. (2004). *The practice of emotionally focused couple therapy: Creating connection* (2nd ed.). New York: Brunner-Routledge.

Johnson, S. M., & Denton, W. (2002). Emotionally focused couple therapy: Creating secure connections. In A. S. Gurman & N. S. Jacobson (Eds.), *Clinical handbook of couple therapy* (3rd ed., pp. 221–250). New York: Guilford Press.

Johnson, S. M., & Greenberg, L. S. (1995). The emotionally focused approach to problems in adult attachment. In N. S. Jacobson & A. S. Gurman (Eds.), *Clinical handbook of couple therapy* (pp. 121–141). New York: Guilford Press.

Johnson, S. M., Hunsley, J., Greenberg, L., & Schindler, D. (1999). Emotionally focused couples therapy: Status and challenges. *Clinical Psychology: Science and Practice, 6,* 67–79.

Johnson, S. M., & Whiffen, V. E. (1999). Made to measure: Adapting emotionally-focused couple therapy to partners' attachment styles. *Clinical Psychology: Science and Practice, 6,* 366–381.

Jolliff, D., & Horne, A. M. (1999). Growing up male: The development of mature masculinity. In A. M. Horne & M. S. Kiselica (Eds.), *Handbook of counseling boys and adolescent males: A practitioner's guide* (pp. 3–23). Thousand Oaks, CA: Sage.

Jordan, J. V., Kaplan, A. G., Miller, J. B., Stiver, I. P., & Surrey, J. L. (1991). *Women's growth in connection: Writing from the Stone Center*. New York: Guilford Press.

Jureidini, R. (2001). Perversion: Erotic form of hatred or exciting avoidance of reality? *Journal of the American Academy of Psychoanalysis, 29*, 195–211.

Kaplan, H. S. (1974). *The new sex therapy: Active treatment of sexual dysfunctions*. New York: Brunner/Mazel.

Kaplan, H. S. (1979). *Disorders of sexual desire and other new concepts and techniques in sex therapy*. New York: Brunner/Mazel.

Kaplan, H. S. (1995). *The sexual desire disorders: Dysfunctional regulation of sexual motivation*. Levittown, PA: Brunner/Mazel.

Kaplan, L. J. (1984). *Adolescence: The farewell to childhood*. New York: Simon & Schuster.

Karpel, M. (1976). Individuation: From fusion to dialogue. *Family Process, 15*(1), 65–82.

Karpel, M. A. (1994). *Evaluating couples: A handbook for practitioners*. New York: Norton.

Karr-Morse, R., & Wiley, M. S. (1997). *Ghosts from the nursery: Tracing the roots of violence*. New York: Oxford University Press.

Kastenbaum, R. (1974). Childhood: The kingdom where creatures die. *Journal of Clinical Child Psychology, 3*(2), 11–14.

Kastenbaum, R. (1995). *Death, society, and human experience* (5th ed.). Boston: Allyn & Bacon.

Kaufman, G. (1980). *Shame: The power of caring*. Cambridge, MA: Schenkman.

Keeley, M. P., & Hart, A. J. (1994). Nonverbal behavior in dyadic interactions. In S. Duck (Ed.), *Dynamics of relationships* (pp. 135–162). Thousand Oaks, CA: Sage.

Keen, S. (1997). *To love and be loved*. New York: Bantam Books.

Kellett, J. M. (2000). Older adult sexuality. In L. T. Szuchman & F. Muscarella (Eds.), *Psychological perspectives on human sexuality* (pp. 355–379). New York: Wiley.

Kelsey, M., & Kelsey, B. (1991). Sex and religion [Electronic version]. Retrieved November 9, 2004, from http://innerself.com/Sex_Talk/Sex_And_Religion.htm

Kenrick, D. T., & Trost, M. R. (1993). The evolutionary perspective. In A. E. Beall & R. J. Sterling (Eds.), *The psychology of gender* (pp. 148–172). New York: Guilford Press.

Kernberg, O. F. (1980). *Internal world and external reality: Object relations theory applied*. Northvale, NJ: Jason Aronson.

Kernberg, O. F. (1991). Aggression and love in the relationship of the couple. In G. I. Fogel & W. A. Myers (Eds.), *Perversions and near-perversions in clinical practice: New psychoanalytic perspectives* (pp. 153–175). New Haven, CT: Yale University Press.

Kernberg, O. F. (1995). *Love relations: Normality and pathology*. New Haven, CT: Yale University Press.

Kerr, M. E., & Bowen, M. (1988). *Family evaluation: An approach based on Bowen theory*. New York: Norton.

Kestenberg, J. S., & Kestenberg, M. (1987). Child killing and child rescuing. In G. G. Neuman (Ed.), *Origins of human aggression: Dynamics and etiology* (pp. 139–154). New York: Human Sciences Press.

Keys, A., Brozek, J., Henschel, A., Mickelsen, O., & Taylor, H. L. (1950). *The biology of human starvation* (Vol. 2). Minneapolis: University of Minnesota Press.

Kindlon, D., & Thompson, M. (1999). *Raising Cain: Protecting the emotional life of boys*. New York: Ballantine Books.

Kinzl, J. F., Traweger, C., & Biebl, W. (1995). Sexual dysfunctions: Relationship to childhood sexual abuse and early family experiences in a nonclinical sample. *Child Abuse and Neglect, 19*, 785–792.

Kipnis, L. (2003). *Against love: A polemic*. New York: Pantheon Books.

Kirkpatrick, L. A. (1998). Evolution, pair–bonding, and reproductive strategies: A reconceptualization of adult attachment. In J. A. Simpson & W. S. Rholes (Eds.), *Attachment theory and close relationships* (pp. 353–393). New York: Guilford Press.

Kirschner, S., & Kirschner, D. A. (1996). Relational components of the incest survivor syndrome. In F. W. Kaslow (Ed.), *Handbook of relational diagnosis and dysfunctional family patterns* (pp. 407–419). New York: Wiley.

Kiselica, M. S. (2001, August). Are attachment disorders and alexithymia characteristic of males? In M. S. Kiselica (Chair), *Are males really emotional dummies? What do the data indicate?* Symposium conducted at the annual meeting of the American Psychological Association, San Francisco, CA.

Klein, Marty. (1992). *Ask me anything: A sex therapist answers the most important questions for the '90s*. New York: Simon & Schuster.

Klein, Melanie. (1975). *The writings of Melanie Klein: Vol. III. Envy and gratitude and other works 1946–1963*. New York: Free Press.

Kleinplatz, P. J. (2001). A critical evaluation of sex therapy: Room for improvement. In P. J. Kleinplatz (Ed.), *New directions in sex therapy: Innovations and alternatives* (pp. xi–xxxiii). Philadelphia: Brunner-Routledge.

Kohut, H. (1977). *The restoration of the self*. New York: International Universities Press.

Kramer, R. (Ed.). (1996). *Otto Rank: A Psychology of Difference: The American Lectures*. Princeton, NJ: Princeton University Press.

Kriegman, D. (1999). Parental investment, sexual selection, and evolved mating strategies: Implications for psychoanalysis. *Psychoanalytic Psychology, 16*, 528–533.

Kupers, T. A. (1997). The politics of psychiatry: Gender and sexual preference in *DSM–IV*. In M. R. Walsh (Ed.), *Women, men, and gender: Ongoing debates* (pp. 340–347). New Haven, CT: Yale University Press.

Laing, R. D. (1967). *The politics of experience*. New York: Ballantine Books.

Lamb, M. E., & Lewis, C. (2004). The development and significance of father–child relationships in two-parent families. In M. E. Lamb (Ed.), *The role of the father in child development* (4th ed., pp. 272–306). New York: Wiley.

Laumann, E. O., Gagnon, J. H., Michael, R. T., & Michaels, S. (1994). *The social organization of sexuality: Sexual practices in the United States*. Chicago: University of Chicago Press.

Laumann, E. O., Paik, A., & Rosen, R. C. (1999). Sexual dysfunction in the United States: Prevalence and predictors. *Journal of the American Medical Association, 281,* 537–544.

Lawrence, D. H. (1920). *Women in love*. London: Penguin Books.

Leahy, R. L. (2001). *Overcoming resistance in cognitive therapy*. New York: Guilford Press.

LeDoux, J. (1996). *The emotional brain: The mysterious underpinnings of emotional life*. New York: Simon & Schuster.

Leiblum, S. R., & Rosen, R. C. (2000). Introduction: Sex therapy in the age of Viagra. In S. R. Leiblum & R. C. Rosen (Eds.), *Principles and practice of sex therapy* (3rd ed., pp. 1–13). New York: Guilford Press.

Lester, D. (1970). Relation of fear of death in subjects to fear of death in their parents. *Psychological Record, 20,* 541–543.

Levant, R. F. (1992). Toward the reconstruction of masculinity. *Journal of Family Psychology, 5,* 379–402.

Levant, R. F. (1998). Desperately seeking language: Understanding, assessing, and treating normative male alexithymia. In W. S. Pollack & R. F. Levant (Eds.), *New psychotherapy for men* (pp. 35–56). New York: Wiley.

Levi-Strauss, C. (1993). The incest prohibition. In D. N. Suggs & A. W. Miracle (Eds.), *Culture and human sexuality: A reader* (pp. 229–236). Pacific Grove, CA: Brooks/Cole. (Original work published 1969)

Lewis, C. S. (1960). *The four loves*. New York: Harcourt Brace.

Lewis, M. (1992). *Shame: The exposed self*. New York: Free Press.

Lewis, T., Amini, F., & Lannon, R. (2000). *A general theory of love*. New York: Vintage Books.

Lieberman, A. F. (2004). Traumatic stress and quality of attachment: Reality and internalization in disorders of infant mental health. *Infant Mental Health Journal, 25,* 336–351.

Lieberman, A. F., Compton, N. C., Van Horn, P., & Ippen, C. G. (2003). *Losing a parent to death in the early years: Guidelines for the treatment of traumatic bereavement in infancy and early childhood*. Washington, DC: Zero to Three.

Lieberman, A. F., & Van Horn, P. (2004). *Don't hit my mommy: A manual for child–parent psychotherapy with young witnesses of family violence*. Washington, DC: Zero to Three.

Liebowitz, M. R. (1983). *The chemistry of love*. Boston: Little, Brown.

Lisak, D. (1994). The psychological impact of sexual abuse: Content analysis of interviews with male survivors. *Journal of Traumatic Stress, 7,* 525–548.

Loftus, E., & Ketcham, K. (1994). *The myth of repressed memory: False memories and allegations of sexual abuse.* New York: St. Martin's Griffin.

LoPiccolo, J. (1978). The professionalization of sex therapy: Issues and problems. In J. LoPiccolo & L. LoPiccolo (Eds.), *Handbook of sex therapy* (pp. 511–526). New York: Plenum.

LoPiccolo, J. (1994). The evolution of sex therapy. *Sexual and Marital Therapy, 9,* 5–7.

Lott, B. (1997). Cataloging gender differences: Science or politics? In M. R. Walsh (Ed.), *Women, men, and gender: Ongoing debates* (pp. 19–23). New Haven, CT: Yale University Press.

Lott, D. A. (1998). Brain development, attachment and impact on psychic vulnerability. *Psychiatric Times, XV*(5). Retrieved September 26, 2004, from http://www.psychiatrictimes.com/p980547.html

Love, P. (with J. Robinson). (1990). *The emotional incest syndrome: What to do when a parent's love rules your life.* New York: Bantam Books.

Love, P. (2001).*The truth about love: The highs, the lows, and how you can make it last forever.* New York: Simon & Schuster.

Love, P., & Brown, J. T. (1999). Creating passion and intimacy. In J. Carlson & L. Sperry (Eds.), *The intimate couple* (pp. 55–65). Philadelphia: Brunner/Mazel.

Love, P., & Robinson, J. (1994). *Hot monogamy: Essential steps to more passionate, intimate lovemaking.* New York: Penguin Books.

Love, P., & Shulkin, S. (1997). *How to ruin a perfectly good relationship.* Austin, TX: Authors.

Lusterman, D. (1995). Treating marital infidelity. In R. H. Mikesell, D. Lusterman, & S. H. McDaniel (Eds.), *Integrating family therapy: Handbook of family psychology and systems theory* (pp. 259–269). Washington, DC: American Psychological Association.

Lyons-Ruth, K., & Zeanah, C. H., Jr. (1993). The family context of infant mental health: I. Affective development in the primary caregiving relationship. In C. H. Zeanah, Jr. (Ed.), *Handbook of infant mental health* (pp. 14–37). New York: Guilford Press.

Maccoby, E. E., & Jacklin, C. N. (1974). *The psychology of sex differences.* Stanford, CA: Stanford University Press.

Mahler, M. S., Pine, F., & Bergman, A. (1975). *The psychological birth of the human infant: Symbiosis and individuation.* New York: Basic Books.

Main, M., & Goldwyn, R. (1984). Predicting rejection of her infant from mother's representation of her own experience: Implications for the abuse–abusing intergenerational cycle. *Child Abuse and Neglect, 8,* 203–217.

Main, M., & Solomon, J. (1986). Discovery of an insecure–disorganized/disoriented attachment pattern. In T. B. Brazelton & M. W. Yogman (Eds.), *Affective development in infancy* (pp. 95–124). Norwood, NJ: Ablex.

Malone, T. P., & Malone, P. T. (1987). *The art of intimacy.* New York: Prentice-Hall.

Manlove, E. E., & Vernon-Feagans, L. (2002). Caring for infant daughters and sons in dual-earner households: Maternal reports of father involvement in weekday time and tasks. *Infant and Child Development, 11,* 305–320.

Manson, W. (1994). *Riddles of eros: Exploring sex, psyche and culture.* Lanham, MD: University Press of America.

Marmor, J. (2004). Changing patterns of femininity: Psychoanalytic implications. *Journal of the American Academy of Psychoanalysis and Dynamic Psychiatry, 32,* 7–20.

Martinson, F. M. (1994). *The sexual life of children.* Westport, CT: Bergin & Garvey.

Masters, W. H., & Johnson, V. E. (1966). *Human sexual response.* Boston: Little, Brown.

Masters, W. H., & Johnson, V. E. (1970). *Human sexual inadequacy.* Boston: Little, Brown.

Masterson, J. F. (1985). *The real self: A developmental, self, and object relations approach.* New York: Brunner/Mazel.

Mathes, E. W. (1991). A cognitive theory of jealousy. In P. Salovey (Ed.), *The psychology of jealousy and envy* (pp. 52–78). New York: Guilford Press.

May, R. (1969). *Love and will.* New York: Dell.

Mazur, R. (2000). *The new intimacy: Open-ended marriage and alternative lifestyles.* San Jose, CA: toExcel Press. (Original work published 1973)

McCarthy, B. W. (1995). Childhood sexual trauma and adult sexual desire: A cognitive–behavioral perspective. In R. C. Rosen & S. R. Leiblum (Eds.), *Case studies in sex therapy* (pp. 148–160). New York: Guilford Press.

McCarthy, B. W. (1997a). Strategies and techniques for revitalizing a nonsexual marriage. *Journal of Sex and Marital Therapy, 23,* 231–240.

McCarthy, B. W. (1997b). Therapeutic and iatrogenic interventions with adults who were sexually abused as children. *Journal of Sex and Marital Therapy, 23,* 118–125.

McCarthy, B. W. (1999). Relapse prevention strategies and techniques for inhibited sexual desire. *Journal of Sex and Marital Therapy, 25,* 297–303.

McCarthy, B., & McCarthy, E. (1998). *Male sexual awareness: Increasing sexual satisfaction* (Rev. ed.). New York: Carroll & Graf.

McCarthy, B., & McCarthy, E. (2003). *Rekindling desire: A step-by-step program to help low-sex and no-sex marriages.* New York: Brunner-Routledge.

McConaghy, N. (2003). Sexual and gender identity disorders. In M. Hersen & S. M. Turner (Eds.), *Adult psychopathology and diagnosis* (4th ed., pp. 506–554). New York: Wiley.

Mead, G. H. (1967). *Mind, self, and society: From the standpoint of a social behaviorist.* Chicago: University of Chicago Press. (Original work published 1934)

Mead, M. (1948). *Male and female: A study of sexes in a changing world.* New York: William Morrow.

Melby, T. (2001). Telling the truth in schools about sex. *Contemporary Sexuality*, 35(5), 1, 4–5.

Mendell, D. (1998). The impact of the mother–daughter relationship on women's relationships with men: The two-man phenomenon. In G. H. Fenchel (Ed.), *The mother–daughter relationship: Echoes through time* (pp. 227–240). Northvale, NJ: Jason Aronson.

Meston, C. M., & Heiman, J. R. (2000). Sexual abuse and sexual function: An examination of sexually relevant cognitive processes. *Journal of Consulting and Clinical Psychology*, 68, 399–406.

Meston, C. M., Heiman, J. R., & Trapnell, P. D. (1999). The relation between early abuse and adult sexuality. *Journal of Sex Research*, 36, 385–395.

Metz, M. E., & McCarthy, B. (2004). A biopsychosocial approach to evaluating and treating premature ejaculation. *Contemporary Sexuality*, 38(5), i–vii.

Miletski, H. (1995). *Mother–son incest: The unthinkable broken taboo: An overview of findings*. Brandon, VT: Safer Society Press.

Miller, A. (1981). *Prisoners of childhood: The drama of the gifted child and the search for the true self* (R. Ward, Trans.). New York: Basic Books. (Original work published 1979)

Miller, A. (1984a). *For your own good: Hidden cruelty in child-rearing and the roots of violence* (2nd ed., H. Hannum & H. Hannum, Trans.). New York: Farrar, Straus, & Giroux. (Original work published 1980)

Miller, A. (1984b). *Thou shalt not be aware: Society's betrayal of the child* (H. Hannum & H. Hannum, Trans.). New York: Farrar, Straus & Giroux. (Original work published 1981)

Miller, G. (2000). *The mating mind: How sexual choice shaped the evolution of human nature*. New York: Anchor Books.

Miller, J. B. (1976). *Toward a new psychology of women*. Boston: Beacon Press.

Miller, J. B., & Stiver, I. P. (1994). *Movement in therapy: Honoring the "strategies disconnection."* (Stone Center Work in Progress #65; pp. 1–13). Wellesley, MA: Wellesley College.

Mitchell, S. A. (2002). *Can love last? The fate of romance over time*. New York: Norton.

Moir, A., & Jessel, D. (1989). *Brainsex: The real difference between men and women*. London: Mandarin.

Montagu, A. (1986). *Touching: The human significance of the skin* (3rd ed.). New York: Harper & Row.

Moore, D. S., & Travis, C. B. (2000). Biological models and sexual politics. In C. B. Travis & J. W. White (Eds.), *Sexuality, society, and feminism* (pp. 35–56). Washington, DC: American Psychological Association.

Morokoff, P. J. (2000). A cultural context for sexual assertiveness in women. In C. B. Travis & J. W. White (Eds.), *Sexuality, society, and feminism* (pp. 299–319). Washington, DC: American Psychological Association.

Morrison, A. P. (1989). *Shame: The underside of narcissism*. Hillsdale, NJ: Analytic Press.

Mullen, P. E., & Fleming, J. (1998, Autumn). Long-term effects of child abuse [Electronic version]. *Issues in Child Abuse Prevention, 9*. Retrieved March 3, 2004, from the National Child Protection Clearinghouse Web site (Melbourne, Australia): http://aifs.org.au/nch/issues9.html

Nagy, M. H. (1959). The child's view of death. In H. Feifel (Ed.), *The meaning of death* (pp. 79–98). New York: McGraw-Hill. (Original work published 1948)

Nealer, J. (2002). Children's gender identity development: A closer look. *Family Therapy Magazine*, 24–27.

Neborsky, R. J., & Solomon, M. F. (2001). Attachment bonds and intimacy: Can the primary imprint of love change? In M. F. Solomon, R. J. Neborsky, L. McCullough, M. Alpert, F. Shapiro, & D. Malan (Eds.), *Short-term therapy for long-term change* (pp. 155–185). New York: Norton.

Nelson, D. A., & Crick, N. R. (2002). Parental psychological control: Implications for childhood physical and relational aggression. In B. K. Barber (Ed.), *Intrusive parenting: How psychological control affects children and adolescents* (pp. 161–189). Washington, DC: American Psychological Association.

Newberger, C. M., & deVos, E. (1988). Abuse and victimization: A life-span developmental perspective. *American Journal of Orthopsychiatry, 58,* 505–511.

Noyes, R., Hoenk, P. R., Kuperman, S., & Slymen, D. J. (1977). Depersonalization in accident victims and psychiatric patients. *Journal of Nervous and Mental Disease, 164,* 401–407.

Oates, R. K. (2004). Sexual abuse and suicidal behavior. *Child Abuse and Neglect, 28,* 487–489.

Oatley, K. (1996). Emotions: Communications to the self and others. In R. Harre & W. G. Parrott (Eds.), *The emotions: Social, cultural and biological dimensions* (pp. 312–316). London: Sage.

Ogilvie, B. A. (2004). *Mother–daughter incest: A guide for helping professionals*. New York: Haworth Press.

Oliver, K. (Ed.). (2002). *The portable Kristeva* (Updated ed.). New York: Columbia University Press.

Olsen, K. L. (1992). Genetic influences on sexual behavior differentiation. In A. A. Gerall, H. Moltz, & I. L. Ward (Eds.), *Handbook of behavioral neurobiology: Vol. 11. Sexual differentiation* (pp. 1–38). New York: Plenum Press.

Orbach, I., Shopen-Koffman, R., & Mikulincer, M. (1994). The impact of subliminal symbiotic vs. identification messages in reducing anxiety. *Journal of Research in Personality, 28,* 492–504.

Orbach, S. (1999). *The impossibility of sex*. New York: Penguin.

Orbach, S. (2004). The body in clinical practice. In K. White (Ed.), *Touch: Attachment and the body: The John Bowlby memorial conference monograph 2003* (pp. 17–47). London: Karnac.

Pagels, E. (1988). *Adam, Eve, and the serpent*. New York: Random House.

Pagels, E. (1995). *The origin of Satan*. New York: Random House.

Park, J. (1995). *Sons, mothers and other lovers*. London: Abacus.

Parker, G. (1983). *Parental overprotection: A risk factor in psychosocial development*. New York: Grune & Stratton.

Parker, R. (1995). *Mother love/mother hate: The power of maternal ambivalence*. New York: Basic Books.

Parrott, W. G., & Harre, R. (1996). Overview. In R. Harre & W. G. Parrott (Eds.), *The emotions: Social, cultural and biological dimensions* (pp. 1–20). London: Sage.

Perris, C., Jacobsson, L., Lindstrom, H., von Knorring, L., & Perris, H. (1980). Development of a new inventory for assessing memories of parental rearing behaviour. *Acta Psychiatrica Scandinavica, 61*, 265–274.

Person, E. S. (1988). *Dreams of love and fateful encounters: The power of romantic passion*. New York: Penguin Books.

Phillips, N. A. (2000). Female sexual dysfunction: Evaluation and treatment. *American Family Physician, 62*, 127–136, 141–142.

Pines, A. M. (1998). *Romantic jealousy: Causes, symptoms, cures*. New York: Routledge.

Pines, A. M. (1999). *Falling in love: Why we choose the lovers we choose*. New York: Routledge.

Pines, A., & Aronson, E. (1983). Antecedents, correlates, and consequences of sexual jealousy. *Journal of Personality, 51*, 108–136.

Pleck, J. H. (1995). The gender role strain paradigm: An update. In R. F. Levant & W. S. Pollack (Eds.), *A new psychology of men* (pp. 11–32). New York: Basic Books.

Pleck, J. H. (1997). Paternal involvement: Levels, sources, and consequences. In M. E. Lamb (Ed.), *The role of the father in child development* (3rd ed., pp. 66–103). New York: Wiley.

Plutchik, R. (2000). *Emotions in the practice of psychotherapy: Clinical implications of affect theories*. Washington, DC: American Psychological Association.

Pollack, W. (1998). *Real boys: Rescuing our sons from the myths of boyhood*. New York: Henry Holt.

Pollack, W., S., & Levant, R. F. (Eds.). (1998). *New psychotherapy for men*. New York: Wiley.

Pope, K. S., & Brown, L. S. (1996). *Recovered memories of abuse: Assessment, therapy, forensics*. Washington, DC: American Psychological Association.

Post, S. G., Underwood, L. G., Schloss, J. P., & Hurlbut, W. B. (2002). General introduction. In S. G. Post, L. G. Underwood, J. P. Schloss, & W. B. Hurlbut (Eds.), *Altruism and altruistic love: Science, philosophy, and religion in dialogue* (pp. 3–12). New York: Oxford University Press.

Prescott, J. W. (1975, November). Body pleasure and the origins of violence. *The Bulletin of the Atomic Scientists*, 10–20. Retrieved February 27, 2004, from http://www.violence.de/prescott/bulletin/article.html

Purcell, D. W., Malow, R. M., Dolezal, C., & Carballo-Dieguez, A. (2004). Sexual abuse of boys: Short- and long-term associations and implications for HIV prevention. In L. J. Koenig, L. S. Doll, A. O'Leary, & W. Pequegnat (Eds.), *From child sexual abuse to adult sexual risk: Trauma, revictimization, and intervention* (pp. 93–114). Washington, DC: American Psychological Association.

Random House. (1998). *Random House Webster's unabridged dictionary* (2nd ed.). New York: Author.

Rank, O. (1941). *Beyond psychology*. New York: Dover.

Rapaport, D. (1951). Toward a theory of thinking. In D. Rapaport (Ed. & Trans.), *Organization and pathology of thought: Selected sources* (pp. 689–730). New York: Columbia University Press.

Reid, P. T., & Bing, V. M. (2000). Sexual roles of girls and women: An ethnocultural lifespan perspective. In C. B. Travis & J. W. White (Eds.), *Sexuality, society, and feminism* (pp. 141–166). Washington, DC: American Psychological Association.

Reik, T. (1941). *Of love and lust: On the psychoanalysis of romantic and sexual emotions*. New York: Farrar-Straus-Giroux.

Reissing, E. D., Binik, Y. M., Khalif, S., Cohen, D., & Amsel, R. (2003). Etiological correlates of vaginismus: Sexual and physical abuse, sexual knowledge, sexual self-schema, and relationship adjustment. *Journal of Sex and Marital Therapy, 29*, 47–59.

Rheingold, J. C. (1964). *The fear of being a woman: A theory of maternal destructiveness*. New York: Grune & Stratton.

Rheingold, J. C. (1967). *The mother, anxiety, and death: The catastrophic death complex*. Boston: Little, Brown.

Richard, D. (2003). 108th: SOS: Sexual health advocates vow to stand tough against the Republican-led 108th Congress. *Contemporary Sexuality, 37*(1), 1, 4–7.

Richman, J. (1986). *Family therapy for suicidal people*. New York: Springer.

Ridley, M. (1993). *The red queen: Sex and the evolution of human nature*. New York: Penguin Books.

Rilke, R. M. (1984). *Letters to a young poet* (S. Mitchell, Trans.). New York: Vintage Books. (Original work published 1908)

Ritter, K. Y., & Terndrup, A. I. (2002). *Handbook of affirmative psychotherapy with lesbians and gay men*. New York: Guilford Press.

Roberts, R., O'Connor, T., Dunn, J., & Golding, J. (2004). The effects of child sexual abuse in later family life; mental health, parenting and adjustment of offspring. *Child Abuse and Neglect, 28*, 525–545.

Rochlin, G. (1967). How younger children view death and themselves. In E. A. Grollman (Ed.), *Explaining death to children* (pp. 51–85). Boston: Beacon Press.

Rogers, A. G. (1994). *Exiled voices: Dissociation and the "return of the repressed" in women's narratives*. (Stone Center Work in Progress #67). Wellesley, MA: Wellesley College.

Rohner, R. P. (1986). *The warmth dimension: Foundations of parental acceptance–rejection theory*. Beverly Hills, CA: Sage.

Rohner, R. P. (1991). *Handbook for the study of parental acceptance and rejection.* Storrs: University of Connecticut.

Romans, S. E., Martin, J. L., Anderson, J. C., Herbison, G. P., & Mullen, P. E. (1995). Sexual abuse in childhood and deliberate self-harm. *American Journal of Psychiatry, 152,* 1336–1342.

Rosen, R. C., & Leiblum, S. R. (1995). Part I: Sexual desire disorders. In R. C. Rosen & S. R. Leiblum (Eds.), *Case studies in sex therapy* (pp. 19–21). New York: Guilford Press.

Rosenberger, J. B. (1998). Female kin: Functions of the meta–identification of womanhood. In G. H. Fenchel (Ed.), *The mother–daughter relationship: Echoes through time* (pp. 63–78). Northvale, NJ: Jason Aronson.

Rothschild, B. (2000). *The body remembers: The psychophysiology of trauma and trauma treatment.* New York: Norton.

Rubin, L. B. (1983). *Intimate strangers: Men and women together.* New York: Harper & Row.

Rubin, L. B. (1990). *Erotic wars: What happened to the sexual revolution?* New York: Farrar, Straus & Giroux.

Rudman, L. A., & Goodwin, S. A. (2004). Gender differences in automatic in-group bias: Why do women like women more than men like men? *Journal of Personality and Social Psychology, 87,* 494–509.

Safran, S. A., Gershuny, B. S., Marzol, P., Otto, M. W., & Pollack, M. H. (2002). History of childhood abuse in panic disorder, social phobia, and generalized anxiety disorder. *Journal of Nervous and Mental Disease, 190,* 453–456.

Sager, C. J., Kaplan, H. S., Gundlach, R. H., Kremer, M., Lenz, R., & Royce, J. R. (1971). The marriage contract. *Family Process, 8,* 311–326.

Salovey, P. (Ed.). (1991). *The psychology of jealousy and envy.* New York: Guilford Press.

Sanford, J. (1985). Projecting our other half. In J. Welwood (Ed.), *Challenge of the heart: Love, sex, and intimacy in changing times* (pp. 82–89). Boston: Shambhala. (Original work published 1980)

Sarwer, D. B., & Durlak, J. A. (1996). Childhood sexual abuse as a predictor of adult female sexual dysfunction: A study of couples seeking sex therapy. *Child Abuse and Neglect, 20,* 963–972.

Schachner, D. A., & Shaver, P. R. (2004). Attachment dimensions and sexual motives. *Personal Relationships, 11,* 179–195.

Scharff, D. E., & Scharff, J. S. (1991). *Object relations couple therapy.* Northvale, NJ: Jason Aronson.

Scharff, J. S. (1995). Psychoanalytic marital therapy. In N. S. Jacobson & A. S. Gurman (Eds.), *Clinical handbook of couple therapy* (pp. 164–193). New York: Guilford Press.

Schiffer, H. B. (2004). *First love: Remembrances*. Santa Barbara, CA: Heartful Loving Press.

Schmidt, G., & Arentewicz, G. (1983). Etiology. In G. Arentewicz & G. Schmidt (Eds.), *The treatment of sexual disorders: Concepts and techniques of couple therapy* (pp. 34–58, T. Todd, Trans.). New York: Basic Books.

Schmitt, D. P., and 118 members of the International Sexuality Description Project. (2003). Universal sex differences in the desire for sexual variety: Tests from 52 nations, 6 continents, and 13 islands. *Journal of Personality and Social Psychology, 85*, 85–104.

Schmitt, D. P., Alcalay, L., Allensworth, M., Allik, J., Ault, L., Austers, I., et al. (2003). Are men universally more dismissing than women? Gender differences in romantic attachment across 62 cultural regions. *Personal Relationships, 10*, 307–331.

Schnarch, D. M. (1991). *Constructing the sexual crucible: An integration of sexual and marital therapy*. New York: Norton.

Schoenewolf, G. (1989). *Sexual animosity between men and women*. Northvale, NJ: Jason Aronson.

Schore, A. N. (1994). *Affect regulation and the origin of the self: The neurobiology of emotional development*. Hillsdale, NJ: Erlbaum.

Segraves. R. T. (1982). *Marital therapy: A combined psychodynamic–behavioral approach*. New York: Plenum Press.

Segraves, R. T., & Balon, R. (2003). *Sexual pharmacology: Fast facts*. New York: Norton.

Sexuality Information and Education Council of the United States. (2002). SIECUS list of life behaviors of a sexually healthy adult. *Contemporary Sexuality, 36*(8), 7.

Sharpsteen, D. J., & Kirkpatrick, L. A. (1997). Romantic jealousy and adult romantic attachment. *Journal of Personality and Social Psychology, 72*, 627–640.

Shaver, P. (1989). Foreword. In G. L. White & P. E. Mullen (Eds.), *Jealousy: Theory, research, and clinical strategies* (pp. v–vi). New York: Guilford Press.

Shaver, P. R., & Clark, C. L. (1994). The psychodynamics of adult romantic attachment. In J. M. Masling & R. F. Bornstein (Eds.), *Empirical perspectives on object relations theory* (pp. 105–156). Washington, DC: American Psychological Association.

Shaver, P. R., Collins, N., & Clark, C. L. (1996). Attachment styles and internal working models of self and relationship partners. In G. J. O. Fletcher & J. Fitness (Eds.), *Knowledge structures in close relationships: A social psychological approach* (pp. 25–61). Mahwah, NJ: Erlbaum.

Shaver, P. R., & Hazan, C. (1993). Adult romantic attachment: Theory and evidence. In D. Perlman & W. Jones (Eds.), *Advances in personal relationships* (Vol. 4, pp. 29–70). London: Jessica Kingsley.

Shaver, P. R., Papalia, D., Clark, C. L., Koski, L. R., Tidwell, M. C., & Nalbone, D. (1996). Androgyny and attachment security: Two related models of optimal personality. *Personality and Social Psychology Bulletin, 22*, 582–597.

Shea, J. D. (1992). Religion and sexual adjustment. In J. F. Schumaker (Ed.), *Religion and mental health* (pp. 70–84). New York: Oxford University Press.

Sheehy, G. (1998). *Understanding men's passages: Discovering the new map of men's lives.* New York: Random House.

Shengold, L. (1989). *Soul murder: The effects of childhood abuse and deprivation.* New Haven, CT: Yale University Press.

Showalter, E. (2001). *Inventing herself: Claiming a feminist intellectual heritage.* New York: Scribner.

Siegel, D. J. (1999). *The developing mind: Toward a neurobiology of interpersonal experience.* New York: Guilford Press.

Siegel, D. J. (2001). Toward an interpersonal neurobiology of the developing mind: Attachment relationships, "mindsight," and neural integration. *Infant Mental Health Journal, 22,* 67–94.

Siegel, D. J., & Hartzell, M. (2003). *Parenting from the inside out: How a deeper self-understanding can help you raise children who thrive.* New York: Jeremy P. Tarcher.

Silverman, D. K. (2003). Mommy nearest: Revisiting the idea of infantile symbiosis and its implication for females. *Psychoanalytic Psychology, 20,* 261–270.

Silverman, L. H., Lachmann, F. M., & Milich, R. H. (1982). *The search for oneness.* New York: International Universities Press.

Silverstein, J. L. (1994). Power and sexuality: Influence of early object relations. *Psychoanalytic Psychology, 11,* 33–46.

Silverstein, L. B., & Auerbach, C. F. (1999). Deconstructing the essential father. *American Psychologist, 54,* 397–407.

Silverstein, L. B., Auerbach, C. F., & Levant, R. F. (2002). Contemporary fathers reconstructing masculinity: Clinical implications of gender role strain. *Professional Psychology: Research and Practice, 33,* 361–369.

Singer, I. (2001). *Sex: A philosophical primer.* Lanham, MD: Rowman & Littlefield.

Slowinski, J. W. (2001). Therapeutic dilemmas: Solving sexual difficulties in the context of religion. *Journal of Sex Education and Therapy, 26,* 272–280.

Sluzki, C. (1989, May/June). Jealousy. *Family Therapy Networker,* 53–55, 78.

Smith, T. W. (1998). American sexual behavior: Trends, socio-demographic differences, and risk behavior. *GSS Topical Report No. 25.* Retrieved January 21, 2004, from the National Opinion Research Center, University of Chicago Web site: http://cloud9.norc/uchicago.edu/dlib/t-25.htm

Solomon, K., & Levy, N. B. (Eds.). (1982). *Men in transition: Theory and therapy.* New York: Plenum Press.

Solomon, M. F. (1997). On love and lust in therapeutic treatment. In M. F. Solomon & J. P. Siegel (Eds.), *Countertransference in couples therapy* (pp. 136–154). New York: Norton.

Solomon, M. F. (2001). Breaking the deadlock of marital collusion. In M. F. Solomon, R. J. Neborsky, L. McCullough, M. Alpert, F. Shapiro, & D. Malan, *Short-term therapy for long-term change* (pp. 130–154). New York: Norton.

Solomon, S., Greenberg, J., & Pyszczynski, T. (1991). A terror management theory of social behavior: The psychological functions of self-esteem and cultural worldviews. *Advances in Experimental Social Psychology, 24,* 93–159.

Spak, L., Spak, F., & Allebeck, P. (1998). Sexual abuse and alcoholism in a female population. *Addiction, 93,* 1365–1373.

Spence, J. T. (1999). Thirty years of gender research: A personal chronicle. In W. B. Swann, Jr., J. H. Langlois, & L. A. Gilbert (Eds.), *Sexism and stereotypes in modern society: The gender science of Janet Taylor Spence* (pp. 255–289). Washington, DC: American Psychological Association.

Spiegel, J. (2003). *Sexual abuse of males: The SAM model of theory and practice.* New York: Brunner-Routledge.

Steele, B., & Alexander, H. (1981). Long-term effects of sexual abuse in childhood. In P. Mrazek & C. Kempe (Eds.), *Sexually abused children and their families* (pp. 223–234). Oxford, England: Pergamon Press.

Stephan, C. W., & Bachman, G. F. (1999). What's sex got to do with it? Attachment, love schemas, and sexuality. *Personal Relationships, 6,* 111–123.

Stern, D. N. (1985). *The interpersonal world of the infant: A view from psychoanalysis and developmental psychology.* New York: Basic Books.

Stern, D. N. (1994). One way to build a clinically relevant baby. *Infant Mental Health Journal, 15,* 9–25.

Stern, D. N. (1995). *The motherhood constellation: A unified view of parent–infant psychotherapy.* New York: Basic Books.

Stern, S. E., & Handel, A. D. (2001). Sexuality and mass media: The historical context of psychology's reaction to sexuality on the internet [Electronic version]. *Journal of Sex Research, 38,* 283–291.

Stiles, W. B. (1999). Suppression of continuity–benevolence assumptions (CBA) voices: A theoretical note on the psychology and psychotherapy of depression. *Psychotherapy, 36,* 268–273.

Stoller, R. J. (1975). *Perversion: The erotic form of hatred.* New York: Dell.

Stoller, R. J. (1991). The term perversion. In G. I. Fogel & W. A. Myers (Eds.), *Perversions and near-perversions in clinical practice: New psychoanalytic perspectives* (pp. 36–56). New Haven, CT: Yale University Press.

Stone, L. (1985, October/November). The strange, secret history of sex. *Utne Reader,* 34–42.

Storr, A. (1968). *Human aggression.* London: Allen Lane/Penguin Press.

Storr, A. (1988). *Solitude.* New York: Ballantine Books.

Stritof, S., & Stritof, B. (2004). Marital sex statistics: Who's doing it and how often? Retrieved January 12, 2004, from http://marriage.about.com/cs/sexual statistics/a/sexstatistics.htm

Strong, B., DeVault, C., & Sayad, B. W. (1999). *Human sexuality: Diversity in contemporary America* (3rd ed.). Mountain View, CA: Mayfield.

Strupp, H. H. (1989). Can the practitioner learn from the researcher? *American Psychologist, 44,* 717–724.

Suggs, D. N., & Miracle, A. W. (1993). *Culture and human sexuality: A reader.* Pacific Grove, CA: Brooks/Cole.

Sullivan, H. S. (1953). *The interpersonal theory of psychiatry.* New York: Norton.

Tannen, D. (1990). *You just don't understand: Women and men in conversation.* London: Virago Books.

Tannen, D. (1997). Women and men talking: An interactional sociolinguistic approach. In M. R. Walsh, *Women, men, and gender: Ongoing debates* (pp. 82–90). New Haven, CT: Yale University Press.

Tedeschi, J. T., & Felson, R. B. (1994). *Violence, aggression, and coercive actions.* Washington, DC: American Psychological Association.

Thakkar, R. R., Gutierrez, P. M., Kuczen, C. L., & McCanne, T. R. (2000). History of physical and/or sexual abuse and current suicidality in college women. *Child Abuse and Neglect, 24,* 1345–1354.

Tiefer, L. (2000). The social construction and social effects of sex research: The sexological model of sexuality. In C. B. Travis & J. W. White (Eds.), *Sexuality, society, and feminism* (pp. 79–107). Washington, DC: American Psychological Association.

Tiefer, L. (2001). Feminist critique of sex therapy: Foregrounding the politics of sex. In P. J. Kleinplatz (Ed.), *New directions in sex therapy: Innovations and alternatives* (pp. 29–49). Philadelphia: Brunner-Routledge.

Tronick, E. (1980). Infant communicative intent. In A. P. Reilly (Ed.), *The communication game: Perspectives on the development of speech, language and non-verbal communication skills* (pp. 4–9). Skillman, NJ: Johnson & Johnson Baby Products.

Tronick, E. Z., Cohn, J., & Shea, E. (1986). The transfer of affect between mothers and infants. In T. B. Brazelton & M. W. Yogman (Eds.), *Affective development in infancy* (pp. 11–25). Norwood, NJ: Ablex.

Tronick, E. Z., & Weinberg, M. K. (1997). Depressed mothers and infants: Failure to form dyadic states of consciousness. In L. Murray & P. J. Cooper (Eds.), *Postpartum depression and child development* (pp. 54–81). New York: Guilford Press.

Turner, P. J. (1991). Relations between attachment, gender, and behavior with peers in preschool. *Child Development, 62,* 1475–1488.

Twomey, H. B., Kaslow, N. J., & Croft, S. (2000). Childhood maltreatment, object relations, and suicidal behavior in women. *Psychoanalytic Psychology, 17,* 313–335.

University of Chicago Harris School. (1994, October 13). *University of Chicago study disputes myths about American sexual habits.* Retrieved October 8, 2002, from the University of Chicago Web site: http://www.harrisschool.uchicago.edu/news/pressreleases/pr_american_sex_stdy.htm

University of Illinois Board of Trustees. (2004). Healthy sexuality. Retrieved October 9, 2004, from the University of Illinois site: http://www.mckinley.uiuc.edu/health-info/sexual/intro/healthse.html

Valliant, L. M. (1997). *Changing character: Short-term anxiety-regulating psychotherapy for restructuring defenses, affects, and attachment*. New York: Basic Books.

Van Horn, P. (1999). [Review of the book *Fear of Intimacy* (back cover)]. Washington, DC: American Psychological Association.

Vergote, A. (1988). *Guilt and desire: Religious attitudes and their pathological derivatives* (M. H. Wood, Trans.). New Haven, CT: Yale University Press. (Original work published 1978)

Wachtel, P. L. (Ed.). (1982). *Resistance: Psychodynamic and behavioral approaches*. New York: Plenum Press.

Wallerstein, J. S., & Blakeslee, S. (1995). *The good marriage: How and why love lasts*. Boston: Houghton-Mifflin.

Walsh, M. R. (Ed.). (1997). *Women, men, and gender: Ongoing debates*. New Haven, CT: Yale University Press.

Waring, E. M. (1988). *Enhancing marital intimacy through facilitating cognitive self-disclosure*. New York: Brunner/Mazel.

Weeks, G. R., & Gambescia, N. (2002). *Hypoactive sexual desire: Integrating sex and couple therapy*. New York: Norton.

Weiner-Davis, M. (2003). *The sex-starved marriage*. New York: Simon & Schuster.

Weinfield, N. S., Sroufe, L. A., Egeland, B., & Carlson, E. A. (1999). The nature of individual differences in infant–caregiver attachment. In J. Cassidy & P. R. Shaver (Eds.), *Handbook of attachment: Theory, research, and clinical applications* (pp. 68–88). New York: Guilford Press.

Welldon, E. V. (1988). *Mother, Madonna, whore: The idealization and denigration of motherhood*. London: Free Association Books.

West, M. L., & Keller, A. E. R. (1991). Parentification of the child: A case study of Bowlby's compulsive care-giving attachment pattern. *American Journal of Psychotherapy, 45*, 425–431.

Westkott, M. C. (1997). On the new psychology of women: A cautionary view. In M. R. Walsh (Ed.), *Women, men, and gender: Ongoing debates* (pp. 362–372). New Haven, CT: Yale University Press.

Wexler, J., & Steidl, J. (1978). Marriage and the capacity to be alone. *Psychiatry, 41*, 72–82.

Whealin, J. (2004). *Child sexual abuse: A National Center for PTSD fact sheet*. Retrieved March 3, 2004, from the National Center for PTSD Web site: http://www.ncptsd.org/facts/specific/fs_child_sexual_abuse.html

Whitaker, C. A., & Malone, T. P. (1953). *The roots of psychotherapy*. New York: Brunner/Mazel.

White, G. L., & Mullen, P. E. (1989). *Jealousy: Theory, research, and clinical strategies*. New York: Guilford Press.

Wile, D. B. (1995). The ego-analytic approach to couple therapy. In N. S. Jacobson & A. S. Gurman (Eds.), *Clinical handbook of couple therapy* (pp. 91–120). New York: Guilford Press.

Willi, J. (1982). *Couples in collusion: The unconscious dimension in partner relationships* (W. Inayat-Khan & M. Tchorek, Trans.). Claremont, CA: Hunter House. (Original work published 1975)

Willi, J. (1984). *Dynamics of couples therapy* (J. Van Heurck, Trans.). Claremont, CA: Hunter House. (Original work published 1978)

Willi, J. (1999). *Ecological psychotherapy: Developing by shaping the personal niche.* Seattle, WA: Hogrefe & Huber.

Wilsnack, S. C., Wonderlich, S. A., Kristjanson, A. F., Vogeltanz-Holm, N. D., & Wilsnack, R. W. (2002). Self-reports of forgetting and remembering childhood sexual abuse in a nationally representative sample of US women. *Child Abuse and Neglect, 26,* 139–147.

Wilson, G. (1981). *The Coolidge effect: An evolutionary account of human sexuality.* New York: William Morrow.

Winnicott, D. W. (1958). *Collected papers: Through paediatrics to psycho-analysis.* London: Tavistock.

Wolfe, T. (1934). *You can't go home again.* New York: Harper & Row.

World Health Organization. (1975). *Education and treatment in human sexuality: The training of health professionals* (World Health Organization Technical Reports Series 55-33, No. 572). Geneva, Switzerland: Author.

Yanak, T. (2004). *The great American history fact-finder: Feminist movement.* Retrieved February 12, 2004, from the Houghton-Mifflin Web site: http://college.hmco.com/history/readerscomp/gahff/html/ff_066300_feministmove.htm

Young, C. (1999). *Ceasefire: Why women and men must join forces to achieve true equality.* New York: Free Press.

Zahn-Waxler, C., Radke-Yarrow, M., Wagner, E., & Chapman, M. (1992). Development of concern for others. *Developmental Psychology, 28,* 126–136.

Zahn-Waxler, C., Robinson, J. L., & Emde, R. N. (1992). The development of empathy in twins. *Developmental Psychology, 28,* 1038–1047.

Zilbergeld, B. (1999). *The new male sexuality* (Rev. ed.). New York: Bantam Books.

Zilboorg, G. (1943). Fear of death. *Psychoanalytic Quarterly, 12,* 465–475.

Zinner, J. (1976). The implications of projective identification for marital interaction. In H. Grunebaum & J. Christ (Eds.), *Contemporary marriage: Structure, dynamics, and therapy* (pp. 293–308). Boston: Little, Brown.

Zoldbrod, A. P. (1998). *Sex smart: How your childhood shaped your sexual life and what to do about it.* Oakland, CA: New Harbinger.

Zurbriggen, E. L., & Freyd, J. J. (2004). The link between child sexual abuse and risky sexual behavior: The role of dissociative tendencies, information-processing effects, and consensual sex decision mechanisms. In L. J. Koenig, L. S. Doll, A. O'Leary, & W. Pequegnat (Eds.), *From child sexual abuse to adult sexual risk: Trauma, revictimization, and intervention* (pp. 135–157). Washington, DC: American Psychological Association.

AUTHOR INDEX

Erlich, H. S., 278
Everaerd, W., 45, *131, 132*
Eyssell, K. M., 85

Fagot, B. I., 100
Fairbairn, W. R. D., 118, 119, 120, 121
Faller, K. C., 63
Fausto-Sterling, A., 45
Feeney, J. A., 122, *132*
Fehr, B., 85
Feldman, S., 205
Feldman, S. S., 90
Felitti, V. J., 66, 137, *168*
Felson, R. B., 47, 79, 198, 207
Fenchel, G. H., 53, 58, 92, 96, 101, 152
Ferenczi, S., 47, 116, 117, 141
Fergusson, D. M., 65
Fierman, L. B., 135, 137, 138
Finnegan, A., 77
Firestone, L., *7*, 36, 71, 129, 163, *195,*
     198, 285–287
Firestone, R. W., *7*, 13, 36, 44, 46, 49,
     50, 53, 54, 56, 57, 58, 59, 62, 66,
     68, 70, 71, 90, 92, 93, 94, 95, 96,
     113, 114, 116, 117, 123, 129,
     136, 137, 138, 139, 140, 141,
     142, 143, 145, 146, 148, 152,
     154, 155, 163, 164, *168*, 172,
     173, 180, 186, 193, *195*, 198,
     208, 213, 214, 216, 219, 229,
     243, 252, 253, 254, *260, 261,*
     279, 281–283
Fischer, K. W., 123
Fisher, H. E., 37, 38, 39, *39*, 45
Fisher, R. L., 49
Fisher, S., 49
Fiske, S. T., 77, 78, 83, 84
Fleming, J., 65, 66, *73*
Foley, S., 162, *169*
Fosha, D., 36, 48
Foster, T. L., 125
Fox, R., 56, *73*
Fraley, R. C., 122, 244, *261*
Francoeur, R. T., 68, 69
Freud, A., 47, 116, 141
Freud, S., 45, 56, 83, 111, 118, 204
Freyd, J. J., 58, 63
Friday, N., 50, 53, 62, *224*
Fried, E., 182
Friedman, R. C., 77

Friedman, S. D., 65
Fromm, E., 32, 119

Gage, R. L., 30
Gagnon, J. H., 12, 50
Galinsky, E., 50
Gambescia, N., 112, 113
Gartner, R. B., 59, 64, 184
Geary, D. C., 98, 99
Geis, F. L., 77
Genevie, L., 92, 114
Gentzler, A. L., 86
Gershuny, B. S., 65
Gerson, R., 48
Gerstein, L. H., 85
Gewirtz, J. L., 48
Ghent, E., 278
Giddens, A., 45
Gilligan, C., 82, 101, *106, 108*
Gilmartin, B. F., 218
Glass, S. P., 197, 202, 206, 209, 216, 220
Glick, P., 78, 84
Goeke-Morey, M. C., 92
Gold, S. N., 65
Goldberg, C., 127, *195*
Goldenberg, J. L., 69, 163, 164, 165, 167,
     207
Golding, J., 65
Goldwyn, R., 22
Goodwin, S. A., 79
Goren, E., *261*
Gottman, J. M., 20, 21, 176
Greenberg, J., 69, 164
Greenberg, L. S., 36, 124, 255
Gridley, B., 85
Grossman, M., 85
Guadagno, R. E., *224*
Guidano, V. F., 127
Gunderson, M. P., 70
Guntrip, H., 118, 119, 120, 121, 139
Gutierrez, P. M., 65

Hagan, R., 100
Hampson, R. B., 47
Handel, A. D., 71
Harding, C., 43
Harlow, H. F., 48
Harlow, M. K., 48
Harmon, E. L., 91, 95

Harper, J. M., *169*
Harper, R. A., 127, 254
Harre, R., 72
Hart, A. J., 21, 176
Hartzell, M., 22, 48
Harvey, J. H., 43
Hatfield, E., 36, 38
Hazan, C., 45, 103, 122, 123, 124
He, Z., 70
Heard-Davison, A. R., 65
Heilman, M. E., 77
Heiman, J. R., 65
Hellinger, B., 146, 148, 155, 156, *169*, 171
Henschel, A., 137
Herbison, G. P., 65
Herdt, G., *74*
Herman, J., 58, 66, 68, 98, 115
Hoenk, P. R., 143
Hogben, M., 89, 125
Hollenbeck, A. R., 48
Holstein, C., 143, 144
Holtzworth-Munroe, A., 205, 215
Hook, M. K., 85
hooks, b., 78
Horne, A. M., 91
Horney, K., 101
Horvath, A. O., 253
Horwood, L. J., 65
Hudson, L., 92
Huh, E., 143, 144
Hunsley, J., 255
Hupka, R. B., 200, 217
Hurlbut, W. B., 30
Hutchinson, G., 205
Hyde, J. S., 75, 86, 89, 100, *106*, 125
Hyun, M., 65

Ickes, W., 77
Ingram, M., *74*
Insel, T. R., 36
Ippen, C. G., *132*

Jacklin, C. N., 53, 125
Jacobsson, L., *224*
Jacot, B., 92
Jain, A., 91, *107*
Jessel, D., *39*, 45

Johnson, E. W., 70
Johnson, S. M., 116, 124, 255, 256, *262*
Johnson, V. E., 111, 112
Jolliff, D., 91
Jordan, J. V., *106*
Jureidini, R., 116

Kalma, A. P., 215
Kaplan, A. G., *106*
Kaplan, H. B., 46
Kaplan, H. S., 45, *105*, 111, 112, 114, 116, 125, 126, 127, 171, 175, 180, 182, 183, 184, 186, 187, 193, *195*, 235, 255, *262*
Kaplan, L. J., 114
Karpel, M. A., 138, 146, 151, 156, *168*, 169
Karr-Morse, R., 22
Kaslow, N. J., 65
Kastenbaum, R., 140
Kaufman, G., 127, *195*
Keeley, M. P., 21, 176
Keen, S., 25, 75, 78, 84
Keller, A. E. R., 58
Kellett, J. M., 235
Kelsey, B., 50
Kelsey, M., 50
Kenrick, D. T., 103
Kernberg, O. F., 70, 100, 118, 119, 121, 122, 221
Kerns, K. A., 86
Kerr, M. E., 22, 128, 129, *132*, 146
Kestenberg, J. S., 56
Kestenberg, M., 56
Ketcham, K., *73*
Keys, A., 137, *168*
Khalife, S., *74*
Kindlon, D., *106*
Kinzl, J. F., *73*, 182
Kipnis, L., 155
Kirkpatrick, L. A., 36, 205
Kirschner, D. A., 65
Kirschner, S., 65
Kiselica, M. S., 99
Klein, Marty, 12
Klein, Melanie, 118, 121
Kleinplatz, P. J., *261*
Koenig, L. J., 65
Kohut, H., 139

Kope, S. A., 162, *169*
Kramer, R., 278
Kriegman, D., 102
Kristjanson, A. F., 64
Krokoff, L. J., 20, 21, 176
Kuczen, C. L., 65
Kunkel, A. W., 85
Kuperman, S., 143
Kupers, T. A., 77, 79

Laan, E. T. M., 45, *131, 132*
Lachmann, F. M., *168*
Lachmann, L. M., 48
Laing, R. D., 35
Lamb, M. E., 86, 98
Lannon, R., 37
Laumann, E. O., 12, 15, *27, 106,* 112, 230
Lawrence, D. H., 34
Leadbeater, B. J., 123
Leahy, R. L., 278
LeDoux, J., 48
Leiblum, S. R., 112, *261*
Lester, D., 140
Levant, R. F., 76, 79, 80, 96, 99, *105, 107*
Levi-Strauss, C., 56, *73*
Levy, N. B., 75
Lewis, C., 86, 98
Lewis, C. S., 30
Lewis, M., 49, 127, 182, *195*
Lewis, T., 37
Li, H., 37
Lieberman, A. F., 68, *132*
Liebowitz, M. R., 38
Lindstrom, H., *224*
Liotti, G., 127
Lipson, A., 143, 144
Lipton, J. E., 207, 217
Lisak, D., 66
Loftus, E., *73*
LoPiccolo, J., 14, 229
Lott, B., 77
Lott, D. A., 48
Love, P., 37, *39,* 59, 60, 61, 95, 96, *105,* 172, 263
Luborsky, L., 253
Lucenko, B. A., 65
Lusterman, D., 202
Lynskey, M. T., 65
Lyons-Ruth, K., *107*

Maccoby, E. E., 53, 125
MacEahron, A. E., 60
Mahler, M. S., 254
Main, M., 22, *27*
Malone, P. T., 128
Malone, T. P., 51, 128
Malow, R. M., 64
Manlove, E. E., 97
Manson, W., 69
Margolies, E., 92, 114
Marmor, J., 88
Martin, G., 65
Martin, J. L., 65
Martinson, F. M., 50
Marzol, P., 65
Mashek, D., 37
Masters, W. H., 111, 112
Masterson, J. F., 58
Mathes, E. W., *224*
May, R., 165
Mazur, R., 218, 221, *224*
McCanne, T. R., 65
McCarthy, B. W., 171, 175, 192, *194, 195,* 258
McCarthy, E., 171, 175, 192, *194, 195*
McCary, J. L., 70
McConaghy, N., 112
McCoy, S. K., 164
Mead, G. H., 76
Mead, M., 89
Melby, T., *131*
Mendell, D., 53, 92, 100
Messman, S. J., 21
Meston, C. M., 65
Metz, M. E., 258
Michael, R. T., 12
Michaels, S., 12
Mickelsen, O., 137
Mikulincer, M., *168*
Miletski, H., 64
Milich, R. H., *168*
Miller, A., 56, 58, 60, 66, 68, 95
Miller, G., 102
Miller, J. B., 82, *106*
Millevoi, A., *224*
Miracle, A. W., 12, *73*
Mitchell, S. A., 172, 173, *195*
Moir, A., *39,* 45
Montagu, A., 48
Moore, D. S., 103, *109*

Morokoff, P. J., 108
Morris, L. A., 60
Morrison, A. P., 127, 195
Mullen, P. E., 65, 66, 73, 200, 203
Munholland, K. A., 123
Murray, C. L., 125

Nagy, M. H., 140
Nealer, J., 98
Neborsky, R. J., 278
Nelson, D. A., 178
Newberger, C. M., 66
Nicastle, L. D., 224
Noller, P., 122
Noyes, R., 143

O'Connor, T., 65
Oates, R. K., 65
Oatley, K., 72
Ogilvie, B. A., 64
Oliver, K., 94
Oliver, M. B., 75, 86, 89, 100, 106, 125
Olsen, K. L., 45
Orbach, I., 168
Orbach, S., 47, 48, 51, 62, 73, 152, 169
Otto, M. W., 65
Oubaid, V., 102

Pagels, E., 69
Paik, A., 112
Papalia, D., 86
Park, J., 90, 95, 96, 114
Parker, G., 58, 91, 107
Parker, R., 46
Parrott, W. G., 72
Patty, J., 122
Pearson, P. T., 124, 216, 254
Perna, F., 168
Perris, C., 224
Perris, H., 224
Person, E. S., 209, 214, 220, 221
Phillips, N. A., 235
Pietromonaco, P. R., 85
Pine, F., 254
Pines, A. M., 37, 197, 199, 200, 205,
    206, 224
Pleck, J. H., 80, 87, 105
Plutchik, R., 203

Pollack, M. H., 65
Pollack, W. S., 80, 90, 91, 96, 98, 99, 105
Pope, K. S., 73
Post, S. G., 30
Prescott, J. W., 68
Purcell, D. W., 64, 65, 66, 115
Putnam, F. W., 66
Pyszczynski, T., 69, 164

Radke-Yarrow, M., 107
Rank, O., 158, 278
Rapaport, D., 141
Rapson, R. L., 36
Raymond, J., 92
Reid, P. T., 83, 100, 107
Reik, T., 29
Reissing, E. D., 74
Rheingold, J. C., 53, 56, 94, 114
Richard, D., 131
Richardson, A. S., 65
Richman, J., 93
Ridley, M., 83, 108
Rilke, R. M., 38
Ritter, K. Y., 260
Roberts, R., 65
Robin, L., 85
Robinson, J., 105
Robinson, J. L., 107
Rochlin, G., 140
Roeger, L., 65
Rogers, A. G., 106
Rohner, R. P., 46
Romans, S. E., 65
Rosen, R. C., 112, 261
Rosenberger, J. B., 83
Ross, D., 53
Ross, S. A., 53
Rothschild, B., 182
Rubin, L. B., 75, 79, 82, 92, 94, 96
Rudman, L. A., 79
Rush, A. J., 125, 143

Sadava, S., 132
Safran, J. D., 36
Safran, S. A., 65
Sagarin, B. J., 224
Sager, C. J., 155, 169
Salovey, P., 199, 200, 203, 224
Samter, W., 85

Wall, S., 180
Waller, N. G., 244
Wallerstein, J. S., 22
Walsh, M. R., 75, *105*
Waring, E. M., *262*
Waters, E., 180
Weber, A. L., 43
Weeks, G. R., 112, 113
Weinberg, M. K., *195*
Weinberger, D. A., 90
Weiner-Davis, M., 171
Weinfield, N. S., 180
Welldon, E. V., 48, 53, 56, 92
Werking, J., 85
West, M. L., 58
Westkott, M. C., 92, *107*
Wexler, J., 138
Whealin, J., 63
Whiffen, V. E., 124
Whitaker, C. A., 51
White, G. L., 200, 203
Wile, D. B., *262*
Wiley, M. S., 22
Willi, J., 146, 156, 158, 257, 258

Wilsnack, R. W., 64
Wilsnack, S. C., 64
Wilson, G., 103
Wilson, M., 83, 206, 214, 217
Winnicott, D. W., *73*, 137
Wolfe, T., 30
Wolitzky, D. L., 23
Wonderlich, S. A., 64
Wood, W., 85, 103
Wright, T. L., 197, 202, 206, 209, 216

Yanak, T., 82
Young, C., 71, 75, 79, 82

Zahn-Waxler, C., *107*
Zeanah, C. H. , Jr., *107*
Zilbergeld, B., 14
Zilboorg, G., 163
Zinner, J., 121, *132*
Zoldbrod, A. P., 43, 50, *73*
Zurbriggen, E. L., 63
Zutter, A., 255

SUBJECT INDEX

Abandonment anxiety, 204–205

Absent fathers, 91, 97

Active receptivity during love making, 88

Adrenaline, 38

Adult ego state, 145–146

Adverse Childhood Experiences (ACE) Study, 74n

Affair of mate, 197–225. *See also* Jealousy

AIDS, 187, 231

American Psychiatric Association, 112, 113, 131n, 203

American Psychological Association's *Guidelines for Psychotherapy with Lesbian, Gay, and Bisexual Clients*, 230, 260n

Antilibidinal ego, 120

Antiself, 141–143, 168n

Attachment perspectives
  on gender differences, 100
  on jealousy, 205
  on love, 36
  self-knowledge and, 27n
  on sexual dysfunctions, 122–125
  on sexual stereotypes, 86

Attitudes toward sex, 50–51. *See also* Cultural influences; Parental impact on adult sexuality

Automatic thoughts, 127, 143, 254

Autonomy. *See* Individuality

Averse Childhood Experiences (ACE), 168n

Behavioral Checklist for Partners, 243, 245, 246, 260n

Benevolent sexism, 84

Betrayal trauma theory, 63–64

Bias of therapists, 230

Biological aspects
  of love, 36–38, 39n
  of sexuality, 45–46

Body image, 51–53
  distorted views of sexuality and human body, 50–53
  touching and, 48–49, 116

Buddhist conception of love, 30–31

Capacity to give and receive love, affection, and sex, 23–24

Child-rearing and sexual stereotypes, 86, 87

Children's sexuality
  attitudes toward one's body, 51–53
  attitudes toward sex, 50–51, 73n
  competition and Oedipal issues, 55–57
  exploitative use of child by parent, 58–62
  female children, sexual abuse of, 63–64
  harsh and negative attitudes, 49, 91, 141
  identification with and imitation of parent of same sex, 53–55
  imitation of parents' views, 50
  interpersonal factors affecting, 46–64
  male children, sexual abuse of, 64
  natural feelings of attraction within families, 62–63
  parental attitudes and behaviors, 46–47, 132n, 283–284
  parental rejection and hostility, 47–49, 142

Child sexual abuse
  adult functioning and sexual relations, effect on, 65–68, 73–74n
  defined, 63
  female children, 63–64, 65–66
  male children, 64, 66
  recovered memories of, 64, 73n
  sexual withholding due to, 182–183
  therapy for adult survivors, 256, 262n

Cleanliness, obsession with, 49

Closeness, 128–129, 132n, 255, 270

Cognitive–behavioral perspectives
on couples therapy, 254
on sexual dysfunctions, 125–127

Communication between genders, 79, 84, 85

Companionate vs. passionate love, 36, 85

Compassion and empathy, 22–23, 85, 264–265

Competition
among partners, 224n
defined, 199
jealousy and, 198–200, 201
parental–child feelings of, 55–57, 90
sexual withholding due to fears of, 180–181

Continuity benevolence assumptions, 144

Continuum of eroticism, 131n

Continuum of sexuality, 114, 144–145

Core attitudes about love and sexuality, 264–266

Corrective suggestions, 167, 266–278, 279n. See also Enhancing sexual intimacy

Couples therapy
approaches to sexual dysfunctions, 253–258
voice therapy as adjunct to, 252, 278
voice therapy in, 234–251

Cultural influences
on jealousy, 203, 217–218
on love, 30–31
on parental attitudes and behaviors, 46
on sexuality, 12, 13, 26n, 68–70, 74n, 281–282
on sexual stereotypes, 105n, 108n

Death anxiety, 136, 140, 163–167, 283

Deception
jealousy and, 216–217
self-deception, 157

Defense formation
death anxiety and, 136, 140, 163–167
fantasy bond, 136, 137–138. See also Fantasy bond
modes of sexual relating, 144–146

psychodynamics and, 137–144
self-parenting process, 138–140
extension into self-gratifying modes, 146–148
voice process, 140–144
manifestations of, 161–162

Destructive thought processes underlying sexual withholding, 185–192

Developmental factors of sexual dysfunctions, 115–118

Diagnostic and Statistical Manual of Mental Disorders (DSM–IV), 112, 113, 131n, 203

Disruption of sexual relations by voices, 230–234

Distortion
of body image, 50–53
fantasy bond and, 149–150
sexual stereotypes and, 78–84

Dopamine, 38, 39n, 45

Double standard, 100

Durex Survey (2003) on American sex practices, 14–15

Dysfunctions. See Sexual dysfunctions

Ego states
adult ego state, 145–146
polarization of parental and childish ego states, 157–159, 168n

Emotional hunger
defined, 34
of parent, 58–59

Emotional incest, 59–62

Emotionally focused therapy (EFT), 255–256, 261–262n

Empathy. See Compassion and empathy

Enhancing sexual intimacy, 263–279
compassion and empathy, 264–265
core attitudes about love and sexuality, 264–266
corrective suggestions, 266–278
for expanding personal boundaries, 269–270
for fantasy bond, 267–269
for goal setting for one's sexual relationship, 270–271
imaginary dialogue with one's parent, 273, 276–277
for jealousy, 222–224
journaling, 273, 274–275

resistance to, 278
for voice disruption, 167, 271–273, 274–275
generosity, 265–266
individuality, 266
overcoming stereotypes, 266
Enmeshed sexual relationship, 124
Envy compared with jealousy, 224n. *See also* Jealousy
Etiology of sexual dysfunctions, 111–132, 284. *See also* Sexual dysfunctions
developmental factors of, 115–118
oral basis of sexuality, 113–115
perspectives on, 113–118
Evolutionary psychologists
on jealousy, 206–208
on mate selection strategies, 102–104, 108n
Exclusive vs. nonexclusive relationships, 218–222. *See also* Jealousy
Expanding personal boundaries, 23–24, 25, 269–270
Experiences in Close Relationships Inventory (ECR–R), 244, 247, 261n
Exploitative use of child by parent, 58–62
Extramarital affair, 197–225. *See also* Jealousy

Family relationships. *See also* Parental impact on adult sexuality
natural feelings of attraction within families, 62–63
as predisposing factors for sexual withholding, 178–185
Family systems theory, 128–129, 132n, 257
Fantasy bond, 136, 137–138
corrective suggestions for, 267–269
defenses against intimacy encouraging, 148–151
distortion and, 149–150
form vs. substance and, 154–157
idealization of partner and, 159
jealousy and, 197, 208–211, 219
loss of independence and sense of separate identity, 160–161
manifestations in couple relationships, 151–161
mutual self-deception and, 157

polarization of parental and childish ego states and, 157–159, 168n
provocation and, 150–151
routinized, impersonal sexuality and, 153, 169n
overcoming, 269–270
selection process and, 148–149
voice therapy and, 259
Fathers. *See* Parental impact on adult sexuality
Feminist movement, 78–79, 82, 106n, 131n
Firestone Assessment of Violent Thoughts (FAVT), 224n
Firestone Voice Scale for Couples (FVSC), 244, 246, 260–261n
Form vs. substance in couple relationships, 154–157
Freudian approach. *See* Psychoanalytical perspective

Gatekeeper mothers, 105–106n
Gender equality, 104–105. *See also* Sexual stereotypes
Gender identity. *See* Sexual stereotypes
Gender relations, 75–76
Gender-role socialization and developmental tasks, 98–102, 105n
Gender studies
on mate selection, 103
on sexual stereotypes, 85–86
Generosity, 265–266
Gestalt therapy, 254
Goal setting for one's sexual relationship, 270–271
Guilt, 59, 87, 93, 115, 116, 195n

Healthy sexuality
criteria used to evaluate, 14–15
defining, 11–12, 14
descriptions of, 14
dimensions of ideal, 15–19
"normal," 11–12
personal traits for, 19–24
perspective on, 13, 285–287
Homosexuals. *See* Same-gendered relationships
Honesty, 20–21, 216–217
Humiliation. *See* Shame

Hypoactive sexual desire (HSD), 126, 187, 195n

Idealization
    of parents, 168n
    of partner, 159
Ideal sexual experience, dimensions of, 15–19
Imaginary dialogue with one's parent, 273, 276–277
Imitation of parents
    children's sexuality and, 50, 89, 93
    distorted views of sexuality and human body, 50
    negative traits of parent, 47, 141
Incest, 56, 63, 66, 67, 73n, 98
    emotional incest, 59–62
Individuality
    loss of, 160–161
    respect for partner's, 21–22
    teaching client couples about, 266
Infants
    gender role identity and, 108n
    need for care-giver proximity, 122
    self-comforting, 137
Infidelity, 197–225. See also Jealousy
Inhibited sexual desire (ISD), 126, 192, 194n, 255
Integrity, 20–21
Internal thought process. See Voice
Internal working models and attachment theory, 123
Internet, 71
Interpersonal factors affecting children's sexuality, 46–64. See also Children's sexuality
Interviews with authors, 281–287
Intimacy
    defenses against, encouraging fantasy bond, 148–151
    enhancing, 263–279. See also Enhancing sexual intimacy

Jealousy, 197–225
    competition and, 198–200, 201
    cultural influences on, 203, 217–218
    deception and, 216–217
    defined, 199

    evolutionary factors influencing, 206–208
    exclusive vs. nonexclusive relationships, perspectives on, 218–222
    fantasy bond and, 197, 208–211, 219
    overcoming negative consequences of, 222–224
    psychoanalytic and attachment theorists' views on, 203–205
    sexual withholding and, 215–216
    subjective experience of, 200–203
    voices intensifying, 211–215
Journaling, 273, 274–275
Judeo–Christian conception of love, 31

Learning theory, 89
Lesbians. See Same-gendered relationships
Loss of independence and sense of separate identity, 160–161
Love, 29–39
    biological aspects of, 36–38
    descriptions of, 30–31
    genuine love, what is not, 34–35
    mystery of, 39n
    passionate vs. companionate, 36
    perspectives on, 31–34, 35–38
    teaching core attitudes about, 264–266

Marriage contracts, 155, 169n
Mate selection. See Selection process
Media
    sexuality in, 70–71
    sexual stereotypes in, 109n
Men's movement, 78
Mixed messages
    sexual withholding and, 175–178
    trust and, 21
Morality, 12
Morbid jealousy, 204
Mortality salience, 207. See also Death anxiety
Mothers. See Parental impact on adult sexuality
Mutual self-deception, 157
Mystery of love, 39n

National Health and Social Life Survey (1992), 112
Natural feelings of attraction within families, 62–63
Nondefensiveness, 19–20
Norepinephrine, 38, 45
"No-sex" marriages, 258

Object relations perspectives
    in couples therapy, 256–257
    on sexual dysfunctions, 119–122
Oedipal issues, 55–57, 95, 101, 108n, 118, 121, 204
Openness, 19–20
Open relationships, 218–222. See also Jealousy
Oprah, 71
Oral basis of sexuality, 113–115
Orgasm
    disorders, 115–116, 131n
    frequency of, 15
Overprotection of son by mother, 94–95, 107n
Oxytocin, 39n, 45

Parental impact on adult sexuality, 89–98. See also Children's sexuality; Imitation of parents; Incest
    emotional hunger, 58–59
    exploitative use of child by parent, 58–62
    fathers and daughters, 96–98
    fathers and sons, 52, 54–55, 57, 90–92, 106n, 127
    imaginary dialogue with one's parent, 273, 276–277
    mothers and daughters, 53–54, 56–57, 64, 92–94, 126–127
    mothers and sons, 64, 94–96
    parental attitudes and behaviors, 46–47, 132n, 283–284
    parental rejection and hostility, 47–49, 142
Parentification, 58
Passionate vs. companionate love, 36, 85
Passive–aggression sexual withholding, 175, 181, 195n
Paternity determination, 102–103
Patriarchal society. See Sexual stereotypes

Penis envy, 101, 108n
Personality of therapist, 253, 261n
Perversion, 131n. See also Sexual dysfunctions
Phenylethylamine, 38
Polarization of parental and childish ego states, 157–159, 168n
Popular culture's representations of sexuality, 70–71
Pornography, 70–71
Posttraumatic stress disorder (PTSD), 182, 202–203
Preoedipal stage, 114, 121
Projective identification, 121
Provocation and fantasy bond, 150–151
Pseudoaggression, 195n
Psyche division into self and antiself, 141–143, 168n
Psychoanalytical perspective
    on female psychosexual development, 101
    on infant's need for care-giver proximity, 122
    on jealousy, 203–205
    on sexual dysfunctions, 111, 118–119
    on unconscious motives, 143
Psychodynamics of defense formation, 137–144
Psychological control of parent, 91, 178
Psychosexual development
    female, 100–102, 108n
    male, 99–100, 108n

Receptivity vs. passivity, 88
Rejection
    infidelity of mate as, 197–225. See also Jealousy
    parental rejection and hostility, 47–49, 142
Rejection sensitivity, 205
Relational diathesis model, 68
Resistance
    to corrective suggestions, 278
    to healthy sexual experiences, 25, 166
    to love, 38
Respect for one's partner, 21–22
Rivalry, 197–225. See also Competition; Jealousy

Routinized, impersonal sexuality and deterioration of sexual relating, 153, 169n
    overcoming, 269–270

Sadomasochistic fantasies or behavior, 116–117
Safe sex, need for, 187, 231
Same-gendered relationships
    jealousy in, 207
    therapist's attitude toward, 230, 260n
    types of sexual activities, 15
Selection process
    evolutionary psychologists on strategies, 102–104, 108n
    fantasy bond and, 148–149
Self-deception, 157
Self-denial as basis for sexual withholding, 173–174, 179–180
Self-differentiation, 128
Self-esteem, 79, 212, 224n
Self-evaluation maintenance (SEM) theory, 224n
Self-parenting process, 138–140
    extension into self-gratifying modes, 146–148
Separation anxiety and sexual experience, 145
Sexism. See Sexual stereotypes
Sexual abuse of children. See Child sexual abuse
Sexual anorexia. See Sexual withholding
Sexual crucible model, 258
Sexual dysfunctions
    attachment approaches to, 122–125
    cognitive–behavioral perspectives on, 125–127
    corrective approaches. See Enhancing sexual intimacy
    couples therapy, approaches to, 253–258
    death anxiety and, 136, 163–167
    defined, 112–113
    developmental factors of, 115–118
    etiology of, 111–132, 284
    as expression of sexual inhibition, 194n
    family systems theory on, 128–129

object relations approaches to, 119–122
oral basis of sexuality and, 113–115
psychoanalytical approach to, 118–119
social learning and, 125–127, 282–283
theoretical approaches to, 118–129
Sexual infidelity, 197–225. See also Jealousy
Sexual Information and Education Council of the United States, 14, 26n
Sexuality. See also Healthy sexuality
    biological factors affecting, 45–46
    children's. See Children's sexuality
    child sexual abuse, effect of, 65–68
    continuum of, 114
    cultural and societal influences, 12, 13, 68–70
    defined, 43
    factors affecting, 43–74
    frequency of sex, 14–15, 27n
    interpersonal factors affecting children's, 46–64. See also Children's sexuality
    media's and popular culture's representations of, 70–71
    oral basis of, 113–115
    types of sexual activities, 15
Sexual rivals, 197–225. See also Competition; Jealousy
Sexual stereotypes, 75–109
    couple relationships and, 155–156
    distorted views, 78–84
        on men, 78–82
        on women, 82–84
    gender research and, 85–86
    gender-role socialization and developmental tasks, 98–102, 105n
    historical perspective
        on men, 78
        on women, 82
    infants and gender role identity, 108n
    mate selection as viewed by evolutionary psychologists, 102–104, 108n
    overcoming, 266
    overview, 76–78
    parental impact on adult sexuality, 89–98

ABOUT THE AUTHORS

Robert W. Firestone, PhD, clinical psychologist and author, has established a comprehensive body of work that focuses on the concept that defenses formed by individuals early in life often impair their ability to develop and sustain intimate adult relationships and interfere with their achieving a healthy, fulfilling sexual life. He was engaged in the private practice of psychotherapy from 1957 to 1979, working with a wide range of patients, expanding his original ideas on schizophrenia, and applying these concepts to a theory of neurosis. In 1979, he joined the Glendon Association in Santa Barbara, California, as its consulting theorist. His major publications include *The Fantasy Bond, Compassionate Child-Rearing, Fear of Intimacy,* and *Creating a Life of Meaning and Compassion: The Wisdom of Psychotherapy.* His studies of negative thought processes led to the development of an innovative therapeutic methodology described in *Voice Therapy, Suicide and the Inner Voice,* and *Combating Destructive Thought Processes.*

Lisa A. Firestone, PhD, clinical psychologist, is the director of research and education at the Glendon Association and an adjunct faculty member at the University of California, Santa Barbara Graduate School of Education. For the past 12 years she has been engaged in private practice, treating couples and individuals struggling with intimacy issues. She has also been involved in clinical training and applied research related to the assessment of suicide and violence potential. She coauthored *Conquer Your Critical Inner Voice* and *Creating a Life of Meaning and Compassion: The Wisdom of Psychotherapy* and has presented these ideas in workshops. She has also discussed these concepts in a video on sexual health from the American Psychological Association. Her recent publications include chapters in edited books: *Katie's Diary: Unlocking the Mystery of Suicide* (D. Lester, Ed.);

Assessment, Treatment, and Prevention of Suicidal Behavior (R. Yufit & D. Lester, Eds.); and *Cognition and Suicide: Theory, Research, and Practice* (T. Ellis, Ed., in press).

Joyce Catlett, MA, author and lecturer, has coauthored four books with Robert W. Firestone and coproduced 37 educational videos for the Glendon Association, including a series on couples and sexuality. She developed the Compassionate Child-Rearing Parent Education Program, a child abuse prevention model curriculum that has been used in six U.S. states, Canada, and Costa Rica. She currently lectures and conducts continuing education workshops at universities and mental health facilities throughout the world.